KIPLING: THE CRITICAL HERITAGE

THE CRITICAL HERITAGE SERIES

GENERAL EDITOR: B. C. SOUTHAM, M.A., B.LITT. (OXON.)

Formerly Department of English, Westfield College, University of London

---

Volumes in the series include

JANE AUSTEN	B. C. Southam
BROWNING	Boyd Litzinger and Donald Smalley
BYRON	Andrew Rutherford
COLERIDGE	J. R. de J. Jackson
DICKENS	Philip Collins
DRYDEN	James and Helen Kinsley
HENRY FIELDING	Ronald Paulson and Thomas Lockwood
THOMAS HARDY	R. G. Cox
HAWTHORNE	J. Donald Crowley
HENRY JAMES	Roger Gard
JAMES JOYCE (2 vols)	Robert H. Deming
KIPLING	Roger Lancelyn Green
D. H. LAWRENCE	R. P. Draper
MILTON	John T. Shawcross
SCOTT	John O. Hayden
SPENSER	R. N. Cummings
SWIFT	Kathleen Williams
SWINBURNE	Clyde K. Hyder
TENNYSON	J. D. Jump
THACKERAY	Geoffrey Tillotson and Donald Hawes
TROLLOPE	Donald Smalley

KIPLING

THE CRITICAL HERITAGE

Edited by
ROGER LANCELYN GREEN
B.Litt., M.A. (Oxon.)

LONDON: ROUTLEDGE & KEGAN PAUL

Published 1971
in Great Britain
by Routledge & Kegan Paul Limited
© *Roger Lancelyn Green 1971*
No part of this book may be reproduced
in any form without permission from
the publisher, except for the quotation
of brief passages in criticism
ISBN 0 7100 6978 2

Printed in Great Britain
by Butler and Tanner Ltd,
Frome and London
Set in 11 pt. on 12 pt. Monotype Bembo

General Editor's Preface

The reception given to a writer by his contemporaries and near-contemporaries is evidence of considerable value to the student of literature. On one side we learn a great deal about the state of criticism at large and in particular about the development of critical attitudes towards a single writer; at the same time, through private comments in letters, journals or marginalia, we gain an insight upon the tastes and literary thought of individual readers of the period. Evidence of this kind helps us to understand the writer's historical situation, the nature of his immediate reading-public, and his response to these pressures.

The separate volumes in the *Critical Heritage Series* present a record of this early criticism. Clearly, for many of the highly productive and lengthily reviewed nineteenth- and twentieth-century writers, there exists an enormous body of material; and in these cases the volume editors have made a selection of the most important views, significant for their intrinsic critical worth or for their representative quality—perhaps even registering incomprehension!

For earlier writers, notably pre-eighteenth century, the materials are much scarcer and the historical period has been extended, sometimes far beyond the writer's lifetime, in order to show the inception and growth of critical views which were initially slow to appear.

In each volume the documents are headed by an Introduction, discussing the material assembled and relating the early stages of the author's reception to what we have come to identify as the critical tradition. The volumes will make available much material which would otherwise be difficult of access and it is hoped that the modern reader will be thereby helped towards an informed understanding of the ways in which literature has been read and judged.

B.C.S.

To
EDMUND BLUNDEN
with gratitude and affection

Contents

CONTENTS

x

CONTENTS

Acknowledgments

I should like to thank the following for their kind permission to reprint and quote copyright material: Mrs. George Bambridge for the various quotations from Kipling's works in prose and verse; John Murray Ltd. for the parody by Barry Pain from the *Cornhill Magazine*; the *Contemporary Review* and his literary executors for the article by J. M. Barrie; William Heinemann Ltd. for the article by Edmund Gosse published by them in his *Questions at Issue* (1893); Methuen & Co. Ltd. for the article on Kipling in *Reading for Pleasure* by R. Ellis Roberts and for the 1893 review by George Saintsbury, collected by J. W. Oliver, A. M. Clarke and A. Muir in *A Last Vintage* (1950); William Blackwood and Sons Ltd. for the article and review by J. H. Millar and for the review by Mrs. Oliphant, which all appeared in *Blackwood's Magazine*; Miss D. E. Collins for the review of *Just So Stories* by G. K. Chesterton, and to her and The Bodley Head Ltd. for extracts from his volume *Heretics*; The Estate of Sir Arthur Conan Doyle and John Murray Ltd. for the extract from *Through the Magic Door*; the Executors of Ford Madox Ford for the extracts from *The Critical Attitude*; the Estates of H. G. Wells and the publishers for extracts from *The New Machiavelli* (now published by Penguin Books) and *The Outline of History* (subsequently revised by G. P. Wells and Raymond Postgate and published by Cassell & Co. Ltd., and Doubleday & Co. Inc.); Mrs. T. S. Eliot and Faber & Faber Ltd. for the review by T. S. Eliot; Mr. Edmund Blunden for the extract from his review of *The Irish Guards,* in the *Nation and Athenaeum*; the *Saturday Review of Literature* (New York) for the review, 'Horace, Book Five', by Christopher Morley; Professor Bonamy Dobrée for his article from the *Monthly Criterion* and the extract from his *Rudyard Kipling: Realist and Fabulist*; the Literary Executors of Gilbert Frankau for the extract from his article in the *London Magazine*; the Cambridge University Press for extracts from F. J. Harvey Darton's *Children's Books in England*; the Kipling Society for papers by L. C. Dunsterville and André Maurois from the *Kipling Journal*; Mr. Dennis Gwynn and Mrs. T. G. Moorhead for the article by their father Stephen Gwynn; The Editor of the *Times Literary Supplement* for the review by T. Humphrey Ward (1890) in *The Times,* and the anonymous obituary

Article from the *T.L.S.* of 25th January 1936; the Literary Executors of George Moore for the extracts from his article on 'Kipling and Loti' reprinted in *Avowals*, published by William Heinemann Ltd.; Mr. Hugh Noyes for the article from the *Bookman* by his father, Alfred Noyes; the Executors of the late Dr. Neil Munro for his article from *Good Words*; the Society of Authors as the literary representative of the Estate of Richard Le Gallienne for his article in *Munsey's Magazine*; J. M. Dent & Sons Ltd. for the extract from *On Some Living Poets* by Sir Arthur Quiller-Couch.

Note on the text

The text of reviews and articles in this volume is taken whenever possible from the original periodical in which each first appeared, and not from subsequent reprints in book form. Where such were made, the original article was usually revised—in some cases many years later, often after Kipling's death. Minor mistakes and misprints (e.g. slips of a word in titles of stories or poems) have been corrected. Longer passages in prose, and more than a few consecutive lines of verse (except when detailed reference is made to them) have been omitted, and references given to the standard editions. In the case of Kipling's prose works, page and line references are to Macmillan's Uniform and Pocket Editions; in the case of the verse to Hodder and Stoughton's *Rudyard Kipling's Verse: Definitive Edition* (1940, frequently reprinted) herein referred to as DV.

Preface

Except in the case of extracts from letters by Robert Louis Stevenson (No. 10), Henry James (No. 11), and Lafcadio Hearn (No. 23), the three reviews by Lionel Johnson (No. 15) (which appeared within about the space of a year) and the two extracts from books by H. G. Wells (No. 46), all the items are arranged in the chronological order of their first appearance. This is of particular interest and importance in the case of Kipling whose critical adventures have been perhaps the strangest experienced by any great writer. And the end is not yet. As explained in the Introduction, the present selection does not carry these adventures further than 1936, the year of Kipling's death. Most of the more outstanding critical essays published since 1940 have already been collected in the volumes edited by Andrew Rutherford and Elliot L. Gilbert described in the Book List at the end of the present volume—where the chief critical and biographical studies of Kipling published in the same period are also listed.

Kipling has taken longer than most writers to pass through the valley of the shadow of criticism: his recent emergence on the further shore has been startling—and is likely to be even more so as his works receive deeper and more dispassionate study in academic and other circles. 'But that is another story.'

ROGER LANCELYN GREEN

Introduction

'It is time that the line should be firmly drawn between criticism and reviewing,' wrote Andrew Lang in 1890; 'the brief contemporary notice is not criticism . . . to me criticism seems more valuable and other . . . [By criticism] I mean reasoned and considered writing on the tried masterpieces of the world, or even ingenious and entertaining writing about new books. To have a clever and accomplished man telling you, in his best manner, what thoughts come into his mind after reading even a new novel, is no trifling pleasure among the pale and shadowy pleasures of the mind.'

Even at its very best criticism is no more than a handmaid to the Muses. The few really great practitioners may produce brief works of literature, but in relation to the works which inspired them, no results can be more than the *hors-d'œuvre* or the dessert to the main meal—however great a relish is added to the banquet by the best additions of even Lamb or Hazlitt, F. R. Leavis or C. S. Lewis.

The best criticism is a stimulant to make the lazy or unobservant reader look for more in the author than he notices at a casual reading. Much of the interest of the sort of early criticism that is half-reviewing is to see the dawning and unfolding of appreciation and realization of a new author with no place then in literature, who is now regarded as a classic. Another interest is of an historical kind: to follow an author's course through the tastes and prejudices and predictions—literary, ethical, social or political—of his period.

Rudyard Kipling is the most controversial author in English Literature. Even today his place on Parnassus remains undecided—though a place there he is generally agreed to have, even if some critics would seek it near the summit while others relegate him to the foothills.

This volume shows the remarkable nature of Kipling's reception by the critics. His sudden leap to the forefront of contemporary authors during the first few months after his return to England at just under twenty-four—hailed as a successor to Dickens by the leading reviewers, and with enthusiasm but a little more discrimination by his contemporaries among novelists; the serious studies as of a major writer by leading critics such as Lang (No. 12) and Gosse (No. 17) in this country,

I

by Howells (No. 28) and Charles Eliot Norton (No. 27) in America during the next ten years; and then the sudden descent into obliquity due almost entirely to political reasons beneath the pens of the Liberal critics of the turn of the century—with no falling off at all among the reading public. And finally the beginnings of his slow climb back towards consideration as a great writer—most of which has come since his death and, as easily available in other volumes, is outside the scope of this book.

As early as 1923, Edward Shanks wrote in the *London Mercury* [Vol. VII, pp. 274-5, 284, January 1923] of Kipling's

leap into a position in English political thought and feeling which, it is safe to say, no other English imaginative writer (even Milton not excepted) has ever occupied. Hence, too, comes the difficulty of looking at him dispassionately as an imaginative writer. We do not often mix together our enjoyment of literature and our partisan interest in politics, but when we do it we do it thoroughly.

So it comes about that we find even critics who maintain that Mr. Kipling does not write well . . . Time, and severe impartial standards, winnowing his work, will winnow much of it away; but they will certainly leave something that is unique.

I

KIPLING IN ENGLISH LITERATURE

The interesting moment of Kipling's eruption into English literature is well described by R. G. Collingwood in *The Principles of Art* (1938). After writing of what he calls 'Magical Art' as 'an art which is representative and therefore evocative of emotion, and evokes of set purpose some emotions rather than others in order to discharge them into the affairs of practical life', he goes on [p. 70]:

The change of spirit which divides Renaissance and modern art from that of the Middle Ages consists in the fact that medieval art was frankly and definitely magical, while Renaissance and modern art was not. I say 'was' not, because the climax of this non-magical or anti-magical period in the history of art was reached in the late nineteenth century, and the tide is now visibly turning. But there were always eddies in the tide-stream. There were cross-currents even in the nineties, when English literary circles were dominated by a school of so-called aesthetes professing the doctrine that art must not subserve any utilitarian end but must be practised for its own sake alone. This cry of art for art's sake was in some ways ambiguous; it did not, for example, distinguish art proper from amusement, and the art which its partisans admired and practised was in fact a shameless amusement art, amusing a select and self-appointed clique; but in one way it was perfectly definite: it ruled out magical art altogether. Into the perfumed and stuffy atmosphere of this china-shop burst Rudyard Kipling, young, nervous, short-sighted, and all on fire with the notion of using his very able pen to evoke and canalize the emotions which in his Indian life he had found to be associated with the governing of the British Empire. The aesthetes were horrified, not because they disapproved of imperialism, but because they disapproved of magical art; Kipling had blundered right up against their most cherished taboo. What was worse, he made a huge success of it. Thousands of people who knew those emotions as the steam in the engine of their daily work took him to their hearts. But Kipling was a morbidly sensitive little man, and the rebuff he had met with from the aesthetes blasted the early summer of his life. Henceforth he was torn between two ideals, and could pursue neither with undivided allegiance.

When Kipling arrived in London in the autumn of 1889 'Art for Art's Sake' was still being preached by Oscar Wilde (No. 16) and practised to a greater or lesser extent by writers such as Robert Louis Stevenson and Henry James (see their correspondence about 'the infant monster of a Kipling', Nos. 10 and 11).

A few years earlier Rider Haggard had set the critical bee-hive humming like Mowgli's hornets' nest with several 'big stones' such as *She* and *Allan Quartermain*. Kipling did not raise a like storm, though Henry James and 'J. K. S.' (No. 13) were anxious to bracket them together.

But the more orthodox view was still given by George Meredith when the American editor S. S. McClure visited him, after hearing of Kipling from Sidney Colvin as 'a new writer who seemed to have red blood in him', and asked: 'Mr. Meredith, Mr. Colvin thinks very highly of a new writer named Rudyard Kipling. He believes he is the coming man. Do you know anything about him?'

'The coming man,' said Meredith emphatically, 'is James Barrie.' [*McClure's Magazine*, Vol. XLII, p. 108, March 1914.]

Stevenson also set Barrie above Kipling, but second to Henry James (No. 10). For, as J. A. Hammerton wrote [in *Barrie: The Story of Genius*, 1929, pp. 140–1]:

The reader whose memory goes back to the year 1889 may recall the thrilling interest which the world of book-lovers was then taking in the performances of two young competitors for literary fame. Kipling, with his sudden spate of shilling story books that had first been 'tried' out on his Anglo-Indian audience and his virile *Barrack-Room Ballads* . . . seemed to shoot ahead of Barrie for the moment . . .

Kipling and Barrie were admittedly the two foremost names among the bright band of new writers who seemed to arrive at the critical moment to breathe a hopeful and purposeful spirit into a literature which, with the decadent trend of the waning century, was threatening to become morbid and joyless. It is true that Stevenson had already brought into contemporary fiction a new sensitiveness to form, and that Meredith, Hardy, and many another good, if lesser, Victorian was still in his vigour . . .

And Barrie himself, who had already achieved his own burst into early fame, greeted his new rival with true generosity: 'The great question is, can he write?' he asked in a short article called 'The Man from Nowhere' [*British Weekly*, 2 May 1890]. 'To which my own answer is that no young man of such capacity has appeared in our literature for years . . . few, if any, novelists who have become great did such promising work at his age.'

The popularity of Kipling's work in the nineties owed a great deal to its novelty. As C. S. Lewis wrote many years later ['Kipling's World' in *Literature and Life*, 1948, pp. 59–60]:

To put the thing in its shortest possible way, Kipling is first and foremost the poet of work. It is really remarkable how poetry and fiction before his time had avoided this subject. They had dealt almost exclusively with men in their 'private hours'—with love-affairs, crimes, sport, illness and changes of fortune . . . With a few exceptions imaginative literature in the eighteenth and nineteenth centuries had quietly omitted, or at least thrust into the background, the sort of thing which in fact occupies most of the waking hours of most men. And this did not merely mean that certain technical aspects of life were unrepresented. A whole range of strong sentiments and emotions—for many men, the strongest of all—went with them. For, as Pepys once noted with surprise, there is a great pleasure in talking of business. It was Kipling who first reclaimed for literature this enormous territory.

With this new literary dimension went also the new use of language —a frankness and a largeness in the use of the 'language of common men' that shocked many, delighted many more, and brought for all a refreshing blast of genuine fresh air into the hot-house atmosphere of the *fin-de-siècle*. 'Here's Literature! Here's Literature at last!' David Masson, elderly Professor of Literature and Rhetoric at Edinburgh is said to have declared to his astonished students, waving over his head a copy of the *Scots Observer* containing 'Danny Deever', in February 1890.

Seventy-five years later Mr Jack Dunman was writing of Kipling in *Marxism Today* (August 1965):

There is in fact no other considerable writer, except Hugh McDiarmid, who

4

has written, or attempted to write, poetry in working-class language; it is a pity that the left-wing poets of the thirties, including Spender and Auden, made no attempt to study his methods . . . There is one other point about the poetry which workers should consider—his deep interest in machinery. No other poet in this country thus far has written so effectively about it. Working-class language is used extensively in the short stories, many of which are about working-class characters and no others . . . He had a profound sense of history, and therefore of change and development; but his history was always human, and human of the common people; never of kings and aristocrats.

And the other great novelty of Kipling's literary achievement was virtually to introduce the short story into English literature—and write perhaps the greatest examples of this genre that we can boast even now.

Curiously enough, only a few months before his discovery of Kipling's short stories, Andrew Lang was writing in the Introduction to a collection of tales from the French, *The Dead Leman, and other Stories* (published in June 1889):

In England, short stories—tales which may be read in half an hour—are not so popular as they are in France. This may perhaps be explained, and certainly it must be regretted. In a brief narrative, or romance, nothing should be wasted, nothing should be superfluous, all should converge rapidly so as to produce the desired effect, or to enhance the interest of the given situation. Hence it is a misfortune that English taste is intolerant of short stories. They are welcomed in a magazine or journal; when collected they are looked on with suspicion. Not long ago a critic in *Blackwood's Magazine* rebuked Mr. Stevenson for publishing a set of *contes* in a volume, as if the performance were almost dishonourable. Some strange prejudice whispers, apparently, that a short story must be a 'pot boiler', or at best a rough sketch. Almost the reverse of this theory is often true.

A writer has an idea, say, a set of characters, or a given situation, which ought to be given in some twenty pages. But he is made to understand that he cannot afford thus to waste his idea. If he treats it as it should be treated, he produces a magazine tale which is not very remunerative; and if he were to write a dozen small masterpieces, and reprint them in a volume, he would have, at best, a little praise as the reward of his toil . . .

In France the *conte*, or short story has always been more fortunate . . . Many circumstances made the short story popular in France. Perhaps the more quick and eager intellect of the people does not dread, as we dread, the effort of awakening the attention afresh a dozen times in one volume. In England, we seem to dislike this effort. We prefer to make it only once, to get interested in the characters once for all, and then to loiter with them through, perhaps, 400,000 words of more or less consecutive narrative. If this theory be correct, short stories will never have much success in England, and, consequently, will not often be well written, because there is no prize in praise or money offered to him who writes them well. It would be hard to mention a single collection of *contes* which has really prospered among English-speaking people, except the stories of Poe. Experience proves that the least excellent of Hawthorne's romances is better liked than his volumes of little masterpieces. We seem to hate literary kickshaws, and to clamour for a round of literary beef. Older authors, Fielding and Dickens, at first mixed up brief tales in their long stories, but such tales were felt to be superfluous. Only one of them is immortal, 'Wandering Willie's Tale' in *Redgauntlet*, that perfect model of a *conte* in whose narrow range, humour, poetry, the grotesque, the terrible are combined as in no other work of man.

Within a year of this, Kipling had entirely altered the literary scene in England with regard to short stories. He arrived with one big volume and six small ones of short stories already written and collected —*Plain Tales from the Hills, Soldiers Three, The Story of the Gadsbys, In Black and White, Under the Deodars, The Phantom Rickshaw* and *Wee Willie Winkie*—and soon had a host of readers waiting for him to collect the stories which were appearing in magazines in 1890 into *Life's Handicap* in 1891.

But it will be noticed how at first most of his critics were suspending judgment until he had written the novel which they assumed he would attempt as the real test of his potentialities as a great writer. *The Light that Failed* at the end of 1890 was written partly as a bid for these laurels—and proved that Kipling had been right in choosing the short story as the literary type most fitted to his genius. *The Naulahka* (1892) proved that he was not to excel in the romance of adventure either; only in 1901 the 'nakedly picaresque' (*Something of Myself,* p. 228) *Kim* showed the one form of longer narrative in which he could write a masterpiece—and *Kim* stands alone, though for convenience sake it is classed as a novel.

This is not the place to enter into the circumstances which made Kipling a writer of short stories but not a novelist in the ordinary sense. Much lay, doubtless, in the whole cast of his mind; something perhaps in the brute fact that for two years he was allowed just the space for a 2,400 word 'Plain Tale' each week in the *Civil and Military Gazette*. But the fact remains that he conquered his reading public in England mainly with collections of short stories in volume form— and from 1890 the short story boomed in England, whether written by Kipling or Stevenson or Maugham, by Conan Doyle or G. K. Chesterton or Saki.

As several critics have pointed out right from the beginning of his career, Kipling learnt to write as a journalist and turned his experiences of daily reporting on Indian papers to good use when he 'graduated into literature'. As Frank Swinnerton put it in his Foreword to Hilton Brown's *Rudyard Kipling* (1945) Kipling was 'the first journalist, since Defoe, to bring a sense of news to the service of fiction, he excelled in the yarn'.

The result of this journalistic background and its unexpected development was well described by Desmond MacCarthy in his obituary article on Kipling in the *Sunday Times* of 19 January 1936:

His style, while loved by the unliterary, often irritated the literary because the aim of his virtuosity was always a *violent precision*. His adjectives and phrases start from the page. He forced you first and foremost to see, to hear, to touch, to smell—above all to see and smell—as vividly as words can make you do those things. When the greatest vividness was inconsistent with an aesthetic impression—well, in his work aesthetic sensitiveness went by the board . . .

Although his style possessed one of the most important qualifications for immense popularity, namely, unflagging vigour, it displayed at the same time an unpopular quality—extreme virtuosity. In his later work, especially, his prose was marked by an acrobatic verbal ingenuity hardly equalled by Meredith. It seems on the face of it strange that an author who is sometimes difficult, an author who must be read slowly, who is so tremendously concentrated and was latterly elliptical, should have continued to appeal to non-literary readers. Kipling is a writer whose phrases must be allowed to soak a moment in the mind before they expand, as those little Japanese pellets do which blossom into flower only when they have lain awhile on the surface of a cup of water.

Yet with all his extravagant and undisguised word-craft, he remained a favourite author of thousands upon thousands of readers who are ordinarily impatient of that kind of writing. No author, too, had a more various audience of admirers, while, oddly enough, it was among literary people, among artists and critics, that this master-craftsman was apt to meet with grudging appreciation. They admitted his genius, his power, but they often wrote and talked as though they were sorry that they had to. What were the qualities which made him admired by millions and yet often crabbed by those who loved, as he did, the painful art of writing?

II

KIPLING AND HIS CRITICS

'The qualities which made him admired by millions' are there for us all to enjoy and discover according to our own individual powers of appreciation and understanding; our own good fortune if we find ourselves naturally in tune with even some of what Kipling wrote in prose or verse, and our ability (and humility) in recognizing his achievements even if we do not admire them.

'Kipling is intensely loved and hated,' said C. S. Lewis. 'Hardly any reader likes him a little.' This should be less true now than when he said it twenty-one years ago since the winnowing process may have made it easier for the uncommitted reader to begin with the best of Kipling, and the passage of time should have brought nearer the happy day when his political opinions will matter no more than those of Milton or Swift or William Morris.

But there is danger here too. Any serious student or reader must read and study all Kipling's stories and all his poems and verses to choose the best—and should do so before reading any criticism or listening to any one else's views on which these are. Even anthologies (several have been issued by Macmillan, one in Dent's Everyman Library, and a number in the United States) should be used only with reserve and read only as introductions—if introduction is deemed necessary.

From time to time during more than forty years since its foundation the Kipling Society (which averages a thousand members) has tried, as a matter of interest, to decide by a majority vote which are Kipling's twelve best (or most popular) stories—but without any very satis-factory results. Even the process of counting votes has only really succeeded in singling out the twelve stories which members feel they should include. But most lists run on the lines: 'Such and such stories obviously ought to be included, but my own favourites are this and that.' One member submitted his twelve favourite stories and the three he disliked most—and those three were included among another member's twelve favourites. On another occasion, at a meeting about fifty strong, a leading Kipling scholar remarked: 'There is probably somewhere in the world a Kipling reader who would include every single one of the stories among his twelve favourites—except, of course, that utterly abominable " —— ".' Whereupon another member immediately exclaimed: 'Oh, that's always been one of my favourites!'

Even among contemporary critics of a single new volume this extraordinary variety of choice is apparent. Thus George Saintsbury (No. 25), when reviewing *Many Inventions*, singled out 'Brugglesmith' and 'Judson and the Empire' as among those he liked best, while Percy Addleshaw in the *Academy* (1 July 1893) included these two with

'The Children of the Zodiac' as 'quite the worst things Mr. Kipling ever wrote—and they are very bad'. Saintsbury liked 'Children of the Zodiac' least, but does not even mention the two, 'In the Rukh' and 'A Matter of Fact', which Addleshaw considered the best. However, Saintsbury's absolute favourites, 'My Lord the Elephant' and 'His Private Honour' were at least admitted to the second class by Addleshaw.

And of the same collection Andrew Lang noted in the *Cosmopolitan* [Vol. XV, p. 616, September 1893]:

Among books of fiction, Mr. Kipling's *Many Inventions* is far the most popular, and deserves its popularity. There are great varieties of excellence in the tales. The fun of 'The Children of the Zodiac' I fail to see, but 'In the Rukh' is a surprising piece of modified were-wolfism; 'The Finest Story in the World' is one of the five or six best stories in the world. 'The Lost Legion' shows a new kind of skill in the supernatural, and the three soldiers are as good as ever, except in 'Love o'Women', which seems to my taste, rather dully disagreeable than really 'powerful'. But it *is* all a matter of taste.

Looking back over the critical reception of his works only a month or two before his death, Kipling wrote in *Something of Myself* [pp. 210–11]:

I am afraid that I was not much impressed by reviews. But my early days in London were unfortunate. As I got to know literary circles and their critical output, I was struck by the slenderness of some of the writers' equipment. I could not see how they got along with so casual a knowledge of French work and, apparently, of much English grounding that I had supposed indispensable. Their stuff seemed to be a day-to-day traffic in generalities, hedged by trade considerations. Here I expect I was wrong but making my own tests (the man who had asked me out to dinner to discover what I had read gave me the notion), I would ask simple questions, misquote or misattribute my quotations; or (once or twice) invent an author. The result did not increase my reverence. Had they been newspaper men in a hurry, I should have understood; but the gentlemen were presented to me as Priests and Pontiffs . . .

With this should be compared Kipling's poem 'In Partibus' and story 'The Three Young Men', written in December 1889 for the *Civil and Military Gazette* and rescued from intended oblivion by the American pirate publication of *Abaft and Funnel* (1909). Otherwise he was absolutely true in saying [*Something of Myself*, pp. 84–5] 'I have never directly or indirectly criticized any fellow-craftsman's output, or encouraged any man or woman to do so; nor have I approached any persons that they might be led to comment on my output.'

There were, of course, obvious exceptions to Kipling's sweeping condemnation of the literary knowledge and basic scholarship of his critics and reviewers. Even in the earlier period he was reviewed and his work studied seriously by men as widely read in European and Classical literature as Lang and Whibley and Henley and Gosse, as well as those who then or later held Chairs in English Literature such as J. H. Millar, Saintsbury, Quiller-Couch and Norton, while Sir William Hunter (No. 3) brought unrivalled knowledge of the Oriental setting of the earlier stories; and his critics also included novelists from Henry James and J. M. Barrie to Ford Madox Ford and Ian Hay, and later on Somerset Maugham and J. B. Priestley, besides poets from Alfred Noyes and Richard Le Gallienne to T. S. Eliot and Edmund Blunden.

But the majority of reviews and much of the criticism that was intended to be more serious were indeed such as Kipling describes, and he rightly ignored them—and understandably paid little attention even to the more worthwhile studies by those better qualified to make them.

For, contrary to much that has been said, Kipling was a truly modest man, and very humble in the conviction that a man's best work came from without—at the promptings of his 'daemon', as he himself would have put it.

Two extracts from the private diary of his closest friend, Rider Haggard, are of interest in this context. [They have been published by Morton N. Cohen in his *Rudyard Kipling to Rider Haggard: The Record of a Friendship* (1965), pp. 84, 100]:

23 March 1915 . . . I asked him what he was doing to occupy his mind amidst all these troubles. He answered, like myself, writing stories, adding, 'I don't know what they are worth, I only know they ain't literature.' Like all big men Kipling is very modest as to his own productions. Only little people are vain . . .
22 May 1918 . . . I commented on the fact that he had wide fame and was known as 'the great Mr. Kipling', which should be a consolation to him. He thrust the idea away with a gesture of disgust. 'What is it worth—what *is* it all worth?' he answered. Moreover he went on to show that anything any of us did *well* was no credit to us: that it came from somewhere else: 'We are only telephone wires.' As example he instanced (I think) 'Recessional' in his own case and *She* in mine. 'You didn't write *She* you know,' he said, 'something wrote it through you!' or some such words.

It should be added that Kipling himself was not only very well read indeed in English and French literature [see *Kipling's Reading* by Ann M. Weygandt (1939) for the majority of references and quotations in his published works], but took a keen interest in most of his contemporaries, and wrote enthusiastically to those whom he knew even slightly. Except in the case of Rider Haggard, whose imaginative achievement he understood and appreciated as few have done, most of these letters remain unpublished. Besides more obvious authors, he wrote letters of praise and criticism to such writers as Barrie and Henley, Conan Doyle, Stanley Weyman and A. E. W. Mason, Mrs Molesworth and E. Nesbit—to name only a few. And contemporary reminiscences and letters bear testimony to his friendly interest and wide appreciation. For example:

Anthony Hope wrote to a friend after meeting Kipling at lunch in November 1900: 'He was kind and interesting about *Quisanté* . . . He is a singularly attractive fellow, genuine and brimming with life.' [Sir Charles Mallet: *Anthony Hope and his Books* (1935), p. 155.]

Baroness Orczy, staying in the same hotel in Bath in 1915, wrote in her autobiography: 'I had many a talk with that very dear and very great man. It would be impossible to imagine anyone distinguished as he was, more simple and unaffected, so full of charm and understanding. He made me very happy with his generous praise of my work, telling me just what he admired in it, and why in his opinion it had been so successful and popular.' [*Links in the Chain of Life* (1947), pp. 147–8.]

A. E. W. Mason wrote in a letter to a friend from Cairo, 29 February 1929: 'Kipling and his wife are out here at this hotel. I never knew him really well before but he is quite charming. He was wildly enthusiastic about [*The Prisoner in the Opal*] which is always pleasant.' [Roger Lancelyn Green: *A. E. W. Mason* (1952), p. 192.]

'F. Anstey' [T. Anstey Guthrie] wrote in his autobiography: 'In 1900 he wrote me an extraordinary kind and generous letter about *The Brass Bottle*, then running as a serial in the pages of the *Strand Magazine*.' [*A Long Retrospect* (1936), p. 147.]

Doubtless Kipling too received many letters of appreciation and criticism from his literary contemporaries, but these have not survived. Like Lang, he destroyed all incoming correspondence, hoping—vainly—that those to whom he wrote would do likewise, objecting to the publication of letters, reminiscences and all forms of 'the higher cannibalism' [*Something of Myself*, p. 191]. 'Seek not to question other than the works I leave behind' (Epilogue to his poetical works), he begged: but it was too much to expect.

As for published criticism, he wrote: 'attacking or attacked, so long as you have breath on no provocation explain'—and held to this rule throughout his career.

'Years ago he gave us fair warning he would not work with an eye to his public, and he never has,' complained a critic in the New York *Bookman* in March 1902. 'There is no sign in Kipling's writings that he has ever learnt anything from his critics or made any concessions to his public's demands. Take it or leave it has been his attitude from the first. In his own good time, after people had despaired of him, he wrote *Kim*. We told him distinctly that was the kind of thing we wanted of him, and asked him to do it again; whereupon he undertook the conduct of the British Government through the agency of bad verse . . . As mere literary pleasure-lovers his readers have a right to complain . . . Other writers have at one time or another paid some attention to criticism. There was George Meredith, for instance, whom no one would accuse of pliancy. He was swerved entirely from his early course by criticism. And Thomas Hardy, the only other living novelist of Kipling's rank, was influenced by it to his own and our advantage. But from Kipling, as from a Tammany watermain, we must take things as they come, knowing that protests are in vain.'

III

CRITICAL RECEPTION

Whether he paid any attention to it or not, Kipling received an immense amount of criticism, from short reviews to full-scale articles by leading critics, followed within ten years of his first appearance in literary London by a flow of book-length studies that by now far exceeds his own original output; if books containing essays and chapters on him are included, the library of the Kipling Society can boast well over two hundred volumes of biography and criticism—and even so cannot claim absolute completeness.

His earliest volumes were reviewed fairly extensively by Indian papers in the English language—but with little realization that here was anything out of the ordinary. Nor did any reviewer do much more than make conventional critical noises.

Departmental Ditties (1886), for example, was greeted by the *Times of India* as 'a very pleasant companion for a lonely half-hour, or to while away the tedium of a railway journey'. The *Indian Daily News* went a little further, declaring that 'the pieces are bright and clever, with occasional touches which indicate that the author may some day reach to higher flights than the lampooning of weak or corrupt officialism'. The *Sind Gazette* went further still, averring that 'they are full of humour and spirit, and, brief as they are, have the genuine ring, and display a poetical faculty of a high order'.

Little more than this was said, except that the *Advocate of India* felt that 'he had attacked the public departments of this country, dealing with them in a spirit of genial fun which reminds one of Bon Gaultier and Aliph Cheem', the *Bombay Gazette* compared 'The Story of Uriah' to *The Biglow Papers*, and *The Englishman* felt that 'they will suffer little by comparison with the best work of Praed or Locker'.

But such fame was purely local. E. Kay Robinson who became editor of the *Civil and Military Gazette* towards the end of 1886, wrote later ['Kipling in India', *McClure's Magazine*, Vol. VII, July 1896]:

Having to my great delight 'discovered' Kipling (though his name was already a household word throughout India) in 1886, I thought that the literary world at home should share my pleasure. He was just then publishing his first little book in India; but the *Departmental Ditties* were good enough, as I thought at the time, and as afterwards turned out, to give him a place among English writers of the day. So I obtained eight copies, and distributed them, with recommendatory letters, among editors of English journals . . . So far as I could ascertain, not a single one of those papers condescended to say a word about the unpretentious little volume.

One copy, however—whether from among Robinson's eight or another source—came into the hands of Andrew Lang, who reviewed it in his monthly causerie, the famous 'At the Sign of the Ship', in *Longman's Magazine* [Vol. VIII, pp. 675-6, October 1886]—the first item (No. 1) in the present volume.

Lang failed to spot the author's name (reproduced in facsimile at the foot of the front wrapper)—or to realize what the signature over 'Assistant—Department of Public Journalism, Lahore District' was: for he notes 'the modest author does not give his name'.

The next step is odd, and has never been fully explained. In October 1887 Kipling wrote to his friend Mrs F. C. Burton (the 'original' of Mrs Hauksbee, to whom *Plain Tales* was dedicated as 'The Wittiest Woman in India'): 'With moderate good luck and the recommendation of a man in London, I get a rather nasty story into *Longman's Magazine* about Christmas time.'

The 'man in London' was Vereker Hamilton; the recommendation came from Ian Hamilton (afterwards General Sir Ian Hamilton), and the story was 'The Mark of the Beast' [later published in the *United Service Magazine* June, and the *Pioneer* 12-14 July 1890, before being collected in *Life's Handicap*, 1891]—possibly in an even 'nastier' version.

The story (apparently with the author unnamed) was shown to Lang by Vereker Hamilton. Lang (who was literary adviser to Charles Longman, editor of *Longman's Magazine*) returned it to Vereker with a letter (no longer extant) containing the sentence: 'I would gladly give Ian a fiver if he had never been the means of my reading this poisonous stuff, which has left an extremely disagreeable impression on my mind.' Surprised by this, but doubtless recollecting Lang's supersensitiveness to any descriptions of cruelty or torture, Vereker took it to William Sharp, 'a man of quite different tastes from Lang'. But Sharp was even more decisive, writing: 'I would like to hazard a guess that the writer is very young and that he will die mad before he has reached the age of thirty.'[1]

(At variance with the usual account, H. B. Marriott-Watson (1863–1921), the novelist, wrote in 1904 that 'The Mark of the Beast', sent by Ian Hamilton, 'reached Mr. Andrew Lang, who read it with interest, and advised the author to get it translated into French, as it would never pass in this country'. Marriott-Watson knew Lang well, and may have had this version of the events from him. [Cutting from unidentified periodical dated 18 July 1904 in the Library of the Kipling Society.])

Lang apparently did not know who had written the story which he found so upsetting (and did not recommend for *Longman's Magazine*). For in 1888 C. F. Hooper, who was learning the publishing business with Thacker and Spink of Calcutta, publishers in that year of Kipling's second book, *Plain Tales from the Hills*, was told 'to try to sell it in London'. Hooper had little success, only sixteen copies being subscribed; but he persuaded the editor of the *Saturday Review* to review it [9 June 1888] (No. 2). [See C. F. Hooper's article 'Kipling's Younger Days', *Saturday Review*, Vol. CLXI, pp. 308–9, 7 March 1936.]

The editor who reviewed *Plain Tales* was Walter Herries Pollock [1850–1926]. Lang was a close friend of his, and wrote each week for the *Saturday Review* at the time—so he cannot have missed seeing the review, and probably reading the book. Certainly it was recorded by Mrs Hill, wife of the Professor with whom Kipling was lodging at Allahabad at the time, in her diary for April 1888: 'I shall never forget the glee with which RK came in one afternoon saying, "What do you suppose I just came across in reading the proof of this week's English letter?" Andrew Lang says: "Who is Mr. Rudyard Kipling?" He was so pleased that they really had heard of him in England, for in all modesty he intends to make his mark in the world.' [Edmonia Hill: 'The Young Kipling', *Atlantic Monthly*, Vol. CLVII, pp. 406–15, April 1936.]

Meanwhile a family friend got a review of *Departmental Ditties* into the *Academy* of 1 September 1888 (No. 3): 'The first analytical essay

by a writer who knew Kipling's background, and knew India', Charles
Carrington calls it in the authorized biography. [Charles Carrington:
Rudyard Kipling—His Life and Work (1955), p. 131.]

Hunter had been on Lord Dufferin's staff, but returned to England to
take up a career in journalism, and Kipling had already addressed a
long (uncollected) ode to him in the *Pioneer* of 1 June 1888, to the effect:

> You're far too good! Ask L[a]ng, ask Ar[no]ld, ask
> The S[avi]lle and the S[ava]ge where men call
> Who nightly gibber 'neath the penny mask,
> And scribble crudities on Time's blank wall,
> How golden is the guerdon of their task,
> Hark! From the weltering Strand the newsboys bawl:
> 'Murder in Paddin'ton! Revoltin' Story!!'
> "Untin' in Injia!' Hunter, is *this* glory?

Somehow, early in 1889, a copy of *Soldiers Three* got to England
and was reviewed anonymously in the *Spectator* of 23 March (No. 4).
But the next definite step was chronicled by Mrs Hill in her diary for
9 March 1889 when she and her husband were already at Calcutta with
Kipling at the beginning of their trip to England via Japan and America,
described in *From Sea to Sea*: 'The covers were torn off from the whole
six of the Wheeler edition on account of some postal law, and the
letterpress sent on to England to Andrew Lang, so that Ruddy may
be already introduced when he arrives in London.' (This may have
been done earlier than the date of the entry, and the books arrived in
time for the *Spectator* review of *Soldiers Three*.)

The six Wheeler paperbound volumes, later collected into two in
England as *Soldiers Three* and *Wee Willie Winkie*, had received only
superficial reviews in India. 'His knowledge of Anglo-Indian human
nature, which is ordinary human nature under great provocation, is
profound—we were going to say awful—and he can go from grave
to gay with the facility of a true artist,' was the most interesting comment the *Home and Colonial Mail* could make; and the *Civil and Military Gazette* followed the same line: 'His pictures of Anglo-Indian life
are finished works of art, full of go and brightness, true to nature in
its many aspects, and enlivened with a quaint fancy, a ready wit, and a
faculty of phrase and expression seldom met with.'

Looking back in 1890, and forgetting that he had not then known
who wrote *Departmental Ditties*, Lang commented on the fact that he
had been the first to review it in England, and went on:

Mr. Kipling's name was new to me, and, much as I admired his verses, I heard no more of him till I received *The Story of the Gadsb's, In Black and White,* and *Under the Deodars.* They were all unpretending little tomes, clad in grey paper, and published in India. Then, on reading them, one saw that a new star in literature had swum into one's ken. [*Harper's Weekly,* 30 August 1890.]

Lang advised Sampson Low, Marston and Co., to publish the Wheeler booklets in England (he is supposed to have exclaimed: 'Eureka! A genius has come to light!' [Edward E. Long: 'The Discovery of Rudyard Kipling', the *London Magazine,* 1926]), and proceeded to review *In Black and White* and *Under the Deodars* in the *Saturday Review* of 10 August 1889 (No. 5). Lang had met Kipling (who arrived in London about 5 October) and introduced him to Haggard [see letter of 26 October to Lang in Morton N. Cohen's *Rudyard Kipling to Rider Haggard* (1965), pp. 25–7] before writing his next review, of *Plain Tales from the Hills* (also anonymous) in the *Daily News* of 2 November.

Lang and others may have prepared the way for Kipling by making his name known to a small public that appreciated good literature and suggesting that critics should look out for him. But on his arrival in London he made his own way into popular fame by the arresting excellence of his stories and poems.

That the word had got about, and his books were being read when he arrived is shown by the recollections of Sidney Low, at that time editor of the *St. James's Gazette:*

I spent an afternoon reading *Soldiers Three* and when I went out to a dinner-party that evening I could talk of nothing but this marvellous youth who had dawned upon the eastern horizon. My host, a well-known journalist and critic of those days, laughed at my enthusiasm which he said would hardly be justified by the appearance of another Dickens. 'It may be,' I answered hotly, 'that a greater than Dickens is here.'

I got Wheeler [Stephen Wheeler, who had been Kipling's first editor on the *Civil and Military Gazette* at Lahore] to put me in touch with Kipling on his arrival in London, and one morning there walked into my office a short, dark, young man with a bowler hat, a rather shabby tweed overcoat, an emphatic voice, a charming smile, and behind his spectacles a pair of the brightest eyes I had ever seen. He told me that he had his way to make in English literature, and intended to do it, though at the time he was young, very poor, and (in this country) quite unknown. I suggested that he might help to keep his pot boiling by writing sketches and short stories for the *St. James's,* which suggestion he willingly accepted . . .

A day or two later he sent me a contribution, which I received with delight and promptly printed. This, so far as I know, was the first piece from Kipling's pen published in England. [D. Chapman-Huston: *The Lost Historian—Sidney Low* (1936), pp. 78-9.]

These stories, which appeared weekly from 21 November ('The Comet of a Season') to 28 December ('The Battle of Rupert Square') were all unsigned (Kipling continued to contribute in prose and verse until the end of March 1890, but some later items were signed and others may not be his), and cannot have helped him to make his name known.

This he did, however, with the aid of the one important introduction which he brought with him, to Mowbray Morris (1847–1911), editor of *Macmillan's Magazine*, who had once been art editor of the *Pioneer* of Allahabad. Even so Kipling began with a pseudonym for his first two poems 'The Ballad of the King's Mercy' and 'The Ballad of East and West', which appeared as by 'Yussuf' in November and December 1889. But the December issue also contained the first signed story, 'The Incarnation of Krishna Mulvaney', and thereafter followed almost monthly such famous stories as 'The Head of the District', 'The Courting of Dinah Shadd', 'The Man Who Was', 'Without Benefit of Clergy', 'On Greenhow Hill', and several poems —all by September 1890, and all signed.

The *Barrack-Room Ballads* began in the *Scots Observer* (edited by W. E. Henley) with 'Danny Deever' on 22 February 1890, and were received with enthusiasm; while stories and poems appeared also in other periodicals such as the *Fortnightly*, *Longman's*, *Lippincott's*, *Harper's* and even the *Fishing Gazette* during that first year with its amazing productivity.

Kipling's meteoric rise to fame is well sketched by J. M. Barrie in his article 'The Man from Nowhere', published over the pseudonym Gavin Ogilvy in the *British Weekly* on 2 May 1890:

... Two society papers made themselves at one time a debating society for discussing Mr. Rudyard Kipling, 'The Man from Nowhere', as he then called himself. That 'everybody knows Mr. Kipling's books', was *The World's* argument, and that 'nobody ever heard of Mr. Kipling', was *Truth's*. As a result, while *The World* and other papers thought Mr. Kipling such a celebrity that they vied with each other in describing the tags of his bootlaces, *Truth* and other papers talked contemptuously of log-rolling.

At the time of the *World–Truth* debate Mr. Kipling was a novelist who, six months previous, was almost quite unknown in this country. Therefore, his detractors seemed to urge, it is absurd that he can be a great man already. No, said his admirers, it is only remarkable, and therefore worth making a greater shout over. They certainly shouted so loudly as to justify the other side in calling him, not the Man from Nowhere, but the Man with many Friends. But to his friends let this folly be charged, not to him. Even if he did take their indiscriminate eulogies a little complacently, can we, with any generosity, blame a young man for liking to hear his work extolled? Whether Mr. Kipling has influential friends is a small matter. The great question is, can he write? To which my own answer is that no young man of such capacity has appeared in our literature for years.

The very next day in the *Scots Observer* (see No. 7 below) W. E. Henley was almost echoing Barrie's words—and Sidney Low's enthusiasm of six months earlier:

When Kipling is writing at his best, of Mulvaney or the Man who would be King, . . . you are made to feel with all your strength that here is such a promise as has not been perceived in English letters since young Mr. Dickens broke in suddenly upon the precincts of immortality as the creator of Pickwick and the Wellers.

And both these echoed an anonymous review of reprints of *Departmental Ditties* and *Soldiers Three* less than a week earlier in the *Athenaeum* [No. 3261, p. 528, 26 April 1890], which might be by Theodore Watts-Dunton:

What position Mr. Kipling may ultimately attain to it is impossible upon his present performances to predict with any certainty; yet if he should prove capable of filling a larger canvas than he has yet essayed, he might conceivably become a second Dickens. His sparkling and cynical trifles are comparable to those *Sketches by Boz* which first brought the great English novelist to the notice of the public; but it remains to be seen whether he can give the public what will answer to a *David Copperfield* or *A Tale of Two Cities*. He has shown himself extraordinarily prolific since his arrival in this country, and some of his later work seems to be of a higher imaginative quality than his earlier studies. What we look for now is that he shall begin '*majora canere*,' and, avoiding the nemesis that waits upon over-productiveness, concentrate his undoubted gifts upon the treatment of more important themes than even the amusing vagaries of Tommy Atkins and the risky situations of Simla society.

All this is confirmed shortly by Kipling in *Something of Myself* [pp. 78–9, 88]:

My small stock-in-trade of books had become known in certain quarters; and there was an evident demand for my stuff. I do not recall that I stirred a hand to help myself. Things happened to me. I went by invitation to Mowbray

Morris, the editor of *Macmillan's Magazine* . . . He took from me an Indian tale and some verses . . .

Then more tales were asked for, and the editor of the *St. James's Gazette* wanted stray articles, signed and unsigned . . .

About this time was an interview in a weekly paper, where I felt myself on the wrong side of the counter and that I ought to be questioning my questioner. Shortly after, that same weekly made me a proposition which I could not see my way to accept, and then announced that I was 'feeling my oats', of which, it was careful to point out, it had given me my first sieveful. Since, at that time, I was overwhelmed, not to say scared, by the amazing luck that had come to me, the pronouncement gave me confidence. If that was how I struck the external world—good! For naturally I considered the whole universe was acutely interested in me only—just as a man who strays into a skirmish is persuaded he is the pivot of the action . . .

I was plentifully assured, *viva voce* and in the Press cuttings—which is a drug that I do not recommend to the young—that 'nothing since Dickens' compared with my 'meteoric rise to fame', etc. (But I was more or less inoculated, if not immune, to the coarser sorts of print.)

'People talked, quite reasonably, of rockets and sticks,' added Kipling, and went on to quote the immortal lines by 'that genius J. K. S.'—'which I would have given much to have written myself' (No. 13).

Besides reproof in verse, parody also could contain genuine—and sometimes devastating—criticism. Barry Pain seems to have been about the first in the field with his parody of a *Plain Tale* in the *Cornhill Magazine* in October 1890 (No. 9)—which shows up some of Kipling's early weaknesses with kindly mockery.

E. V. Lucas (1868–1938) late in 1892 in the *Privateer* (an ephemeral magazine issued at University College, London, which survived only for eleven numbers) included in a series of amusing 'Literary Recipes' one for 'Kipling Chutnee':

This pickle has a peculiar mordant quality which distinguishes it from all others. The chief ingredient is unwashed English, chopped, broken, and bruised with a brazen instrument. Then work in chips and fragments of cynicism, 'B.V.' [James Thomson, author of *The City of Dreadful Night*]'s poems, the seven cardinal sins, the *Soldier's Pocket Book*, the *Civil Service Regulations*, Simla manners, profanity, an Ekka pony, the Southern Cross, and genius. Spice with a Tipperary brogue.

Again, Owen Seaman in 'The Ballad of the Kipperling' in *Punch* (13 January 1894), hits off very neatly the facility of some of Kipling's verse, and his inordinate delight in 'jargon'. But later examples tend to be vindictive without conveying any real criticism, as in the case of Max Beerbohm's 'P.C., X, 36' in *A Christmas Garland* (1912), pp. 11-20. At least nine caricatures and two critical articles emanated from the pen of the unconscionable Max, as well as this parody: 'This incomparable master of the smirk and titter,' wrote Charles Carrington, 'was, as a rule, gentle, except when he touched upon one topic. He hated Rudyard Kipling. He set himself to destroy Kipling's reputation and, later, to assure the world that it had been destroyed, with no small degree of success among the literary coteries, but with no visible effect upon Kipling's ever-growing fame and influence in wider circles.' [*Rudyard Kipling*, p. 341.]

Such parodies as R. C. Lehmann's 'Burra Murra Boko', Number Two of the second series of Mr Punch's Prize Novels [*Punch*, Vol. XCIX, p. 173, 11 October 1890]; Anthony C. Deane's 'A Very Nearly Story' [*Punch*, Vol. CXXIII, p. 248, 8 October 1902] and the Kipling item in St John Hankin's *Lost Masterpieces* [*Punch*, Vol. CXXV, p. 254, 14 October 1903] are little more than mildly amusing and do not have much to say as criticism. Lehmann also wrote an attack on 'The Islanders' [*Punch*, Vol. CXXII, p. 52, 15 January 1902], from a political rather than a literary angle which, Kipling declared, nearly made him break his rule of never answering criticism:

I had written during the Boer War a set of verses based on unofficial criticisms of many serious junior officers . . . Nobody loved them, and indeed they were not conciliatory; but *Punch* took them rather hard. This was a pity because *Punch* would have been useful at that juncture. I knew none of its staff, but I asked questions and learned that *Punch* on this particular issue was—non-Aryan 'and German at that' . . . I swallowed my spittle at once. Israel is a race to leave alone. It abets disorder. [*Something of Myself*, pp. 223-4.]

But indeed from the end of the century onwards most parody of Kipling was from a political angle, as most criticism soon tended to become. His role as prophet was neatly summed up, and without animus, in an anonymous Alphabet of Authors contributed to the *London Magazine* about 1902:

> K is for Kipling
> A builder of rhymes,
> Who 'lest we forget'
> All our national crimes
> Sets them forth at great length
> In large type in *The Times*.

A little earlier, in their *Lives of the 'Lustrious* (1901) C. L. Graves and E. V. Lucas had also made gently satiric protest against Kipling's new role:

KIPLING, RUDYARD, Poet Laureate and Recruiting Sergeant, was born all over the world, some eighteen years ago. After a lurid infancy at Westward Ho! in the company of Stalky & Co., he emigrated to India at the age of six and swallowed it whole. In the following year the British Empire was placed in his charge, and it is still there. A misgiving that England may have gone too far in the matter of self-esteem having struck him in 1897, he wrote 'The Recessional', but there are signs that he has since forgotten it . . . He lives in Cape Colony, which is a suburb of Rottingdean, and at intervals puts forth a fascinating book, or a moral essay in *The Times* . . . [Quoted in full in E. V. Lucas: *Reading, Writing and Remembering* (1932), pp. 212–13.]

Whether or not Kipling was 'The Man with Many Friends', even those most interested in his success mingled blame with their praise, and by no means practised the gentle art of log-rolling. To take one example, Andrew Lang who had done more to help Kipling to make his way in the literary world than any other of his earlier critics shows by a selection of his more casual utterances that he did not necessarily admire all that Kipling wrote:

What *does* Kipling mean by that story in *Longman's*? 1 admire him awfully, but one or two such performances as that would make me set about a volume of selections. [Unpublished letter to Rider Haggard: April 1890.] [The story was the uncollected 'For One Night Only'.]
    I don't care for *The Light that Failed*! [Unpublished letter to Walter Herries Pollock: 3 April 1891.]
    'Love-o'-Women' seems to my taste, rather dully disagreeable than really 'powerful'. [*Cosmopolitan* (N.Y.), Vol. XV, p. 616, September 1893.]
Of new books here, Mr. Rudyard Kipling's *Jungle Book* is perhaps the most interesting, certainly the most original. One likes to hear dull owls hoot that Mr. Kipling will 'write himself out'. Nobody is less likely to exhaust his stores of reflection, humour and observation . . . [Mowgli and the wolves] are delightful to read about, for 'grown-ups', and the pretty volume is a paradise for children . . . Oh, blessed province of fancy, and dear jungle of the imagination, whither we can flee and be at peace, if he who guides us, like Mr. Kipling, has the secret of the branch of gold. [*Cosmopolitan*, Vol. XVII, p. 503, August 1894.]
As my sympathies are not wholly engaged with *Stalky and Co.* in their long and successful combat with their masters, I prefer to say very little about these heroes. Whatever they may be they are not normal schoolboys. Their eternal use of the word 'giddy' is teasing; their slang is not 'of the centre' . . . More

agreeable fellows are Mr. Eden Phillpots's heroes in that delightful book *The Human Boy* . . . Then I am wholly captivated by those perfect little trumps, Mrs. Nesbit's characters in *The Treasure Seekers* . . . [*Longman's Magazine*, Vol. XXXV, p. 184, December 1899.]

Mr. Kipling in *Kim* in *Cassell's Magazine* is once more the Mr. Kipling who first won our hearts. His theme is India, where he is always at his best; and we learn more of the populace, the sects, the races, the lamas, the air, the sounds, scents and smells from a few pages than from libraries of learned authors. [*Longman's Magazine*, Vol. XXXVII, p. 570, April 1901.]

Before political bias took the place of literary criticism, beginning with Robert Buchanan's 'The Voice of the Hooligan' (No. 33) in 1899, the more scholarly critics had attempted to treat fully and dispassionately of such work as was before them from the simple standpoint of literature. Lang at the beginning of 1891 (No. 12) was followed by Barrie (No. 14) and Gosse (No. 17) and Henry James (No. 21), with a more grudging acceptance from Francis Adams (No. 20) and the fuller studies by Charles Eliot Norton (No. 27) and J. H. Millar (No. 29).

Millar's lengthy and leisurely pontification in *Blackwood's Magazine* in 1898 is typical—and the best—of a number of anonymous studies of great length in the 'Reviews'; Rowland Prothero, Baron Ernle (1851–1937) wrote twenty pages on 'The Tales of Mr. Kipling' in the *Edinburgh Review* [Vol. CLXXIV, pp. 132–51] in July 1891; the Rev. William Barry, Catholic apologist, (1849–1930) thirty pages on 'Mr. Rudyard Kipling's Tales' in the *Quarterly Review* [Vol. CLXXV, pp. 132–61] in July 1892, and Henry Heathcote Statham, authority on art and music, (1839–1924) preceded Millar with an article of twenty-two pages on 'The Works of Mr. Rudyard Kipling' in the *Edinburgh Review* [Vol. CLXXXVII, pp. 203–26] in January 1898.

After them Kipling became the butt of political prejudice, and his literary attainments were more and more ignored by critics, or assumed not to exist outside the popular fancy. An occasional reviewer broke away from what was fast becoming a stereotyped ready-made label; but on the whole no serious criticism of Kipling was written during the first two decades of the present century.

An honourable exception was Holbrook Jackson (1874–1948) in his excellent study *The Eighteen Nineties* (1913), where he gave Kipling a whole chapter of sensible and well-balanced description, setting him reasonably in his period, and attempting no overall judgments.

The first award of the Nobel Prize for Literature to Kipling in 1907 did little to reinstate him as a great writer in his own country. Books of the stature of *Puck of Pook's Hill* (1906) and *Rewards and Fairies* (1910) were dismissed on the back pages of periodicals as scarcely worthy of notice: the *Athenaeum's* note on the former is typical:

In his new part—the missionary of empire—Mr. Kipling is living the strenuous life. He has frankly abandoned story telling, and is using his complete and powerful armoury in the interest of patriotic zeal. [No. 4119, p. 404, 6 October 1906.]

It was, of course, understandable when Kipling was appealing for conscription and warning the country of its unreadiness for the European war which he foresaw as imminent, in public speeches, in impassioned verses set up 'in large type in *The Times*', and even in such stories as 'The Army of a Dream '[*Morning Post*, 15–18 June 1904; collected in *Traffics and Discoveries* the same year] and 'The Edge of the Evening' [*Pall Mall Magazine*, December 1913; collected in *A Diversity of Creatures*, 1917] and the allegory of 'The Mother Hive.' [*Windsor Magazine*, December 1908; collected in *Actions and Reactions*, 1909], that those who disagreed with him should look with suspicion on all else that he wrote.

Naturally an author's deeply-held convictions may find some reflection in most of what he writes, and Kipling did see parallels between past and present in his historical stories (which is only to repeat the cliché that history repeats itself); but though the Puck stories became immediately popular—among his most popular works, in fact—it took a generation before they were considered seriously as important historical fiction. Then the historian G. M. Trevelyan set them at the top of Kipling's achievement, declaring in 1953 that:

He tells us tale after tale of the ancient history of England, as he imagines it, with a marvellous historical sense, I think . . . As a piece of historical imagination I know of nothing in the world better than the third story in *Puck* called 'The Joyous Venture', in which the Viking ship coasts Africa to find gold, and fight gorillas in the tropical forest. I can see no fault in it, and many a merit. [See further in his *A Layman's Love of Letters* (1954), pp. 27–35. Also on Kipling's historical stories see J. I. M. Stewart in the *Kipling Journal*, No. 153, p. 9, March 1965, and his other writings on Kipling.]

The First World War proved Kipling right in many respects—as he said in his poetic tribute to Lord Roberts, it was 'the War that he had descried'. But prophets of woe are usually execrated before the event and seldom praised for their prescience after it.

Perhaps Kipling was considered harmless, a toothless tiger, by early postwar writers—even as approaching the image of a 'grand old man of letters'—and he was often described (with an implied shrug) as 'an institution'.

Overseas Maurice Hutton, lecturing in Montreal in 1918, felt able to take Kipling as a serious craftsman [the *University Magazine*, Montreal, Vol. XVII, No. 4, pp. 589-618, December 1918]; but in England the first attempt came, surprisingly, from the greatest poet of the new literary movement, T. S. Eliot, in a review of Kipling's verse in the *Athenaeum* of 9 May 1919 (No. 50).

The real beginning of modern Kipling criticism, however, came from Professor Bonamy Dobrée in a long article in the *Monthly Criterion* for December 1927 (No. 55)—later enlarged and reprinted in his *The Lamp and the Lute* (1929, revised 1964)—a prelude to his full-scale study *Rudyard Kipling: Realist and Fabulist* (1967).

But in 1919 E. T. Raymond [Edward Raymond Thompson] was writing in his *All and Sundry* [pp. 177-85], with much second-hand and facile generalizations, the startling conviction that 'Mr. Rudyard Kipling is not perhaps a spent force. But it seems safe to say that he will never again be more than a minor one.'

Though there were dissenting murmurs in America (see Nos. 53 and 54 below), this remained the general critical opinion until well after Kipling's death on 18 January 1936. That event brought forth the usual chorus of polite tributes—of little critical value and remarkable in this case for their extreme caution. The best of the obituary studies seem to have been the article by Desmond MacCarthy quoted earlier in this Introduction, and the anonymous essay in the *Times Literary Supplement* which concludes the present volume (No. 61). A good study of the reaction—or lack of it—after Kipling's death is given by Hilton Brown in the first chapter of his *Rudyard Kipling: A New Appreciation* (1943).

IV

SALES, HOME AND OVERSEAS

The critical reaction against Kipling seems to have made little difference to his popularity. Sales figures are not available, as one would expect with an author who valued his privacy as highly as Kipling did, but it can be stated from reliable evidence that the only sharp falling-off in sales, and that only a temporary one, came in 1919 after a 'boom' period during the War.

Charles Carrington who, though even he did not have full access to the sales figures, was able to make some kind of estimate of the overall picture, wrote in 1955 [*Rudyard Kipling*, p. xxi]:

According to the verdict of the critics, Kipling's literary credit reached its zenith in the early eighteen-nineties, declined and was almost extinguished before his death, to be revived by some connoisseurs in the nineteen-forties. By another criterion, his reputation moved through quite different phases. Not only his most approved writings but all his authorized work, year after year, and decade after decade, remained in the class that the book trade calls 'best-sellers', and were still in that class twenty years after his death, although these books were never issued in cheap editions . . . Kipling, like Dickens and Defoe, was a popular writer whose work had a 'sensational' success that did not die with the season, that did not need puffing by the reviewers. From 1890 to 1932, and even to 1955, there was no lack of buyers for this line of goods even though the publicists no longer urged the public to acquire it. When his politics were most out of fashion, he still had no lack of readers . . .

And Charles Morgan, writing the history of Kipling's publishers in 1943 [*The House of Macmillan*, pp. 151–2] had already described how, during Kipling's lifetime—

It became, as the years passed, almost a game to invent new dresses for his work —uniform editions, pocket editions, the Edition de Luxe in red and gold, the Bombay Edition, the Service Edition intended for the pack or pocket of soldiers in the 1914 War. There were, also, school editions, and gigantic volumes in which all the dog stories or all the Mowgli stories or all the humorous stories were assembled, and year by year the wise men held their breath and wondered whether by now the public demand for old wine in new bottles was exhausted. The cautious feared it might be, but they were always wrong.[2]

Only the magnificent Sussex Editions, prepared by Kipling during the last year of his life though not published until 1937–8, failed to sell as quickly as was anticipated, and some of the 525 sets (35 volumes at £87 10s. 0d. per set) were unsold in 1940 and perished in the Blitz. Very few, however, seem to have been destroyed, and the remaining majority of sets average £500 to £600 when they come up for sale two or three times a year.

In the United States the Kipling sales seem to have been less steady, but at least as great on aggregate—beginning with a host of pirate editions before the 1891 Copyright Act, and once more proliferating in paperbacks as the earlier volumes go out of copyright under the different system, which dates from first publication and not, as here, from author's death.

The critical reception seems to have been much the same as in England, but a little slower in recognizing a major author.

Speaking a bit sarcastically of American popular taste, Andrew Lang wrote [*Harper's Weekly*, 30 August] in 1890:

I do not anticipate for Mr. Kipling a very popular popularity. He does not compete with Miss Braddon or Mr. E. P. Roe. His favourite subjects are too remote and unfamiliar for a world that likes to be amused with matters near home and passions that do not stray far from the drawing-room or the parlor.

And he was shown to have hit off the American reaction pretty fairly by an anonymous writer a month later in *Harper's Magazine* [October 1890, Vol. LXXXI, pp. 801–2]:

It is pathetic that people read Haggard and Rudyard Kipling when such artistic and important books as Harold Frederic's are available.

And the author (possibly the Editor, H. M. Alden, 1869–1919) goes on to speak contemptuously of 'the Rudyard Kipling fad'.

But the 'fad' grew by leaps and bounds, and Roger Burlingame records [*Of Many Books*, 1946, p. 249] the extraordinary success of *Departmental Ditties* and *Barrack-Room Ballads*:

These verses were, of course, novel in subject and rhythm; they caught on surprisingly in America—being so British in substance—until Kipling's public here equalled or exceeded that in the homeland.

He records, however, that by the end of the century 'Kipling and Barrie were no longer among the ten at the top: Gilbert Parker, William J. Locke and Mrs. Humphrey Ward took their places.'

The reaction at the beginning of the twentieth century seems to have been almost as strong in America as in England, and may be typified by quotation from Arthur Bartlett Maurice's review of *Kim* in the New York *Bookman* [Vol. XIV, pp. 146–9] in October 1901:

There was, once upon a time—somehow it seems very many years ago—a young man who left his home in English India and came to Europe and America, bringing with him a dressing case filled with the manuscripts of marvellous tales about soldiers and civilians . . . That, in a word, was the Mr. Kipling of other days whom men deservedly called great. Unfortunately, it is not the Mr. Kipling of today.

It should be understood that mediocre and meaningless though *Kim* is, it is not to be classed with some of Mr. Kipling's other recent literary efforts—especially with some attempts at verse of which he has of late been guilty. For instance, there was 'The Lesson', an alleged poem, which treated of England's political and military mistakes in the war in the Transvaal. Now, 'The Lesson' was absolutely and flatly unspeakable bosh . . .

[After an inaccurate synopsis] And there you have *Kim*, a jumble of native phrases, of extraneous conversations, of Eastern mysticism, redeemed and brought into a certain concrete form by that craft which Mr. Kipling could not fail to acquire in the years of his apprenticeship and of his genius. It is all so cold, so dead, so lifeless. Mr. Kipling seems to have gone raking through the cinders of his youth in search of the bits of half-burned coals with which to make a little flame and warmth. The old spontaneous fire seems to have irrevocably gone.

On the continent of Europe Kipling took and still holds a high place which seems to have suffered little from adverse political climates— even, strangely enough, in Germany and Russia. His books have been continuously translated into most languages, French taking precedence over a close tie between German, Italian and Swedish.

When he was at his lowest ebb with English critics, one finds no change on the continent. In 1902 Guido Milanesi [in *Rivista d'Italia: Lettere Scienze ed Arte*, Rome, May 1902] is prophesying immortality for *The Seven Seas* and *The Jungle Books*, describing Kipling as a poet—'the poet of the practical spirit'—and accusing English critics of underestimating the greatness of *Plain Tales from the Hills* because they cannot accept its extreme realism.

André Chrevillon [*Revue de Paris*, 15 February 1908] was hailing Kipling six years later as a literary genius—even if some of his political ideas were out of fashion. And J. Castellanos was translating his poems into Spanish and lecturing on them as the work of a great contemporary writer in 1914 [published in *Los Optimistas: Ensayos Literarios*, Madrid, c. 1918]. 'Public taste has shifted to Meredith, Wells, Shaw and Joyce,' wrote André Chaumeix in 1933 [*Le Mois*, April]. 'But Rudyard Kipling can wait serenely for the judgement of the future.' And in his obituary article ['La Grandeur de Kipling', *Revue de France*, 15 February 1936] Claude Farrere ended a glowing tribute with the assertion that 'Rudyard Kipling is better understood by certain French readers than by the immense majority of the British public.'

Kipling himself, always a Francophil, and one who had read French as easily as English since his schooldays, claimed [*Something of Myself*, pp. 227–8] that Prévost was the subconscious inspiration of *The Light that Failed*, and goes on: 'I was confirmed in my belief when the French took to that *conte* with relish, and I always fancied that it walked better in translation than in the original.'

By the time of his death Kipling's works could be found in translation (other than European) ranging from Bengali, Hindustani and Urdu to Chinese, Japanese, Korean, Brazilian and Yiddish. [See Flora V. Livingston: *Supplement to Bibliography of the Works of Rudyard Kipling*, Cambridge, Mass., 1938, pp. 201–31 for a good representative list.]

As far as post-revolutionary Russia is concerned an interesting note appeared in the *Author*, winter number, in 1958, drawn from the findings of the Director of the All Union Chamber of Publications in Moscow:

According to statistics he has produced for the years 1918 to July 1st 1958, more than 77 million copies of works by British authors (including works appearing in anthologies) have been published in the USSR. The number of British authors represented is 236, and the number of languages in which their works have been published is 54. Dickens comes top of the list with nearly ten million copies to his credit (18 languages). He is followed by Wells with nearly seven million copies (16 languages). Conan Doyle, Kipling and Swift are in the next group—between four and five million each, Kipling being published in 34 languages, Swift in 42 and Conan Doyle in 9. In the three-to-four-million group come Defoe, Galsworthy, Shakespeare and Scott; Defoe being the most translated of the three (36 languages). Between two and three million are Robert Louis Stevenson and A. J. Cronin (15 and 6 languages respectively), and in the one-to-two-million group comes James Aldridge, with Jerome K. Jerome. A large group in the half-million area includes Byron, Burns, Charlotte Brontë, Hardy, Walter Greenwood, Conrad, Thackeray, Fielding and Shaw.

During a visit paid to Oxford by a group of Russian professors of English literature the same year, the *Guardian* (21 July 1958) noted that: 'They are surprised by the different value given to certain English writers by Russian and English critical opinion—notably the importance attached to Lawrence and Joyce here and our neglect of Kipling and Galsworthy.' And 'Atticus' in the *Sunday Times* of 6 May 1962 recorded a conversation between the English poet Edwin Brock and the young Russian poet Evgeni Evtushenko:

'For my last book,' said the Russian modestly, 'there were orders for 200,000 copies.' He seemed amazed when Brock murmured that a young British poet was lucky to sell a thousand copies . . .

'I shouldn't think anyone here has made a living out of poetry since Tennyson,' ventured Brock.

'Kipling must have made money out of poetry,' said Evtushenko. 'You know, the most popular poet in Moscow is Kipling.'

'But Kipling was an imperialist.'

The Russian smiled and quoted Kipling in Russian with evident approval.

Kipling's popularity throughout the British Empire seems to have been at least as great as in the mother country—and it does not seem to have suffered for long as former dominions and colonies achieved their varying forms of independence.

Thus, in the early years of Kipling's fame we find the Australian novelist 'Rolf Boldrewood' [Thomas Alexander Browne, 1826–1915, quoted in Simon Nowell-Smith's *Letters to Macmillan*, 1967, p. 213] writing to his publisher on 20 July 1891:

I have just been reading your edition of *The Light that Failed*. In my humble opinion Mr. Rudyard Kipling is the strongest and most original writer in his own department since Dickens.

From the middle of his career a Canadian writer, Edgar Pelham [*University Magazine* (Montreal), Vol. VII, pp. 261–5, April 1908, in an article on 'English Poetry since Tennyson'] contrasted Kipling's 'kettledrums in the street' with Yeats's 'flute in the hushed forest', and compared the realism of the one with the idealism of the other. Kipling, he maintained, was inferior to Yeats in harmony and imagination, but Kipling was original in 'introducing into poetry the primitive nature sentiment', though he did not lean on traditional, literary primitivism. Kipling, 'rather than conveying the beauty of ocean, best conveys its mystery and strength'.

In the same year, an Indian writer, Kiran Nath Dhar ['Some Indian Novels' in the *Calcutta Review*, Vol. CXXVII, pp. 561–83, October 1908] declared that Kipling 'was more truly Anglo-Indian than any other writer. His short stories are vivid, and a genuine sympathy for all things Indian pervades his works.'

Between then and independence Indian writers naturally tended to denigrate Kipling and credit him less and less with any understanding of the native Indian outlook and point of view. But with independence an accomplished fact, political axes ceased to be ground far more quickly than they have here, and in 1957 as eminent a writer and critic as Nirad C. Chaudhuri was writing [in *Encounter*, Vol. VIII, pp. 47–53, April 1957]:

'In *Kim* its author wrote not only the finest novel in the English language with an Indian theme, but also one of the greatest of English novels in spite of the theme. This rider is necessary, because the association of anything in English literature with India suggests a qualified excellence, an achievement which is to be judged by its special standards, or even a work which in form and content has in it more than a shade of the second-rate. But *Kim* is great by any standards that ever obtained in any age of English literature.

KIPLING CRITICISM TO-DAY

But it is not proposed to deal in the present volume with the Kipling criticism of the last thirty years. The most important critical essays have been collected by Andrew Rutherford in *Kipling's Mind and Art* (1964) and by Elliot L. Gilbert in *Kipling and the Critics* (1965); and there have been several individual studies. The official biography, *Rudyard Kipling: His Life and Work* (1955) by Charles Carrington contains many quotations from earlier criticism, besides its author's own expert and judicious comments. In 1959 J. M. S. Tompkins produced her full-scale study *The Art of Rudyard Kipling*, the best and fullest critical assessment so far made, and other writers since then have written on various sides of his literary achievement. (See Select Bibliography on pp. 396-7 of the present volume.)

In his Preface to Hilton Brown's book quoted above, Frank Swinnerton wrote: 'Until Mr. T. S. Eliot caused consternation among the genteel by analysing his virtues as a poet he was safely dismissed by them as a sort of literary bounder who was somehow responsible for the Boer War.'

Eliot's essay, a study in thirty-two pages, introduced *A Choice of Kipling's Verse* in 1941, and is also too well known and easily accessible to quote here. He was not quite the first to treat Kipling seriously, if we include a rather cautious and non-committal lecture by W. L. Renwick published in the *Durham University Journal* [Vol. XXXII, pp. 3-16] in January 1940, and collected by Rutherford. Edmund Wilson had also just preceded Eliot with his notorious article 'The Kipling that Nobody Read' in the *Atlantic Monthly* [Vol. CLXVII] of February and March 1941 and reprinted at the end of the year in his *The Wound and the Bow* (also included by Rutherford in his collection). And both of these had been forestalled by Edward Shanks in his book *Rudyard Kipling: A Study in Literature and Political Ideas* published in 1940—a volume still not altogether superseded.

But Eliot's determination to treat Kipling as a major writer provoked a good deal of strenuous confutations and expressions of opinion, notably from Boris Ford in *Scrutiny* (11 January 1942), George Orwell in *Horizon* [Vol. V, pp. 111-25, February 1942] and Lionel Trilling in *Nation* [New York: Vol. CLVII, pp. 436 etc., 16 October 1943] —all collected in Elliot L. Gilbert's volume and the second two by Rutherford.

The best re-assessment preceding the volumes by Carrington and Tompkins was, however, the lecture on 'Kipling's World' delivered by C. S. Lewis before the English Association and first published in their *Literature and Life* (1948), since when it has been reprinted in several places, and is included in Gilbert's volume.

Lewis insisted that Kipling 'was a very great writer', even if there were certain things about him which you did not like or even considered a serious blot. To Lewis the blot on Kipling was that 'he is the slave of the Inner Ring'; to other critics it can be his supposed streak of cruelty, his insistence on the Law, or his conviction (for a time at least) that the British Empire offered the best hope of world peace and prosperity.

Critics are apt to be led into over-emphasizing their personal views or special pre-occupation—and others seem unable or unwilling to make the necessary historical metempsychosis to understand the outlook of Kipling's contemporaries—forgetting that the greatest social and intellectual change in recorded history has taken place since Kipling was a young man in India nearly a century ago.

Some critics seem to be 'too clever by half', looking for double-meanings and hidden allegories and allusions. They may add to a reader's enjoyment, even if they cannot prove their points. A good example of this is in the excellent study *Aspects of Kipling's Art* (1964) by Professor C. A. Bodelsen which treats several of the stories, notably the final one, 'Teem: A Treasure-Hunter', as if they were literary Chinese-puzzles, carved ivory ring within ring. There is much amusement in it for the reader, and he often underlines meanings that we may have missed. But we are too often left at the end with the uneasy feeling that we have been sharing in an amusing game, like that played by the Sherlock Holmes Society, rather than arriving at a truer understanding of Kipling's stories.

More dangerous is the psychological approach initiated by Edmund Wilson, who found distrust, hate and cruelty as dominant traits of Kipling's work, and then set to work conscientiously to prove his thesis by exaggerating the unhappy period at Southsea, the harshness of the 'twelve bleak houses by the shore' at Westward Ho! and the 'seven years hard' in India. Most of this has been either disproved, or shown to be in need of drastic toning-down and re-statement by the biographical works published since Wilson's essay; but the attitude still persists as more than a mere echo of Robert Buchanan and H. G. Wells.

Another approach is the frankly clinical psychoanalysis. But so far this seems to have been inept, and based on such shaky foundations of pre-conception and sheer ignorance as to be hardly worth considering.

As an example of this so-called criticism may be taken the article by Thomas N. Cross, M.D., 'Rudyard Kipling's Sense of Identity', published in the *Michigan Quarterly Review* [Vol. IV, No. 4, pp. 245–53] in October 1965. This also bases Kipling's literary and political outlook on his sufferings as a child at Southsea. But it can easily be disproved. The 'Devil Boy' whose cruelties were described by Kipling in the story 'Baa, Baa, Black Sheep' and forty years later in his autobiographical fragment *Something of Myself*, is called 'Harry' in the story, and his parents are 'Uncle Harry' and 'Auntie Rosa' (Dr Cross adds a note that Kipling and his sister called Mrs Holloway 'Auntie Rosa', though 'she was not a relative as various biographers have assumed' —I have not so far discovered any of those 'biographers'). And he goes on:

In all that he wrote—more than thirty-six volumes—Kipling used thousands of names; but never once did he use the name Harry. He did, however, use the expression 'By the Lord Harry!'—reflecting, I think, at least something of Harry's power over him.

Mr R. E. Harbord, the President of The Kipling Society, who has been preparing a Reader's Guide to Kipling's works for the last twenty years, writes: 'There are 4 Harrys and 11 Henrys in the Verse; 14 Harrys and 20 Henrys in the Prose—total 49.'

The names given to the couple and their son in the story should surely have been considered by any serious scholar as fictional, unless he could prove that they were the actual names. Dr Cross could have discovered from the *Kipling Journal*, No. 139 (September 1961) that the names of the parents were Captain Pryse Agar Holloway and Sarah Holloway. Their son's name eluded research until about the time the article was written, but was only published after it: he was, in fact, Henry Thomas Holloway [see my *Kipling and the Children* (1965), pp. 29–30].

As for the expression 'By the Lord Harry!' it was a common ejaculation much used in the nineties, and may be found easily in the works of Rider Haggard, Conan Doyle and any other writer of the period.

Conclusions based on such flimsy evidence and ignorance of the very rudiments of research can surely be dismissed as worthless.

Before turning from the end to the beginning of Kipling criticism, as exhibited in the following pages, we can do no better than read and take to heart the opening paragraph of Professor Dobrée's *Rudyard Kipling: Realist and Fabulist*:

Rudyard Kipling, it is now coming generally to be acknowledged, has been more grotesquely misunderstood, misrepresented, and in consequence denigrated, than any other known writer. I have attempted here to present him as outside any of the camps into which careless readers have wished to, indeed have, put him, either in praise or in blame. I say 'careless readers' because I have found that most of those who so readily label him have not really read him, or have done so with preconceived notions of what he wished to impart. Not long ago a distinguished man of letters and lecturer wrote to me: 'People are not only blinded, but *deafened* by prejudice. If you talk (as I sometimes do . . .) about him, *nobody hears what you say*. They simply switch off their aids, or have an automatic cut-out.' Thus I have not attempted, except by occasional incidental remarks, to refute the ill-based accusations made against him. An unbiased view of the totality of his work makes such labour unnecessary.

NOTES

1 Vereker Hamilton: *Things That Happened* (1925), pp. 186–9; Ian Hamilton: *Listening for the Drums* (1944), p. 203; Coulson Kernahan: *Nothing Quite Like Kipling Had Happened Before* (1944), p. 47; Ian B. W. Hamilton: *The Happy Warrior: A Life of General Sir Ian Hamilton* (1966), p. 77.

2 There seem to have been twenty-one Collected Editions of Kipling's works between 1890 and 1965, nine of these limited sets at high prices: eleven (three of them early and not completed) in America, ten in England and one (Tauchnitz, 19 volumes) on the Continent. This does not include school editions, translations into foreign languages, nor such selections— each of more than a thousand pages—as *The One Volume Kipling* (1928) and *A Kipling Pageant* (1935), both published in America; nor the various editions of his Collected Verse of which there seem to have been nine before the *Definitive Edition* of 1940.

1. Andrew Lang introduces Kipling's First Book

1886

The earliest review in Great Britain so far discovered was contained in Andrew Lang's monthly *causerie* 'At the Sign of the Ship' in *Longman's Magazine*, Vol. VIII, pp. 675–6, October 1886. (Lang did not realize that the name in facsimile handwriting on the 'envelope' was that of the author. See pages 13–14 of Introduction.)

Andrew Lang (1844–1912), poet, scholar, folklorist and essayist, was the leading literary critic and reviewer of the last two decades of the century. He was among the first to recognize and encourage many writers of the period, notably Stevenson, Bridges, Kipling and De la Mare, besides the romance-writers from Haggard, Doyle and Weyman to A. E. W. Mason and John Buchan.

There is a special variety of English *Vers de Société*, namely the Anglo-Indian species. A quaint and amusing example of this literature has reached me, named *Departmental Ditties*. The modest author does not give his name. The little book is published in the shape of an official paper, 'No. 1. of 1886'. The envelope is the cover. No poem, and this is an excellent arrangement, occupies more than one of the long narrow pages. Would that all poems were as brief. The Radical should read *Departmental Ditties* and learn how gaily *Jobus et Cie* govern India:

> 'Who shall doubt' the secret hid
> Under Cheops' pyramid,
> Was that the contractor 'did'
>   Cheops out of several millions?

> Or that Joseph's sudden rise
> To Comptroller of Supplies,
> Was a fraud of monstrous size
>   On King Pharaoh's swart civilians?

34

Here we learn how Ahasuerus Jenkins, merely because he 'had a tenor voice of super Santley tone', became a power in the state.

Very curious is the tale of Jones, who left his newly-wedded bride, and went to the Hurrom Hills above the Afghan border, and whose heliographic messages home were intercepted and interpreted by General Bangs.

> With damnatory dash and dot he'd heliographed his wife
> Some interesting details of the General's private life.

On the whole, these are melancholy ditties. Jobs, and posts, and pensions, and the wives of their neighbours appear (if we trust the satirist) to be much coveted by her Majesty's Oriental civil servants. The story of Giffen, who was broken and disgraced, and saved a whole countryside at the expense of his own life, and who is now worshipped (by the natives) in Bengal, is worthy of Bret Harte.

The Indian poet has kept the best wine to the last, and I like his poem 'In Spring-time' so much that (supreme compliment!) I have copied it out here . . . [the poem is quoted in full: see DV, p. 78].

2. *Plain Tales from the Hills*
Reaches England

1888

Anonymous review of *Plain Tales from the Hills* (Thacker and Spink, London and Calcutta, 1888) in the *Saturday Review*, No. 1702, Vol. LXV, pp. 697–8 (9 June 1888) under the heading 'Novels and Stories', with seven other novels by various authors —none now remembered.

Probably by Walter Herries Pollock (1850–1926), the editor— author of minor verse, fiction, criticism, etc. C. F. Hooper (then a member of the firm of Thacker and Spink) recorded in an article 'Kipling's Younger Days'—*Saturday Review*, 7 March 1936, that he was trying to sell *Plain Tales* in London, but had no success until he persuaded the Editor of the *Saturday Review* to review it.

There is a good deal in a title. Could there be a much less attractive title than *Plain Tales from the Hills*? Residents in British India and subscribers to the *Civil and Military Gazette* may know what it means, and hasten to get hold of the book accordingly; but to the untravelled inhabitants of London and the United Kingdom generally it would seem almost as hopeful to undertake the perusal of a volume entitled *Straight Talks from Beulah*. We should suggest to Mr. Kipling to change the name of his book to *The Other Man; and Other Stories*, not because 'The Other Man' is his best plain tale, which it is not, but because it would look well on the bookstalls. There are forty plain tales, of which twenty-eight have appeared separately in a newspaper, and the other twelve are, in the modest words of the author, 'more or less new'. Each tale is extremely short, the average length being just under seven pages. Nevertheless, for the profitable disposal of odds and ends of time or for a cross-country journey in stopping trains on Sunday it would be hard to find better reading. Mr. Kipling knows and appreciates the English in India, and is a born story-teller and a man of humour into the bargain. He is also singularly versatile, and equally at home in humour and pathos. 'Thrown Away', a story of a commonplace youth who killed himself in despair merely for want of proper training, is little short of genuine tragedy, and is full of a grim humour which is decidedly telling. 'The Three Musketeers' and 'A Friend's Friend' are farce of a high order. Four of the stories—and four of the best—concern the British private in regiments stationed in India. An inimitable Irishman appears in each of them, and relates his experiences with a delightful freshness and good humour. The following extract occurs in an astonishing story of the taking of a town by Burmese Dacoits. The British detachment could not discover where the Dacoits abode; but

evenshually we *puckarowed* wan man. 'Trate him tinderly,' sez the Lift'nint. So I tuk him away into the jungle, wid the Burmese Interprut'r an' my clanin'-rod. Sez I to the man: 'My paceful squireen,' sez I, 'you shquot on your hunkers an' dimonstrate to *my* frind here, where *your* frinds are whan they're at home.' Wid that I introjuced him to the clanin'-rod, an' he comminst to jabber; the Interprut'r inturprutin' in betweens, an' me helpin' the Intelligince Departmint wid my clanin'-rod whan the man misremimbered.

It has been explained just before that: 'Tis only a *dah* and a Snider that makes a dacoit. Widout thim he's a paceful cultivator, an' felony for to shoot.'

Another remarkable military story is 'The Madness of Private Ortheris'. Ortheris goes out shooting with his friend Mulvaney and the author . . . [26 lines, mainly quotations from the story, with synopsis] . . . The military stories happen to have been dwelt on here, but there are many tales of civilians, and indeed of natives, that arc really quite as good. The reader should not omit to peruse the head-notes of the stories, especially when they are in verse. It seems probable that a considerable proportion are Mr. Kipling's own. One advantage in the extreme shortness of the stories is that, as they are read in a few minutes, their incidents are easily forgotten, and they may be read again with fresh pleasure after a short interval. For this reason, and because it is small, the book is one to buy, and not merely to get from the library.

3. Sir William Hunter on Departmental Ditties

1888

Signed review in the *Academy*, No. 852, pp. 128–9 (1 September 1888).

Sir William Wilson Hunter (1840–1900) was a well-known Indian civilian, historian and publicist, author of several learned works on India, notably *The Indian Empire: its Peoples, History and Products* (1895), and a member of the Governor-General's Council 1881–7.

Charles Carrington calls this review 'the first analytical essay by a writer who knew Kipling's background, and knew India'.

Mr. Kipling's ditties have well earned the honours of a third edition. They possess the one quality which entitles *vers de société* to live. For they reflect with light gaiety the thoughts and feelings of actual men and women, and are true as well as clever. Neither wit nor sparkling epigram, nor the laboriously laughable rhyme, but this element of truth alone can save the poet of a set from oblivion.

As Pope admits us to a real belle's toilette in the reign of Queen Anne and allows us to look over her hand at ombre; or as Praed preserves alive the political coterie-life of half-a-century ago; or as Bret Harte, in his sadder way, places us down among the saloon-gamblers of the West with their stray gleams of compunction and tenderness— so Mr. Kipling achieves the feat of making Anglo-Indian society flirt and intrigue visibly before our eyes. It is not, as he discloses it, a very attractive society. Its flirtations will seem rather childish to a London coquette, its intrigues very small to a parliamentary wire-puller. But, if Mr. Kipling makes his little Simla folk rather silly, he also makes them very real. The Mayfair matron, accustomed to calmly play her musical pawns at her matinées, will indeed marvel that any woman should take the trouble which the Simla lady took to capture one singing subaltern. The 'Legend of the Indian Foreign Office' may seem to the diplomatic youth whose windows look out on Downing Street to be better suited to the civic parlour of some small pushing mayor. Although, however, Mr. Kipling's stage is a narrow one, his players are very much alive, and they go through their pranks in quite fresh dresses, and with all the accessories of true tears and ogles, audible sighs and laughter.

It is a curious little world to which he introduces us. The few English men of letters who have passed a portion of their lives in India, from Philip Francis to Macaulay, and the still rarer stray scholar from foreign parts, like Csoma de Koros, who has sojourned there, seem to have found Anglo-Indian society sometimes bizarre, and more often intolerably dull. It is this weariness of uncongenial social surroundings which gives to Sir Alfred Lyall's poems their note of peculiar pathos. In spite of the brilliance of his own career, India is ever to him the Land of Regrets. The merry little people who flirt through Mr. Kipling's ditties look out on the scene with altogether different eyes. They may detest the country and dislike the natives, but they find their own small lives vastly amusing. Their personal tastes and their code of public morals are equally simple. Their highest ideal of enjoyment would seem, according to Mr. Kipling, to be a stringed band and a smooth floor. Their most serious aim in life, we learn from the same observer, is 'an appointment'—signifying thereby not an opportunity for doing work, but a device for drawing pay. This great object of existence in the ditties is apparently best to be achieved by flirting, fibbing, and conjugal collusion. Thus Mr. Potiphar Gubbins, the hero of one poem, gets hoisted over the heads of his brother engineers by the fascinations of his wife—an attractive and a complaisant young person who, for reasons of her own, has married Potiphar, although 'coarse as a chimpanzee'. Another piece relates how Mr. Sleary, an impecunious subaltern secretly engaged to a lady in England, obtains an appointment by proposing to the daughter of an Indian official. Having secured the post, he frightens his fiancée Number Two out of the engagement by pretending to have epileptic fits, then nobly marries fiancée Number One, and lives with her happily ever after on the produce of his fraud. In the ditty of Delilah, a veteran Simla charmer wheedles a State secret out of an aged Councillor and betrays it to a younger admirer, who, in turn, promptly betrays it to the press. In the story of Uriah, an officer is despatched to Quetta and dies there, in order that his wife may more freely amuse herself at Simla with the senior who got him sent out of the way. A private secretary-ship is the well-earned reward of a young gentleman who receives a kiss by mistake at a masked ball, and who has the extraordinary chivalry or prudence not to publish the lady's name. These little *contes*, with various duller, if more decorous, jobs like that of the Chatham colonel, may seem poor stuff for verse. But Mr. Kipling handles each situation with a light touch and a gay malice, which make it difficult to be quite sure whether he sincerely admires his pretty marionettes, or whether he is not inwardly chafing and raging at the people among whom he is condemned to live. He very calmly expounds the scheme of creation in his curious Anglo-India world:

[quotes first four stanzas of 'A General Summary': DV p. 4]

If this were Mr. Kipling's highest flight his poems would scarcely have reached a third edition. But in the midst of much flippancy and cynicism come notes of a pathetic loneliness and a not ignoble dis-content with himself, which have something very like the ring of genius. Making verses, however clever, for the mess-room and the lawn tennis-club cannot be an altogether satisfying lifework. To Mr. Kipling, as to Sir Alfred Lyall in our own time, or to poor Leyden in the past, and, indeed, to every man of the true literary temperament who has had to spend his years in India, that country is still the 'sultry and sombre Noverca—the Land of Regrets'. There are many stanzas and not a few poems in this little volume which go straight to the heart of all who have suffered or are now suffering, the long pain of tropical exile. For besides the silly little world which disports itself throughout most of the ditties, there is another Anglo-Indian world which for high aims, and a certain steadfastness in effort after the personal in-terest in effort is well nigh dead, has never had an equal in history. Some day a writer will arise—perhaps this young poet is the destined man—who will make that nobler Anglo-Indian world known as it really is. It will then be seen by what a hard discipline of endurance our countrymen and countrywomen in India are trained to do England's greatest work on the earth. Heat, solitude, anxiety, ill-health, the never-ending pain of separation from wife and child, these are not the experiences which make men amusing in after-life. But these are the stern teachers who have schooled one generation of Anglo-Indian administrators after another to go on quietly and resolutely, if not hopefully, with their appointed task. Of this realistic side of Anglo-

Indian life Mr. Kipling also gives glimpses. His serious poems seem to me the ones most full of promise. Taken as a whole, his book gives hope of a new literary star of no mean magnitude rising in the east. An almost virgin field of literary labour there awaits some man of genius. The hand which wrote 'The Last Department' in this little volume is surely reserved for higher work than breaking those poor pretty Simla butterflies on the wheel.

4. An Early Review of *Soldiers Three*

1889

Anonymous review from the *Spectator*, Vol. LXII, pp. 403–4, 23 March 1889; reprinted in the *Kipling Journal*, Vol. VII, No. 52, pp. 27–30, December 1939.

There is no evidence as to who wrote this review, but it may well have been by John St. Loe Strachey (1860–1927), at that time on the staff of the *Spectator* (of which he was editor and proprietor from 1898 to 1925), who was a family friend of the Lockwood Kiplings.

As a wholesome corrective to what may be called the oleographic style of depicting military life, now so much in vogue, Mr. Kipling's brilliant sketches of the barrack-room, realistic in the best sense of the word, deserve a hearty welcome. Here be no inanities of the officers' mess, no apotheosis of the gilded and tawny-moustachioed dragoon, no languid and lisping lancer, no child-sweethearts—none, in fact, of the sentimental paraphernalia familiar to readers of modern military fiction. Here, instead, we have Tommy Atkins as the central figure: and not Tommy on parade, but in those moods when the natural man finds freest expression—amorous, pugnacious, and thievish—a somewhat earthy personage on the whole, but with occasional gleams of chivalry and devotion lighting up his cloudy humanity. Too many so-called realists seem to aim at representing man as continuously animal, without any intervals in which his higher nature emerges at all. But Mr. Kipling happily does not belong to this school. The actualities of barrack-room life are not extenuated, but the tone of the whole is sound and manly. The author does not gloss over the animal tendencies of the British private, but he shows how in the grossest natures sparks of nobility may lie hid.

He has taken three widely different types of British soldier, a Yorkshireman, a Cockney, and a 'Paddy from Cork', and in spite of the savagery of the first, the cynicism of the second, and the thrasonical complacency of the third, we can fully comprehend the attractions which their company is supposed to have offered to the narrator. Of a truth it must indeed have been 'better to sit out with Mulvaney than to dance many dances', if Mulvaney in the flesh was at all like his literary representation. 'Hit a man an' help a woman, and ye can't be far wrong, anyways'—one of his own maxims—sums up very adequately the philosophy of this combative but chivalrous warrior, whose voluble tongue and droll humour render him the most conspicuous figure of this quaintly assorted but most attacked trio. Private Mulvaney—he was 'a Corp'ril wanst', but he was 'rejuced aftherwards'—he is really a humorist of a very high order, witness the following passage:

[quotes 'Black Jack', *Soldiers Three*, p. 100, lines 11–20]

Mr. Kipling has a genius for reproducing quaint and characteristic Hibernicisms. How expressive for example are the words in which Mulvaney describes the court paid by an unscrupulous officer to a girl whom he wished to elope with him: 'So he went menowderin', and minanderin', and blandandherin' round an' about the Colonel's daughter.' In another place he speaks of some men who 'can swear so as to make green turf crack'. Who but an Irishman again would think of addressing a ghost as 'ye frozen thief of Genesis', or who would speak of a 'little squidgereen' of an officer?

Some of the stories in this collection introduce us to the realities of warfare in a surprisingly vivid fashion, and here also Mulvaney's sayings are full of life and originality. For example, he tells how in a peculiarly bloody engagement with some hill tribes, an Irish soldier was anxious to avenge a comrade: "Tim Coulan'll slape aisy to-night", sez he wid a grin (after bayoneting a Pathan): and the next minute his head was in two halves, an' he went down grinnin' by sections.'

There is a strange power in the following grim picture of another episode of the same fight:

[quotes 'With the Main Guard', *Soldiers Three*, p. 70, line 20, to p. 71, line 10]

Mr. Kipling is equally at home in the Yorkshire and Whitechapel dialects; and perhaps the most purely humorous narrative in the book is 'Private Learoyd's Story', a tale of successful imposture, in which the dog-fancying instinct of the Yorkshireman has full scope. The victim is thus described by the narrator; the last sentence speaks volumes:

[quotes 'Private Learoyd's Story', *Soldiers Three*, p, 17, lines 10 to 19]

Another very happy touch is Private Learoyd's contemptuous dismissal of the caressing nonsense which womenkind lavish upon dogs, as 'thot sort o' talk, at a dog o' sense mebbe thinks nowt on, tho' he bides it by reason o' his breedin' '.

The point of this story consists in the successful substitution of a very vicious cur for a fox-terrier, for the theft of which the Eurasian lady described above had offered a very heavy bribe to the narrator. How this was done is best described in the words of two of the conspirators. Mulvaney was the first to conceive the idea of palming off another dog on their covetous friend:

[quotes 'Private Learoyd's Story', *Soldiers Three*, p. 24, line 10, to p. 25, line 11]

The perusal of these stories cannot fail to inspire the reader with the desire to make further acquaintance with the other writings of the author. They are brimfull of humanity and a drollery that never degenerates into burlesque. In many places a note of genuine pathos is heard. Mr. Kipling is so gifted and versatile, that one would gladly see him at work on a larger canvas. But to be so brilliant a teller of short stories is in itself no small distinction.

5a. Andrew Lang on 'Mr. Kipling's Stories'

1889

Unsigned review of *In Black and White* and *Under the Deodars* from the *Saturday Review*, Vol. LXVIII, pp. 165–6, 10 August 1889. Lang had recently received the six Wheeler's Railway Library booklets, and was recommending their publication in England to Sampson Low, Marston & Co. (See Introduction, pp. 15–16.)

The worst of recommending Mr. Wheeler's publications, which we do very heartily, is that apparently they are difficult to procure. They appear in paper-covered little volumes; but these volumes are not found on English railway bookstalls. Very little that is so new and so good can be discovered in those shrines of fugitive literature. Mr. Kipling is a new writer, or a writer new to the English as distinct from the Anglo-Indian public. He is so clever, so fresh, and so cynical that he must be young; like other people, he will be kinder to life when he has seen more of it. Clever people usually begin with a little aversion, which is toned down, in life as in love, to a friendly resignation, if it is not toned up to something warmer by longer experience. Mr. Kipling's least cynical stories are those in *In Black and White*, studies of native life and character. He is far happier with Afghan homicides and old ford-watchers, and even with fair Lalun, 'whose profession was the most ancient in the world', and whose house was built upon the city wall, than with the flirts and fribbles of the hills. His 'black men' (as Macaulay would have called them) are excellent men, full of courage, cunning, revenge, and with points of honour of their own. We are more in sympathy with their ancient semi-barbarism than with the inexpensive rank and second-hand fashion of Simla.

An invidious critic might say, and not untruly, that Mr. Kipling has, consciously or unconsciously, formed himself on the model of Mr. Bret Harte. He has something of Mr. Harte's elliptic and allusive manner, though his grammar is very much better. He has Mr. Harte's liking for good qualities where they have the charm of the unexpected. Perhaps the similarity is increased by the choice of topics and events on the fringes of alien civilizations. It may also be conjectured that Mr. Kipling is not ignorant of 'Gyp's' works. In any case he has wit, humour, observation; he can tell a story, and he does not always disdain pathos, even when the pathetic is a little too obvious. People will probably expect Mr. Kipling, with all these graces of his, to try his hand at a long novel. We are a nation that likes quantity. But it may very probably turn out that Mr. Kipling is best at short stories and sketches.

Perhaps the most excellent of his tales is 'Dray Wara Yow Dee', the confession to an Englishman of a horse-dealer from the Northern frontier. This character, in his cunning and his honesty, his madness of revenge, his love, his misery, his honour, is to our mind a little masterpiece. There is a poetry and a melancholy about the picture which it would be hard, perhaps impossible, to find in more than one or two barbaric or savage portraits from a European hand. His confession must be read; we shall not spoil it by analysis. The 'Judgment of Dungara' is as good, in a comic and cynical manner; so is the tale of a 'sahib, called Yankum Sahib'. Missionaries ought to get the former by heart, and magistrates the latter. 'Gemini', the story of Ram Dass and Durga Dass, might make a Radical Indophile laugh, and might teach him a good deal about his clients. 'In Flood Time' is a little prose idyl of epical strength; there is something primitive in the adventure and something very sympathetic in the old warder of the ford who tells the tale. The 'Sending of Dana Da' is an Icelandic kind of miracle worked on esoteric Buddhists to their confusion and sorrow. The sending wherewith Dana Da vexed Lone Sahib was a sending of kittens, not nice young vivacious kittens, but kittens in their babyhood, and they vexed Lone Sahib sore. 'On the City Wall' is the last, and certainly one of the very best, of the stories; the tale of conspiracy, riot, prison-breaking, organized by Lalun the Fair and Wali Dad, 'a young Mahommedan who was suffering acutely from Education of the English variety, and knew it'. This Wali Dad is as clever a study as that of the Pathan horse thief; his modern melancholy, infidelity, *Weltschmerz*, and all the rest of it, leave him at bottom as thorough a Moslem fanatic as ever yelled 'Ya Hasan! Ya Hussain!' How the British soldiers quell a multitude of yelling fanatics, without drawing a bayonet or firing a shot, is pleasant to read. And, at the end of the riot, there we find Agnostic Wali Dad, 'shoeless, turbanless, and frothing at the mouth; the flesh on his chest bruised and bleeding from the vehemence with which he had smitten himself'. Wherefore we part from Wali Dad respecting him rather more than in his character of educated Unbeliever; for the attitude and actions of the fanatic were more sincere than the sighs and sneers of 'the product'.

On the whole, Mr. Kipling's *Under the Deodars* is more conventional and less interesting than his studies of native life. There is comparatively little variety in 'playing lawn-tennis with the Seventh Commandment'. Mr. Kipling, in his preface, intimates that Anglo-Indian society has other and more seemly diversions. Any persons who wish to see the misery, the seamy, sorry side of irregular love affairs, may turn to 'The Hill of Illusion'. It is enough to convert a man or woman on the verge of guilt by reminding them that, after all, they will be no happier than they have been, and much less respectable. 'A Wayside Comedy' contains a tragedy almost impossible in its absurd and miserable complexity of relations. Only a very small and very remote Anglo-Indian station could have produced this comedy, or tolerated it; and yet what were the wretched men and women to do on this side of suicide? The freaks of Mrs. Hauksbee and Mrs. Mallowe are more commonplace and rather strained in their cleverness. But, on the whole, the two little volumes, with Mr. Kipling's *Departmental Ditties*, give the impression that there is a new and enjoyable talent at work in Anglo-Indian literature.

5b. Andrew Lang welcomes 'An Indian Story-teller'

1889

Unsigned review of *Plain Tales from the Hills* in the *Daily News* (2 November 1889).

'Who will show us some new thing?' is the constant demand of criticism. As Jeames grew tired of beef and mutton, and wished that some new animal was invented, so the professional student of contemporary fiction wearies, ungratefully, of the regular wholesome old joints—of the worthy veteran novelists. This fastidiousness has its good side, it gives every beginner a chance of pleasing; but, on the other hand, it tempts people to overestimate an author merely because he is not yet stale and hackneyed, or at least familiar. We know pretty well what the eminent old hands can do, they seldom surprise us agreeably. What the new hand does is likely to have the merit of a surprise. Thus Mr. Rudyard Kipling's *Plain Tales from the Hills* (Thacker and Co.) take us captive, pretty much as his friend, Private Mulvaney, with twenty-five naked recruits, took the Burmese town of Lungtungpen. It was the dash, the strangeness, and the unexpectedness of Private Mulvaney's expedition that did the business; the fort was not captured according to the theories of war. Thus we must be more on the watch than the Burmese garrison, and must not surrender at discretion to a literary recruit. This warning is needful because Mr. Kipling's tales really are of an extraordinary charm and fascination, not to all readers no doubt, but certainly to many men. His is more a man's book than a woman's book. The 'average' novel reader, who likes her three stout volumes full of the love affairs of an ordinary young lady in ordinary circumstances, will not care for Mr. Kipling's brief and lively stories. There is nothing ordinary about them. The very scenes are strange, scenes of Anglo-Indian life, military and official; of native life; of the life of half-castes and Eurasians. The subjects in themselves would be a hindrance and a handicap to most authors,

c   47

because the general reader is much averse to the study of Indian matters, and is baffled by *jhairuns*, and *khitmatgars*, and the rest of it. Nothing but the writer's unusual vivacity, freshness, wit, and knowledge of things little known—the dreams of opium smokers, the ideas of private soldiers, the passions of Pathans and wild Border tribes, the magic which is yet a living force in India, the loves of secluded native widows, the habits of damsels whose house, like Rahab's, is on the city wall— nothing but these qualities keeps the English reader awake and excited. It may safely be said that *Plain Tales from the Hills* will teach more of India, of our task there, of the various peoples whom we try to rule, than many Blue Books. Here is an unbroken field of actual romance, here are incidents as strange as befall in any city of dream, any Kôr or Zu-Vendis, and the incidents are true.

Mr. Kipling's romances are not all of equal value; far from it. Several of them might indeed be left out with no great loss. But the best are very good indeed. For example, to read 'The False Dawn' is to receive quite a new idea of the possibilities of life, and of what some people call 'the potentialities of passion'. Cut down to the quick, it only tells how a civil servant, in love with one sister, proposed to another in the darkness of a dust storm. But the brief, vivid narrative; the ride to the old tomb in the sultry tropical midnight, 'the horizon to the north, carrying a faint, dun-coloured feather, the hot wind lashing the orange trees; the wandering, blind night of dust; the lightning spurting like water from a sluice; the human passions breaking forth as wildly as the fire from Heaven; the headlong race in the whirlwind and the gloom; the dust-white, ghostly men and women'— all these make pictures as real as they are strange. 'I never knew anything so un-English in my life,' says Mr. Kipling; and well he may. It is more like a story from another world than merely from another continent. A window is opened on the future, and we have a glimpse of what our race may become when our descendants have lived long in alien lands, in changed conditions—for example, in the electric air of South Africa. There will be new and passionate types of character in 'the lands not yet meted out'.

The natives of India have been dwelling for countless centuries in the region which can make even Englishmen 'un-English'. Mr. Kipling's tales of native life are particularly moving and unwonted. Perhaps the very best, the account of a Hindoo and Moslem riot, called 'On the City Wall' is not in this volume, and we miss here the Pathan story of love and revenge. But, if anyone wishes to 'grue', as the Ettrick Shepherd has it, to shudder, he may try 'In the House of Suddhoo'. He will not only be taught to shiver, though the magic employed was a mere imposture, but he will learn more of what un-educated natives believe, than official records and superficial books of travel can tell him. There is nothing approaching it in modern litera-ture, except the Pakeha Maori's account of a native séance in a Tohun-ga's hut in New Zealand. The Voice, the twittering, spiritual Voice that flew about the darkness, talking now from the roof, now from the floor, now without, now within, impressed the Pakeha Maori till it said, 'Give the priest my gun'. Then the English observer began to doubt the genuine nature of the ghost. In the same way when the dead head of the native child spoke as it floated on the brass basin in the haunted house of Suddhoo, the English spectator can hardly help being moved, till the dry lips declare that the fee of the sorcerer must be doubled. 'Here the mistake from the artistic point of view came in.' But the tragic consequences came in too, inevitably. Mr. Kipling acts Asmodeus here, and, as it were, lifts the roof from the native house. The roof is only half lifted, with a terrible effect, in the roman-tic story 'Beyond the Pale', the half-told and never-to-be-finished record of an Englishman's *amour* with a young native widow. On the other hand, in 'The Gate of a Hundred Sorrows', the whole life of a half-caste opium smoker, all the spectacle of will and nerve hopelessly relaxed and ruined, is transparent and masterly. At first three pipes enabled him to see the red and yellow dragons fight on his neighbour's cap. Now it needs a dozen pipes, and soon he will see their last battle, and slip into another sleep, in 'The Gate of a Hundred Sorrows'. The tales of English existence, official and military, are often diverting and witty; occasionally flippant and too rich in slang. Mr. Kipling may have the vivacity of Guy De Maupassant, but he has neither his pessim-ism, nor, unluckily, the simplicity of his style. There is yet a good deal to be learned by this born storyteller, and there is always the danger that, with experience and self-restraint, may come timidity and lack of force. The last story of the volume promises, or seems to promise, a novel on a theme quite untouched, the existence of a broken-down Englishman, a white pariah fallen among the dark places of 'the Serzi where the horse-traders live'. These stories, whatever their merits, are an addition to the new exotic literature, of which M. Pierre Loti is the leader in France. They have not M. Loti's style, nor his romantic gloom and desolation; their defects are a certain knowingness and familiarity, as of one telling a story in a smoking-room rather late in the evening. But that is a very curable fault, and it is natural to expect much from a talent so fresh, facile, and spontaneous, working in a field of such unusual experiences.

6. 'Mr. Kipling's Writings'

1890

Anonymous article in *The Times*, 25 March 1890. The Editor of the *Times Literary Supplement* kindly informs me that it was by Humphrey Ward.

Thomas Humphrey Ward (1845–1926)—husband of the novelist 'Mrs. Humphrey Ward'—was a Fellow and Tutor of Brasenose College, Oxford, and joined the staff of *The Times* in 1881. He is best remembered for his edition of *The English Poets*, 1881. There is no evidence that he had ever met Kipling when he wrote this article.

India has given us an abundance of soldiers and administrators but she has seldom given us a writer. There is no question, however, that she has done this in the person of the author of the numerous short stories and verses of which we give the titles below. Mr. Rudyard Kipling has the merit of having tapped a new vein, and of having worked it out with real originality. He is even now a very young man, in spite of his seven or eight small volumes; in fact, we believe he is not yet twenty-five. The son of an Englishman who has long been head of the Government School of Art at Lahore, Mr. Kipling was, in the usual way, sent home in early childhood to be educated, and at sixteen or so returned to India to earn his bread. He soon showed that his faculties of keen observation and incisive writing were already developed to an extent far beyond his years. Circumstances appear to have thrown him into journalism, and his talent soon found its proper scope in the stories that he wrote for different Indian papers, especially for the *Week's News*. They made an impression, and when they came to be reprinted Mr. Kipling found himself famous in Indian society as the writer of sketches which were generally accepted as representing, with a fair amount of truth and a great amount of pungency, scenes of a very diverse kind. For he does not confine himself to one class of subjects. He is at home at Simla, and in the life of 'the station', but he is very far from considering that the English ladies and gentlemen there assembled either constitute the whole of India, or, indeed, are the personages best worth studying there. He deals also with that unfortunate result of our settlement in India, the Eurasian, and some of the most brilliant of his tales have this seldom successful growth for their topic. Again, one of his favourite studies lies in the lower ranks of the British Army, and he may, indeed, be almost called the discoverer, as far as India is concerned, of 'Tommy Atkins' as a hero of realistic romance. But if English ladies and gentlemen are, numerically speaking, almost as nothing in comparison with the millions of natives, the private soldiers are not much more numerous, and it was not to be expected that a writer so open-eyed as Mr. Kipling should represent these as including all that was worth description in the life of that vast continent. Accordingly some of the best and most penetrating of the *Plain Tales from the Hills* and the whole of the little collection called *In Black and White* deal with various aspects of native life, and in this department Mr. Kipling's serious and seemingly almost instinctive knowledge is not less evident than in his stories of European life. In fact, from the artistic point of view we should be inclined to place these stories at the top of all his compositions. That very grim story 'In the House of Suddhoo', the tragedy called 'Beyond the Pale', and one or two of the 'Black and White' series seem to be almost the best of Mr. Kipling's writings, perhaps because they appear to lift the veil from a state of society so immeasurably distant from our own and to offer us glimpses of unknown depths and gulfs of human existence.

Nothing is more difficult to review than a collection of short stories. Three-fourths of the charm must lie in the stories themselves, in the plot, and in the characters whom the author can at most indicate by a few strong touches. The reviewer, however, cannot follow him, and cannot tell the stories again one after another; and the only alternative left to him, that of generalizing as to the writer's method and the world in which he moves, is at best unsatisfactory. But Mr. Kipling provides

a certain connection between the stories that make up his different
books; he does not leave his labyrinth entirely without a thread.
There is, for example, a strong family likeness among the tales which
he tells of his 'Three Musketeers'—three private soldiers of the Indian
army, linked together by a close and romantic friendship, different
as are their races and characters. The Irishman, Mulvaney, the cockney,
Ortheris, and the big Yorkshireman, Learoyd, are comrades in weal
or woe, proud of the regiment, devoted to each other, given to a
certain amount of quarrelling over their cups, and of horseplay at any
time, but at bottom admirable specimens of their class and profession,
and interesting by the tenacity of their affection for one another.
Whether they have their exact personal counterparts in real life, we
cannot say; probably Mr. Kipling, like a true novelist, has taken but
the germs of these characters from fact and developed them by his
imagination alone. But they are singularly consistent, and poor Mulvaney especially, the strongest and the best of the three, who was a
corporal once but had to be 'rejuced' for drunkenness, is a truly
attaching creature from his strength and his little weaknesses. The
comedy, the dull hard work, and the not unfrequent tragedy of life in
the ranks are admirably given in the stories which concern these three
soldiers. In some of them we see hard fighting, as in that called 'With
the Main Guard', which contains a truly brilliant account, put in the
mouth of the Irishman, of a struggle between the 'Tyrone' regiment
and the Afghans. In 'Black Jack' a section of the same imaginary
regiment is set upon murdering its sergeant, and Mulvaney tells how he
was able to upset the little conspiracy. 'In the Matter of a Private' is a
gruesome tale of a soldier who literally runs amuck with his Martini-
Henry in a fit of heat hysteria; and we may here remark that in nothing
is Mr. Kipling more successful than in his truly lurid descriptions and
indications of what Indian heat can be, and what its effect on the minds
and bodies of the Europeans who have to suffer it. We in England seem
to take for granted that India is hot, but scarcely one of us makes any
attempt to realize what that heat really means, especially to the men
on whom our power there really reacts, our private soldiers, with their
few comforts, their dreary, enforced leisure, and their almost irresistible temptations for getting into mischief. Mr. Kipling has used to the
full the novelist's right and the novelist's power of bringing home a
practical fact like this to his readers, and although his aim is artistic in
the first place and practical only in the second, he will certainly not be
unwilling that the British Government as well as the British people

should come nearer to realizing what these terrible conditions of life actually imply. It is not, however, all tragedy and all horror with Private Mulvaney and his friends. Persons with so keen a sense of humour as these three are likely to find plenty of occupation for it even in India, and this we are happy to say Mr. Kipling's heroes do.

Plain Tales from the Hills is the longest of the volumes, and, as its title implies, it deals mostly with Simla life. The picture that Mr. Kipling gives is not altogether a pleasant one; but then he does not profess to be an optimist or to represent society as all varnish and veneer. And probably he himself would be the last to maintain that his Mrs. Reiver and Mrs. Mallowe, and even the great Mrs. Hauksbee, 'the most wonderful woman in India', represent Anglo-Indian society as a whole, or that even at Simla men and women have nothing to do but to make love where they ought not. Still, those who have had the most experience in India—by which we do not mean those who have moved longest and most smoothly along the official groove—will recognize that in many respects these stories give a true picture of what is at all events not an inconsiderable section of Indian society. If it fails of being quite a first-rate picture, it is because Mr. Kipling, though an admirably direct writer, is comparatively wanting in style. People have compared him with Guy de Maupassant, not, let it be observed, that he shows any disposition to emulate the French writer in his choice of subjects, (which would be, indeed, even now, an impossibility for an Englishman), but because of his incisive power of drawing vignette portraits and of representing in half-a-dozen pages a complete action. There is, however, an important difference. Guy de Maupassant is a stylist of the first order, and this Mr. Kipling is not yet, whatever he may come to be. His admirers, however, may fairly hope that, in this respect as in others, he may go very much further than he has yet gone. Many of the stories which he has lately published in the English magazines—for he has returned to England, probably for good—show a distinct advance in artistic power on any of those he published in India, and the volume called *Departmental Ditties*, clever and bright as it is, is in no respect on the same level as certain verses which have appeared with and without his name during the present year in British periodicals. Even so, we are far from asserting that Mr. Kipling has yet made any claim to a place in the first rank of contemporary writers. He has given evidence of a knowledge of Indian life which would be extraordinary in any writer and is phenomenal in one so young. He has shown a truly remarkable power of telling a story dramatically and vividly. He has written a number of amusing occasional verses, not without point and sting. But, as yet, he has not attempted 'the long distance race', and the question in which the rapidly-growing number of his readers are now most interested is the question whether he possesses staying power. We sincerely hope that he does, and that he will show it in good time; but, meanwhile, it is to be hoped he will not write himself out. Modern magazines and their eager editors are a dangerous snare in the way of a bright, clever, and versatile writer, who knows that he has caught the public taste.

7. W. E. Henley on 'The New Writer'

1890

Anonymous review of *Soldiers Three, Plain Tales from the Hills* and *Departmental Ditties* in the *Scots Observer* (3 May 1890). Besides evidence of style, a reference in a letter quoted by John Connell in his *W. E. Henley* (1949, p. 194) makes the ascription to Henley virtually certain.

William Ernest Henley (1849–1903) is best known as a minor poet. But 'as a critic', wrote Meredith, 'he was one of the main supports of good literature in our time', and Kipling called him 'a jewel of an editor'. Besides other noteworthy ventures he edited the *Scots* (later *National*) *Observer* from 1889 to 1894 and published in it most of Kipling's *Barrack-Room Ballads*, beginning with 'Danny Deever' on 22 February 1890. His other contributors ranged from R. L. Stevenson, Thomas Hardy, J. M. Barrie and Andrew Lang to W. B. Yeats, H. G. Wells, Alice Meynell and Kenneth Grahame.

Mr. Kipling is so fervently engaged just now in cutting his old records and making himself new records to cut that perhaps it is hardly fair to discuss him in respect of the works of his youth. But himself has challenged criticism; and as the aforesaid works of youth are marked by most of the qualities that distinguish those of his riper years—(he is, we believe, a man of five- or six-and-twenty)—it may be well to take him pretty much as he is revealed in them, and see what are his faults, his virtues what, and what his chances in the future.

To begin with the spots upon the sun: Mr. Kipling is not nearly so complete a master of the tongue that Shakespeare spake as he is of the atrocious lingo—a mixture of all the slangs in the world with a rank, peculiar flavour of its own—of Thomas Atkins. In writing English he is often inadequate, he is often pert, and he is sometimes even common; but in dialect he is nearly always an artist. That is, he has so steeped himself in Atkinsese, he is so thoroughly conscious of its capacities and so quick with the essentials of its genius, that he can and does use it not only to state facts and express ideas withal but also as a means of producing those effects in the arrangement of words that belong to pure art. This, of course, is less true of *Soldiers Three* than of certain *Barrack-Room Ballads* known to readers of this journal; but it is true in a sense of much of the speech of Mulvaney and Learoyd, while in the later work the medium is handled to a purpose that could not, it seems, have been achieved in any other. The material is of the vilest—is the very dregs of language, in fact; but the artist has come that way, and has produced an effect—by the orchestration as it were of such low-lived and degraded vocables as (say) the equivalents of 'bloomin' ' and 'beggar'—that in its way and degree is comparable to that of those great Miltonic polysyllables which seem to have been dictated by Apollo himself. Once, and only once, has Mr. Kipling done anything of the sort in plain English; and even then—it was in that noble 'Ballad of East and West' which remains thus far his master-piece, alike in inspiration and in execution—the quality of the result was by no means extraordinary. And this is really the principal count in our indictment. What he has to tell is now and then of such un-common excellence that one resents the faults of his method with a sense of peculiar exasperation. The stuff is so good of the one part that it is a sin and a shame it is not better of the other. True it is in many of his stories in prose he abounds in worrying little tricks and mannerisms; that at times he is self-conscious to the point of being well-nigh unbearable; that he is capable of being so clever as to con-trive to miss his point and go out with the face of his intention veiled from the eyes of man; that he has sometimes no story to tell you, and that sometimes he does but spoil his story in the telling. But all these are maladies most incident to youth, and one regards them not: they are there, and they will pass, and no more need be said about them. What concerns one chiefly is the fact that the man's style has commonly so rich and curious a savour of newspaperese and is—unless he is pro-jecting himself into somebody else, and uttering that somebody else in dialect—unworthy of the matter it conveys.

For, the truth is, that matter is often of so extraordinary a quality that in these days one knows not where to look for its like. Mr. Kipling has been thrice fortunate in experience, and it is a thing to reflect upon with pride and a lively sense of favours to come that here at last is something that may well turn out to be a force in literature. His verse may be, and often is, pure doggerel; but it hits you. His prose may be, and often is, self-conscious, jerky, incapable of persuasiveness; but when he is putting it to the best use of which it is thus far capable—when, for instance, Mulvaney is delivering himself of that terrific experience of his at Silver's Theatre, or you are listening to the delirium of Mrs. Gadsby, or that crazy Sancho of the blackguard, red-haired Quixote that wanted to be king is telling what came of his chief's desire—then you have to attend with all your ears, and then you are made to feel with all your strength that here is such a promise as has not been perceived in English letters since young Mr. Dickens broke in suddenly upon the precincts of immortality as the creator of Pickwick and the Wellers. Mr. Kipling, indeed, has that rarest gift of all—the gift of not merely suggesting character and emotion but of so creating and so realising character that the emotion it expresses appears the living and unalterable truth. Sir Walter had it when he liked, Dickens had it often, Thackeray had it now and then, Mr. Meredith has it sometimes; Mr. Kipling has shown more than once that he, too, has it in him to be great as these were great, and that in the presentation of character and emotion he may hope, if he keep the right way, to vie with the heroes until himself attains to heroism. It is a far cry from now to then, of course; but to be five-and-twenty, and have put Kamal and the Colonel's Son on their feet, and set them face to face with each other, and made them swagger it out as they do—to have done that, we say, is to have given hostages to expectation, and placed oneself in the position of them of whom much is asked, and whose failure were a national misfortune, even as their triumph is a triumph for the race. Mr. Kipling has but to be patient, to forget that he is somebody before his time, to be prepared to meet failure half-way, to put off the vanity of superfluous industry, to avoid cleverness as he would avoid the devil, to write—(as Mozart wrote *Don Juan*) 'for himself and two or three friends'; and the issue is not doubtful.

It is late in the day to begin talking of Mulvaney and Ortheris and Learoyd; so we shall let them go on speaking for themselves—speaking as surely three of Her Imperial Majesty's army never spoke before. It is late, too, for anybody to discuss the merits and demerits of a book in everybody's hands, which appears to be what is the matter with *Plain Tales from the Hills*; so no more shall here be said of it than that 'The Taking of Lung-Tung-Pen' and 'The Madness of Private Ortheris' are good enough to be read at least three times apiece and then remembered with the good things of minor literature. And this fourth edition of *Departmental Ditties* is not particularly suggestive either.

There is a convention of Anglo-Indian verse, of course; and of course it is worth noting that the poet of Potiphar Gubbins and Pagett, M.P., is no prodigy but the result of a certain process of evolution. He is the best, perhaps; for he has sung the dirge of Jack Barrett, and is the maker of a certain 'Ballad of Burial' and 'Possibilities' and 'The Undertaker's Horse'—(all three of them clamouring for better technique)—and has told the strange and moving story of how Giffen—Giffen the drunkard and the renegade—became the local god. But there were Anglo-Indian poets before him as there were men of might before Agamemnon; and it may be that his supremacy is largely an effect of the effort that preceded his and the convention he found ready to his hand. Of the ten new numbers included in the present edition, the three best —'The Ballad of Fisher's Boarding-House' and 'The Grave of the Hundred Heads' and 'The Galley Slave'—are out of place in their environment. The themes of them are tragic, the manner befits the theme, the effect is spoiled by a certain sense of incongruity, and to get the full of it you have to go back on them and take them apart from their surroundings. They have so little in common, indeed, with Sleary and Delilah Aberystwith and the light loves and lighter chatter of Simla that their introduction is felt and resented as a mistake in art. It would not have mattered so much had they been bad; but all are good—'The Galley Slave', in especial, being almost good enough to vie with 'The Ballad of East and West' for the place of honour in Mr. Kipling's whole metrical achievement. In a sense too, it is typical of the writer. The rhythm is coarse, and the *facture* by no means irreproachable; but to read it without emotion is impossible. It is a man's work done for men; and it puts before you the feeling of the Anglo-Indian for the Indian Empire in terms so single-hearted and so strong as to make you glory in the name of Briton and exult in the work your race has done.

8. Charles Whibley on 'Good Stuff and Bad'

1890

Anonymous review of reprints of *In Black and White* and *The Story of the Gadsbys* in the *Scots Observer* (20 September 1890). Credited to Whibley by John Connell in his *W. E. Henley* (1949, p. 194).

Charles Whibley (1859–1930), scholar, critic and wit was a close friend of W. E. Henley with whom he worked in most of the latter's editorial ventures, and with whom he produced the Tudor Translations series. Later he contributed 'Musings Without Method' each month to *Blackwood's Magazine* for twenty-five years. Carrington describes him as 'a scholarly *bon-viveur* with a well-earned liver complaint'.

It was one of Matthew Arnold's justest canons that a man of letters must be appraised by his best work. If you wish to appreciate the poems of Wordsworth, he said in effect, or the collection of books known as the New Testament, you must first strip them of their absurdities and irrelevancies and there will then remain for your enjoyment a pearl of great price. The surest winnower, indeed, is Time, who suffers no chaff on his threshing-floor. But the man of genius never lived that did not give the hostile among his contemporaries reason to blaspheme. It would be an easy matter, by an unscrupulous choice of examples, to prove that Mr. Kipling was little better than a smart journalist; but if we boldly attempt to anticipate the work of Time and discard what is merely 'copy', there will be left a very great deal to which only a man of genius could set his name.

The misfortune is that good and bad are sent out into the world together. The alliance is not a permanent one, but though it endures but a brief while it is imprudent. *In Black and White* exhibits the same glaring inequalities to which Mr. Kipling has accustomed us. When the two stories are set side by side it is difficult to believe that the author of 'In Flood-Time' also wrote 'The Sending of Dana Da'. The latter is perhaps worthy to beguile a railway journey; the former is one of the finest examples of its genre in the language. He who can read it without a thrill is dead to words. Never has the relentless might of the flood found clearer expression. The rain-swollen river dashes and swirls through the whole story. The horror of the populous stream is set forth in the simplest terms, and yet it grips the reader as the Mariner's skinny hand gripped the Wedding Guest. 'There were dead beasts in the driftwood on the piers, and others caught by the neck in the lattice-work—buffaloes and kine, and wild pig, and deer one or two, and snakes and jackals past counting. Their bodies were black upon the left side of the bridge.' When the Strong One of Barhwi, rising above the 'wave of the wrath of the river', puts forth his hand to swim and it falls on the knotted hair of a dead man, it is impossible to repress a shudder. With such skill and restraint is the scene presented, its darkness and awe overwhelm you. And not only has Mr. Kipling arranged his material with the perception of the artist, but as a piece of English the description could not be bettered. The words fit the idea like a garment, and you are conscious all the while of receiving the precise impression which the writer intended to convey. To achieve which is a triumph of art.

No less masterly is 'Dray Wara Yow Dee'. Its theme is the fury and passion of jealousy. The local colour is luridly Eastern, and none but Mr. Kipling, who knows the native of India as he was never known before, could so rightly have felt, so rightly have expressed, the situation. The Oriental's ferocity is curiously tinctured with a heart-whole trustfulness in fate.

'Surely I shall overtake him,' says the seeker after vengeance, 'surely God hath him in the hollow of His hand against my claiming! There shall no harm befall Daoud Shah till I come; for I would fain kill him quick and whole with the life sticking firm in his body. A pomegranate is sweetest when the cloves break away unwilling from the rind. Let it be in the daytime, that I may see his face and my delight may be crowned.'

If it is by work such as this that Mr. Kipling is to be judged, it may be claimed for him that he is among the most distinguished of those who have enriched English literature with short stories. But no man may spend his life fashioning masterpieces, whether small or great: and were *In Black and White* robbed of the stories we have named little enough would be left. 'At Twenty-Two' has its moments, it is true, and 'On the City Wall' contains an admirable sketch of Lalun, 'a member of the most ancient profession in the world', as well as a street-fighter described with energy and gusto. But it does not hold together, and it emphatically fails to give the impression of completion and achievement which in 'Dray Wara Yow Dee' and 'In Flood-Time' is irresistible.

There have been men who learned Greek in their cradle, and Mr. Kipling was born with an insight into life. The knowledge of human feeling and human impulse he displays in *The Story of the Gadsbys* would be miraculous did we not reflect that it is intuitive: he probably knew as much at fifteen as he does at twenty-five. The book is intensely dramatic, and is packed with action and emotion. It has serious faults of diction which are all the more irritating to the reader because they might so easily have been avoided. In more than one scene Mr. Kipling crosses the line which divides art from reporting. He seems to forget that the written word does not produce the same effect as the spoken. A duologue conducted in the slang of the mess-room only becomes vulgar when it is crystallised into literary form. Words and phrases have one value in life, another in literature, and it is the artist's business to translate, not to transcribe. The reader wearies of such expressions as 'regimental shop o' sorts', and the jarring note lingers long in the brain. By a bolder generalisation Mr. Kipling might have given the impression that all his characters were talking slang, and refrained from using a single doubtful phrase. But his characters, though their accent is not always irreproachable, have the blood and bone of reality. There is not one but lives and convinces the reader of his life. Captain Gadsby's explanation with Mrs. Herriott is done with amazing dexterity and with that impartial recognition of the facts that holds the scales of sympathy even. There is a haunting pathos in 'The Valley of the Shadow', and the situation, almost new to literature, is handled with a fine discretion. When Gadsby, uncertain if his wife will live another hour, stumbles into the garden and merely says in answer to Mafflin's inquiry, 'Your curb's too loose,' the touch is so true that it is hard to believe that Mr. Kipling was not a witness of the scene. None, except Count Tolstoi, has introduced the unimportant in an emotional crisis with better tact. And with how sure a hand is drawn the picture of Gadsby 'funking a fall on parade!' The effect of marriage upon the Captain of the Pink Hussars is the result of inspiration rather than of observation. The man who 'led at Amdheran after Bogul-Deasin went under, and came out of the show dripping like a butcher,' is afraid to gallop in column of troop! Where in literature has the demoralisation of comfort found clearer and stronger expression?

9. 'The Sincerest Form of Flattery'

1890

Anonymous parody first published in the *Cornhill Magazine*, N.S. Vol. XV, pp. 367-9 (October 1890).

By Barry Pain (1864-1928), the 'inventor' of 'The New Humour' exemplified in his *In a Canadian Canoe* (1891) and in the writings of Jerome K. Jerome. He wrote excellent parodies in prose and verse, the earlier examples of which were collected in his *Playthings and Parodies* (1892)—in which the following parody of *Plain Tales* occupies pp. 3-8.

This is not a tale. It is a conversation which I had with a complete stranger. If you ask me why I talked to him, I have no very good reason to give. I would simply tell you to spend three hours of solitude in that same compartment on that same line. You may not know the line; which is neither your loss nor the company's gain. I do, and I had spent three hours alone on it; and at the end of three hours I longed for human converse. I was prepared to talk Persian poetry to an assistant commissioner; I was ready to talk to anyone about anything; I would have talked to a pariah dog; talked kindly, too.

So when the complete stranger got in I began at once. You see, I did not know then that he was an inaccurate young man. I thought he was a nicely-dressed average specimen. It never does to judge from appearances. I once knew a T.G., or rather, Tranter of the Bombay side knew him; but that is another story. First we talked weather, and then we talked horse. He smoked my cheroots, and I told him several things which were quite true. He began to look a little uneasy, as if he were not used to that kind of talk. Then he told me the story of the little mare which he bought in Calcutta. He gave RS.175 for her. It was thought by his friends at the time that he had been too generous; she had a very bad cough and a plaintive look in the eyes.

'I have now had her for two years,' he said, slowly removing my cheroot from his lips, 'and she has not got over that cough yet. She also continues to look plaintive. But she is fast. The other day I drove her sixty miles along the road in an *ekka*.'

I was given to understand that the time had been five hours, twenty minutes, and a decimal. Well, a country-bred mare will go almost any pace you like to ask. I should have thought about believing the man if he had not put in the decimal. As it was, I never really wanted to call him a liar until he picked up the book which I had been reading. It was a copy of *Plain Tales from the Hills*, and it lay on the seat by my side. I have a liking for that book, and I often read it. It is a good book.

'Can you understand,' he asked, 'why that book is so popular in England? Perhaps you will allow me to explain. I understand books as well as I understand horses and men. First, note this. Even in your schooldays you probably saw the difference between the prose of Cicero and the conversational Latin of Plautus.'

This last remark enabled me to place the man. He was, it seemed, a full-sized Oxford prig. They are fond of throwing their education about like that. Which is loathly in them. But they do it. I explained to him that I had never been to school.

'Well, then, to come down to your level,' he continued. 'You have read English books, and you must have seen that written English is not like spoken English. When we speak, for instance—to take quite a minor point—we often put a full stop before the relative clauses— add them as an afterthought.'

Which struck me as being true.

'But when we write we only put a comma. The author of *Plain Tales from the Hills* saw this, and acted on the principle. He punctuated his writing as he did his speaking; and used more full stops than any man before him. Which was genius.'

I think—I am not sure, but I think—that at this point I blushed.

Secondly, the public want to be mystified. They like references to things of which they have never heard. They read the sporting papers for that reason. So this man wrote of Anglo-Indian life, and put very little explanation into it. It was all local colour. Do you suppose the average cockney knows what 'P.W.D. accounts' are? Of course he doesn't. But he likes to be treated as if he did. The author noted this point. And that also shows genius. Thirdly, the public do *not* like the good man, nor do they like the bad man. They like the man-who-has-some-good-in-him-after-all. 'I am cynical,' says our author, 'and desperately worldly, and somewhat happy-go-lucky, yet I, the same man, am interested in children. Witness my story of Tods and my great goodness to Muhammed Din. With all my cynicism I have a kind heart. Was I not kind even unto Jellaludin? I am the man-who-has-some-good-in-him-after-all. Love me!' Genius again. Fourthly, take the subject-matter—soldiers, horses, and flirts. Of these three the public never weary. It may not have been genius to have seen that. And the public like catch-words. I knew a girl once who did the serio-comic business at the————; but that is another story. To recognise the beauty of catch-words may not be genius either. But it *is* genius to say more than you know, and to seem to know more than you say—to be young and to seem old. There are people who are connected with the Government of India who are so high that no one knows anything about them except themselves, and their own knowledge is very superficial. Is our author afraid? Not a bit. He speaks of them with freedom but with vagueness. He says Up Above. And the public admire the freedom, and never motice the vagueness. Bless the dear public!

The train and the complete stranger stopped simultaneously. I was not angry. 'How do you come to know the workings of the author's mind?' I asked.

I put the question calmly, and I waited to see him shrivel.

He never shrivelled. He was getting his gun-case out from under the seat. 'I am the author,' he said blandly. 'Good afternoon.' Then he got out.

He was so bland that I should have quite believed him if I had not written the book myself. As it is, I feel by no means sure about it.

Which is curious.

10. Extracts from Robert Louis Stevenson's Letters

1890-94

Extracts from letters by Robert Louis Stevenson (1850–1894), the most popular of the great writers of the Nineties—until the appearance of Kipling. These are taken from the Tusitala Edition of Stevenson's works, to which references are given below—except in the case of the letter to Richard Le Gallienne which was published in that writer's *The Romantic Nineties* (1926, p. 81). It should be remembered that R.L.S. set 'style' above all else in his literary judgments.

To Henry James. August 1890. Vol. XXXIII, p. 306:
'Kipling is too clever to live.'

To Henry James. 29 December 1890. Vol. XXXIV, p. 45:
'Kipling is by far the most promising young man who has appeared since—ahem—I appeared. He amazes me by his percocity and various endowment. But he alarms me by his copiousness and haste. He should shield his fire with both hands "and draw up all his strength and sweetness in one ball". ("Draw all his strength and all his sweetness up into one ball?" I cannot remember Marvell's words.) So the critics have been saying to me; but I was never capable of—and surely never guilty of—such a debauch of production. At this rate his works will soon fill the habitable globe; and surely he was armed for better conflicts than these succinct sketches and flying leaves of verse? I look on, I admire, I rejoice for myself; but in a kind of ambition we all have for our tongue and literature I am wounded. If I had this man's fertility and courage, it seems to me I could heave a pyramid.

Well, we begin to be old fogies now; and it was high time *something* rose to take our places. Certainly Kipling has the gifts; the fairy godmothers were all tipsy at his christening: what will he do with them?'

To Charles Baxter. 18 July 1892. Vol. XXXIV, pp. 208–9:
'Glad to hear Henley's prospects are fair: his new volume [*The Song of the Sword, and Other Verses*] is the work of a real poet. He is one of those who can make a noise of his own with words, and in whom experience strikes an individual note. There is perhaps no more genuine poet living, bar the Big Guns . . . How poorly Kipling compares! He is all smart journalism and cleverness; it is all bright and and shallow and limpid, like a business paper—a good one, *s'entend*; but there is no blot of heart's blood and the Old Night; there are no harmonics, there is scarce harmony to his music; and in Henley—all these; a touch, a sense within sense, a sound outside the sound, the shadow of the inscrutable, eloquent beyond all definition.'

To Henry James. 5 December 1892. Vol. XXXIV, p. 273:
'Hurry up with another book of stories. I am now reduced to two of my contemporaries, you and Barrie—O, and Kipling—you and Barrie and Kipling are now my Muses Three. And with Kipling, as you know, there are reservations to be made. And you and Barrie don't write enough. I should say I also read Anstey when he is serious . . . But Barrie is a beauty, *The Little Minister* and *The Window in Thrums*, eh? Stuff in that young man; but he must see and not be too funny. Genius in him, but there's a journalist at his elbow—there's the risk.'

To Richard Le Gallienne. 28 December 1893. *The Romantic Nineties*, p. 81:
'You are still young, and you may live to do much. The little artificial popularity of style in England tends, I think, to die out; the British pig returns to his true love, the love of the style-less, of the shapeless, of the slapdash and the disorderly. Rudyard Kipling, with all his genius, his Morrowbie-Jukeses, and At-the-end-of-the-Passages, is a move in that direction, and it is the wrong one. There is trouble coming, I think; and you may have to hold the fort for us in evil days.'

To Will H. Low. 15 January 1894. Vol. XXXV, p. 111:
'Here is a long while I have been waiting for something *good* in art; and what have I seen? Zola's *Débâcle* and a few of Kipling's tales . . .'

[Note by Sidney Colvin, editor of Stevenson's *Letters*, in the Tusitala Edition, Vol. XXXIV, pp. 45–46. 'In 1890, on first becoming acquainted with Mr. Kipling's *Soldiers Three*, Stevenson had written off his congratulations red-hot. "Well and indeed, Mr. Mulvaney," so ran the first sentences of his note, "but it's as good as meat to meet in with you sir. They tell me it was a man of the name of Kipling made ye; but indeed and they can't fool me; it was the Lord God Almighty that made you." Taking the cue thus offered, Mr. Kipling had written back in the character of his own Irishman, Terence Mulvaney, addressing Stevenson's Highlander, Alan Breck Stewart . . .'

Colvin includes Stevenson's answer to this, in the character of Alan —but it is of little interest and contains no criticism. The rest of Stevenson's original letter, and any others in the correspondence, have not so far been traced.]

11. Extracts from Letters of Henry James

1890–99

Henry James (1843–1916), American novelist resident in England, was an early acquaintance of Kipling's at the Savile Club, but got to know him well via their mutual friendship for Wolcott Balestier with whom Kipling was collaborating in *The Naulahka* by July 1890. He wrote an Introduction to the American collection of Kipling's stories, *Mine Own People*, in 1891 (see No. 21, below). For the other side of the correspondence with Stevenson see No. 10 above.

The extracts from his letters are quoted from *The Letters of Henry James* (2 vols.), edited by Percy Lubbock in 1920, except for two from Charles Carrington's *Rudyard Kipling*, 1955.

To Robert Louis Stevenson. 21 March 1890. *Letters*: Vol. I, p. 158: 'We'll tell you all about Rudyard Kipling—your nascent rival; he has killed one immortal—Rider Haggard; the star of the hour, aged 24 and author of remarkable Anglo-Indian and extraordinarily observed barrack life—Tommy Atkins—tales.'

To Robert Louis Stevenson. 12 January 1891. *Letters*: Vol. I, p. 182:
'The only news in literature here—such is the virtuous vacancy of our consciousness—continues to be the infant monster of a Kipling. I enclose, in this, for your entertainment a few pages I have lately written about him, to serve as the preface to an (of course authorized) American *recueil* of some of his tales. [*Mine Own People*. See No. 21.] I may add that he has just put forth his longest story yet—a thing in *Lippincott* ['The Light that Failed'—shorter version with happy ending—in January 1891 number of *Lippincott's Monthly Magazine*, Vol. XLVII, pp. 3–97] which I also send you herewith—which cuts the ground somewhat from under my feet, inasmuch as I find it the most youthfully infirm of his productions (in spite of great 'life'), much wanting in composition and in narrative and explicative, or even implicative, art.'

To Robert Louis Stevenson. 30 October 1891. Carrington, p. 188:
'That little black demon of a Kipling will perhaps have leaped upon your silver strand by the time this reaches you. He publicly left England to embrace you many weeks ago—carrying literary genius out of the country with him in his pocket.' [Kipling reached New Zealand on 18 October—but was not able to get to Samoa to see Stevenson.]

To William James. 6 February 1892. Carrington, p. 193:
'I saw the Rudyard Kiplings off by the *Teutonic* the other day ... She was poor Wolcott Balestier's sister and is a hard devoted capable little person whom I don't in the least understand his marrying ... Kipling strikes me personally as the most complete man of genius (as distinct from fine intelligence) that I have ever known.'

To Robert Louis Stevenson. 19 March 1892. *Letters*: Vol. I, p. 193:
'We lately clubbed together, all, to despatch to you an eye-witness in the person of the genius or the *genus*, in himself, Rudyard, for the concussion of whose extraordinary personality with your own we are beginning soon to strain the listening ear. We devoutly hope that this time he will really be washed upon your shore. With him goes a new little wife—whose brother—Wolcott Balestier, lately dead, in much youthful promise and performance (I don't allude, in saying that, especially to the literary part of it,) was a very valued young friend of mine.' [Again Kipling failed to reach Samoa, this time on account of

the failure of his bank which left him almost penniless in Yokohama on 9 June 1892 on his wedding trip round the world.]

To Jonathan Sturges. 5 November 1896. *Letters*: Vol. I, p. 256:
'... We will talk of many things—and among them of Rudyard Kipling's *Seven Seas*, which he has just sent me. I am laid low by the absolutely uncanny talent—the prodigious special faculty of it. It's all *violent*, without a dream of nuance or a hint of 'distinction'; all prose trumpets and castanets and such—with never a touch of the fiddle-string or a note of the nightingale. But it's magnificent and masterly in its way, and full of the most insidious art. He's a rum 'un—and one of the very few first *talents* of the time. There's a vilely idiotic reference to his 'coarseness' in this a.m.'s. *Chronicle*. The coarseness of 'The Mary Gloster' is absolutely one of the most triumphant 'values' of that triumphant thing.'

To Grace Norton. 25 December 1897. *Letters*: Vol. I, p. 278:
'His ballad future may still be big. But my view of his prose future has much shrunken in the light of one's increasingly observing how little life he can make use of. Almost nothing civilized save steam and patriotism—and the latter only in verse, where I *hate* it so, especially mixed up with God and goodness, that that half spoils my enjoyment of his great talent. Almost nothing of the complicated soul or of the female form or of any other question of *shades*—which latter constitutes, to my sense, the real formative literary discipline. In his earliest time I thought he perhaps contained the seeds of an English Balzac; but I have given that up in proportion as he has come down steadily from the simple in subject to the more simple—from the Anglo-Indians to the natives, from the natives to the Tommies, from the Tommies to the quadrupeds, from the quadrupeds to the fish, and from the fish to the engines and screws.'

To Charles Eliot Norton. 28 November 1899. Vol. I, p. 349:
'The great little Rudyard struck me as quite on his feet again, and very sane and sound and happy. Yet I am afraid you will think me a very disgusted person if I show my reserves again, over *his* recent incarnations. I can't swallow his loud, brazen patriotic verse—an exploitation of the patriotic idea, for that matter, which seems to me not really much other than the exploitation of the name of one's mother or one's wife. Two or three times a century—yes; but not every month. He is,

however, such an embodied little talent, so economically constructed for all use and no waste, that he will get again upon a good road—leading *not* into mere multitudinous noise. His talent I think quite diabolically great; and this in spite—here I am at it again!—of the misguided, the unfortunate Stalky. Stalky gives him away, aesthetically, as a man in his really now, as regards our roaring race, bardic condition, should not have allowed himself to be given. That is not a thing, however, that, in our paradise of criticism, appears to occur to so much as three persons, and meanwhile the sale, I believe, is tremendous.'

12. Andrew Lang on 'Mr. Kipling's Stories'

1891

Critical essay from Andrew Lang's *Essays in Little* (published January 1891), pp. 198–205.

For Lang's earlier writings on Kipling see above, pp. 44–50 etc.

The wind bloweth where it listeth. But the wind of literary inspiration has rarely shaken the bungalows of India, as, in the tales of the old Jesuit missionaries, the magical air shook the frail 'medicine tents', where Huron conjurors practised their mysteries. With a world of romance and of character at their doors, Englishmen in India have seen as if they saw it not. They have been busy in governing, in making war, making peace, building bridges, laying down roads, and writing official reports. Our literature from that continent of our conquest has been sparse indeed, except in the way of biographies, of histories, and of rather local and unintelligible *facetiæ*. Except the novels by the author of 'Tara', and Sir Henry Cunningham's brilliant sketches, such as 'Dustypore', and Sir Alfred Lyall's poems, we might almost say that India has contributed nothing to our finer literature. That old haunt of history, the wealth of character brought out in that confusion of races, of religions, and the old and new, has been wealth untouched, a treasure-house sealed: those pagoda trees have never been shaken. At last there comes an Englishman with eyes, with a pen extraordinarily deft, an observation marvellously rapid and keen; and, by good luck, this Englishman has no official duties: he is neither a soldier, nor a judge; he is merely a man of letters. He has leisure to look around him, he has the power of making us see what he sees; and, when we have lost India, when some new power is ruling where we ruled, when our empire has followed that of the Moguls, future generations will learn from Mr. Kipling's works what India was under English sway.

It is one of the surprises of literature that these tiny masterpieces in prose and verse were poured, 'as rich men give that care not for their gifts', into the columns of Anglo-Indian journals. There they were thought clever and ephemeral—part of the chatter of the week. The subjects, no doubt, seemed so familiar, that the strength of the handling, the brilliance of the colour, were scarcely recognised. But Mr. Kipling's volumes no sooner reached England than the people into whose hands they fell were certain that here were the beginnings of a new literary force. The books had the strangeness, the colour, the variety, the perfume of the East. Thus it is no wonder that Mr. Kipling's repute grew up as rapidly as the mysterious mango tree of the conjurors. There were critics, of course, ready to say that the thing was merely a trick, and had nothing of the supernatural. That opinion is not likely to hold its ground. Perhaps the most severe of the critics has been a young Scotch gentleman, writing French, and writing it wonderfully well, in a Parisian review. He chose to regard Mr. Kipling as little but an imitator of Bret Harte, deriving his popularity mainly from the novel and exotic character of his subjects. No doubt, if Mr. Kipling has a literary progenitor, it is Mr. Bret Harte. Among his earlier verses a few are what an imitator of the American might have written in India. But it is a wild judgment which traces Mr. Kipling's success to his use, for example, of Anglo-Indian phrases and scraps of native dialects. The presence of these elements is among the causes which have made Englishmen think Anglo-Indian literature tediously provincial, and India a bore. Mr. Kipling, on the other hand, makes us regard the continent which was a bore as an enchanted land, full of marvels and magic which are real. There has, indeed, arisen a taste for exotic literature: people have become alive to the strangeness and fascination of the world beyond the bounds of Europe and the United

States. But that is only because men of imagination and literary skill have been the new conquerors—the Corteses and Balboas of India, Africa, Australia, Japan, and the isles of the southern seas. All such conquerors, whether they write with the polish of M. Pierre Loti, or with the carelessness of Mr. Boldrewood, have, at least, seen new worlds for themselves; have gone out of the streets of the over-populated lands into the open air; have sailed and ridden, walked and hunted; have escaped from the fog and smoke of towns. New strength has come from fresher air into their brains and blood; hence the novelty and buoyancy of the stories which they tell. Hence, too, they are rather to be counted among romanticists than realists, however real is the essential truth of their books. They have found so much to see and to record, that they are not tempted to use the microscope, and pore for ever on the minute in character. A great deal of realism, especially in France, attracts because it is novel, because M. Zola and others have also found new worlds to conquer. Yet certain provinces in those worlds were not unknown to, but were voluntarily neglected by, earlier explorers. They were the 'Bad Lands' of life and character: surely it is wiser to seek quite new realms than to build mud huts and dunghills on the 'Bad Lands'.

Mr. Kipling's work, like all good work, is both real and romantic. It is real because he sees and feels very swiftly and keenly; it is romantic, again, because he has a sharp eye for the reality of romance, for the attraction and possibility of adventure, and because he is young. If a reader wants to see petty characters displayed in all their meannesses, if this be realism, surely certain of Mr. Kipling's painted and frisky matrons are realistic enough. The seamy side of Anglo-Indian life: the intrigues, amorous or semi-political—the slang of people who describe dining as 'mangling garbage'—the 'games of tennis with the seventh commandment'—he has not neglected any of these. Probably the sketches are true enough, and pity 'tis 'tis true: for example, the sketches in *Under the Deodars* and in *The Gadsbys*. That worthy pair, with their friends, are to myself as unsympathetic almost, as the characters in *La Conquête de Plassans*. But Mr. Kipling is too much a true realist to make their selfishness and pettiness unbroken, unceasing. We know that 'Gaddy' is a brave, modest, and hard-working soldier; and, when his silly little bride (who prefers being kissed by a man with waxed moustaches) lies near to death, certainly I am nearer to tears than when I am obliged to attend the bed of Little Dombey or of Little Nell. Probably there is a great deal of slangy and unrefined Anglo-Indian society; and, no doubt, to sketch it in its true colours is not beyond the province of art. At worst it is redeemed, in part, by its constancy in the presence of various perils—from disease, and from 'the bullet flying down the pass'. Mr. Kipling may not be, and very probably is not, a reader of 'Gyp'; but *The Gadsbys*, especially, reads like the work of an Anglo-Indian disciple, trammelled by certain English conventions. The more Pharisaic realists—those of the strictest sect—would probably welcome Mr. Kipling as a younger brother, so far as *Under the Deodars* and *The Gadsbys* are concerned, if he were not occasionally witty and even flippant, as well as realistic. But, very fortunately, he has not confined his observation to the leisures and pleasures of Simla; he has looked out also on war and on sport, on the life of all native tribes and castes; and has even glanced across the borders of 'The Undiscovered Country'.

Among Mr. Kipling's discoveries of new kinds of characters, probably the most popular is his invention of the British soldier in India. He avers that he 'loves that very strong man, Thomas Atkins'; but his affection has not blinded him to the faults of the beloved. Mr. Atkins drinks too much, is too careless a gallant in love, has been educated either too much or too little, and has other faults, partly due, apparently, to recent military organisation, partly to the feverish and unsettled state of the civilised world. But he is still brave, when he is well led; still loyal, above all, to his 'trusty chum'. Every Englishman must hope that, if Terence Mulvaney did not take the city of Lungtung Pen as described, yet he is ready and willing so to take it. Mr. Mulvaney is as humorous as Micky Free, but more melancholy and more truculent. He has, perhaps, 'won his way to the mythical' already, and is not so much a soldier, as an incarnation, not of Krishna, but of many soldierly qualities. On the other hand, Private Ortheris, especially in his frenzy, seems to shew all the truth, and much more than the life of, a photograph. Such, we presume, is the soldier, and such are his experiences and temptations and repentance. But nobody ever dreamed of telling us all this, till Mr. Kipling came. As for the soldier in action, the 'Taking of Lungtung Pen', and the 'Drums of the Fore and Aft', and that other tale of the battle with the Pathans in the gorge, are among the good fights of fiction. They stir the spirit, and they should be distributed (in addition, of course, to the *Soldier's Pocket Book*) in the ranks of the British army. Mr. Kipling is as well informed about the soldier's women-kind as about the soldier; about Dinah Shadd as about Terence Mulvaney. Lever never instructed us on these matters:

Micky Free, if he loves, rides away; but Terence Mulvaney is true to his old woman. Gallant, loyal, reckless, vain, swaggering, and tender-hearted, Terence Mulvaney, if there were enough of him, 'would take St. Petersburg in his drawers'. Can we be too grateful to an author who has extended, as Mr. Kipling in his military sketches has extended, the frontiers of our knowledge and sympathy?

It is a mere question of individual taste; but, for my own part, had I to make a small selection from Mr. Kipling's tales, I would include more of his studies in Black than in White, and many of his excursions beyond the probable and natural. It is difficult to have one special favourite in this kind; but perhaps the story of the two English adventurers among the freemasons of unknown Kafiristan (in the 'Phantom Rickshaw') would take a very high place. The gas-heated air of the Indian newspaper office is so real, and into it comes a wanderer who has seen new faces of death, and who carries with him a head that has worn a royal crown. The contrasts are of brutal force; the legend is among the best of such strange fancies. Then there is, in the same volume, 'The Strange Ride of Morrowbie Jukes', the most dreadful nightmare of the most awful Bunker in the realms of fancy. This is a very early work; if nothing else of Mr. Kipling's existed, his memory might live by it, as does the memory of the American Irishman by the 'Diamond Lens'. The sham magic of 'In the House of Suddhu' is as terrible as true necromancy could be, and I have a *faiblesse* for the 'Bisara of Pooree'. 'The Gate of the Hundred Sorrows', is a realistic version of 'The English Opium Eater', and more powerful by dint of less rhetoric. As for the sketches of native life—for example, 'On the City Wall'—to English readers they are no less than revelations. They testify, more even than the military stories, to the author's swift and certain vision, his certainty in his effects. In brief, Mr. Kipling has conquered worlds, of which, as it were, we knew not the existence.

His faults are so conspicuous, so much on the surface, that they hardly need to be named. They are curiously visible to some readers who are blind to his merits. There is a false air of hardness (quite in contradiction to the sentiment in his tales of childish life); there is a knowing air; there are mannerisms, such as 'But that is another story'; there is a display of slang; there is the too obtrusive knocking of the nail on the head. Everybody can mark these errors; a few cannot overcome their antipathy, and so lose a great deal of pleasure.

It is impossible to guess how Mr. Kipling will fare if he ventures on one of the usual novels, of the orthodox length. Few men have succeeded both in the *conte* and the novel. Mr. Bret Harte is limited to the *conte*; M. Guy de Maupassant is probably at his best in it. Scott wrote but three or four short tales, and only one of these is a masterpiece. Poe never attempted a novel. Hawthorne is almost alone in his command of both kinds. We can live only in the hope that Mr. Kipling, so skilled in so many species of the *conte*, so vigorous in so many kinds of verse, will also be triumphant in the novel; though it seems unlikely that its scene can be in England, and though it is certain that a writer who so cuts to the quick will not be happy with the novel's almost inevitable 'padding'. Mr. Kipling's longest effort, *The Light which Failed*, can, perhaps, hardly be considered a test or touchstone of his powers as a novelist. The central interest is not so powerful, the characters are not so sympathetic, as are the interest and the characters of his short pieces. Many of these persons we have met so often that they are not mere passing acquaintances, but already find in us the loyalty due to old friends.

13. J. K. Stephen: 'A Protest in Verse'

1891

First published in the *Cambridge Review* (February 1891) and collected the same year in '*Lapsus Calami*, by J.K.S.'.

James Kenneth Stephen (1859–1892), son of Sir James Fitzjames Stephen, was a barrister and Fellow of Trinity College, Cambridge. He produced two slim volumes of superb parodies and light verse, *Lapsus Calami* and *Quo, Musa, Tendis?*, both published in 1891 shortly before his tragically early death in February 1892.

Kipling wrote in *Something of Myself* (1937), pp. 92–3: 'People talked, quite reasonably, of rockets and sticks; and that genius, J.K.S., brother to Herbert Stephen, dealt with Haggard and me in some stanzas which I would have given much to have written myself . . . It ran joyously through all the papers. It still hangs faintly in the air and, as I used to warn Haggard, may continue as an aroma when all but our two queer names are forgotten.'

To R.K.

As long I dwell on some stupendous
and tremendous (Heaven defend us!)
Monstr'-inform'-ingens-horrendous
Demoniaco-seraphic
Penman's latest piece of graphic
BROWNING

Will there never come a season
Which shall rid us from the curse
Of a prose which knows no reason
And an unmelodious verse:
When the world shall cease to wonder
At the genius of an Ass,
And a boy's eccentric blunder
Shall not bring success to pass:

When mankind shall be delivered
From the clash of magazines,
And the inkstand shall be shivered
Into countless smithereens:
When there stands a muzzled stripling,
Mute, beside a muzzled bore:
When the Rudyards cease from kipling
And the Haggards Ride no more.

14. J. M. Barrie on 'Mr. Kipling's Stories'

1891

Signed article from the *Contemporary Review*, Vol. LIX, pp. 364–372 (March 1891).

James Matthew Barrie (1860–1937), though now remembered for his plays, was at first considered to be the great coming novelist on the strength of his sketches of Scottish character in *Auld Licht Idylls* (1888) and *A Window in Thrums* (1889). Both Meredith and Stevenson set him above Kipling, and were not disappointed when he too essayed the full-length novel in 1891 with *The Little Minister*. Barrie had already welcomed his young rival with typical generosity a year earlier in an article 'The Man from Nowhere' in the *British Weekly* (2 May 1890): for quotations from this see Introduction pp. 17–18.

The best of our fiction is by novelists who allow that it is as good as they can give, and the worst by novelists who maintain that they could do much better if the public would let them. They want to be strong, but the public, they say, prohibits it. In the meantime, Mr. Kipling has done what we are to understand they could do if they dared. He has brought no mild wines from India, only liqueurs, and the public has drunk eagerly. His mission is to tell Mr. Grant Allen and the others that they may venture to bring their 'Scarlet Letter' out of their desks and print it. Mr. Kipling has done even more than that. He has given the reading public a right not to feel ashamed of itself on second thoughts, which is a privilege it seldom enjoys. Now that the Eurekas over his discovery are ended we have no reason to blush for them. Literary men of mark are seldom discovered; we begin to be proud of them when they are full-grown, or afterwards. True, every other season a new writer is the darling of London, but not by merit, and presently he is pilloried for standing on the pedestal where our whim placed him. Mankind has no mercy for the author about whom it has deceived itself. But here is a literary 'sensation' lifted on high because he is worth looking at. Doubtless the circumstances were favourable. Most writers begin with one book, but he came from India with half a dozen ready, and fired them at the town simultaneously. A six-shooter attracts more attention than a single barrel. Alarming stories of his youth went abroad at the same time, and did him no harm among a people who love to say 'Oh my! and 'Fancy!' over precocity. Many men have begun to write as early as Mr. Kipling, but seldom so boldly. His audacity alone might have carried him shoulder-high for a brief period. His knowledge of life, 'sufficient to turn your hair grey', would have sent ladies from the musical prodigies whom they fed on sweets, and the theatrical prodigies who (according to the interviews) play when at home with dolls, to the literary prodigy whose characters swear most awful. From the first only the risky subjects seem to have attracted Mr. Kipling. He began by dancing on ground that most novelists look long at before they adventure a foot. His game was leapfrog over all the passions. One felt that he must have been born *blasé*, that in his hurry to be a man he had jumped boyhood, which is perhaps why his boy and girl of *The Light that Failed* are a man and woman playing in vain at being children. The task he set himself was to peer into humanity with a very bright lantern, of which he holds the patent, and when he encountered virtue he passed it by respectfully as not what he was looking for. It is a jewel, no doubt, but one that will not gleam sufficiently in the light of that lantern. In short, he was in search of the devil (his only hero so far) that is in all of us, and he found him and brought him forth for inspection, exhibiting him from many points of view in a series of lightning flashes. Lightning, however, dazzles as well as reveals, and after recovering their breath, people began to wonder whether Mr. Kipling's favourite figure would look like this in daylight. He has been in no hurry to answer them, for it is in these flashes that the magic lies; they are his style.

'It would be a good thing,' Mr. Mark Twain says, 'to read Mr. Kipling's writings for their style alone, if there were no story back of it.' This might be a good thing if it were not impossible, the style being the story. As well might one say, 'It would be a good thing to admire a Rubens for the way it is painted alone, though there were no picture back of it;' or, 'It would be a good thing to admire correct spelling, though there were no word back of it.' Words are what we spell ideas with. Here, then, is the difference between style and matter. The ideas are the matter, and the spelling is the style. But style and matter, we have been saying, are one. So they are, even as the letters that make a word are the word. Unless we have the right letters arranged in the one way we do not have the word, and, similarly, without the right words arranged in the one way, we do not get the idea. Were we as capable at spelling ideas as at spelling words, we could estimate a writer as easily as a schoolmaster corrects a boy's exercise. Unfortunately, when we sit down to criticise we must write at the top of our paper, 'But we don't know the way ourselves'. The author under our lens is at the same time our teacher, for we only know how the idea he is putting together should be spelled after we have seen him spell it. So difficult is his task that he has done a big thing if the spelling is nearly right; if, that is to say, we can recognise the idea, as we know a word though there may be a letter missing or upside down. An idea correctly spelled is so beautiful that we read the truth in its face. It carries conviction. How does Mr. Kipling spell his ideas? therefore, is a way of asking what is his style, which sums up his worth. Most will admit that of our living novelists Mr. Meredith and Mr. Hardy spell the greatest ideas best. Doubtless Mr. Stevenson is correct more often than any of his contemporaries, certainly a dozen times for Mr. Kipling's once; but, on the other hand, it should be said that the younger writer tries to spell the bigger ideas. While Mr. Stevenson sets his horse at ideas of one syllable and goes over like a bird, Mr. Kipling is facing Mesopotamia and reaching the other side, perhaps on his head or muddy. Still he has got through it, if not over it. He rides a plucky little donkey that shies at nothing and sticks in nothing. We have his style in that sentence in which Mulvaney wakes from a drunken bout and 'feels as tho' a she-cat had littered in my mouth'. This is not an idea perfectly spelled. *She*-cat is unnecessary; Tom-cats do not litter. But though it is by coarseness that Mr. Kipling gains his end, which is to make us feel suddenly sick, he does gain it, and so he is an artist. Some admit his humour, his pathos, his character-drawing, his wonderful way of flashing a picture before our eyes till it is as vivid as a landscape seen in lightning—in short, his dramatic power—and yet add with a sigh, 'What a pity he has no style!' This surely is saying in one breath that he is and he isn't. These qualities they have allowed him are his style. They are his spelling of ideas. Nevertheless, he is to Mr. Stevenson as phonetic spelling is to pure English. He is not a Christian, but a Kristyān. His words are often wrong, but he groups them so that they convey the idea he is in pursuit of. We see at once that his pathos is potatoes. It is not legitimate, but it produces the desired effects. There are sentences without verbs. He wants perpetually to take his readers by surprise, and has them, as it were, at the end of a string, which he is constantly jerking. With such a jerk he is usually off from one paragraph to the next. He writes Finis with it. His style is the perfection of what is called journalese, which is sometimes not on speaking terms with Lindley Murray.[1]

He owes nothing to any other writer. No one helped to form him. He never imitated, preparatory to making a style for himself. He began by being original, and probably when at school learned calligraphy from copy lines of his own invention. If his work suggests that of any other novelists, it is by accident; he would have written thus though they had never existed. By some he has been hailed as a Dickens, which seems mere cruelty to a young man. A Dickens should never be expected. He must always come as a surprise. He is too big to dream about. But there is a swing, an exuberance of life in some of Mr. Kipling's practical jokes that are worthy of the author of 'Charles O'Malley'. Rather let us say that certain of Lever's roaring boys are worthy of Mr. Kipling. 'The Taking of Lungtungpen' and 'The Man who would be King' are beyond Lever; indeed, for the second of these two stories, our author's masterpiece, there is no word but magnificent. It is about two scamps, stone-broke, who, as they can get no other employment, decide to be kings. They borrow a map of India, fix upon their territory, and become monarchs after a series of adventures that make the reader's head swim. Finally, their weakness for women and liquor dethrones them, and the one is sent back to civilised parts with the other's head in a bag. Positively it is the most audacious thing in fiction, and yet it reads as true as *Robinson Crusoe*. Daniel Dravot the First throws Mulvaney. I like to think that he was Mulvaney all the time. Thus should that warrior's career have closed. It is Mr. Bret Harte that Mr. Kipling most resembles. He, too, uses the lantern flash; Mulvaney would have been at home in Red Gulch and Mr. Oakhurst in Simla. Let us, in fanciful mood, suppose we presented a town to our novelists and asked each to write a book about the persons in it that interested him most. The majority would begin their novel as soon as they found a young man and woman who made forty years between them. Without mentioning names, we know who would wait for a murder as the beginning of all good things, and who would go to the East-end in search of a lady from the West, and who would

[1] [Author of the standard *English Grammar*, 1795]

stroll into the country and who would seek (and find) a Highlander, and who would inquire for a pirate with no female connections. But Mr. Harte and Mr. Kipling would discover their quarry in the ne'er-do-wells and treat them not dissimilarly. Mr. Kipling has one advantage. He is never theatrical as Mr. Harte sometimes is. Both are frequently pathetic, but the one ever draws back from bathos, while the other marches into it, and is fitly rewarded if we smile instead of weep. There is more restraint in Mr. Kipling's art. But Mr. Harte is easily first in his drawing of women. It is in their women that most of our leading novelists excel. No doubt (the sex tells us so) the women are all wrong, for no man really knows anything about women except that they are a riddle. It is enough, however, to put the riddle delightfully, as so many do, Mr. Harte among them. We are in love with his girls, and so all is well. Here, unfortunately, Mr. Kipling fails. Mr. Stevenson is in the same predicament, but that, one almost dares to conclude, is because he lacks interest in the subject; he cunningly contrives men who can get on without the other sex, and such is his fascination that we let this pass. The 'duel between the sexes', however, is Mr. Kipling's theme (which increases his chances of immortality), and there is a woman in most of his stories. Yet who remembers her? The three soldiers' tales are often about women, and these wonderful soldiers you could not forget if you would, but the women are as if they had never been. The author's own favourite is Mrs. Hauksbee, the grass widow, whom the 'boys' love, and she is an adept at drawing back from the brink, while they go over or are saved according to her whim. She is clever and good-natured, and has a sense of humour, and that she is a pernicious woman is no subject for complaint. She belongs to the dirty corner, of which we have to speak presently. But she is drawn with little subtlety. We only know her superficially. We should forget her like the rest did she not appear so frequently. The real Mrs. Hauksbee is to be found in the works of other novelists. Yet she is better than the usually vulgar girls of Simla, to whom she occasionally restores a lover. Girlhood is what is wanted, and so far it has proved beyond him. In *The Light that Failed*, Maisie, the heroine, is utterly uninteresting, which is the one thing a heroine may not be. We never know her, and this is not because she is an intricate study. She is merely offered as a nice girl, with an ambition to have her person and paint-brush described in the *Star's* fashionable column. But she is colourless, a nonentity. On the other hand, she has a friend called 'the red-haired girl', whom we do care for, but probably only because we see her in three brief flashes. If she came into the light of day she might prove as dull as Maisie.

Some have taken Mr. Kipling's aim to be the representation of India as it is, and have refused to believe that Indian life—especially Anglo-Indian life—is as ugly as he paints it. Their premiss granted, few would object to their conclusion except such as judge England by the froth of society or by its dregs. But Mr. Kipling warns us against this assumption. In the preface to one of his books—a preface that might stand in front of all—he 'assures the ill-informed that India is not entirely inhabited by men and women playing tennis with the Seventh Commandment . . . The drawback of collecting dirt in one corner is that it gives a false notion of the filth of the room.' The admission of his aim herein contained contracts his ambition into a comparatively little thing, but it should silence much of the hostile criticism. That he is entitled as an artist to dwell chiefly on the dirty corner of the room will surely be admitted. A distinguished American writer maintains that certain subjects taken up by daring novelists should be left to the doctors; but is not this a mistake? The novelist's subject is mankind, and there is no part of it of which he has not the right to treat. By his subject never, by his treatment of it always, should he be judged. If he does not go about the work honestly, so much the worse for him. If his motives are unworthy, nothing is surer in this world than that tomorrow, if not today, he will be found out. Many in England seem to have forgotten this, and Mr. Kipling has done noble work in reminding them of it by example. He refuses to be caged, and that is all a novelist need do to be free. The dirty corner is Mr. Kipling's, to write about if he chooses, and he may do it with the highest motives, that is to say, as an artist, and according as he does it well or ill shall we esteem him. From all points of view but one he does it amazingly well. Assuredly we are made to see that dirty corner. We get it from north, south, east and west. But we are never allowed to estimate its size; there is no perspective; the blaze of light is always on the one spot; we never see the rest of the room. It is not enough for Mr. Kipling to say that he is only concerned with the corner, and so can keep the room in darkness. By all means let the corner be his subject; but we shall never know all about it until we can fit it into that of which it is a part. In other words, we must be shown the room in order to know the corner. Suppose an artist, instead of choosing the human figure for his subject, were to limit himself to the human hand, his work might be as fine as Mr. Kipling's, and yet it would be incomplete. We should not know whether that hand needed sixes or nines in gloves, unless we saw the person it belonged to, and the artist could not satisfy us by merely intimating that the figure is not all hand, as Mr. Kipling remarks that the room is not all dirty corner. We want to see the whole room lighted up that we may judge the dirty corner by comparison. No doubt it is this want of perspective that has made many uneasy about Mr. Kipling's work. He has startled them, and then left them doubtful whether it was done legitimately. There is something wrong, they feel, and they have a notion that they could put their finger on it if the stories were English instead of Indian, and long instead of short. Hence, apparently, has arisen a noisy demand for English novels from him. They are to be his test. In answer, one may conclude, to this request, he has written several English stories recently, one of them his 'first long story'. Mr. Kipling, having a respect for his calling, always writes as well as he can, and these stories, we are told, have been rewritten as many times as Mr. Ruskin would have lovers serve years for their ladies. It is, however, by the result alone that he is to be judged, and the result is not great. Those of the stories that deal with 'Society', are more ambitious than the *feuilletons* of the Society journals, but merit no longer life. *The Record of Badalia Herodsfoot* is much better; but it is merely a very clever man's treatment of a land he knows little of. We are only shown the conventional East-end, and there is something grim in Mr. Kipling become conventional. The only point the story has in common with the Indian sketches is that it makes straight for the dirty corner. But it has one inspired moment, when Badalia dances on the barrow. As for *The Light that Failed*, one hasty critic finds not even cleverness in it; while another says it would make ninety-seven ordinary novels, and proves his argument by pointing out that Mr. Kipling knows there are three kinds of soap. Mr. Kipling knows even more than this; but despite its vigour and picturesqueness, the story would probably have attracted little notice had it been an unknown man, and such as it might have got would have been won by its almost brutal cynicism. High as the author stands as a writer of short stories, *The Light that Failed* proves that the moment he takes to writing novels he has many contemporaries to make up upon, as also that, if he is to do it, he must abandon some of his own methods in favour of some of theirs.

His chief defect is ignorance of life. This seems a startling charge to bring against one whose so-called knowledge of life has frightened the timid. But it is true. One may not often identify an author with any of his characters, but if Dick Heldar had written instead of painted, or Mr. Kipling had painted instead of written, it would have been difficult to distinguish the one artist from the other. Dick gives us his views on art and life in *The Light that Failed*, and his creator in that story and others, and they correspond. They are very smart views, and gaudy. Mr. Kipling is most tender in his treatment of Dick become blind. Such a man would not, we think, have fallen in love with Maisie the characterless, and instead of sitting in his blindness turning her letters over in his hand, and purring placidly when she is willing, in pity, to be his, he would probably have blown out his brains. But Dick and the letters make an affecting picture. There is something else in the story, however, far more touching; and the author is not aware of it, which adds greatly to the pathos. It is the revolting cynicism of Dick, who thinks he is at least a man, and is really anything but that. Though Dick had kept his eyesight, he could not have become a great artist without growing out of the ideas he was so proud of. He was always half blind to the best in life, just as Mr. Kipling is. Yet he was so brilliant, so honest, so streaked with good, that one does not sneer at his boyish cynicism, but is sad because he became blind before he ever saw properly. He is under the curse of thinking he knows everything. He believes that because he has knocked about the world in shady company he has no more to learn. It never dawns on him that he is but a beginner in knowledge of life compared to many men who have stayed at home with their mothers. He knows so little where is the fire in which men and women are proved that he has crossed a globe for it, which is like taking a journey to look for one's shadow. He is so ignorant of art as to think it the greatest thing in the world. Poor Dick comes to London, gloating over the stir he is to make, and thus addresses a row of semi-detached villas: 'Oh, you rabbit-hutches! Do you know what you have to do later on? You have to supply me with men-servants and maid-servants'—here he smacked his lips—'and the peculiar treasure of kings. Meantime I'll get clothes and boots, and presently I will return and trample on you.' And why is Master Dick to trample on these people? Because they have not the artistic instinct. This is what it is to be a heaven-born artist according to Messrs. Heldar and Kipling. We know it from scores of the stories. There is no sympathy with humanity, without which there never was and never will be a great novelist. Sympathy is the blood of the novel. True, Mr. Kipling has an affection for the Mulvaney type, but it is only because they too, are artists in their own way. When full of drink

85

and damns they are picturesque, they have a lordly swagger, they are saved by being devil-may-cares. But if they drank tea instead of whisky, if it was their own wives they walked out with, if they were not ashamed to live respectably in semi-detached villas, if they were grocers who thought almanacks art, or double-chinned professional men who only admired the right picture when they had an explanatory catalogue in their hand, if they were costermongers whose dissipation was the People's Palace, then would they be as cattle. Ninety-nine in every hundred of the population are for trampling on. With the mass of his fellow-creatures Mr. Kipling is out of touch, and thus they are an unknown tongue to him. He will not even look for the key. At present he is a rare workman with a contempt for the best material.

Should Mr. Kipling learn that he can be taught much by grocers, whose views of art are bounded by Adelphi dramas and Sunday-school literature, he may rise to be a great novelist, for the like of him at his age has seldom been known in fiction. His work of the past twelve months is a flat contradiction to the statement that he is written out. Some of the recent stories in *Macmillan's Magazine* rank among his best. It has been pointed out that 'he cannot go on writing these sketches for ever', that they must lose in freshness, that all his characters will soon be used up. But this only means that we could not write them for ever, which is quite true, as we could not have written them at all. We have no right to demand long novels from him, we should be content to revel in the sketches, but if, as we have been led to believe, his intentions run in that direction, we know enough of him to be convinced that he should lay his scene in India. The cry for an English novel has been curiously unreasonable. The example our great novelists have set him is not to write of England, but of what he knows best. If by an accident it has usually been England with them, it is India by accident with him.

The Light that Failed is not much, but, like *The Story of the Gadsbys*, it reveals the great gift of character-drawing by means of dialogue, and as a first attempt in a new method it is in one respect little short of a triumph. Hitherto he had always worked by means of the lantern flash. He took an hour of a man's life and condensed it into a moment. What we were shown was less a printed page that had to be read than a picture which we could take in at once. He had it thus before himself. He could grip it all in his hand. He never required to wonder how one part should play into another. Not in this way can the novel be written. It does not aim at immediate and incessant effects. The chapter, which could swallow half-a-dozen sketches, is not considered by itself, but as the small part of the whole, and it is as a whole that the novel is judged. To forget this is to lose thought of symmetry. No doubt Scott wrote too quickly, but his speed was a real advantage in one way, for it kept his mind on the story as a whole. Having mastered the flash, one might have feared that Mr. Kipling had also become its slave. In *The Story of the Gadsbys* he uses it as much as in the short sketches. That tale is in eight chapters, but each is complete in itself. We get eight events in the Gadsbys' life squeezed into eight minutes, and the result is not a novel. It is only a series of fine pictures. But when he began *The Light that Failed*, Mr. Kipling had realised that the novel in flashes will no more do than liqueurs in tumblers. He broke away from the old method, and he has produced a real novel, though not a great one. Here is proof that there are latent capabilities in him which may develop, and show him by-and-by grown out of knowledge. If he is as conscientious in the future as he has been in the past, and discovers that nothing lives in literature save what is ennobling, he may surprise us again.

15. Three Reviews by Lionel Johnson

1891-2

Three signed reviews which appeared in the *Academy*, Vol. XXXIX, pp. 319–20 (4 April 1891); Vol. XL, pp. 327–8 (17 October 1891) and Vol. XLI, pp. 509–10 (28 May 1892). Subsequently collected in *Reviews and Critical Papers* by Lionel Johnson, (1921) pp. 17–51.

Lionel Pigot Johnson (1867–1902) minor poet and critic. Besides volumes of poems, and a number of reviews such as those collected in the 1921 volume, Johnson wrote *The Art of Thomas Hardy* (1894) and on Irish poetry.

---

(1). *The Light that Failed* (1891)

'Good Lord! who can account for the fathomless folly of the public?' 'They're a remarkably sensible people.' 'They're subject to fits, if that's what you mean; and you happen to be the object of the latest fit among those who are interested in what they call art. Just now you're a fashion, a phenomenon, or whatever you please.'

This is part of a conversation between Dick Heldar, a young artist whose work has taken the public, and his best friend Torpenhow. Mr. Kipling will not think me discourteous, if I confess that these wise words bear for me a second application to himself. Thanks to the incessant criticism, panegyric, detraction and talk inflicted upon his work in the last year, one feels an unreasoning desire, either to defer the study of Mr. Kipling till the hubbub die down, or to assume an indifference towards him, in the name of sober sense. Either course would be foolish, and neither is possible. Whatever else be true of Mr. Kipling, it is the first truth about him that he has power: not a clever trick, nor a happy knack, nor a flashy style, but real intrinsic power. The reader of contemporary books, driven mad by the distracting affectations, the contemptible pettiness of so much modern work, feels his whole heart go out towards a writer with mind and muscle in him, not only nerves and sentiment. To get into the grip of a new writer; not to saunter arm in arm with him, listening to his tedious and familiar elegancies: that is what we want. Style, the perfection of workmanship, we cannot do without that; but still less can we endure the dexterous and polished imitation of that. It is easy enough to find fault with Mr. Kipling, to deplore certain technical failures, to cry out against his lack of grace; but perfect workmanship is the last good gift, and granted only to the faithful and the laborious in literature. A writer whose first books have flesh and blood, mind and meaning in them, has the right to hope for all things. But the public is less kind than uncritical, when it admires 'achieved perfection' in writings that have achieved much else that is good, but not yet that.

The present volume gives us the story 'as it was originally conceived by the writer', not as it appeared in *Lippincott's Magazine*. There, as most of us know, the story has a pleasant and conventional close, with a marriage of the consolatory sort, familiar to English readers. It is difficult to think well of Mr. Kipling in this matter; such a conclusion was impossible, upon the stated premises. But the book in its true form is finely and desperately logical. Briefly expressed, this is the idea: A boy and a girl, brought up together not too happily, part as chidlren, when the boy's sentiments of mere companionship begin to deepen into love, of a childish sort indeed, yet perfectly real. The boy leads a rough, adventurous life about the world, and after the most varied experiences, wins a sudden and perhaps precarious success in art. His life has been that of an Elizabethan adventurer, in the altered manner of this century: a life of the reckless sort, wild and free, with all the virtues of *camaraderie*, and with few of the more decorous moral excellences. Settled, more or less, in London, he meets the girl again, whom he has never forgotten; she, too, is an artist, full of ambition, eager for recognition, and singularly selfish. She refuses to think of love and marriage; and he devotes himself, half in hopes, half in despair, to her service in art. From the effect of an early wound he grows blind; and the culminating point of interest is reached when the question presents itself to the girl, whom he has loved and served, whether now, in mere compassion and self-respect, she will marry him, and so pay back his devotion by an act of willing self-denial. In sheer selfishness, perfectly natural and immensely strong, she prefers her freedom and her foolish dreams of fame. He cannot endure the idle agony of his life, cut off from all the best things in the world; and he makes his way out to the Soudan, the old scene of his early life, and is there killed, dying in his friend's arms.

The story has a double interest: the interest of character in Maisie the heroine, and the interest of dramatic life and action in Dick the hero and in his friends. Hero and heroine are not the right words, but let that pass. Now the first thought that occurs to one well acquainted with Mr. Kipling's work, upon reading this, his longest book, is of this sort: why is the interest of character so slight and the interest of action and of life so strong? Scenes of superb vigour and animation, passages of wonderful force and movement, these have struck us and taken hold upon us; but the characters, emotions, the mind and soul of Maisie and Dick have not been felt, and do not remain with us. We remember how they looked, talked, bore themselves in various situations; we still hear their characteristic phrases, we still see their attitudes and motions; but themselves, their inner reality, for all the power and mind of the book, are strange to us. Perhaps this may be the reason. Mr. Kipling, before all things, is an observer, not a thinker. Certainly no one can observe life without colouring or shaping his observations by his thoughts; each has his own way of observing life, according to his own habit and cast of mind. But it is not so much the reflections upon life, as the reflections of life, that Mr. Kipling values; and he leaves the bare facts, in all their intensity and vividness, to create the impression which he desires us to receive. There must be no waste of words, no flow of sentiment, no dwelling upon motives; take the facts, he seems to say, as lifelike as I can show them, and make what you can of them. This may be called cynicism, but it need not be that. Without question it is an effective literary method; but, and here is the difficulty, it is a method of very limited application. It will excellently serve for a brilliant sketch of certain scenes, where the men and women act and speak in character, with all the appropriate peculiarities of manner and speech. A third-class smoking-carriage full of soldiers, labourers and city clerks, each with his personal or professional dialect and style, and with that curious force and energy which belong to the less cultured—Mr. Kipling's manner serves perfectly to give us that. But a drawing-room full of more sophisticated and of less intelligible persons, all possessing the complicated emotions and using the subtile language of a life externally refined: what will his robust method make of that? Here we turn to Mr. Henry James. He will in twenty pages bring home to us the passion or the intellect at work in that room, perhaps during one hour only; yet each word will be essential and indispensable. If Mr. James try his hand upon coarser material, he fails at once: witness many pages of *The Princess Casamassima*. Hitherto Mr. Kipling has been successful when dealing with life of a certain vehement intensity, not only in the emotions of it, but in the outward manner: his soldiers, with their heartiness, or roughness, or swagger, or strength, men 'of strange oaths'—full of experience, yet children after all in many things—these are admirable. Or his natives of India, whose circumstances, sordid or picturesque, dignified or pathetic, are felt to be impressive—these he can present to us in perfection. But in whatever he handles well, there must be salient points rather than delicate shades. 'One crowded hour of glorious life', splendid and intoxicating, he can render into words of marvellous intensity; some scene of touching pitifulness, quite simple and human, he can draw with touches absolutely true and right. He is master of human nature in the rough, in its primitive or unconventional manifestations. His rapid sketches, carefully as they are designed, give an impression rather of an immense capacity of eye than of a fineness of sympathy and understanding. His work of this 'coloured and figured' sort is unrivalled, and stands alone; no one has done anything quite like it. But Mr. Kipling is, or seems to be, so fascinated by these lively effects that he wishes to treat everything in the same way, which is irritating. He appears almost to despise whatever is not vivid and impressive; to look at everything from the standpoint of a man who knows camps and barracks, wild countries and native quarters. He attempts to play Othello to his ignorant reader's Desdemona, in a manner almost ludicrous. A writer may be intimate with Valparaiso and Zanzibar without being superior to the reader, who knows only Bloomsbury and Kensington, or Oxford and Manchester. It is impossible to take English life of all kinds by storm, for literary purposes, with the methods applicable to military stations in India. And so, whilst in this book the scenes in the Soudan, and the riotous humours of special correspondents, are convincing and true to the inexperienced reader, there is a great deal which rings false. Torpenhow's warning comes into our mind, 'Take care, Dick: remember, this isn't the Soudan'. When Mr. Kipling is concerned with Maisie's character, and the less obvious emotions of life, we are constantly thinking, take care: remember, this isn't an Irish private. One striking fact illustrates this comparative incapacity for treating delicate or sophisticated sentiments: we cannot remember the phrases used.

Professional terms, technical slang, all varieties of masculine dialect and expression, are easily remembered by Mr. Kipling's readers; everything forcible and boisterous. But of Dick's conversation with Maisie, of the sentiment and psychological description, we can quote not one word. Take away from Mr. Kipling his salient points and lively effects, and then his style becomes merely commonplace. And even in his best passages, the strained expression, the unrelaxed determination to be vigorous, grows wearisome. Contrast with Mr. Kipling the enchanting style of Pierre Loti; that strangely ironical and gentle style, so caressing and unforgettable. For *Les trois Dames de la Kasbah*, we would give many a Plain Tale from the Hills. And, ultimately, Mr. Kipling's incessant vigilance, lest he fall into the hackneyed and the tame, produces an effect of brilliant vulgarity: an effect wholly unjust to Mr. Kipling, yet an inevitable result of his method, when carried to excess. Surely, one protests, we do not want special correspondence, even composed with genius.

Apart from this mannerism, Mr. Kipling's work has innumerable good qualities. Restraint, a dislike of the superfluous, how rare is that just now! To take one small instance: Mr. Kipling makes Dick quote Emerson and Marvell, but he does not mention them by name. In actual life, we do not mention the authors of our quotations; we quote what we suppose familiar to our companions. But in books there seems to come upon the writer a desire to exhibit his reading; he mentions Emerson and Marvell. It is an infinitely small matter, but it is precisely characteristic of Mr. Kipling. Directness, also; only Mr. Meredith, Mr. Hardy, and Mr. Stevenson, to name three very varied writers, can so give us the absolutely right and infallible phrase. Mr. Kipling, with 'his eye on the object', is astounding; with no accumulation of detail, no tiresome minuteness, he brings before us the very reality of life and of character, so far as character can be shown in sketches of talk and action. For there are these limitations to Mr. Kipling's art; within them I recognise with gratitude and admiration a fine writer. But, outside them, I seem to see, if I may make a vigorous quotation in Mr. Kipling's manner, 'another good man gone wrong'. Let us hope for the best, and enjoy what is already in so great a measure so excellent.

(2). *Life's Handicap: Being Stories of Mine Own People* (1891)

Mr. Kipling has gathered into a volume twenty-seven stories: the best of them have been already recognised by readers of the magazines as

Mr. Kipling's finest work. The book is so characteristic, for good and bad, of its author, that it may be interesting to attempt a classification of these twenty-seven stories. Eight of them, with certain limitations, are excellent: 'The Incarnation of Krishna Mulvaney', 'The Courting of Dinah Shadd', 'On Greenhow Hill', 'The Man Who Was', 'Without Benefit of Clergy', 'Through the Fire', 'The Finances of the Gods', and 'Little Tobrah'. To these may be added the Preface. They deal with the famous triumvirate of privates, with the British army, and with the comedy and tragedy of native life and character. Two stories, 'At the End of the Passage' and 'The Mark of the Beast', are concerned with the grim and terrible possibilities and impossibilities of sickness, weariness, fear, superstition, climate, work, and, to put it plainly, the devil, as shown by the experiences of Englishmen in India. Three more, 'The Return of Imray', 'Bubbling Well Road', and 'Bertran and Bimi', are powerful stories of the horrible, without any mixture of mystery and impossibility. Three, 'The Mutiny of the Mavericks', 'The Head of the District' and 'Namgay Doola', have, more or less directly, a political moral wrapped up in them. Five more, 'The Amir's Homily', 'Jews in Shushan', 'The Limitations of Pambe Serang', 'The City of Dreadful Night' and 'The Dream of Duncan Parrenness', are mediocre examples of Mr. Kipling's various manners; and of these the fourth is the most striking. The remaining six, in my sincere and humble opinion, do not deserve publication: 'The Lang Men o'Larut', 'Reingelder and the German Flag', 'The Wandering Jew', 'Moti Guj', 'Georgie Porgie' and 'Naboth'. The volume ends with some of Mr. Kipling's best verses.

This is, of course, merely a classification made according to the mind of one particular reader, with his own tastes and prejudices. Among the stories which I think the worst, is one which many readers have ranked among the best. But, upon the whole, I think that most readers would accept the classification in its spirit and intention.

The one great fault in Mr. Kipling's work is, not its 'brutality', nor its fondness for strong effects, but a certain taint of bad manners, from the literary point of view. He insists upon spicing his stories with an ill-flavoured kind of gossip, wholly irrelevant, and very offensive. For example: 'The Man Who Was', an admirable story, full of that indefinable spirit, military patriotism and regimental pride, is spoilt by this pointless passage:

And indeed they were a regiment to be admired. When Lady Durgan, widow of the late Sir John Durgan, arrived in their station, and after a short time had been proposed to by every single man at mess, she put the public sentiment very neatly when she explained that they were all so nice that unless she could marry them all, including the colonel and some majors already married, she was not going to content herself with one hussar. Wherefore she wedded a little man in a Rifle Regiment, being by nature contradictious: and the White Hussars were going to wear crape on their arms, but compromised by attending the wedding in full force, and lining the aisle with unutterable reproach. She had jilted them all—from Bassett-Holmer, the senior captain, to little Mildred, the junior subaltern, who could have given her four thousand a year and a title.

I hate to mutilate a book; but I hope to read this story often; and, rather than meet the offence and the annoyance of that silly stuff, in a story otherwise splendid, I have obliterated the passage. Too often, in reading Mr. Kipling, we are forced to say, 'That would make a good special report', or 'That's a telling bit of war correspondence': yet special reports and war correspondence are good things of their kind. But the passage just quoted shows merely the contemptible smartness of a society journal; and of a very inferior specimen. I do not say that the thing did not, could not, or should not, happen: I do say that Mr. Kipling, as an artist, one careful to preserve the tone and the proportion of his work, commits a grave offence against his art by such a fall from the fine to the trivial, without just cause. And from the frequency of his offence, in every book that he has written, it would seem that he does not feel the common sentiments of natural good breeding and of artistic reticence. Two expressions in a stirring passage of the same story jar upon us in the same way:

The talk rose higher and higher, and the regimental band played between the courses, as is the immemorial custom, till all tongues ceased for a moment with the removal of the dinner-slips, and the first toast of obligation, when an officer rising said, 'Mr. Vice, the Queen,' and little Mildred from the bottom of the table answered, 'The Queen, God bless her,' and the big spurs clanked as the big men heaved themselves up and drank the Queen, upon whose pay they were falsely supposed to settle their mess bills. That sacrament of the mess never grows old, and never ceases to bring a lump into the throat of the listener wherever he be by sea or by land.

What is the point here of dragging in the familiar fact that the Queen's pay is insufficient for a modern officer under modern circumstances? It sounds like the petty, ill-conditioned criticism of some Cockney money-lender: it is a crying false note, coming just in that place. Again, 'toast of obligation' and 'sacrament of the mess' are phrases in which it is difficult not to see a flippant reference to two ecclesiastical and sacred terms. These things are fatal to the perfection of a story: and Mr. Kipling's taste for them is his worst enemy. But it may be observed that they do not occur except when Mr. Kipling is dealing with English officers and civilians: his 'common' soldiers and his Indian natives, under all circumstances and conditions, talk, and are treated by Mr. Kipling, without these petty offences against good taste. Ortheris and Mulvaney, Ameera and Khoda Dad Khan, in every mood or situation, are allowed by Mr. Kipling to live without those peculiar tricks and tones, which in his stories are the essential notes of the English gentleman in India. His officers and his civil servants, Orde, Tallentire, Hummil, Spurstow, Lowndes, Mottram, Strickland, and 'I', one and all talk with a strained intensity, a bitter tone, a sharp conciseness, an abbreviation of epigram, a clever slang, which are meant to denote, partly their cultured intellects and partly that sentiment of fatality and dogged endurance which Mr. Kipling would have us believe to be the invariable result of official work in India. The Empire, the Administration, the Government, become in Mr. Kipling's hands necessary and yet amusing powers, in whose service Englishmen are willing to toil and sweat, knowing that *il n'y pas d'homme necessaire*, but content to go on, relieved by making cynical epigrams about life and death, and everything before, between, or after them. The consciousness of duty becomes the consciousness of a mechanical necessity: the sentiment of loyalty is caricatured into a cynical perseverance. One thinks of Dalhousie and of the Lawrences. Mr. Kipling has had experience of English life and work in India: his readers, for the most part, have not. But I would ask any reader, who has known English officers and civilians, before, during, and after their Indian service, whether he has found them quite so brilliant or quite so ill-bred, quite so epigrammatic or quite so self-conscious, as these creatures of Mr. Kipling. Is it that before leaving home, or while home on leave, or when done with India, they are natural Englishmen; but that an Indian climate, and a share in Indian administration, turn them into machines: men who seem to talk like telegrams, and to think in shorthand, and to pose, each as a modern Atlas, helping to uphold the Indian Empire, and swearing pessimist oaths at its weight? Mr. Kipling presents English rule in India, for purposes of effective fiction, as a huge and ironical joke, or, to use one of his favourite words, as a 'grim' comedy. In fact, whenever he gives us the views of life held by men of education and official responsibility, they are the views expressed by his title, *Life's Handicap.* You start with your chances and make the best of the race, sure to be tripped up half-way by the irony of the fates and powers, or baulked at the very finish. In 'The Head of the District', a dying man sees his wife crossing the river to meet him, and knows that she will come too late; and his last words are: 'That's Polly,' he said simply, though his mouth was wried with agony. 'Polly and—the grimmest practical joke ever played on a man. Dick—you'll—have—to—explain.'

The one story in the book, admirable from first to last, is 'The Courting of Dinah Shadd': the tragedy of his life, told by Mulvaney. The Irishman's story is told with perfect truth and pity: Mr. Kipling makes not one mistake in sentiment. But had Mulvaney's colonel told the story of *his* life, Mr. Kipling would have filled it with cheap jests and cynicisms, gall and bitterness.

Years ago, *Werther* first, and *Childe Harold* afterwards, brought into fashion the philosophy of woe and want, and tragic heroics: a perverted sensibility, an affectation of misery and despair: its victims or devotees wept over their sorrows and shrieked at their gods. But the posture was tiring, and at last literature renounced it. Just now, a new philosophy is coming into fashion: it is required of a man that he be virile, robust and bitter. Laugh at life, and jest with the world: waste no words and spare no blushes: whatever you do, do it doggedly, and whatever you say, put a sting into it. In sentiment, let Voltaire talking Ibsen be your ideal: in life, rival the Flying Dutchman for recklessness, the Wandering Jew for restlessness, and the American rowdy for readiness to act. Life is short, so stuff it full: art is long, so cut it short. Various men have various methods: some writers cut art short by reducing it to impressions, some by reducing it to epigrams. Whichever you do, care nothing for beauty and truth, but everything for brevity and effect. You may lead your readers to believe that you have stayed at home and analysed yourself till you were sick of yourself; or that you have raged round the world and found all hollow, without you and within. You can make literature an affair of nerves or an affair of blood: you may paint life grey, or paint it red. But if you would be a modern man of letters, before all else, ignore the Ten Commandments and the Classics. Swear by the sciences, which you have not studied, and the foreign literature, which you read in translation: if you want to make a hit, bring the *Iliad* up to date: you need only double the bloodshed, and turn the long speeches into short, smart, snapping cynicisms.

Some of these follies, which many writers now take for virtues, are but the accidental vices of Mr. Kipling's work; and it is because he can write so well that I have ventured to suggest that he often writes far too badly. A writer suddenly and deservedly welcomed with great praise is at once imitated by all sorts of incapable persons; and for one story which has something of his real charm and power, there are twenty with nothing but his casual levities and unfortunate mannerisms. For example, 'The Mark of the Beast' is a story of an incident among the more unnecessary horrors of life in India, brought about by 'the power of the Gods and Devils of Asia'. An Englishman pays a drunken insult to Hanuman, the monkey-god, in his temple at night: a leper, a 'Silver Man', just drops his head upon the man's breast, and nothing more. And gradually, with dreadful warnings and signs, the man's nature is changed into a beast's, a wolf's. It is an uncanny, haunting story, told with a singular power: but Mr. Kipling does not seem to know wherein consist the real horror and fascination of his own work. A passage of pure and perfect excellence is often followed by one of simple bad taste and feebleness. For example: while Fleete, the were-wolf, is lying bound in the house, with his two friends watching, the cry of the Silver Man is heard outside. They determine to capture him, and go into the garden: and 'in the moonlight we could see the leper coming round the corner of the house. He was perfectly naked, and from time to time he mewed and stopped to dance with his shadow.' That sentence gave me a literal shudder of sudden fear, like the fear of a child in the dark: for complete effectiveness, in the narration of a fearful story, it could not be beaten. It is horrible, but the horror is not strained and emphasised; the simple words do their work naturally. The two men succeed in capturing the leper; they resolve to torture him into removing the spell from their friend. 'When we confronted him with the beast, the scene was beyond description. The beast doubled backwards into a bow as though he had been poisoned with strychnine, and moaned in the most pitiable fashion.' Well, that is right enough in its way; but Mr. Kipling adds, 'several other things happened also, but they cannot be put down here'. And 'Strickland shaded his eyes with his hands for a moment, and we set to work. This part is not to be printed.' A row of asterisks follows. Now this suggestion of un-mentionable horror is a piece of the very worst possible art: Mr. Kipling means to thrill us with absolute horror, to fill us with shudder-ing apprehensions of absolute fearfulness. He fails: we feel nothing but wonder and contempt, to find so able a writer fall into so pitiable a device. And he is constantly leading us up to the doors of a sealed chamber of horrors, and expecting us to be smitten with dread. The fearful and the terrible are not necessarily loathsome to the senses, matters of blood and noisome pestilence: they are produced by appeals to the imagination and to the intellect. Running through Mr. Kipling's work, and spoiling its value, is this strain of bad taste: irritated by silly sentiment, he takes up silly cynicism; angry with foolish shamefacedness, he adopts a foolish shamelessness. Rather than let his work win its way by the subtle powers of its ideas, he prefers to force our attention by the studied abruptness of his phrases. It is characteristic of the times: General Booth and Mr. Stanley, the German Emperor and General Boulanger, have done much the same thing in practical affairs. But Mr. Kipling, in his profession, is a greater man than they in theirs and we continue to hope against hope for his ultimate purification and perfection.

(3). *Barrack-Room Ballads and Other Verses* (1892)

The two divisions of this book disclose the strength and the weakness of Mr. Kipling: triumphant success and disastrous failure. Certainly, there are weak things among the strong, and strong things among the weak; but the good and the bad, for the most part, are separated, the wheat from the tares. The 'Barrack-Room Ballads' are fine and true; the 'Other Verses', too many of them, are rhetorical and only half true. It is more important, then, as it is more pleasant, to consider first, and at the greater length, the 'Barrack-Room Ballads'.

They are written in the dialect of 'the common soldier', of 'Tommy Atkins'; they are composed in his spirit also. It is a curious reflection that the British Army at large, and the British soldier in particular, have received so little attention in literature of any excellence. We have plenty of heroic poems, as Mr. Henley and many others know well; plenty of verse alive with the martial spirit, with the 'pomp and circumstance of glorious war'; plenty of things hardly less great than Wordsworth's 'Happy Warrior', or the Laureate's 'Ode on Wellington'. But of the British Army, as a way of daily life, as composed of individual men, as full of marked personal characteristics and peculiarities, our poets great and small have had little conception. What Smollett in prose, and Dibdin in verse, did for the Navy, no one has yet done for the Army. Famous achievements and signal successes of armies, or of regiments, or of individual men, have been sung. Agincourt, Flodden, Blenheim, Waterloo, the Crimea, the Mutiny, have inspired praises, not always stilted and official; but the personal sentiments of the British soldier have not been the theme of any British poet worth naming. Certain criticisms which I have read of these Ballads have dwelt upon the technical difficulty of their dialect. Such criticism is of a piece with the prevailing apathy and ignorance concerning the Army. Little wonder that Special Committees and Royal Commissions are required to look into its state, while so many critics of literature, whose pride and business it is to be omniscient, are baffled by the technical terms or the appropriate slang of these Ballads. Poems thick with archaeological terms, with foreign phrases, with recondite learning and allusions, are accepted without demur. Mr. Kipling's Indian stories have roused no protest; but when he sings the common soldier in a common way, these omnivorous critics are aghast at the uncouth and mysterious language.

There are twenty of these Ballads; and there can hardly be said to be one failure among them, although two or three are of marked inferiority to the rest, and although the greater number look poor by the side of the four or five masterpieces. The most noticeable thing about them, on a first reading, is their swinging, marching music. The accents and beat of the verse fall true and full, like the rhythmical tramp of men's feet. Take such rhythms and measures as

> For it was—'Belts, belts, belts, an' that's one for you!'
> An' it was—'Belts, belts, belts, an' that's done for you!'

Or as

> When first under fire, an' you're wishful to duck,
> Don't look nor take 'eed at the man that is struck,
> Be thankful you're livin', and trust to your luck,
>   And march to your front like a soldier.
>   Front, front, front, like a soldier,
>   Front, front, front, like a soldier,
>   Front, front, front, like a soldier,
>   So-oldier *of* the Queen!

Or, best of all, as

> On the road to Mandalay,
> Where the old Flotilla lay;
> Can't you 'ear their paddles chunkin' from Rangoon to Mandalay?
> On the road to Mandalay,
> Where the flyin' fishes play,
> An' the dawn comes up like thunder outer China 'crost the bay!

They go with a swing and a march, an emphasis and a roll, which may delude the inexperienced into thinking them easy to 'rattle off'. I should be greatly surprised to hear that Mr. Kipling thought the same.

The Ballads deal with a few marked incidents, experiences, and emotions from the private soldier's point of view; some general and unlocalised, but most peculiar to military life in the East. All Mr. Kipling's undiverted and undiluted strength has gone into these vivid Ballads; phrase follows phrase, instinct with life, quivering and vibrating with the writer's intensity. No superfluity, no misplaced condescension to sentiment, no disguising of things ludicrous or ugly or unpleasant; Tommy Atkins is presented to the ordinary reader, with no apologies and with no adornments.

> We aren't no thin red 'eroes, nor we aren't no blackguards too,
> But single men in barricks, most remarkable like you,

he sings: in a genial and, at the same time, an acute expostulation with the people, who exalt him in war but despise him in peace, in the amiable manner lately described by the Duke of Connaught. But no panegyrics could give the civilian a truer sense of the soldier's life, in its rough and ready hardships, than the experiences of camp and battle in these pages; their grim pleasantry in describing the little accidents of a battery charge, the perversities of the commissariat camel, the dangers that await the "arf made' recruits in the East, the humours of the 'time-expired', the fascinations of 'loot', the joys of the 'cells', the fatigue and the exhilaration of 'route marchin' '. Then we have the generous recognition of 'Fuzzy-Wuzzy', the Soudanese:

> So 'ere's to you, Fuzzy-Wuzzy, at your 'ome in the Soudan;
> You're a pore benighted 'eathen, but a first-class fightin' man;
> An' 'ere's to you, Fuzzy-Wuzzy, with your 'ayrick 'ead of 'air—
> You big black boundin' beggar—for you broke a British square!

And an eulogy no less generous is bestowed upon the native water-carrier, 'our regimental bhisti, Gunga Din'.

The most poetical, in the sense of being the most imaginative and heightened in expression, is 'Danny Deever', hanged for shooting a comrade.

> ''Is cot was right-'and cot to mine,' said Files-on-Parade.
> ''E's sleepin' out an' far to-night,' the Colour-Sergeant said.
> ' I've drunk 'is beer a score o' times,' said Files-on-Parade.
> ''E's drinkin' bitter beer alone,' the Colour-Sergeant said.

And perhaps the most winning of them all is 'Mandalay': the Burmese girl and her lover, the British soldier, his sickness and disgust at London and England after those old times in the East.

> I'm learnin' 'ere in London what the ten-year soldier tells,
> 'If you've 'eard the East a-callin', you won't never 'eed naught else'

—which would seem to be the experience of Mr. Kipling also.

There is plenty of matter in these Ballads to which 'inquisiturient' critics, to use Milton's word, can take objection: the moral and dogmatic theology of the soldier, as indicated by Mr. Kipling, is somewhat unauthorised and lax. But Mr. Kipling has no ambition to paint him, except in his own colours; and, very seriously contemplated, these Ballads give a picture of life and character more estimable and praiseworthy for many rugged virtues of generosity, endurance, heartiness, and simplicity, than are the lives and characters of many 'gentlemen of England, who stay at home at ease'.

Mr. Kipling's 'Other Verses' are less pleasant reading. Their rhetorical energy is splendid. At times they ring true to nature; but for the most part they are spasmodic, ranting, overstrained. For example, the volume opens with a poem to the praise of one whose death Mr. Kipling has an especial right to lament, while all lovers of literature have also their regrets. It imagines the great dead in a Valhalla of the windiest sort. There, beyond the farthest ways of sun, or comet, or star, or 'star-dust', 'live such as fought, and sailed, and ruled, and loved, and made our world'. There 'they sit at wine with the Maidens Nine and the Gods of the Elder Days'; and

> 'Tis theirs to sweep through the ringing deep where Azrael's outposts are,
> Or buffet a path through the Pit's red wrath when God goes out to war
> Or hang with the reckless Seraphim on the rim of a red-maned star.

There 'they whistle the Devil to make them sport who know that Sin is vain;' but that is not all:

> And ofttimes cometh our wise Lord God, master of every trade,
> And tells them tales of His daily toil, of Edens newly made;
> And they rise to their feet as He passes by, gentlemen unafraid.

It is a Paradise, an Elysium, a Valhalla, of 'the Strong Men'.

The hollow insincerity of this rhetoric is little short of marvellous; not, I need hardly say, that I impute any insincerity to the writer's spirit and intention. I mean, that the imaginative design of the poem, aiming at the heroic and the sublime, falls into a bathos worthy of

Nat Lee. 'The reckless Seraphim', to put it quite frankly, are absurd; and so is the whole attempt, by a mystical use of vague astronomy, to represent in a new fashion the home and the life of the great dead. I can attach no meaning to the jumble of 'Maidens Nine' and 'Gods of the Elder Days' and 'Azrael' and 'the Pit' and 'the Devil' and 'our wise Lord God': if it be all metaphorical, a large and half-Oriental dream, it loses all semblance of reality; if it be more soberly meant, I prefer not to characterise it, but rather turn to Dante or to Virgil. Dante has no lack of strength and power; and I am more at home, with reverence be it said, in his *Paradiso*, with *il santo atleta*, than with the self-satisfied 'Strong Men' of Mr. Kipling. Yet, like all that he writes with any degree of excellence, these lines have fine things in them: witness the description of him who walked from his birth 'in simpleness and gentleness and honour and clean mirth': a just and noble praise.

Mr. Kipling has run riot in chaunting the glories of action; for still, as Mr. Stevenson has it,

> For still the Lord is Lord of might;
> In deeds, in deeds, he takes delight.

It is very true; but he takes delight in other things also; and this glorification of the Strong, the Virile, the Robust, the Vigorous is fast becoming as great a nuisance and an affectation as were the True and the Beautiful years ago. It is so easy to bluster and to brag; so hard to remember that 'they also serve who only stand and wait'. Indeed, there seems to be no virtue which Mr. Kipling would not put under the head of valour; virtue, to him, is *virtus*, and all the good qualities of man are valorous. From that point of view, saints and sinners, soldiers and poets, men of science and men of art, if they excel in their chosen works, are all Strong Men. That may be fair enough as a view of the matter to be sometimes emphasised; but we can have too much of it.

In some of the finest pieces Mr. Kipling is a prey to the grandiose aspect of things. 'The English Flag', for example, in which the Winds of the World witness to England's greatness, is grievously spoiled by exaggeration of tone. We know that England is great, that Englishmen have done great things, that the fame of her glory has filled the corners of the earth; but we have no occasion to shriek about it, to wax hysterically wroth with those who deny it. Shakespeare's great burst of loyal pride, Milton's solemn utterance, Wordsworth's noble verses, Browning's 'Home Thoughts from Abroad', the Laureate's stately lyrics, do not brag and bluster and protest. 'What should they know of England, who only England know?' cries Mr. Kipling; as though nothing short of ocular demonstration and a tourist's ticket could make the 'poor little street-bred people' believe in the greatness of England by North, South, East and West. The occasion upon which the verses were written may justify some of this agitated declamation; but the tone is habitual with Mr. Kipling. Again, the delightful satire of 'Tomlinson', the man with no soul of his own, whose God and whose virtues and whose rites came all 'from a printed book', would be far more telling if there were some recognition of the fact that a man may be equally contemptible who 'posts o'er land and ocean without rest', with no more soul than a thistledown. I am duly sorry to rely so much upon 'printed books'; but I remember certain exhortations to the theoretic life in Plato and Aristotle, certain passages in Dante about *l'antica Rachele*, the Lady of Contemplation, and in Milton about 'the cherub Contemplation', whom he wished for 'first and chiefest'. Doubtless, this is to take Mr. Kipling's satire too seriously, and to have no sense of humour; but I am in Mr. Kipling's debt for so great a number of delights that I am the more moved to exclaim against his defects. I want to enjoy all that he writes. All that he urges against the effeminate, miserable people who take their whole standard of life and conduct from the opinions that they meet, and the society that surrounds them, is admirable; but it is not the whole truth. Perhaps, as Mr. Stevenson suggests, there is no such thing as the whole truth.

Of the remaining poems, far the best are the 'Ballad of East and West', a thing to stir the blood like a trumpet; the 'Conundrum of the Workshops', a charming satire upon critics and criticism; and the ballads of the 'Clampherdown' and the 'Bolivar'. The fierce and stinging verses against the Irish members concerned in the famous Commission are too virulent in their partisanship to be quite successful, even in the eyes of those who agree with them in the main. Of the Indian legends and ballads, we may say nothing; most of them have some force and spirit, but they do not equal the similar work of Sir Alfred Lyall.

Let me conclude by expressing my thanks once more for the 'Barrack-Room Ballads'; in them, their unforced vigour and unexaggerated truth, I can forget all excesses of rhetoric, all extravagances of tone.

16. Oscar Wilde: Two Extracts

1891

Extracts from 'The True Function and Value of Criticism' (The *Nineteenth Century*, Vol. XXVIII, July, September 1890; reprinted with additions, bracketed below, in *Intentions* 1891) and a letter about a criticism of the above published in *The Times* (25 September 1891), under the heading 'An Anglo-Indian's Complaint'.

Oscar Wilde (1854–1900) was a great dramatist and minor story-teller and versifier. His occasional criticism lacked depth but supplied a number of brilliant and sometimes telling epigrams. Kipling began by imitating him (e.g. in 'Ave Imperatrix' and in his early, and mainly uncollected, Indian sketches and stories), but ended by writing in *Something of Myself* of 'the suburban Toilet-Club school favoured by the late Mr. Oscar Wilde'.

(1) ... He who would stir us now by fiction must either give us an entirely new background or reveal to us the soul of man in its innermost workings. The first is for the moment being done for us by Mr. Rudyard Kipling. As one turns over the pages of his *Plain Tales from the Hills*, one feels as if one were seated under a palm-tree reading life by superb flashes of vulgarity. The jaded, second-rate Anglo-Indians are in exquisite incongruity with their surroundings. The mere lack of style in the story-teller gives an odd journalistic realism to what he tells us. From the point of view of literature Mr. Kipling is a genius who drops his aspirates. From the point of view of life, he is a reporter who knows vulgarity better than anyone has ever known it. Dickens knew its clothes [and its comedy]. Mr. Kipling knows its essence [and its seriousness]. He is our first authority on the second-rate [and has seen marvellous things through keyholes, and his backgrounds are real works of art].

(2) ... There is no reason why Mr. Rudyard Kipling should not select vulgarity as his subject-matter, or part of it. For a realistic artist,

certainly, vulgarity is a most admirable subject. How far Mr. Kipling's stories really mirror Anglo-Indian society I have no idea at all, nor, indeed, am I ever much interested in any correspondence between art and nature. It seems to me a matter of entirely secondary importance.

17. Edmund Gosse: 'Rudyard Kipling'

1891

Signed article in the *Century Magazine*, Vol. XLII, pp. 901–10 (October 1891). Much of this was reprinted in the author's *Questions at Issue* (1893).

Sir Edmund William Gosse (1849–1928) was a minor poet and a major critic and biographer throughout most of Kipling's working life. He is remembered for his 'grim memoir' *Father and Son* (1907), but in his day was an influential critic. He was one of the circle at the Savile Club who welcomed Kipling's advent to literary London at the end of 1889. He introduced him to Wolcott Balestier, and he, with his wife and son, made up half the congregation at Kipling's wedding to Balestier's sister in January 1892.

Two years ago there was suddenly revealed to us, no one seems to remember how, a new star out of the East. Not fewer distinguished men of letters profess to have 'discovered' Mr. Kipling than there were cities of old in which Homer was born. Yet, in fact, the discovery was not much more creditable to them than it would be, on a summer night, to contrive to notice a comet flaring across the sky. Not only was this new talent robust, brilliant, and self-asserting, but its reception was prepared for by a unique series of circumstances. The fiction of the Anglo-Saxon world, in its more intellectual provinces, had become curiously femininized. Those novel-writers who cared to produce subtle impressions upon their readers, in England and America, had become extremely refined in taste and discreet in judgment. People who were not content to pursue the soul of their next-door neighbor through all the burrows of self-consciousness had no choice but to take ship with Mr. Rider Haggard for the 'Mountains of the Moon'. Between excess of psychological analysis and excess of superhuman romance, there was a great void in the world of Anglo-Saxon fiction. It is this void which Mr. Kipling, with something less than one hundred short stories, one novel, and a few poems, has filled by his exotic realism and his vigorous rendering of unhackneyed experience. His temperament is eminently masculine, and yet his imagination is strictly bound by existing laws. The Evarras of the novel had said: 'Thus gods are made,/And whoso makes them otherwise shall die,' when, behold, a young man comes up out of India, and makes them quite otherwise, and lives.

The vulgar trick, however, of depreciating other writers in order to exalt the favorite of a moment was never less worthy of practice than it is in the case of the author of Soldiers Three. His relation to his contemporaries is curiously slight. One living writer there is, indeed, with whom it is not unnatural to compare him—Pierre Loti. Each of these men has attracted the attention, and then the almost exaggerated admiration, of a crowd of readers drawn from every class. Each has become popular without ceasing to be delightful to the fastidious. Each is independent of traditional literature, and affects a disdain for books. Each is a wanderer, a lover of prolonged exile, more at home among the ancient races of the East than among his own people. Each describes what he has seen, in short sentences, with highly colored phrases and local words, little troubled to obey the laws of style if he can but render an exact impression of what the movement of physical life has been to himself. Each produces on the reader a peculiar thrill, a voluptuous and agitating sentiment of intellectual uneasiness, with the spontaneous art of which he has the secret. Totally unlike in detail, Rudyard Kipling and Pierre Loti have these general qualities in common, and if we want a literary parallel to the former, the latter is certainly the only one that we can find. Nor is the attitude of the French novelist to his sailor friends at all unlike that of the Anglo-Indian civilian to his soldier chums. To distinguish we must note very carefully the difference between Mulvaney and *mon frère Yves*; it is not altogether to the advantage of the latter.

The old rhetorical manner of criticism was not meant for the discussion of such writers as these. The only way in which, as it seems to me, we can possibly approach them, is by a frank confession of their personal relation to the feelings of the critic. I will therefore admit that I cannot pretend to be indifferent to the charm of what Mr. Kipling writes. From the first moment of my acquaintance with it it has held me fast. It excites, disturbs, and attracts me; I cannot throw off its disquieting influence. I admit all that is to be said in its disfavor. I force myself to see that its occasional cynicism is irritating and strikes a false note. I acknowledge the broken and jagged style, the noisy newspaper bustle of the little peremptory sentences, the cheap irony of the satires on society. Often—but this is chiefly in the earlier stories—I am aware that there is a good deal too much of the rattle of the piano at some café concert. But when all this is said, what does it amount to? What but an acknowledgment of the crudity of a strong and rapidly developing young nature? You cannot expect a creamy smoothness while the act of vinous fermentation is proceeding.

> Wit will shine
> Through the harsh cadence of a ruggèd line;
> A noble error, and but seldom made,
> When poets are by too much force betray'd;
> Thy generous fruits, though gather'd ere their prime,
> Still show a quickness, and maturing time
> But mellows what we write to the dull sweets of rime.

In the following pages I shall try to explain why the sense of these shortcomings is altogether buried for me in delighted sympathy and breathless curiosity. Mr. Kipling does not provoke a critical suspension of judgment. He is vehement, and sweeps us away with him; he plays upon a strange and seductive pipe, and we follow him like children. As I write these sentences, I feel how futile is this attempt to analyse his gifts, and how greatly I should prefer to throw this paper to the winds, and listen to the magician himself. I want more and more, like Oliver Twist. I want all those 'other stories'; I wish to wander down all those by-paths that we have seen disappear in the brushwood. If one lay very still and low by the watch-fire, in the hollow of Ortheris's great-coat, one might learn more and more of the inextinguishable sorrows of Mulvaney. One might be told more of what happened, out of the moonlight, in the blackness of Amir Nath's Gully. I want to know how the palanquin came into Dearsley's possession, and what became of Kheni Singh, and whether the seal-cutter did really die in the House of Suddhoo. I want to know who it is who dances the *Halli Hukk*, and how, and why, and where. I want to know what happened at Jagadhri, when the Death Bull was painted. I want to know all the things that Mr. Kipling does not like to tell—to see the devils of the East 'rioting as the stallions riot in spring'. It is the strength of this new story-teller that he re-awakens in us the primitive emotions of curiosity, mystery, and romance in action. He is the master of a new kind of terrible and enchanting peepshow, and we crowd around him begging for 'just one more look'. When a writer excites and tantalizes us in this way, it seems a little idle to discuss his style. Let pedants, then, if they will, say that Mr. Kipling has no style; yet if so, how shall we designate such passages as this, frequent enough among his more exotic stories?

Come back with me to the north and be among men once more. Come back when this matter is accomplished and I call for thee. The bloom of the peach orchards is upon all the valley, and *here* is only dust and a great stink. There is a pleasant wind among the mulberry trees, and the streams are bright with snow-water, and the caravans go up and the caravans go down, and a hundred fires sparkle in the gut of the pass, and tent-peg answers hammer-nose, and pony squeals to pony across the drift-smoke of the evening. It is good in the north now. Come back with me. Let us return to our own people. Come!

The private life of Mr. Rudyard Kipling is not a matter of public interest, and I should be very unwilling to exploit it, even if I had the means of doing so. The youngest of living writers should really be protected for a few years longer against those who chirp and gabble about the unessential. All that needs to be known, in order to give him his due chronological place, is that he was born in Bombay in Christmas week, 1865, and that he is therefore only in his twenty-sixth year yet. The careful student of what he has published will collect from it the impression that Mr. Kipling was in India at an age when few European children remain there; that he returned to England for a brief period; that he began a career on his own account in India at an unusually early age; that he has led life of extraordinary vicissitude, as a journalist, as a war correspondent, as a civilian in the wake of the army; that an insatiable curiosity has led him to shrink from no experience that might help to solve the strange riddles of Oriental existence; and that he is distinguished from other active, adventurous, and inquisitive persons in that his capacious memory retains every impression that it captures. Beyond this, all that must here be said about the man is that his stories began to be published—I think about eight years ago—in local newspapers of India, that his first book of verse, *Departmental Ditties*, appeared in 1886, while his prose stories were not collected from a Lahore journal, of which he was the sub-editor, until 1888, when a volume of *Plain Tales from the Hills* appeared in Calcutta. In the same year six successive pamphlets or thin books appeared in an 'Indian Railway Library', published at Allahabad, under the titles of *Soldiers Three*, *The Gadsbys*, *In Black and White*, *Under the Deodars*, *The Phantom Rickshaw*, and *Wee Willie Winkie*. These formed the literary baggage of Mr. Rudyard Kipling when, in 1889, he came home to find himself suddenly famous at the age of twenty-three.

Since his arrival in England Mr. Kipling has not been idle. In 1890 he brought out a Christmas annual called *The Record of Badalia Herods-foot*, and a short novel, *The Light that Failed*. Already in 1891 he has published a fresh collection of tales called (in America) *Mine Own People* [*Life's Handicap*] and a second miscellany of verses. This is by no means a complete record of his activity, but it includes the names of all his important writings. At an age when few future novelists have yet produced anything at all, Mr. Kipling is already voluminous. It would be absurd not to acknowledge that a danger lies in this preco-cious fecundity. It would probably be an excellent thing for every one concerned if this brilliant youth could be deprived of pens and ink for a few years and be buried again somewhere in the far East. There should be a 'close time' for authors no less than for seals, and the extra-ordinary fullness and richness of Mr. Kipling's work does not com-pletely reassure us.

The publications which I have named above have not, as a rule, any structural cohesion. With the exception of *Badalia Herodsfoot* and *The Light that Failed* which deal with phases of London life, their contents might be thrown together without much loss of relation. The general mass so formed could then be re-divided into several coherent sections. It may be remarked that Mr. Kipling's short stories, of which, as I have said, we hold nearly a hundred, mainly deal with three or four distinct classes of Indian life. We may roughly distinguish these as the British soldier in India, the Anglo-Indian, the Native, and the British child in India. In the following pages I shall endeavor to characterize his treatment of these four classes, and finally to say a word about him as a poet.

There can be no question that the side upon which Mr. Kipling's talent has most delicately tickled British curiosity, and British patriot-ism too, is his revelation of the soldier in India. A great mass of our countrymen are constantly being drafted out to the East on Indian service. They serve their time, are recalled, and merge in the mass of our population; their strange temporary isolation between the civilian and the native and their practical inability to find public expression for their feelings make these men—to whom, though we so often forget it, we owe the maintenance of the English Empire in the East—an absolutely silent section of the community. Of their officers we may know something, although 'A Conference of the Powers' may perhaps have awakened us to the fact that we know very little. Still, people like Tick Boileau and Captain Mafflin of the Duke of Derry's Pink Hussars are of ourselves; we meet them before they go out and when they come back; they marry our sisters and our daughters; and they lay down the law about India after dinner. Of the private soldier, on the other hand, of his loves and hates, sorrows and pleasures, of the way in which the vast, hot, wearisome country and its mysterious inhabitants strike him, of his attitude towards India, and of the way in which India treats him, we know, or knew until Mr. Kipling enlightened us, absolutely nothing. It is not surprising, then, if the novelty of this portion of his writings has struck ordinary English readers more than that of any other.

This section of Mr. Kipling's work occupies the seven tales called *Soldiers Three* and a variety of stories scattered through his other books. In order to make his point of view that of the men themselves, not spoiled by the presence of superior officers or by social restraint of any sort, the author takes upon himself the character of an almost silent young civilian who has gained the warm friendship of three soldiers, whose intimate companion and chum he becomes. Most of the military stories, though not all, are told by one of these three, or else recount their adventures or caprices. Before opening the book called *Soldiers Three*, however, the reader will do well to make himself familiar with the opening pages of a comparatively late story, 'The Incarnation of Krishna Mulvaney', in which the characteristics of the famous three are more clearly defined than elsewhere. Mulvaney, the Irish giant, who has been the 'grizzled, tender, and very wise Ulysses' to successive generations of young and foolish recruits, is a great creation. He is the father of the craft of arms to his associates; he has served with various regiments from Bermuda to Halifax; he is 'old in war, scarred, reckless, resourceful, and in his pious hours an unequalled soldier'. Learoyd, the second of these friends, is 'six-and-a-half feet of slow-moving, heavy-footed Yorkshireman, born on the wolds, bred in the dales, and educated chiefly among the carriers' carts at the back of York railway-station'. The third is Ortheris, a little man as sharp as a needle, 'a fox-terrier of a cockney', an inveterate poacher and dog-stealer.

Of these three strongly contrasted types the first and the third live in Mr. Kipling's pages with absolute reality. I must confess that Learoyd is to me a little shadowy, and even in a late story, 'On Greenhow Hill', which has apparently been written in order to emphasize the outline of the Yorkshireman, I find myself chiefly interested in the incidental part, the sharp-shooting of Ortheris. It seems as though Mr. Kipling required, for the artistic balance of his cycle of stories, a third figure, and had evolved Learoyd while he observed and created Mulvaney and Ortheris, nor am I sure that places could not be pointed out where Learoyd, save for the dialect, melts undistinguishably into an incarnation of Mulvaney. The others are studied from the life, and by an observer who goes deep below the surface of conduct. How penetrating the study is, and how clear the diagnosis, may be seen in one or two stories which lie somewhat outside the popular group. It is no superficial idler among men who has taken down the strange notes on military hysteria which inspire 'The Madness of Ortheris' and 'In the Matter of a Private', while the skill with which the battered giant Mulvaney, who has been a corporal and then has been reduced for misconduct, who to the ordinary view and in the eyes of all but the wisest of his officers is a dissipated blackguard, is made to display the rapidity, wit, resource, and high moral feeling which he really possesses, is extraordinary.

We have hitherto had in English literature no portraits of private soldiers like these, and yet the soldier is an object of interest and of very real, if vague and inefficient, admiration to his fellow-citizens. Mr. Thomas Hardy has painted a few excellent soldiers, but in a more romantic light and a far more pastoral setting. Other studies of this kind in fiction have either been slight and unsubstantial, or else they have been, as in the baby-writings of a certain novelist who has enjoyed popularity for a moment, odious in their sentimental unreality. There seems to be something essentially volatile about the soldier's memory. His life is so monotonous, so hedged in by routine, that he forgets the details of it as soon as the restraint is removed, or else he looks back upon it to see it bathed in a fictitious haze of sentiment. The absence of sentimentality in Mr. Kipling's version of the soldier's life in India is one of its great merits. What romance it assumes under his treatment is due to the curious contrasts it encourages. We see the ignorant and raw English youth transplanted, at the very moment when his instincts begin to develop, into a country where he is divided from everything which can remind him of his home, where by noon and night, in the bazaar, in barracks, in the glowing scrub jungle, in the ferny defiles of the hills, everything he sees and hears and smells and feels produces on him an unfamiliar and an unwelcome impression. How he behaves himself under these new circumstances, what code of laws still binds his conscience, what are his relaxations, and what his observations, these are the questions which we ask and which Mr. Kipling essays for the first time to answer.

Among the short stories which Mr. Kipling has dedicated to the British soldier in India there are a few which excel all the rest as works of art. I do not think that any one will deny that of this inner selection none exceeds in skill or originality 'The Taking of Lungtungpen'. Those who have not read this little masterpiece have yet before them the pleasure of becoming acquainted with one of the best short stories not merely in English but in any language. I do not know how to praise adequately the technical merit of this little narrative. It possesses to the full that masculine buoyancy, that power of sustaining an extremely spirited narrative in a tone appropriate to the action, which is one of Mr. Kipling's rare gifts. Its concentration, which never descends into obscurity, its absolute novelty, its direct and irresistible appeal to what is young and daring and absurdly splendid, are unsurpassed. To read it, at all events to admire and enjoy it, is to recover for a moment a little of that dare-devil quality that lurks somewhere in the softest and the baldest of us. Only a very young man could have written it, perhaps, but still more certainly only a young man of genius.

A little less interesting, in a totally different way, is 'The Daughter of the Regiment', with its extraordinarily vivid account of the breaking-out of cholera in a troop-train. Of 'The Madness of Ortheris' I have already spoken; as a work of art this again seems to me somewhat less remarkable, because carried out with less completeness. But it would be hard to find a parallel, of its own class, to 'The Rout of the White Hussars', with its study of the effects of what is believed to be supernatural on a gathering of young fellows who are absolutely without fear of any phenomenon of which they comprehend the nature. In a very late story, 'The Courting of Dinah Shadd', Mr. Kipling has shown that he is able to deal with the humors and matrimonial amours of India barrack-life just as rapidly, fully, and spiritedly as with the more serious episodes of a soldier's career. The scene between Judy Sheehy and Dinah, as told by Mulvaney in that story, is pure comedy, without a touch of farce.

On the whole, however, the impression left by Mr. Kipling's military stories is one of melancholy. Tommy Atkins, whom the author knows so well and sympathizes with so truly, is a solitary being in India. In all these tales I am conscious of the barracks as of an island in a desolate ocean of sand. All around is the infinite waste of India, obscure, monotonous, immense, inhabited by black men and pariah dogs, Pathans and green parrots, kites and crocodiles, and long solitudes of high grass. The island in this sea is a little collection of young men, sent out from the remoteness of England to serve 'the Widder', and to help to preserve for her the rich and barbarous empire of the East. This microcosm of the barracks has its own laws, its own morals, its own range of emotional sentiment. What these are the new writer has (not told us, for that would be a long story) but shown us that he himself has divined. He has held the door open for a moment, and has revealed to us a set of very human creations. One thing, at least, the biographer of Mulvaney and Ortheris has no difficulty in persuading us, namely, that 'God in his wisdom has made the heart of the British soldier, who is very often an unlicked ruffian, as soft as the heart of a little child, in order that he may believe in and follow his officers into tight and nasty places.'

The Anglo-Indians with whom Mr. Kipling deals are of two kinds. I must confess that there is no section of his work which appears to me so insignificant as that which deals with Indian 'society'. The eight tales which are bound together as *The Story of the Gadsbys* are doubtless very early productions. I have been told, but I know not whether on good authority, that they were published before the author was twenty-one. Judged as the observation of Anglo-Indian life by so young a boy, they are, it is needless to say, astonishingly clever. Some pages in them can never, I suppose, come to seem unworthy of later fame. The conversation in 'The Tents of Kedar', where Captain Gadsby breaks to Mrs. Herriott that he is engaged to be married, and absolutely darkens her world to her during 'a Naini Tal dinner for thirty-five', is of consummate adroitness. What a 'Naini Tal[1] dinner' is I have not the slightest conception, but it is evidently something very sumptuous and public, and if any practised hand of the old social school could have contrived the thrust and parry under the fire of

[1][Naini Tal is a hill station near Lucknow.]

seventy critical eyes better than young Mr. Kipling has done, I know
not who that writer is. In quite another way the pathos of the little
bride's delirium in 'The Valley of the Shadow' is of a very high,
almost of the highest, order.

But, as a rule, Mr. Kipling's 'society' Anglo-Indians are not drawn
better than those which other Indian novelists have created for our
diversion. There is a sameness in the type of devouring female, and
though Mr. Kipling devises several names for it, and would fain
persuade us that Mrs. Herriott, and Mrs. Reiver, and Mrs. Hauksbee
possess subtle differences which distinguish them, yet I confess I am
not persuaded. They all—and the Venus Annodomini as well—appear
to me to be the same high-colored, rather ill-bred, not wholly spoiled
professional coquette. Mr. Kipling seems to be too impatient of what
he calls 'the shiny top-scum stuff people call civilization' to paint these
ladies very carefully. 'The Phantom Rickshaw', in which a hideously
selfish man is made to tell the story of his own cruelty and of his
mechanical remorse, is indeed highly original, but here it is the man,
not the woman, in whom we are interested. The proposal of marriage
in the dust-storm in 'False Dawn', a theatrical, lurid scene, though
scarcely natural, is highly effective. The archery contest in 'Cupid's
Arrows' needs only to be compared with a similar scene in 'Daniel
Deronda' to show how much more closely Mr. Kipling keeps his eye
on detail than George Eliot did. But these things are rare in this class
of his stories, and too often the Anglo-Indian social episodes are choppy,
unconvincing, and not very refined.

All is changed when the central figure is a man. Mr. Kipling's
officials and civilians are admirably vivid and of an amazing variety.
If any one wishes to know why this new author has been received with
joy and thankfulness by the Anglo-Saxon world, it is really not
necessary for him to go further for a reason than to the moral tale of
'The Conversion of Aurelian McGoggin'. Let the author of that tract
speak for himself.

Every man is entitled to his own religious opinions;

but no man—least of all a junior—has a right to thrust these down other men's
throats. The government sends out weird civilians now and again; but McGoggin was the queerest exported for a long time. He was clever—brilliantly
clever—but his cleverness worked the wrong way. Instead of keeping to the
study of the vernaculars, he had read some books written by a man called
Comte, I think, and a man called Spencer, and a Professor Clifford. [You will
find these books in the Library.] They deal with people's insides from the point

of view of men who have no stomachs. There was no order against his reading them, but his mama should have smacked him. . . . I do not say a word against this creed. It was made up in town, where there is nothing but machinery and asphalt and building—all shut in by the fog. . . . But in this country [India], where you really see humanity—raw, brown, naked humanity—with nothing between it and the blazing sky, and only the used-up, over-handled earth under-foot, the notion somehow dies away, and most folk come back to simpler theories.

Those who will not come back to simpler theories are prigs, for whom the machine-made notion is higher than experience. Now Mr. Kipling, in his warm way, hates many things, but he hates the prig for preference. Aurelian McGoggin, better known as the Blastoderm, is a prig of the over-educated type, and upon him falls the awful calamity of sudden and complete nerve-collapse. Lieutenant Golightly, in the story which bears his name, is a prig who values himself for spotless attire and clockwork precision of manner; he therefore is mauled and muddied up to his eyes, and then arrested under painfully derogatory conditions. In 'Lispeth' we get the missionary prig, who thinks that the Indian instincts can be effaced by a veneer of Christianity. Mr. Kipling hates 'the sheltered life'. The men he likes are those who have been thrown out of their depth at an early age, and taught to swim off a boat. The very remarkable story of 'Thrown Away' shows the effect of preparing for India by a life 'unspotted from the world' in England; it is as hopelessly tragic as any in Mr. Kipling's somewhat grim repertory.

Against the régime of the prig Mr. Kipling sets the régime of Strickland. Over and over again he introduces this mysterious figure, always with a phrase of extreme approval. Strickland is in the police, and his power consists in his determination to know the East as the natives know it. He can pass through the whole of Upper India, dressed up as a fakir, without attracting the least attention. Sometimes, as in 'Beyond the Pale', he may know too much. But this is an excep-tion, and personal to himself. Mr. Kipling's conviction is that this is the sort of man to pervade India for us, and that one Strickland is worth a thousand self-conceited civilians. But even below the Indian prig, because he has at least known India, is the final object of Mr. Kipling's loathing, 'Pagett, M.P.', the radical English politician who comes out for four months to set everybody right. His chastisement is always severe and often comic. But in one very valuable paper, which Mr. Kipling must not be permitted to leave unreprinted, 'The

Enlightenments of Pagett, M.P.', he has dealt elaborately and quite seriously with this noxious creature. Whether Mr. Kipling is right or wrong, far be it from me in my ignorance to pretend to know. But his way of putting these things is persuasive.

Since Mr. Kipling has come back from India he has written about society 'of sorts' in England. Is there not perhaps in him something of Pagett, M.P., turned inside out? As a delineator of English life, at all events, he is not yet thoroughly master of his craft. Everything he writes has vigor and picturesqueness. But 'The Lamentable Comedy of Willow Wood' is the sort of thing that any extremely brilliant Burman, whose English, if slightly odd, was nevertheless unimpeachable, might write of English ladies and gentlemen, having never been in England. *The Record of Badalia Herodsfoot* was in every way better, more truly observed, more credible, more artistic, but yet a little too cynical and brutal to come straight from life. And last of all there is the novel of *The Light that Failed*, with its much-discussed two endings, its oases of admirable detail in a desert of the undesirable, with its extremely disagreeable woman, and its far more brutal and detestable man, presented to us, the precious pair of them, as typical specimens of English society. I confess that it is *The Light that Failed* that has wakened me to the fact that there are limits to this dazzling new talent, the éclat of which had almost lifted us off our critical feet.

The conception of Strickland would be very tantalizing and incomplete if we were not permitted to profit from his wisdom and experience. But, happily, Mr. Kipling is perfectly willing to take us below the surface, and to show us glimpses of the secret life of India. In so doing he puts forth his powers to their fullest extent, and I think it cannot be doubted that the tales which deal with native manners are not merely the most curious and interesting which Mr. Kipling has written, but are also the most fortunately constructed. Every one who has thought over this writer's mode of execution will have been struck with the skill with which his best work is restrained within certain limits. When inspiration flags with him, indeed, his stories may grow too long, or fail, as if from languor, before they reach their culmination. But his best short stories—and among his best we include the majority of his native Indian tales—are cast at once, as if in a mould; nothing can be detached from them without injury. In this consists his great technical advantage over almost all his English rivals; we must look to France or to America for stories fashioned in this way. In several of his tales of Indian manners this skill reaches its highest because most complicated expression. It may be comparatively easy to hold within artistic bonds a gentle episode of European amorosity. To deal, in the same form, but with infinitely greater audacity, with the muffled passions and mysterious instincts of India, to slur over nothing, to emphasize nothing, to give in some twenty pages the very spicy odour of the East, this is marvelous.

Not less than this Mr. Kipling has done in a little group of stories which I cannot but hold to be the culminating point of his genius so far. If the remainder of his writings were swept away, posterity would be able to reconstruct its Rudyard Kipling from 'Without Benefit of Clergy', 'The Man who Would be King', 'The Strange Ride of Morrowbie Jukes', and 'Beyond the Pale'. More than that, if all record of Indian habits had been destroyed, much might be conjectured from them of the pathos, the splendor, the cruelty, and the mystery of India. From 'The Gate of the Hundred Sorrows' more is to be gleaned of the real action of opium-smoking, and the causes of that indulgence, than from many sapient debates in the British House of Commons. We come very close to the confines of the moonlight-colored world of magic in 'The Bisara of Pooree'. For pure horror and for the hopeless impenetrability of the native conscience there is 'The Recrudescence of Imray'. In a revel of color and shadow, at the close of the audacious and Lucianic story of 'The Incarnation of Krishna Mulvaney', we peep for a moment into the mystery of 'a big queen's praying at Benares'.

Admirable, too, are the stories which deal with the results of attempts made to melt the Asiatic and the European into one. The red-headed Irish–Thibetan who makes the king's life a burden to him in the fantastic story of 'Namgay Doola' represents one extremity of this chain of grotesque Eurasians: Michele D'Cruze, the wretched little black police inspector, with a drop of white blood in his body, who wakes up to energetic action at one supreme moment of his life, is at the other. The relapse of the converted Indian is a favorite theme with this cynical observer of human nature. It is depicted in 'The Judgment of Dungara', with a rattling humor worthy of Lever, where the whole mission, clad in white garments woven of the scorpion nettle, go mad with fire and plunge into the river, while the trumpet of the god bellows triumphantly from the hills. In 'Lispeth' we have a study—much less skilfully worked out, however—of the Indian woman carefully Christianized from childhood reverting at once to heathenism when her passions reach maturity.

The lover of good literature, however, is likely to come back to the four stories which we named first in this section. They are the very flower of Mr. Kipling's work up to the present moment, and on these we base our highest expectations for his future. 'Without Benefit of Clergy' is a study of the Indian woman as wife and mother, uncovenanted wife of the English civilian and mother of his son. The tremulous passion of Ameera, her hopes, her fears, and her agonies of disappointment, combine to form by far the most tender page which Mr. Kipling has written. For pure beauty the scene where Holden, Ameera, and the baby count the stars on the housetop for Tota's horoscope is so characteristic that, although it is too long to quote in full, its opening paragraph must here be given as a specimen of Mr. Kipling's style in this class of work.

Ameera climbed the narrow staircase that led to the flat roof. The child, placid and unwinking, lay in the hollow of her right arm, gorgeous in silver-fringed muslin, with a small skull-cap on his head. Ameera wore all that she valued most. The diamond nose-stud that takes the place of the Western patch in drawing attention to the curve of the nostril, the gold ornament in the center of the forehead studded with tallow-drop emeralds and flawed rubies, the heavy circlet of beaten gold that was fastened round her neck by the softness of the pure metal, and the clinking curb-patterned silver anklets hanging low over the rosy ankle-bones. She was dressed in jade-green muslin, as befitted a daughter of the Faith, and from shoulder to elbow and elbow to wrist ran bracelets of silver tied with floss silk; frail glass bangles slipped over the wrist in proof of the slenderness of the hand, and certain heavy gold bracelets that had no part in her country's ornaments, but, since they were Holden's gifts, and fastened with a cunning European snap, delighted her immensely.

They sat down by the low white parapet of the roof, overlooking the city and its light.

What tragedy was in store for the gentle astrologer, or in what darkness of waters the story ends, it is needless to repeat here.

In 'The Strange Ride of Morrowbie Jukes' a civil engineer stumbles by chance on a ghastly city of the dead who do not die, trapped into it, down walls of shifting sand, on the same principle as the ant-lion secures its prey, the parallel being so close that one half suspects Mr. Kipling of having invented a human analogy to the myrmeleon. The abominable settlement of living dead men is so vividly described, and the wonders of it are so calmly, and, as it were, so temperately discussed, that no one who possesses the happy gift of believing can fail to be persuaded of the truth of the tale. The character of Gunga Dass, a Deccanee Brahmin whom Jukes finds in this reeking village, and who, reduced to the bare elements of life, preserves a little, though exceedingly little, of his old traditional obsequiousness, is an admirable study. But all such considerations are lost, as we read the story first, in the overwhelming and Poe-like horror of the situation and the extreme novelty of the conception.

A still higher place, however, I am inclined to claim for the daring invention of 'The Man who Would be King'. This is a longer story than is usual with Mr. Kipling, and it depends for its effect, not upon any epigrammatic surprise or extravagant denouement of the intrigue, but on an imaginative effort brilliantly sustained through a detailed succession of events. Two ignorant and disreputable Englishmen, exiles from social life, determine to have done with the sordid struggle, and to close with a try for nothing less than empire. They are seen by the journalist who narrates the story to disappear northward from the Kumharsan Serai disguised as a mad priest and his servant starting to sell whirligigs to the Ameer of Kabul. Two years later there stumbles into the newspaper office a human creature bent into a circle, and moving his feet one over the other like a bear. This is the surviving adventurer, who, half dead and half dazed, is roused by doses of raw whisky into a condition which permits him to unravel the squalid and splendid chronicle of adventures beyond the utmost rim of mountains, adventures on the veritable throne of Kafiristan. The tale is recounted with great skill as from the lips of the dying king. At first, to give the needful impression of his faint, bewildered state, he mixes up his narrative, whimpers, forgets, and repeats his phrases; but by the time the curiosity of the reader is fully arrested, the tale has become limpid and straightforward enough. When it has to be drawn to a close, the symptoms of aphasia and brain-lesion are repeated. This story is conceived and conducted in the finest spirit of an artist. It is strange to the verge of being incredible, but it never outrages possibility, and the severe moderation of the author preserves our credence throughout.

It is in these Indian stories that Mr. Kipling displays more than anywhere else the accuracy of his eye and the retentiveness of his memory. No detail escapes him, and, without seeming to emphasize the fact, he is always giving an exact feature where those who are in possession of fewer facts or who see less vividly are satisfied with a shrewd generality.

In Mr. Kipling's first volume there was one story which struck quite a different note from all the others, and gave promise of a new delineator of children. 'Tods' Amendment', which is a curiously constructed piece of work, is in itself a political allegory. It is to be noticed that when he warms to his theme the author puts aside the trifling fact that Tods is an infant of six summers, and makes him give a clear statement of collated native opinion worthy of a barrister in ample practice. What led to the story, one sees without difficulty, was the wish to emphasize the fact that unless the Indian government humbles itself, and becomes like Tods, it can never legislate with efficiency, because it never can tell what all the *jhampanis* and *saises* in the bazaar really wish for. If this were all, Mr. Kipling in creating Tods would have shown no more real acquaintance with children than other political allegorists have shown with sylphs or Chinese philosophers. But Mr. Kipling is always an artist, and in order to make a setting for his child-professor of jurisprudence, he invented a really convincing and delightful world of conquering infancy. Tods, who lives up at Simla with Tods' mama, and knows everybody, is 'an utterly fearless young pagan', who pursues his favorite kid even into the sacred presence of the Supreme Legislative Council, and is on terms of equally well-bred familiarity with the Viceroy and with Futteh Khan, the villainous loafer *khit* from Mussoorie.

To prove that 'Tods' Amendment' was not an accident, and also, perhaps, to show that he could write about children purely and simply, without any afterthought of allegory, he brought out, as the sixth instalment of the 'Indian Railway Library', a little volume entirely devoted to child-life. Of the four stories contained in this book one is among the finest productions of its author, while two others are very good indeed. There are also, of course, the children in *The Light that Failed*, although they are too closely copied from the author's previous creations in 'Baa, Baa, Black Sheep'; and in other writings of his children take a position sufficiently prominent to justify us in considering this as one of the main divisions of his work.

In his preface to *Wee Willie Winkie* Mr. Kipling has sketched for us the attitude which he adopts towards babies. 'Only women,' he says, but we may doubt if he means it, 'understand children thoroughly; but if a mere man keeps very quiet, and humbles himself properly, and refrains from talking down to his superiors, the children will sometimes be good to him, and let him see what they think about the world.' This is a curious form of expression, and suggests the naturalist more than the lover of children. So might we conceive a successful zoologist describing the way to note the habits of wild animals and birds, by keeping very quiet, and lying low in the grass, and refraining from making sudden noises. This is, indeed, the note by which we may distinguish Mr. Kipling from such true lovers of childhood as Mrs. Ewing. He has no very strong emotion in the matter, but he patiently and carefully collects data, partly out of his own faithful and capacious personal memory, partly out of what he observes.

The Tods type he would probably insist that he has observed. A finer and more highly developed specimen of it is given in *Wee Willie Winkie*, the hero of which is a noble infant of overpowering vitality, who has to be put under military discipline to keep him in any sort of domestic order, and who, while suffering under two days' confinement to barracks (the house and veranda), saves the life of a headstrong girl. The way in which Wee Willie Winkie—who is of Mr. Kipling's favorite age, six—does this is at once wholly delightful and a terrible strain to credence. The baby sees Miss Allardyce cross the river, which he has always been forbidden to do, because the river is the frontier, and beyond it are bad men, goblins, Afghans, and the like. He feels that she is in danger, he breaks mutinously out of barracks on his pony and follows her, and when she has an accident, and is surrounded by twenty hill-men, he saves her by his spirit and by his complicated display of resource. To criticize this story, which is told with infinite zest and picturesqueness, seems merely priggish. Yet it is contrary to Mr. Kipling's whole intellectual attitude to suppose him capable of writing what he knows to be supernatural romance. We have therefore to suppose that in India infants 'of the dominant race' are so highly developed at six, physically and intellectually, as to be able to ride hard, alone, across a difficult river, and up pathless hilly country, to contrive a plan for succoring a hapless lady, and to hold a little regiment of savages at bay by mere force of eye. If Wee Willie Winkie had been twelve instead of six, the feat would have been just possible. But then the romantic contrast between the baby and his virile deeds would not have been nearly so piquant. In all this Mr. Kipling, led away by sentiment and a false ideal, is not quite the honest craftsman that he should be.

But when, instead of romancing and creating, he is content to observe children, he is excellent in this as in other branches of careful natural history. But the children he observes, are, or we much misjudge him, himself. 'Baa, Baa, Black Sheep' is a strange compound of work at

121

first and second hand. Aunty Rosa (delightfully known, without a suspicion of supposed relationship, as 'Anti-rosa'), the Mrs. Squeers of the Rocklington lodgings, is a sub-Dickensian creature, tricked out with a few touches of reality, but mainly a survival of early literary hatreds. The boy Harry and the soft little sister of Punch are rather shadowy. But Punch lives with an intense vitality, and here, without any indiscretion, we may be sure that Mr. Kipling has looked inside his own heart and drawn from memory. Nothing in the autobiographies of their childhood by Tolstoi and Pierre Loti, nothing in Mr. R. L. Stevenson's 'Child's Garden of Verses', is more valuable as a record of the development of childhood than the account of how Punch learned to read, moved by curiosity to know what the 'falchion' was with which the German man split the Griffin open. Very nice, also, is the reference to the mysterious rune, called 'Sonny, my Soul',[1] with which mama used to sing Punch to sleep.

By far the most powerful and ingenious story, however, which Mr. Kipling has yet dedicated to a study of childhood is 'The Drums of The Fore and Aft'. 'The Fore and Aft' is a nickname given in derision to a crack regiment, whose real title is 'The Fore and Fit', in memory of a sudden calamity which befell them on a certain day in an Afghan pass, when if it had not been for two little blackguard drummer-boys, they would have been woefully and contemptibly cut to pieces, as they were routed, by a dashing troop of Ghazis. The two little heroes, who only conquer to die, are called Jakin and Lew, stunted children of fourteen, 'gutter-birds' who drink and smoke and 'do everything but lie', and are the disgrace of the regiment. In their little souls, however, there burns what Mr. Pater would call a 'hard, gem-like flame' of patriotism, and they are willing to undergo any privation, if only they may wipe away the stigma of being 'bloomin' non-combatants'. In the intervals of showing us how that stain was completely removed, Mr. Kipling gives us not merely one of the most thrilling and effective battles in fiction, but a singularly delicate portrait of two grubby little souls turned white and splendid by an element of native greatness. It would be difficult to point to a page of modern English more poignant than that which describes how 'the only acting-drummers who were took along',—and—left, behind, moved forward across the pass alone to the enemy's front, and sounded on drum and fife the return of the regiment to duty. But perhaps the most remarkable feature of the whole story is that a record of shocking British retreat

[1] [The hymn 'sun of my soul . . .']

and failure is so treated as to flatter in its tenderest susceptibilities the pride of British patriotism.

Mr. Kipling's début was made in a volume of verse, called *Departmental Ditties*, which has continued to enjoy considerable popularity and has frequently been reprinted. This collection of comical and satirical pieces representative of Indian official life has, however, very slight literary value. The verses in it are mostly imitations of popular English and American bards, with but here and there a trace of the true accent of the author in such strong though ill-executed strains as 'The Story of Uriah', and 'The Song of the Women'. In other cases they follow, but more faintly, the lines of the author's prose stories. It cannot be said that in this collection Mr. Kipling soars above the 'Ali Babas' and 'Aliph Cheems' who strike an agreeable lyre for the entertainment of their fellow Anglo-Indians. No claim for the title of poet could be founded on literary baggage so slight as *Departmental Ditties*.

Of late years, however, Mr. Kipling has put forward, in a great variety of directions, essays in verse which deserve much higher consideration. He has indulged the habit of prefixing to his prose stories fragments of poems which must be his own, for there is nobody else to claim them. Some of these are as vivid and tantalizing as the tiny bits we possess of lost Greek tragedians. Among them is to be found this extract from a 'barrack-room ballad' used to introduce the story of 'The Madness of Private Ortheris':

> Oh! where would I be when my froat was dry?
> Oh! where would I be when the bullets fly?
> Oh! where would I be when I come to die?
>   Why,
> Somewheres anigh my chum,
>   If 'e's liquor 'e'll give me some,
> If I'm dying 'e'll 'old my 'ead,
> An' 'e'll write 'em 'ome when I'm dead.
>   God send us a trusty chum!

There must have been not a few readers who, like the present writer, on finding this nugget of ballad-doggerel, felt that here was a totally unworked field just touched by the spade, and left. Happily, Mr. Kipling has digged farther and deeper, and he has written a series of barrack-room ballads which are unique in their kind, and of which scarcely one but is of definite and permanent value. The only writer who has, to my mind, in any degree anticipated the mixture of vulgar

and realistic phraseology with the various elements of pathos combined in the lives of rough young men exiled from home is the
Australian poet Adam Lindsay Gordon, whom Mr. Kipling greatly
excels in variety of metre and force of language. Except in its sardonic
form, humor has never been a prominent feature of Mr. Kipling's
prose. I hardly know an instance of it not disturbed by irony or
savagery, except the story of 'Moti Guj', the mutineer elephant. But
in some of the *Barrack-Room Ballads* there is found the light of a genuine
humor. What can be more delightful, for instance, than this appreciative description of Fuzzy-Wuzzy, by one of the Soudan force who
has had to deal with him in the bush?

[quotes last stanza of 'Fuzzy-Wuzzy': DV, pp. 400–1]

But more often, underneath the rollicking storm of the verses, there
may be heard the melancholy which is characteristic of so much of
the best modern writing, the murmur of that *Weltschmerz* which is
never far off, at all events, from Mr. Kipling's verse. It sometimes
seems as though it were the author himself who speaks to us in the
soldier's impatience at the colorlessness and restraint of Western life.
And it is with the exquisite melody of his own ballad of 'Mandalay'
that we leave the author who has so strangely moved and fascinated
us, who has enlarged our horizon on one wholly neglected side, and
from whom, in the near future, we have a right to expect so much
imaginative invigoration. But what is he saying?

> Ship me somewhere east of Suez where the best is like the worst,
> Where there are n't no Ten Commandments, an' a man can raise a thirst;
> For the temple-bells are callin', an' it's there that I would be—
> By the old Moulmein Pagoda, lookin' lazy at the sea—
>   On the road to Mandalay,
>   Where the old flotilla lay,
> With our sick beneath the awnings when we went to Mandalay!
>   Oh, the road to Mandalay,
>   Where the flyin'-fishes play,
> An' the dawn comes up like thunder out er China 'crost the bay!

Ah, yes! Mr. Kipling, go back to the far East! Yours is not the
talent to bear with patience the dry-rot of London or of New York.
Disappear, another Waring, and come back in ten years' time with a
fresh and still more admirable budget of precious loot out of Wonderland!

18. The *Bookman* estimate; 'Kipling'

1891

Two articles from the *Bookman* (London), Vol. I, pp. 28–30 and
63–6 (October and November 1891), signed 'Y. Y.', and both
headed 'The Work of Rudyard Kipling'.

The author has not so far been identified. Works of reference all
give him as Robert Lynd (1879–1949) who used this pseudonym
—but in 1891 Lynd was only twelve years old, and there were
earlier essays and verses signed 'Y. Y.' even than this.

PART I

This attempt to estimate the work of Mr. Kipling shall be mainly
illustrated from his last book, *Life's Handicap*, which is fairly representative, and will be freshest in the reader's memory. Is such an
estimate premature? Is it unfair? I think not, and for this reason. If his
career is not yet closed, at least one phase of it is. Nothing he may yet
do is likely to alter, to enhance or impair, the rank he has already
taken as an Observer and Recorder of what he has seen of Nature and
Man. For such he is—nothing less, nor more.

On the very threshold lie three stumbling-blocks. First, the perplex-
ing form in which his work has been presented to us. From time to
time his stray stories have been hunted up and issued in small volumes,
arranged on no apparent principle. Many were not worth re-printing—
mere doting-Colonel-yarns of the nullah-in-the-foreground type,
mess-room practical jokes, and dingy Simla scandals. These I shall
simply ignore. All his best work might well have been wrought into
his two books, *Black and White* and *Soldiers Three*. Secondly, he is
furiously popular. His books sell like the *Sporting Life* or Dr. Farrar's
Sermons—and to the same buyers. He has been cuddled by the lewd
people of the baser sort, who fancy themselves Athenians because they
rave over Τι καινότερον—Robert Elsmeres, Shes, Hes, Hermaphrodites,
or what not. Lastly, he has been imported as an Infant Prodigy all the

way from India, where he has performed with applause before all the crowned, uncrowned and discrowned heads. Here we at once get into the heart of the question.

Mr. Kipling is neither an Infant—if he ever was one—nor a Prodigy; but his training has been prodigious, if you like—at least in our sleek days. His writings as yet contain no avowedly autobiographical element. It would therefore be impertinent to repeat all that I have been privileged to learn about his early career, and I apologise for mentioning even so much as is directly to my purpose. His gifts of eye and mind are hereditary. Exiled to England like other Indian children he at last broke his chain, found his way back, and sacrificing the advantages of a finished education entered as a mere youth the hard school of journalism. Thus much, and no more.

'But oh, think how wonderfully young!' Granted. Young he was— young he still is—in savage energy, fearless dash, careless confidence; but in other respects old—wonderfully old. He had seen much, heard much, noted much—more perhaps than is well for a lad—while other youthful eyes were riveted mostly on lexicons and cricket-stumps. And that too in a land of varied races and rival civilisations and strange old obsolete, yet living religions, where even a boy who will see and think becomes perforce somewhat of a philosopher. True, he has not been ground small in our educational mill. But is that loss or gain? To us, I think, almost wholly gain. We have enough and to spare of prize graduates, quite as clever as he, who are going to turn out Bacons, Gibbons, and Matthew Arnolds. But somehow they are all so dreadfully alike. Send them to India—as we do in fact. Tell them to look at a jungle, or a Jain temple; they will see just what Ruskin taught them to look for and nothing beyond. Bid them discourse of sepoys, priests, zenanas, village life; they will give you only the same views that other cautious, well-expressed persons have cautiously expressed so well before them. Ask them to judge, to criticise; they will try to tell you not what they themselves think, but what they think the majority of their cultured tribe must be thinking. Among so many Levites surely we have room for one sturdy Ishmael. He has never been taught to see, hear, reflect and describe in the proper Levitical, academical, second-hand way. He just has to do the best he can. What is that best? How has it been developed by his exceptional training? Space only permits me to hastily touch a few points.

As an observer and recorder Mr. Kipling is not really an Impression-ist, but rather a Selecter. He does not—even in his 'City of Dreadful

Night'—give us a mere sidelight on a passing mood; he seems to see the whole, and make us see it too, by selecting and dashing down a very few intensely significant points. I do not mean that he draws a skeleton of the man or the landscape for our fancy to clothe at will. He takes the skeleton for granted, and just accentuates those half-dozen features of physiognomy which give the keynote to our first view and our last lingering memory of a man or a picture. Those who have visited or read much about India have the background and general composition already in their mind's eye; Mr. Kipling adds the magic touches—and the picture lives. His method is the reverse of Balzac's, but to me at least, as satisfying.

This power of selection naturally involves dramatic art, the instinct of construction and the ineffable tact of omission. These gifts he sometimes misuses and abuses, and too often wholly neglects, as in the ill-judged introductions to some of his stories. But at its best his art is supreme. 'The Finances of the Gods' is a masterpiece—so tiny, so compact, so homogenous—prologue, legend and epilogue, so simply graceful, so paternally tender, such an interior—one almost fancies Metsu painting an Indian conversation-piece—such a seeming lightness, such a deep undercurrent of significance—nothing less than the infiltration, the saturation of a nation's whole life by a Faith to us impossibly grotesque! You think this exaggeration? then clearly you have only skimmed the story instead of studying, analysing, and dissecting it. Another short sketch, 'Little Tobrah', illustrates still more signally the instinctive knowledge of what to omit. Its intense directness is electric. But enough, for pages would not suffice for analysing the varied forms of Mr. Kipling's dramatic art, varied because unconventional.

Again, note his youthful confidence. Right or wrong he never hesitates, balances, shuffles, sees both ways at once—clearly he never practised writing essays for the headmaster.

Humour he possesses, but it is of the grim, broad, not wholly happy, Yorkshire type—the humour of experience. His wit is less striking, save in his felicitous and pregnant epigrams; for example take this—'the Russian is a delightful person till he tucks in his shirt', or this—'East of Suez, some hold, the direct control of Providence ceases'.

His narrative style may lack symmetry and taste, but now and then phrases flash out of native force and beauty. This of a caged wild beast asleep—'troubled by some dream of the forests of his freedom'—or this of the Amir—'His word is red law; by the gust of his passion falls the leaf of man's life, and his favour is terrible'—though here perhaps we may trace an Oriental model. Indeed, long passages might be selected of vivid, nay majestic force, or pathetic beauty marred only by a few blemishes. When he observes most keenly, he describes most eloquently, as you will own if you study the perfect sentence on page 37 about the Indian starlight. And above all he has never learnt the trick of reeling off neat pages of something or other about nothing.

One other feature in his rich variety—variety, look you, not versatility. His method never changes, but he applies it with equal force to such varied material, such diverse experiences—for experiences they must surely be. His German, his Fenian, his Rajah, his Yorkshire Methodist, his Malay murderer, his Burmese priest, his Moslem mullah, even Bimi the orang-outang, are as Shakspearian as his Soldiers Three—that is, each is a veritably individual specimen of a district generic type. Once rightly conceive the relations of individual, species and genus—that is, if you can—and you may conjure up a living man in ten lines, instead of manufacturing him in a whole chapter.

The final result of this peculiar self-training is an attitude, a manner, a style of presentation wholly personal and individual. There is something like it in much of the nervous, high-pressure work of the best American, and probably also Anglo-Indian, journalism. Yet not quite the same. Mr. Kipling will of course find imitators, but among his predecessors, can we point to a single page which could be mistaken for his best work? Whether it be good, whether it be bad, he has added yet another to the many forms of English literature.

Such are the more obvious merits of his books, viewed from the purely literary and artistic side. But he has also *les défauts de ses qualités*. These, and with them far deeper and more suggestive questions—the moral significance, the human interest, the philosophic bearing, the present achievement and the future promise of his work—remain yet untreated.

PART II

It has been already hinted that Mr. Kipling has the defects which spring from his merits. His quick, bold style of presentation often strains and fatigues the attention; his scenic construction, when extended to trifles, sometimes sinks to burlesque; his dogmatic assurance and daring satire is bound to stab many a respectable prejudice. Further, a self-formed style must always seem a tacit outrage upon the great accepted models unless itself rises to the rank of a model. Mr.

Kipling's style is no model, nor is it even quite original. Tainted with the flippancy of journalism and the distressing smartness of trans-Atlantic buffoonery, it is by no means that of the artless child of Nature who 'pipes but as the throstles sing'. Superfine vulgarians have called him vulgar. Vulgar he is not. His occasional untowardness or forwardness has no real affinity to the innately vulgar and subtly vulgarising tone of a Charles Reade or a Theodore Hook. To me, indeed, his errors of taste seem but the price we pay for the unconventional evolution of his genius. And so far we gain more than we lose.

Good print is well; good style is better; best of all is good matter. Such, at least, is the due order of excellence in the eyes of the sober Bookman, who would not love books so well, loved he not knowledge more. In Mr. Kipling's manner I have pointed to some admirable qualities marred by a few glaring yet pardonable blemishes. It remains to ask what is it that he has to say—wherein and how far are we the richer or the better for it?

One verdict has been given already. The big battalions of railway-readers on whose *popularis aura* our writers are now wafted to fame—that myriad-eyed Argus intent on Tit-bits, Scraps and Orts, has long since decided with the enviable promptitude to be expected of a critic who sees his way at a glance into the inmost Secret of Bradshaw. *Life's Handicap* has amused and excited him—what more would you have? Yet the oracles of the smoking carriage are truer than their echoes in the penny press. The morning paper which at present I take in, in a brief notice just admires and quotes the (really unsatisfactory) Preface, decides that the stories are 'very smart and imbued with a strong worldly philosophy', and closes by singling out three as 'especially striking', of which the first, I own, is excellent, the second peculiarly inartistic and repulsive, the third the one palpable failure in the series. Yet even such criticism serves its turn. Few care to dig deeper. The popular interest in Humanity is mainly centred on its choicest specimen—oneself. Millions ride in cabs; only hundreds criticise the horse; only tens study the cabman. Smart and worldly—such is the very last word of the railroad critics who only read as they run.

He who leisurely turns the pages will seek and will find more than amusement. Much that seems, much that is, wholly new will startle him; he will ask himself: are these things true? how did the author get hold of them? what does he really think about them? what would he have me think? what do I think? Of some such train of thought, limited to his best prose work, here are a few results.

His avowed purpose is described in the Preface thus—'Chiefly I write of Life and Death, and men and women and Love and Fate'. This is true enough, though the Preface is but a disingenuous mystification contradicted by its business-like last sentences—a mere clever *jeu d'esprit* composed to bind together a random collection of stories. Men, and in a less degree women and children—even brutes, as dogs, apes and elephants, in so far as they present inchoate human elements—are Mr. Kipling's absorbing theme.

His peculiar attitude towards Nature proves this. True, he has the artist-eye. His reading of Indian scenery is, I am assured, not less exactly truthful than it seems. But he has nothing of the Wordsworthian, vague, yearning sympathy with Nature. His marvellous, often terrible, pictures of elemental phenomena—seasons, heat, cold, rain and flood—are always drawn in the light of man's enjoyment or misery. If ever his landscape lacks some foreground figures their place is supplied by a human suggestion of loneliness. He is no pious Pantheist to whom the earth is but a great globular god, with Rydal Mount for its pole—an all-sufficing Paradise sadly marred by the intrusion of Adam's children with their odious railways and waterworks. True, in a splendid night description he says: 'the earth was a grey shadow more unreal than the sky. We could hear her breathing lightly in the pauses between the howling of the jackals and the movement of the wind in the tamarisks;' but then he adds his touches of human interest, the 'fitful mutter of musketry-fire leagues away', a 'native woman singing in some unseen hut', and the 'mail-train thundering by'. For this 'even breathing of the crowded earth' is not the charming repose of flowers and trees and pretty birds; he is thinking of the mighty Indian soil strewn with myriad tired, stark men, as it were some vast beach at the tremulous pause of the low tide of humanity. To him the earth is the Lord's and the fulness thereof, but that lord is Mankind. No mystical hypostatic union of the human Soul with the divine Nature of sunsets, waterfalls, larks, and lesser celandines: Nature, the world, is simply the home, the environment of man, the mere scenery of the supreme drama of human struggle, failure, or success.

In what spirit, by what method, has he studied men? The answer is involved in the further question of his veracity. And here I find myself at fault. On the one hand a high—perhaps the very highest—authority on India tells me that Mr. Kipling's portraitures of native character and opinions are simply brilliant imaginative creations based only on limited and superficial observation. On the other hand, I confess that my own experience seldom clashes with his European characters, and that his Oriental element, which is infinitely the more interesting, seems to strengthen, but never conflict with the impressions left by such masters as Burton and Meadows Taylor, and by the only Hindu of first-rate intellect and real learning whose mind I ever studied at leisure. This presumption I do not justify, but may fairly palliate by large concessions. I grant that in his coarser work Mr. Kipling has contented himself with conventional types like his Simla flirts, and wooden officials; that he has never penetrated the inner working of the mighty machine of Government; that of the highest class, both native and English, he has little to say, and that mostly in a vein of comic exaggeration and contemptuous raillery, for all this is patent. For instance, he makes the 'Very Greatest of All the Viceroys' promote a native pet from Bengal to the North West Service. Surely this was beyond the power even of the Most Mischievous of All the Mediocrities, though the satire is fair enough in principle. Again, in his satirical and allegorical sketches he takes strange licences; for example, in 'Namgay Doolah' a savage family with three-fourths of Thibetan and only one-fourth of Irish blood, all have red hair, and by pure hereditary instinct cut off cows' tails, wear black masks, and take blood-money to betray their own kin. But this, like 'Naboth', is clearly allegory. Again, elephant yarns are probably the Indian equivalent for English dog-stories; hence the farcical exaggerations of 'Moti Guj'. Granted, too, that so young a man cannot possibly have studied profoundly and exhaustively every inch of the ground he covers, granted much more—for these concessions are but my own suggestions—the dilemma remains, either a creative genius well-nigh incredible, or a very considerable basis of experience. For my own part, inclining to the latter, I would fain combine both views, and in this way. Where Mr. Kipling is careless, or deficient, or wrong is precisely where we have no lack of trustworthy guides. Great men, great matters, great theories—not such are his true province, but the infinitely little, yet supremely significant trifles which cling closest round the core of humanity. Of these, the statesman, the statistician, the traveller is silent. They will tell you correctly all about the Native—his land-system, his creed, his literature, his social system, his customs, his manners, his general un-Englishism—and you wonder at the odd creature. The Storyteller takes up the lifeless image, adds a few bold touches, making it odder than ever, but you cease to wonder—it seems after all but a man of like passions with yourself, to be either familiarly kicked, or taken by the hand. It seems—nay, it is. For correctness is not truth. The practised eye may detect in these native portraits many discrepancies, errors, and omissions; the outsider, rightly or wrongly, will feel them to be true, and deny that even genius can make bricks without straw. He will even doubt whether the high official mind can fully gauge the opportunities for seeing and hearing which a varied, more or less Bohemian, unofficial life may have afforded. On these Mr. Kipling has built up a definite body of opinion. Little of personal reminiscence can be detected, save in his short novel; most of his stories have been picked up, some wholly invented, but into each he weaves the already arranged and labelled results of his observation—each at least reads like a first-hand experience. Whether an Observer or a Creator, he is equally original. It may be that, like Darwin with his Cirripedia, he at first concentrated himself on a few typical characters, and by this training matured his power of rapidly discriminating each new type he comes across. He does not present, of course, George Eliot's close analysis of complex and conflicting motive—his men are active animals, not ruminants—but in a masterly way he does single out what we may call the main efficient cause of conduct, whether it be a ruling passion or a momentary impulse. And to find it he goes down to the very depths.

Mark, too, his careful racial discrimination. He never confounds the turns and tricks of thought of his Irish, Yorkshire, and Cockney soldiers, or of his varied Orientals. How boldly in 'Pambe Serang' does he contrast the Malay and African traits! How grandly he brings out in the 'Amir's Homily' the secret of Eastern despotism! How exquisitely in the last pages of 'Without Benefit of Clergy' that loveliest of Oriental traits, the courteous, unobtrusive, reverent sympathy with one stricken of God. Vambéry, Burton, Morier, even Palgrave, no doubt bring us nearer to the secret of Moslem character; he alone is at home with all sorts and conditions of men. Take the rigmarole evidence of the coolies (p. 12); there you have the Bengali as ages of servitude have made him, a well-meaning, fawning, crafty, yet transparent liar— the liar of instinct of self-preservation. Or take 'Through the Fire', or 'Little Tobrah'; how utterly un-European is every feeling, every motive, every standard of conduct, yet how utterly human! Correct or not, it is—surely it must be—true.

And it would be truer still if he dared. We live a century too late and too soon for speaking out; but sometimes, as in 'On the Wall', he throws off the fetters. Bold or reticent by turns, he never discloses his ethical system. Probably it is yet incomplete. Like Zola, he never comments or moralises, but so artfully arranges the facts that the inferences become irresistible. In 'Without Benefit of Clergy'—the very title is polemical—those inferences amount to a homily.

If his ethics are obscure, they are always manly. Courage, endurance, fidelity, discipline, the joy of living, of working, of fighting—every spring of virile conduct he delights in. This naturally implies a certain tincture of brutal coarseness, already sufficiently bewailed by the critics. I will therefore only say—and say emphatically—that to this coarseness we owe the purity, the depth, and the intensity of his pathos. In that superb study, 'Greenhow Hill', are a few lines, the death of 'Liza' when for a brief moment the Woman survives the Saint, to which I know no parallel whatever in literature, so poignant its feeling, so profound its philosophy, so instinctive its truth. He only who has studied the coarse animalism of strong men can understand and portray their flashes of supreme tenderness and their numb, speechless grief. Herein we trace the only true affinity to the work of Mr. Bret Harte. Rugged yet affecting pathos is perhaps the highest attribute of Mr. Kipling's genius, and it comes of his penetrating insight into the hearts of men, not indeed the whole heart—a Tito Melema is beyond his grasp—but its inmost part, its most strenuous pulsation, the secret of its very self.

I pass lightly over his two most obvious errors of conception, both results of an imperfect training. Sometimes he stoops to the Supernatural, sinking as low as the prophecies in 'Dinah Shadd', the dog rubbish in 'Imray', the snake lies on page 232, and that vile tale, 'The Mark of the Beast'. Again, he has not yet shaken off his morbid love of journalistic 'horrors', 'shocking discoveries'—that is to say, putrid corpses, painful suffering, and spilled blood. Such 'horrors' do not shock—they only disgust.

Finally, his attitude towards the world of men is very much that of an eager, attentive, observant, sharp-eyed sight-seer. Much in him that looks like sympathy is really only strong interest. He always preserves a certain cynical aloofness; he never, like Dickens, fondles his puppets; none of them, not even Mulvaney, seems dearer to him than another. Hence his somewhat repellent, unfriendly personality as an author. Contrast him with Lamb or Montaigne or Rabelais; of them in no sense could Flaubert say: '*l'œuvre est tout, l'homme est rien.*' And why? Because no one doubts the rounded completeness of the philosophy which Rabelais chose to conceal, or disdained to explain. Mr. Kipling's reticence is less suggestive. I doubt whether he yet has, or ever will have, a philosophy—a broad universal scheme into which all his thoughts and experiences can be harmoniously fitted. But without it no great, creative work is possible. Fielding had his great, tender humanity, Dickens his sentimental optimism, Goethe his belief in Spirit, Scott his trust in providential justice—one has the Christian faith, another fatalism—but all have some sheet anchor. Mr. Kipling, like so many of us, has none. And mark this—it is just when genius after its first daring flights is settling down for maturer triumphs that the lack of early discipline is felt. As it is with the painter so is it with the author. For then the mind, grasping to attain some higher, firmer, wider standpoint, falls back upon the half-forgotten, long-despaired, but never wholly eradicated teaching of school and college; self-discipline reproduces an echo of the ferule; law, order, precept, method, system, resume their sway, and Genius, now heated to fluidity in the fires of life, at last pours smoothly into the matrix chiselled for it by the master-spirits of all the ages. The scholar has become a man, both are fused into the philosopher. I wish, but dare not hope, that Mr. Kipling may yet attain that rich, ripe, sober, benevolent spirit, that repose of the heart, that balance of the brain, which makes the great humanist. His fresh start, *The Light that Failed*, was a false one. He may go on multiplying for our delight his Indian experiences; he may study new types in the West; but can a man feel a youth's quick impressions, or describe them with a youth's audacious energy? He may strengthen, but cannot alter his place in literature. That place is not beside the great masters of imperishable fiction, but high among those vivid, veracious, but fragmentary painters of life and manners by whose inestimable aid, as de Caylus aptly says: '*on sait vivre sans avoir vécu.*'

19. Mrs. Oliphant reviews *Life's Handicap*

1891

From an anonymous review of new books under the general heading of 'The Old Saloon' in *Blackwood's Magazine*, Vol. CL, pp. 728–35 (November 1891), credited to Mrs. Oliphant by *The Wellesley Index*.

Margaret Oliphant (1828–1897), well-known Scottish novelist, historian and biographer, had a life-long connection with *Blackwood's Magazine* in which much of her fiction appeared, as well as reviews: she also wrote the history of the publishing firm of William Blackwood and Sons. Kipling quotes from her best-known novel, *A Beleagured City* (1880) in *Stalky and Co.* (p. 123).

We know of no recent success in the world of literature which is at all equal to that of the young man who came to us from India a few years ago with a name unknown, and in that very short period has made himself such a reputation that everything he writes is not only looked for with eagerness by readers, but is enough to make the temporary fortune of any newspaper or cheap print which is fortunate enough to secure the blazon of that name. When we say he came to us unknown, we do not mean to ignore the fact that he brought with him from that distant empire of which the mass of us, who are not connected with any of the Indian services (a large exception, by the way), are so little acquainted—a blast of reputation and the work upon which that reputation was founded, the *Plain Tales*, in which the great Mulvaney and his comrades were first made known to the world: along with some other views of Indian soldiers and Indian civilians equally novel and wonderful. These revelations of a new world, pure gold of genius and poetic insight, were alloyed by many conventional and quite distasteful visions of something odious beyond the other developments of that generally odious thing 'society'—in the East: which no doubt had appeared, in various mess-rooms, club-rooms, and drawing-rooms, acquainted with Mrs. Hauksbee in her various incarnations, to be 'the real thing', more thrilling and full of interest than mere stories about natives and private soldiers. Mrs. Hauksbee was much in the front of our young man's productions when he came to us with those early works, not perhaps quite sure of his own genius nor of what was its strength, and disposed to think (as we have been credibly informed) in his youthful over-acquaintance and inacquaintance with life, that his own precocious success was merely a 'boom', and would not last. His last volume has completely proved, if proof had been necessary, the inappropriateness of this conclusion. Mr. Rudyard Kipling, we imagine, must now have discovered himself, his wonderful powers, and the just direction of them, as he has discovered so many other things. Not that it is easy to limit the application of these powers. He came from India, the country of his education, and, we understand, predilection, which he understands as few do, and cast his eyes by some chance upon the slums of London—of which he forthwith produced a tremendous picture, such as made into instant and vivid life the scenes which a hundred ineffectual pens and voices have endeavoured to lay before us. We saw the paper in which this extraordinary *aperçu* of a situation and characters [*sic*] which must have been entirely new to the writer only long enough for a single hurried reading; but it was enough to make the London of those awful streets, and their strange but entirely true heroine, as real to us as any of the masterpieces of fiction. The name of the woman was absurd. She was called Badaliah Hindsfoot[1]—a name impossible both for fact and fiction; but this was the only thing unreal about her. The story was also, perhaps, too painful for a trim and permanent new edition; yet we hope we may have it so ere long.

Those, however, who wish to avoid pain must not go to Mr. Rudyard Kipling for pleasure. The thrill of emotion which he has the gift to send tingling through and through his reader is not of the easy kind. It is far from being the best of all possible worlds which he reveals to us; but it is something better. It is a world in which every cruel ill is confronted by that struggling humanity which is continually overborne, yet always victorious—victorious in defeat, in downfall, and in death: the spirit of man made, even when he knows it not, in the image of God. His conception of the race is the same as that which Browning died singing:

One who never turned his back, but marched breast forward.

[1] [Badalia Herodsfoot, reprinted in *Many Inventions*, 1893]

Yet his conception of life is not, as Browning's was, optimistic. Perhaps indeed he has no clearly developed conception of life: he knows that the strangest effort often ends in overthrow; perhaps he may believe that it can do no other. Yet while we stand by his Indian civilian, cut down unnoted in the vast world of darkness against which he is struggling in the name of law and mercy; his soldiers slaughtered in some battle the very name of which will never be known—our souls are penetrated not by the sense of failure, but of the terrible and splendid warfare of everlasting good against overwhelming yet temporary evil. It is something very different from the story of the Good Apprentice; living happy ever after is not the fate to which his heroes, or even his heroines, attain. His men are not always moral; they are distinguished by none of the niceties of the drawing-room (that is to say, those among them who are so, are odious, and surrounded by still more odious womankind); they are faulty, troublesome, impracticable. The soldiers get drunk as often as they can, and swear freely on all occasions; they are not too scrupulous about bloodshed. Yet what our young missionary makes us see with the clearness of light is, that these rough fellows are struggling too, in their way, on the side of righteousness, and that when all this hay, straw, and stubble of mortal error is swept away, the meaning and purpose and essence of the men will not be lost.

Along with this, and perhaps the highest result of Mr. Rudyard Kipling's work is to roll away for us the veil which covers that vast and teeming world, the responsibility of which, for good or evil, before God, the British nation has taken upon its shoulders—India, in so many of its differing nations and phases, and what is going on within it. How he has acquired his marvellous acquaintance, so impartial and so complete, we have no means of knowing; each scene bears so strong a stamp of reality that, as with a portrait painted by one of the masters of human physiognomy and expression, we say instinctively: 'This must be a perfect likeness': the men prove themselves, from the Head of the District to the drummers of the Fore and Aft, from the little naked brown child in the bazaar to the old devotee who has retired to await his death in the temple. The landscape, the atmosphere, even the temperature—that stifling of awful heat, those breakings of great storms, the dust, the blaze, the air that burns, all rise before us; but chiefly, and above all, the servants of that majesty of England, of whom, when they are not our sons and brothers, we know so little. The reader may study a hundred authentic and instructive works upon India without coming to a knowledge of the way in which that Government is carried on, which a glimpse at this record will give him. The civilians out in obscure districts, with neither hopes of fame nor wealth, who live there knowing that far the likeliest thing is that they will die there, and never be heard of more, one man following another with a grim heroism, knowledge of all the risks, and determined indifference to them—is of itself a revelation which sweeps away in a moment all the modern cant of a weakened race and unheroic age. Unheroic! With the commonplace Competition Wallah marching up into the dust and glare to relieve a comrade who is dying or succeed one who is dead, at a moment's notice, knowing that he will probably be relieved himself after a horrible year or two, or month or two, in the same grim way—Smith dead, Brown to take his place—a mere item in a list, nothing more. The breast tightens, the eyes fill, as we read. They lie in the desert where they fell, scores, nay, hundreds of them, the British supremacy built up upon their tombstones—if they have so much as that to show where they lie to form its foundations; and what they suffer in the meantime only themselves and Mr. Rudyard Kipling knows. Here is the *mise-en-scène*—the place and the men:

[quotes 'At the End of the Passage', *Life's Handicap*, pp. 182, line 1, to 185, line 5]

We may add the account these same men give of the various occupations from which they have come to the spare entertainment of the engineer's hut. The explanation is made apropos of a speech read to them out of an English paper in which appointments in India were described as retained for 'scions of the aristocracy who took care to maintain their lavish scale of incomes, to avoid or stifle any enquiries into the nature and conduct of their administration, while they themselves force the unhappy peasant to pay with the sweat of his brow', etc. The civil servant describes his position with various amusing and instructive details:

[quotes 'At the End of the Passage', *Life's Handicap*, pp. 188, line 21, to 189, line 27]

The engineer who is the host is worst off of all. His English subcontractor has died 'accidentally' by the going off of his gun, and he himself is half mad with sleeplessness, but will not ask for leave because the man who would relieve him has a delicate wife at Simla, whom he can visit weekly where he is, and who would insist on following were he sent to Hummil's desert post. 'It's murder to bring a woman here just now. Burkett hasn't the physique of a rat. If he came here he'd go out: and I know she hasn't any money, and I'm pretty sure she'd go out too. I'm salted in a sort of way, and I'm not married. Wait till the rains, and then Burkett can get thin down here.' The story of this hero, and how he perishes at the post he will not let another man encounter the dangers of, is told in the terrible story called the 'End of the Passage'. So much for the servants of the English Government in the burning plains. We ourselves think this story one of the most sad and terrible in the book, though perhaps the 'Man who Was' is still more piteously tragic. The great horror of the volume, the 'Mark of the Beast', affects our particular imagination less, insomuch as it has, as the children say, a happy ending, the man being set free from the horrible enchantment. But it is idle to call these marvellous glimpses into a strange life stories, in the ordinary sense of the word—they are revelations, of what men can do, of what perhaps devils may.

The soldiers, again, are portrayed with more love and sympathy than the civilians, and with not less vivid touches. The 'Drummers of the Fore and Aft' (not in this book) is an epic which has seized upon every man from the age of ten upwards—and we say not man invidiously, as shutting out woman, but collectively as including her. These have entered into the English language, and are, though so young, mere babies of tales, rooted like Shakespeare. The soldiers, even in their most tragic moments, are gayer than the civil servants. The battle in the 'Main Guard' (also not in this volume) is like Homer or Sir Walter. The Pathans and the Englishmen, drunk with fighting, love and applaud each other as each cuts down his man, and the sergeant, withdrawn for a moment from the deadly struggle, who sits on the 'little orficer bhoy' to keep his immature strength out of it, while the youngster struggles and roars threats of punishment, is an immortal group. We will not attempt to quote anything from stories so well known, except in the little unconsidered details which a hasty reader full of excitement for the narrative might slip over in his haste. Here is an indication of the ways of the bivouac and the relations between officers and men, accustomed to lead and follow in the real and awful game of war, though for the moment only playing at it in the manœuvres of a sham campaign.

[quotes 'The Courting of Dinah Shadd', *Life's Handicap*, pp. 42, line 33, to 43, line 25; and p. 47, lines 6 to 16]

This is a very pretty picture of one of the armies in the world in which there is the greatest distance between officers and men—'the men moaning melodiously' after the lieutenant is one of the happiest touches.

This, however, is not all that we owe to Mr. Rudyard Kipling. Behind those bands of Englishmen, Scotsmen (he gives our countrymen but little attention, yet introduces one here and there for a moment, just to show that he can give the speech and accent of a Scot without ridicule or mistake, the all-comprehending boy), and Irishmen, whom he loves, and to whom he does full justice, lies the vast world of India, which also, in the great and unfathomable experience of his less than thirty years, this wonderful youth has penetrated and made his own. The niggers whom foolish young officers scorn—the wily and flattering races that bow down before the Sahibs; the fierce Borderers, who own their master when they see him, but are ready, like children, to take immediate advantage of a priest's murmur that the British Raj is over; the pathetic feminine creatures, half children, half women, whom the white men love and ride away; the old sages squatted in the cool recesses of the temples; the noble chief, who, having been poor himself and worked for his living, has no mercy on the vagabond who steals to live. These are stories, no doubt, and most entertaining stories, full of human nature, piquant in its difference, overwhelming in its resemblances to our own— with all the strange circumstances of ignorance and wisdom, unlike ours, that make it a revelation to us. There has been a question lately in the papers, of a decoration for literature, a share in the honours so freely going about the world, for literary men. Some of the debaters— indeed most of them—have taken a high tone, and attributed to writers the ineffable pretension of being above everything of the kind. Why? We do not pretend to know, the writers of books being but men, not contemptuous of any good thing that their trade may bring them, were it no more (but what is more?—the Garter itself is only that) than a piece of ribbon. If her Majesty's Ministers will be guided by us (which perhaps is not extremely probable; yet we confess we should like the command of a Minister's ear for several shrewd suggestions), they will bestow a Star of India without more ado upon this young man of genius, who has shown us all what the India empire means. Perhaps Lord Salisbury has not time, poor gentleman! with all the weight of State upon him, to refresh his soul with stories; but we dare be bound Mr. Balfour has, who, to speak as do the children of today, is up to everything. Sir Edwin Arnold had a good right to that star, probably suggested by his own poem, which showed us Buddha in his more-than-half Christianity—wonderful shadow of the Christ that was to be, not to be lightly touched by the ignorant missionary; and we would award it to a few others we know of—the author, for instance, of the 'City of Sunshine',[1] and perhaps he of 'Mr. Isaacs'.[2] But there is no Indian potentate, no general, no political agent, no member of council, who has a better right to the Indian decoration than this errant storyteller. We have all read a great deal about that vast continent, and the extraordinary British rule which is over it, without in most cases understanding very much. But here it lies, a hundred nationalities, a world unknown, under the blazing sky— innumerable crowds of human creatures, like the plains they inhabit, stretching into distance further than any eye can see. Never was there a more astonishing picture than that, all done in black and white, which is called the 'City of Dreadful Night'. We pant in the air which is no air, we sicken for the evanescent breath of dawn, we walk between the white bodies asleep, not dead, that lie in every corner, we hear the *muezzin* climb the stairs to give forth his cry upon the stillness, as if we were there in bodily sight and hearing. It is a magic, it is an enchantment. If her Majesty herself, who knows so much, desires a fuller knowledge of her Indian empire, and how it is ruled and defended and fought for every day against all the Powers of Darkness, we desire respectfully to recommend to the Secretary for India that he should place no sheaves of despatches in the royal hands, but Mr. Rudyard Kipling's books. There are only two volumes of them, besides sundry small *brochures*. A good bulky conscientious three-volume novel holds as many words. But there lies India, the most wonderful conquest and possession that any victorious kingdom ever made, the greatest fief, perhaps, that ever was held for God. These are great words: and the young magician upon whose lips we hang does not hesitate to show us by what imperfect instruments the Raj of the white empire is upheld, by men themselves stumbling and labouring upon the path of life, taking that great name as often in vain as speaking it in reverence— storming, fighting, sinning, forgetting themselves often, yet never forgetting the strong rule and curb with which, a handful themselves

---

[1] [*City of Sunshine* (1877) by Alexander Allardyce]
[2] [*Mr. Isaacs* (1882) by F. Marion Crawford]

they hold millions, always with an obdurate and steadfast direction towards Justice and Truth.

No patriot leader could do a better work. We dwell upon none of the literary qualities of this achievement. These are for lesser efforts. What Mr. Rudyard Kipling has done is an imperial work, and worthy of an imperial reward. The Star of India! a small thing the critic might say; but in this modern condition of affairs, when it is no longer the fashion to give a man as much land as he can ride round in a summer day—as much as there is to give. It would be a good beginning of a new system in respect to that unacknowledged craft which is bid to content itself with what little good it can do in its generation and the fickle applauses of popular fame. It is well to consider, however, another good thing that Mr. Kipling has done. He has proved that the public, though apt to be beguiled by Mr. Jerome K. Jerome and the 'Mystery of a Hansom Cab',[1] has yet sense enough to recognise something better when it sees it—for which also we are much beholden to him: it restores our faith in human nature: though how Mulvaney and his friends can share the quarters, even on a railway bookstall, of the sentimental Bootles[2] and his men and babies, we confess we are at a loss to conceive.

It was said, we believe, of our young man, that though superlative in the art (which he has brought so strongly into fashion) of the short story, he was incapable of writing a long one. In answer to which, his daemon produced at a sitting *The Light that Failed*. We remember sitting up to read that story through the moonlight hours of an Italian midnight, until the blueness of the morning began to lighten over the sea, and the grey olives twinkled silvery in that first dawn which comes before the sun. Much experience hath made us calm, and might, as one would think, take the edge off any interest or excitement of a tale. But it is not so; and like a youth with the spell of strong feelings upon us, we seized the pen to write to the author. But paused, as Gobind in Dhunni Bhagat's Chubara might have done; for youth in these days is apt to contemn experience, and better loves the praises of his kind. Here, however, by the dignified hand of Maga, the ever young, is that letter which was never written, bidding the young genius All-hail! and more power to his elbow, to relapse into vernacular speech, which is always more convincing than the high-flown.

---

[1] [1886. By 'Fergus Hume']
[2] [*Bootles' Baby*, by John Strange Winter]

20. Francis Adams on 'Rudyard Kipling'

1891

Signed article from the *Fortnightly Review*, Vol. LVI, pp. 686–700 (November 1891).

Francis William Lauderdale Adams (1862–1893), minor poet and essayist of promise who died young, also wrote a long article on 'Mr. Kipling's Verse' in the *Fortnightly Review*, Vol. LX, pp. 185–216 (November 1893)—but in it politics triumph over literary criticism even more than here. With Kipling, Adams tells us, 'the drop is always straight from the stars into the puddles'—but he equates stars with sentimental Liberal views and puddles with Tory imperialism.

It was inevitable that sooner or later someone should make a systematic effort, in the interests (say) of literature and art, to exploit India and the Anglo-Indian life. England has awakened at last to the astonishing fact of her world-wide Empire, and has now an ever-growing curiosity concerning her great possessions *outre mer*. The writer who can 'explain', in a vivid and plausible manner, the social conditions of India, Australia, Canada, and South Africa—who can show, even approximately, how people there live, move, and have their being, is assured of at least a remarkable vogue. Several vogues of this sort have already been won on more or less inadequate grounds: have been won, and lost and the cry is still: 'They come!' From among them all, so far, one writer alone, led on to fortune on this flood-tide in the affairs of men, has consciously and deliberately aimed high; taken his work seriously, and attempted to add something to the vast store of our English literature. The spectacle of a writer of fiction who is also a man of letters, and not merely a helpless caterer for the circulating libraries and the railway bookstalls, is unfortunately as rare among us as it is frequent among our French friends. Literature and Art are organized in France, and have prestige and power. In England they are impotent and utterly at the mercy of Philistine and imperfectly-educated newspaper men, who, professed caterers for the ignorant and stupid cravings of the average English person, male and female (and especially female), foist upon us painters, poets, novelists, and musicians of the most hopeless mediocrity. In France this sort of thing is impossible. Such efforts would only provoke a smile. People would say to you when you were taking seriously a poet (for instance) like Mr. Lewis Morris, or Sir Edwin Arnold, or a novelist like Mr. Besant or Mr. Haggard: 'Why, you must be joking! These gentlemen are not writers—are not artists at all. Surely you know that what they concern themselves with is the nourishment of the babes and sucklings who have to be provided with pap somehow; but serious workers, contributors to critical and creative thought—*allez!*' It seems something to be at last able to go to our French friends, and say: 'Well, here at any rate we have a young Englishman who has won a remarkable vogue, and for all that *is* a serious worker, *is* a contributor to critical and creative thought, *is* an artist, *is* a writer'—to be able to go and say this, and to advance reasons for our belief in it of sufficient cogency to extort, perhaps, from our friends a genuine assent. If for this alone, we ought to be grateful to Mr. Rudyard Kipling, our Anglo-Indian story-teller.

From the very beginning Mr. Kipling struck a strong and solemn personal note. To his first booklet, *Soldiers Three*, a collection of seven 'stories of barrack-room life', and designed to 'illustrate' one of 'the four main features of Anglo-Indian life', viz., the military, he attached the following sombre, proud, and yet pitiful *envoi*:

[quotes 'A Dedication' (DV. pp. 637-8) in full]

Certainly three of these tales constituted something very like a revelation not only of one of 'the four main features of Anglo-Indian life', but also of a new writer of considerable force and originality. Nothing like either 'The Big Drunk Draf', or 'With the Main Guard', had been presented to the reading public before, and the praise of the long *bazaar* was justifiable enough. But as a gallery of characters, as manifest fictional creations, the success of the book is not great. Indeed, one of the weakest sides of all Mr. Kipling's work is just the want of this very gift, on the assured possession of which he seems to pique himself. His characterization is never excellent; often it is mediocre; sometimes it is abominable. He cannot escape from his own subjectivity. Never was work more acutely personal than his. Never did a

writer consciously or unconsciously insist with such passionate persistence on the special form of milieu which has given him what he
feels to be (so far at least) the dominant factor in his view of things.
And this is why, in nine cases out of ten, his dramatis personae melt
away so rapidly in the memory, leaving us with nothing but the
impression of an admirably piquant and clever delineation. He has
probably spent more time and trouble over his 'Soldiers Three',
Mulvaney, Ortheris, and Learoyd, than over any other of the characters of his tales; yet Mulvaney alone is recognizable as anything approaching an organic creation. Mr. Kipling sacrifices everything to his
mordant individuality. Mulvaney, the drunken, pugnacious, loqua-
cious, kindly Irish ruffian of the old school, will tell you how, 'Brazenose walked into the gang wid his sword, like Diarmid av the Gowlden
Collar,' and will not mention the name of the Queen in ordinary
conversation without devoutly invoking upon her the blessing of the
Creator! Ortheris, the little vulgar rascal of a cockney, urges his comrade on to an adventure with the quotation:

> Go forth, return in glory,
>   To Clusium's royal 'ome:
> And round these bloomin' temples 'ang
>   The bloomin' shields o' Rome.

And, when he is rebuked for loquacity under trial, inquires: 'D'you
stop your parrit screamin' of a 'ot day when the cage is a-cookin' 'is
pore little pink toes orf?' Similarly a regimental carpenter likens the
splitting open of a boat to 'a cock-eyed Chinese lotus', or a London
street-girl entreats: 'But cou-couldn't you take and live with me till
Miss Right comes along? I'm only Miss Wrong, I know, but I'd,' etc.,
etc. I respectfully submit that the speaker here is Mr. Rudyard Kipling,
not Mulvaney, nor Ortheris, nor another. Instances of this sort of
utterly inartistic insertion of little bits of Mr. Rudyard Kipling into
Mr. Rudyard Kipling's 'rude figures of a rough-hewn race', are very
plentiful, and are certainly not edifying samples of the way he shows
his god-like 'power over these'. But how, when taken from the larger
point of view, this defect limits the value of his criticism of the main
features of Anglo-Indian life, which he designs to 'illustrate'! Today
we are all full of eagerness and curiosity to know of what sort our
short-service soldiers are. Mr. Kipling dedicates his booklet to 'that very
strong man, T. Atkins', who is surely the very person in question. But
what does he tell us about him? Little or nothing. It is the old long-service

man who is his game. Into the mouth of Mulvaney, who gives us most of the military criticism, is put the ancient and stock abuse of the short-service system, backed up with the stock and ancient chauvinism about the glory and gain of the good old gentleman officer, all of the olden time, the individual with the courage of a mastiff and the brains of a rabbit. The poor old Irishman in his degradation is even made consolingly to kick himself with the reflection that, if he could have kept out of one big drink a month, he would have been an honorary lieutenant by this time, 'a nuisance to my betthers, a laughin' stock to my equils, an' a curse to meself'. And thus we settle the modern military question, incidentally throwing in a few jeers at Lord Wolseley as a drawing-room man, who doesn't know his business. With what heartfelt rapture, on the other hand, do we approach the sacred exhibitions of the Old Style! Take the first toast at the mess, which is the same as Mulvaney's loyal conversational prayer. 'That Sacrament of the Mess', says Mr. Kipling solemnly and deliberately in his own person, 'never grows old and never ceases to bring a lump into the throat of the listener, be he by sea or by land.' Dirkovitch [a mere unregenerate Cossack] 'rose with his "brothers glorious", but he did not understand. *No one but an officer* [the italics are mine] can tell what that means; and the bulk', etc., etc. And this in the year of grace 1891! Now what I want to know is this. Does Mr. Rudyard Kipling, in his most calm and disillusionized hours, in the dead unhappy night, and when the rain is on the roof, seriously believe in this sort of thing? If so, then he is indeed in a condition past even that in which the Lord might be asked to have mercy on his soul. For 'with stupidity the gods themselves contend in vain'. There are other excesses to which the sightless tradition of the old hide-bound, Jingoistic, Anglo-Indian officialism leads Mr. Kipling, but they are excusable and even defensible. It is only abject silliness which can be neither defended nor excused. None the less, he carries some of these excesses to considerable length. Dickie, the most gentle and lovable of his male characters, blind, and going to his death, 'stretches himself on the floor' [of a carriage in an armed train at Suakim] 'wild with delight at the sounds and the smells' of the machine-gun, pouring out lead through its five noses upon hapless Arabs, fighting for their freedom in their native land. ' "God is very good—never thought I'd hear this again. Give 'em hell, men! oh, give 'em hell!" he cried.'

The exceeding goodness of God in relation to Englishmen and 'niggers' seems always to consist in the opportunity and ability of the former to give the latter 'hell'. Never once in his tales does Mr. Kipling appear to be aware that these same miserable aliens may have a point of view of their own—they also. There is always the tacit assumption of the fact that they are made merely to be fought with, conquered, and ruled, which is simply the sentiment of the Exeter Hall of the Jingoes, who should surely look with greater favour than they do on their Christian brethren. For are they not both after the same thing? The missionary going even one better in his desire for the servitude not only of the body but of the spirit, which of course is *his* special way of 'giving 'em hell'. I am not quarrelling with this genial and enlightened manner of treating the 'inferior races'. I am only saying that in the case of Mr. Rudyard Kipling it makes one feel how much less interesting and valuable his criticism on the Indian people is than it might be. Ah, if only kindly nature had given him as much brain-power as she has given him pictorial talent, what a rendering of the Anglo-Indian life we might have had! It would have been final. There would have been no need for anyone even to try to do this contemporary phase of it over again.

Pieces of his description of fighting have been spoken of as un-paralleled. Wonderful as was his first effort in this direction, the 'jam' in 'the gut betune two hills, as black as a bucket an' as thin as a gurl's waist', where the Pathans waited 'like rats in a pit', for the onslaught of the two regiments, one of which (the Black Tyrone) 'had seen their dead'—wonderfully as this was presented in the Mulvaneyan brogue, when Mr. Kipling trusted to himself alone he did better and achieved a masterpiece. 'The Drums of the Fore and Aft' is one of those performances which are apt to reduce criticism to the mere tribute of a respectful admiration. It is absolutely and thoroughly well done. It 'explains' everybody and everything. We follow the raw-recruited regiment step by step in the process of its demoralization. We feel the approach of the inevitable catastrophe. Equally clear is the demon-stration of the personal incident of the two little drummer-boys, who are to be on this occasion the chance gods from the machine. It all passes before us like a piece of illuminated life. And with what dramatic power is it all gathered together and swept forward to the culminating scene, where the two lads step out from the rocks with drum and fife, 'and the old tune of the old Line shrills and rattles'. Then from the purely descriptive writing which follows, take a specimen like this:

'The English were not running. They were hacking and hewing and stabbing ... The Fore and Aft held their fire till one bullet could drive through five or six men, and the front of the Afghan force gave on the volley. They then selected their men, and slew them with deep gasps and short hacking coughs, and groanings of leather belts against strained bodies.'

Scarcely less fine is the charge of the Lancers, which

'detached the enemy from his base as a sponge is torn from a rock, and left him ringed about with fire in that pitiless plain. And as a sponge is chased round the bath-tub by the hand of the bather, so were the Afghans chased.'

Whenever Mr. Kipling touches on a battle-scene, especially a mêlée, he writes with this absolute mastery of it all. It is real pictorial magic. The charge of Arabs on the square on the Nile bank (*The Light that Failed*, chap. ii.) is too long for full quotation here, and too perfect to be mutilated; the following may be taken as a sample of the way in which he can render a personal incident in such surroundings. It is from a tale in his last book, *Life's Handicap*, 'The Mutiny of the Mavericks', which is for the most part a worthless piece of special pleading, but which ends with this admirable portrayal of the madness of a coward:

Dan and Horse Egan kept themselves in the neighbourhood of Mulcahy. Twice the man would have bolted back in the confusion. Twice he was heaved, kicked, and shouldered back again into the unpaintable *inferno* of a hotly contested charge. At the end, the panic excess of his fear drove him into madness beyond all human courage. His eyes staring at nothing, his mouth open and frothing, and breathing as one in a cold bath, he went forward demented, while Dan toiled after him. The charge checked at a high mud wall. It was Mulcahy who scrambled up tooth and nail and hurled down among the bayonets the amazed Afghan who barred his way. It was Mulcahy, keeping to the straight line of the rabid dog, who led a collection of ardent souls at a newly unmasked battery and flung himself on the muzzle of a gun, as his companions danced among the gunners. It was Mulcahy who ran wildly on from that battery into the open plain, where the enemy were retiring in sullen groups. His hands were empty, he had lost helmet and belt, and he was bleeding from a wound in the neck . . . Dan and Horse Egan, panting and distressed, had thrown themselves down upon the ground by the captured guns, when they noticed Mulcahy's charge. . . . The last of a hurrying crowd of Afghans turned at the noise of shod feet behind him, and shifted his knife ready to hand. This, he saw, was no time to take prisoners. Mulcahy tore on, sobbing; the straight-held blade went home through the defenceless breast, and the body pitched forward almost before a shot from Dan's rifle brought down the slayer. The two Irishmen went out to bring in their dead.

'Description,' said Byron, in his riper time, when he had begun to understand himself a little, 'description is my *forte*'. It is also Mr. Rudyard Kipling's.

The second of the four main features of the Anglo-Indian life is the domestic, and Mr. Kipling chooses *The Story of the Gadsbys* as his typical illustration of it. The difference, however, between the 'domestic' feature and the last of the four, which he denominates the 'social' feature, is slight, and the latter term is quite comprehensive enough for the two. Here, indeed, he is on his special ground. Here his critical limitations do not come into play; his pet prejudices and theories are unaffected, and he sets himself to render Anglo-Indian 'society' as seen and felt from within as well as from without, with an unimpeachable disinterestedness. *The Story of the Gadsbys* showed, in at least one scene of that dramatized 'tale without a plot' ('The Tents of Kedar'), a really remarkable gift of dialogue. It was true drawing-room comedy of a high order, and indeed throughout the whole of the piece the talking and gesturing of the puppets were undeniably actual. In the *Soldiers Three* there was a piece of first-rate dialogue ('The Solid Muldoon', pp. 45, 46, the talk between Mulvaney and Annie Bragin), but it is obviously one thing to write two pages of conversation and quite another to write eighty. The characters chosen for analysis, however, are on a rather low plane and prove tedious when treated at such length. Seven pages of the silly delirium of a silly girl are rather too large an instalment of predetermined pathos on one note, coming on the top of two even larger and more monotonous instalments of honeymooning and conjugal 'tiffing'. An obviously much-experienced I.C.S. man has a felicitous phrase for the Anglo-Indian 'society' ladies, married or single. He calls them 'fire-balloons', and every type of 'fire-balloon', from the empty-headed little girl aforesaid (whose maiden experience so soon corroborates the touching aphorism of her maiden friend that 'being kissed by a man who *didn't* wax his moustache was like eating an egg without salt') through the savage man-exploiting Mrs. Reiver up to Mrs. Hauksbee, 'the most wonderful woman in India',—everyone of them he treats with a loving, patient, and elaborate detail. Some of them are not worth it, 'the most wonderful woman in India' among them (he dedicates *Plain Tales from the Hills*, with a mild fatuity, 'to the wittiest woman in India', who must run that terrible Mrs. Hauksbee close);[1] but others

[1] [They were, in fact, the same: Mrs. F. C. Burton]

are drawn with the hand of a master, and are among his most living creations. The same is to be said of most of the men.

Here, then, we have at last the Anglo-Indian 'society' life of today, and we see it from every side. Duty and red tape tempered by picnics and adultery—it is a singular spectacle. But we are to ascribe much, very much, to the climate. Simla holds 'the only existence in this desolate land worth the living'. For the rest, it is six months purgatory and six months hell. 'One of the many curses of our life in India is the want of atmosphere in the painter's sense. There are no half-tints worth noticing. Men stand out all crude and raw, with nothing to tone them down, and nothing to scale them against.' For instance, we speak of 'all the pleasures of a quiet English wooing, quite different from the brazen businesses of the East, when half the community stand back and bet on the result, and the other half wonder what Mrs. So-and-so will say to it'. Thus Minnie Threegan competes successfully with her 'poor, dear mamma' (who is not precisely a widow) for Mr. Gadsby, who, in his turn, throws over Mrs. Herriott (also apparently not a widow to any alarming extent) in order to enter into the matrimonial 'garden of Eden'. Out of the six tales specially designed to 'illustrate' the 'social' life of the Anglo-Indians, five are based, some more, some less, on adultery. In the way of short stories Mr. Kipling has done nothing better than the three central ones— 'At the Pit's Mouth', 'A Wayside Comedy', and 'The Hill of Illusion'; the last containing the most admirably sustained piece of dialogue he has yet written. The other side to the picture of the reckless, light-hearted revelry of the Hills is to be found in the doggedly heroic work of, at any rate, the male portion of these people down in the Plains. Picnics, rides and drives, with garden-parties and promenades, are suddenly forgotten in a scene like this:

The atmosphere within was only 104°, as the thermometer bore witness, and heavy with the foul smell of badly-trimmed kerosene lamps; and this stench, combined with that of native tobacco, baked brick and dried earth, sends the heart of many a strong man down to his boots, for it is the smell of the Great Indian Empire when she turns herself for six months into a house of torment.

The temper induced by this sort of thing, when mixed up well with fever and finally flavoured with cholera *ad libitum*, is scarcely likely to be lamb-like. 'It's an insult to the intelligence of the Deity,' observes one of the sufferers, 'to pretend we're anything but tortured rebels.' Who shall be surprised, then, that when the tortured rebels go away for a holiday to 'the only existence in this desolate land worth the living', they are devotees of the gospel of eating, drinking, and being merry, for only too obvious reasons? At the bad times this same gospel leads to astonishing effects in the way of kindliness and self-sacrifice. A savage Stoicism holds all things cheap, even death. 'Bah! how these Christians funk death!' It is the grim and contemptuous jeer of the eternal heathen, whose heart says to him with a fraternal candour, 'Dust thou art, and to dust thou shalt return, and what on earth does it matter?' Yet what a depth of passion and emotion lies in these Stoics, and how paltry and factitious all other men seem beside them— children babbling of the moon or cowards sucking at their spiritual opium pipes to drug their 'funk' into 'faith'. Mr. Kipling loves his heathens with all his heart, and even the silliest of his 'fire-balloons' seeks not succour 'from on high' in the troubles and agonies of 'life's handicap'. As for his men, they have all more or less of the nature of the eternal barbarian, the atavistic impulse of ruthless action which lies so deeply and so ineradicably in almost all of us, under the thin veneer of our civilized refinement and 'good manners'. Speaking of his Dickie, he calls it the

go-fever, which is more real than many doctor's diseases, waking and raging, urging him, who loved Maisie beyond anything in the world, to go away and taste the old, hot, unregenerate life again—to scuffle, swear, gamble, and live light lives with his fellows; to take ship and know the sea once more, and by her beget pictures; to talk to Binat among the sands of Port Said, while Yellow Tina mixed the drinks. . . .

and so on. Very little respect or care has he, therefore, for those who shout to us perpetually: 'Great is the Respectability of the English people!' 'Oh, you rabbit hutches!' cries out Dickie, in the black hour of his poverty in London, 'do you know what you've got to do later on? You have to supply me with men-servants and maid-servants'— here he smacked his lips—'and the peculiar treasure of kings. Meantime I'll get clothes and boots, and presently I will return and trample on you.' Strange, passing strange, that in the throat of men who talk like this a lump should rise, 'be they by sea or by land', at the mystic formula which sums up the cult of the Sovereign who doesn't rule. Yet such, it appears, are we English, a 'peculiar people' in all conscience. Nor is even the saving grace of humour denied to our Anglo-Indian storyteller, to temper the foolisher aspects of that bilious and fiery jingoism of the devastated and terrible clime. The preface to *Life's*

Handicap is a delicious proof of this, and paragraphs, sentences and phrases, that have the true piquant flavour, are rarely to seek. Yet his touch is not by any means always certain. His false characterization has its parallel in false criticism, sometimes merely the smart super-ficialities of the imperfectly-educated journalist (to whom culture stands for nothing more than 'culchaw), at other times quite shocking tributes of respect and admiration to tenth-rate personages. Mr. Kipling knows little beyond modern English prose. The secret of the art and literature of the great Continental peoples is hid from him. He is too young, and he has lived too hard, not to be considerably in the dark about himself. The pose he prefers to take is that of the utmost smartness and cocksureness available. How else is one to ex-plain the insertion of work absolutely vile and detestable in his latest book? The *sacra fames auri* might explain such composition; but it is another thing in the full flood-tide of your vogue, with name, and fame, and fortune all at your hand, to write in this way of your work:

> The depth and dream of my desire,
>   The bitter paths wherein I stray,
> Thou knowest Who hast made the fire,
>   Thou knowest Who hast made the clay.

> One stone the more swings to her place
>   In that dread Temple of Thy worth—
> It is enough that thro' Thy grace
>   I saw nought common on Thy earth.

> Take not that vision from my ken;
>   Oh, whatso'er may spoil or speed,
> Help me to need no aid from men
>   That I may help such men as need!

to write like this, and then to present to us such unspeakably mediocre and wretched stuff as 'The Lang Men o' Larut' or 'Namgay Doola!' 'Under any circumstances, remember,' says the sagacious Dickie, in the character of the pictorial journalist in the heyday of his London vogue, 'four-fifths of everybody's work must be bad. But the remnant is worth the trouble for its own sake.' Very true: but is this any reason that a man who can give us such a splendid sample of storytelling as 'The Courting of Dinah Shadd', or touch the very spring of the *lacrimae rerum* in the piteous narrative of 'The Man who was', should proceed to inflict on us work which even the most sympathetic criticism can only designate as beneath contempt? Mr. Kipling asks too much of his most devoted admirers when he leaves them to try and justify the existence of 'Namgay Doola' and 'The Lang Men o' Larut', and even 'The Incarnation of Krishna Mulvaney'. Balzac could not afford to sign his name to such rubbish. For Mr. Rudyard Kipling to do so, is to send snakes to strangle his reputation in its cradle.

'In India,' he says, speaking in his proper person, 'you really see humanity—raw, brown, naked humanity—with nothing between it and the blazing sky, and only the used-up, over-handled earth under foot.' One of the results of the overwhelming nature of this fact is that, at any rate in any close consideration of the 'native feature' you are soon driven to take refuge in 'simpler theories' than those current among the benighted English home officials. Herein, of course, is the great difference between these and the Anglo-Indian officials. The latter have ever treated the native feature from the simpler theory point of view. Hence the stupendous success of our Indian administration as an administration from the days of Clive to those of Lord Lytton and onwards. Our sympathetic comprehension of the races we have ruled, our intimate knowledge and appreciation of their religious and social feelings; all this is due to the simpler theories of our Anglo-Indian officials, civil and military. The events of the year 1857 were the crowning proof of this. In that year we simplified even these simpler theories into the one simplest theory of all. 'We gave 'em hell' to an extent that they have never forgotten, and Mr. Kipling smiles cunningly over the still active native prejudice against being blown away from the mouths of cannons. The foolish person in search of a little disinterested information about things may find the so-called Indian Mutiny an unexplained historical phenomenon and eagerly hope for some enlightenment on the subject from a writer who is 'illustrating' the native feature. He will get little or none from Mr. Kipling. Firstly, he will find the scantiest mention or even allusion to the social movements of the natives. They are viewed merely as a huge mass of raw, brown, naked humanity to be manipulated by the civil and military officials for the arcane purposes of the Great Indian Empire, or by the inspired amateur detective (Strickland is Mr. Kipling's name for him) as material for his dexterous energy and sagacity, or by the male portion of the Anglo-Indians as a happy hunting-ground for more or less animating, if monotonous, sexual experiences 'without benefit of clergy'. We see the officials perpetually hustling the child-like natives about all over the country. We see Strickland or somebody else, not quite so clever perhaps, but still far too clever for child-like natives, perpetually exposing their villainies. We see rows of Anglo-Indian bachelors of all sorts (some the most commonplace sorts) inspiring dark-eyed little native girls with dog-like adorations.

There is in these narratives all the ability of the thoroughly good storyteller we know, here and there bits of excellent dialogue (the final scene in 'The Sending of Dana Da', for example), the same exquisite little descriptive cameos, the same rapid and piquant dogmatism—one has nothing less to praise here than in the tales of the 'military' feature, but unhappily also nothing more. Now and then vivid touches seem to bring us into contact with the peculiar and essential nature of the more active members of the alien races, and we realize for a moment something of the qualities in them which have made history; but how rare and partial such glimpses are! Thus Mr. Kipling shows us the Afghan Amir in his Court, and 'the long tail of feudal chiefs, men of blood, fed and cowed with blood'. But such things are not his game. It is the little personal experiences and the 'begetting of pictures' from the same that he is keen for. This is what interests and absorbs him. 'If I were Job ten times over,' says one of his characters in the most unnatural manner for the character, and in the most natural manner for Mr. Rudyard Kipling, 'I should be so interested in what was going to happen next that I'd stay in and watch'. And he makes his Mrs. Hauksbee repeat the sentiment. 'Colour, light, and motion,' he says elsewhere with his own voice, 'without which no man has much pleasure in living'. He loves the demonstrative instinct of the Oriental. 'You cannot explain things to the Oriental. You must show.' He has in him, too, the Oriental love of storytelling for its own sake; and even their superstition strikes a responsive chord in him. 'I have lived long enough in this India,' he says, 'to know that it is best to know nothing'. And on the force of this he mars a little masterpiece like 'The Courting of Dinah Shadd' with a large allowance of second-rate second-sight prediction, which is fulfilled to the letter. I cannot tell whether it is simply due to the benumbing chill of incredulity, but his deliberately supernatural tales, from 'The Phantom Rickshaw' downwards, impress me as distinct failures. On the other hand, when he deals in natural horror (take 'At the Pit's Mouth' as a sample, or 'The Other Man') I often find him a master.

But do not let me seem to strike with too great insistence the note of depreciation and disappointment. That would be to be unjust as well as ungracious. The best Mr. Kipling has to give, he gives, and the best of that best is veritably good, and what more should we ask of him? Nowhere in his more elaborate efforts to delineate child-life (and some of them are something rather like successes) does he give us so perfect a piece of work as the little child-idyll called 'The Story of Muhammad Din': nowhere does this gift of natural horror find more artistically harrowing expression than in 'The Gate of the Hundred Sorrows', or in 'Bubbling Well Road': nowhere does he paint the *ewig Weibliche* with a more liquid depth of simple love than in 'Lispeth' or 'Beyond the Pale'. And all of these are stories that illustrate the native feature.

There is one obvious quality in all literary work without which the name or fame of a writer has no possible chance of survival, and that is the literary quality. Its manifestations are many, far more diverse, indeed, than jejune critics like Matthew Arnold will admit. Arnold loved to quote a line of Sophocles above a line of Homer, a line of Dante below a line of Shakspeare, and to assure us that these were all perfect samples of 'style'. The fact is, that of style in the sense known to Sophocles or Milton, Shakspeare and Homer had little, and Dante had less. Shakspeare achieves his immortality through a verbal magic unequalled in the world's literature. No man ever created such lines and phrases. Dante (to take his case alone) achieves his immortality by something quite different—by a sheer and simple sincerity of outlook. He watches, and watches, and watches, till he sees things before him with an actuality that burns achingly into his sight, and what he sees he puts down simply—as he sees it; but style in the sense of Sophocles, verbal magic in the sense of Shakspeare, he has little or none of either.

Our business here is obviously with things on a smaller scale, but the same line of judgment must be held as with those of the largest. No one can claim for Mr. Kipling the possession of a real prose style, or, indeed, of anything approaching it. He cannot even, at least in this respect, for a moment be placed beside his French contemporaries and fellow storytellers—Maupassant and Bourget, let alone the great names of French and English prose. Such style, *qua* style, as he has is mere ephemeral and journalistic smartness, and he never begins to do good work till he has consciously forgotten all about it, and has set himself down to paint his 'pictures' or express his emotions as he best may. Neither has he that sheer and simple sincerity of outlook, that patient and relentless realism which (for example) lifts the best work of Zola so high. His youth and ardour, worked to white-heat by the Indian climate and his hard life, have intensified his individualism to such a pitch that he cannot get out of himself—cannot render anyone or anything objectively. The types he hates he caricatures, and mingles up men, and women, and children with puppets tricked out in semblance of the same, with a splendid want of discrimination. What side, then, of this precious, this indispensable quality does he possess as the 'Open, Sesame', of the years to come, where newspaper 'boomers' cease from troubling and serious workers are at rest? The reply can happily be given without much hesitation. Beyond all question (to put it in the particular form) he has the gift, both of the happy simile and of the happy phrase. 'You pass through big still deodar forests, and under big still cliffs, and over big still grass-downs swelling like a woman's breasts; and the wind across the grass, and the rain among the deodars says: "Hush—hush—hush." ' A touch of verbal trickery here, and Nature is rendered purely in the focus of the spectator's subjectivity, but how well she is rendered! Or, again:

A large, low moon turned the tops of the spear-grass to silver, and the stunted camelthorn-bushes and sour tamarisks into the likeness of trooping devils. The smell of the sun had not left the earth, and little aimless winds, blowing across the rose-gardens to the southward, brought the scent of dried roses and water.

He is almost as keen a connoisseur of scents and smells as M. Guy de Maupassant. He realizes their powers. Several such samples have been given already. Here are the Himalayas from the nasal point of view.

The monkeys sang sorrowfully to each other as they hunted for dry roots in the fern-wreathed trees, and the last puff of the day-wind brought from the unseen villages the scent of damp wood-smoke, hot cakes, dripping under-growth, and rotting pine-cones. That is the true smell of the Himalayas, and if once it creeps into the blood of a man, that man will, at the last, forgetting all else, return to the hills to die.

Admirable, indeed, are these little descriptive cameos, which he strews broadcast. Sometimes they are enclosed in two or three lines. 'The witchery of the dawn turned the grey river-reaches to purple, gold, and opal: and it was as though the lumbering barge crept across the splendour of a new Heaven.' Again he achieves the same result in one single perfect epithet. 'The drinking earth'—three words to describe the drought-laden Indian land under the heavy, unceasing downpour of the longed-for, welcome rains. 'Nothing save the spikes of the rain without and the smell of the drinking earth in my nostrils.' Verbal magic of this sort is of the poet: it is thrown out whole, so to say, not constructed. Or take this: 'There was nothing but grass everywhere, and it was impossible to see two yards in any direction. *The grass-stems held the heat exactly as boiler tubes do.*' No more: not another word. Oh, veritably in Art the part is ever greater than the whole. Naturally enough, when he deliberately sets himself down to exploit this supreme gift of his, he succeeds but moderately. 'The City of Dreadful Night' may be taken as a good example. It is excellent better-class journalism, and all the third-rate 'word-painters' are in raptures over it, but (alas!) it is not the third-rate, or the second-rate, or even the first-rate word painters who precisely know what they are talking about. Yet (alas! once more) for how much do they and their wrong-headed praise and undiscriminating enthusiasm count in the creation of vogues! Must a man ever owe three-fourths of his temporary success to his defects and limitations? Smartness and superficiality, Jingoism and aggressive cock-sureness, *rococo* fictional types and overloaded pseudo-prose, how much too much have these helped to make the name of our young Anglo-Indian storyteller familiar to the readers of the English-speaking race all over the earth!

Grant to him, however, as we surely must, the possession of verbal magic, of this striking aspect of our precious and indispensable literary quality, and add to it such gifts as have been enumerated in our short review of his work, and surely the case for taking it and its creator seriously has been clearly made out. On the other hand, we must not for a moment lose sight of the fact with which we started in our consideration of his claims to a permanent literary position. We are dealing with things on a scale which can only be called small, and his limitations, his aberrations are very real and very grave. The time is past when a writer of talent could win such a position, even for a generation, by the most nimble and vivid variations of a 'criticism of life' adapted to the use of the nursery or the schoolroom. Loud-tongued, fractious and numerous though it still is, the Noble Army of Blockheads no longer exercises that perfect tyranny it did fifteen or twenty years ago. It is yet able to dispense the loaves and fishes, but its judgments, overwhelming though they be for a short time, are being perpetually upset by the small, but ever-growing section of the public that begins in Art and Literature to know its right hand from its left. It will not be long before people come to tell Mr. Kipling that they are sick to death of his continual efforts to galvanize his most puppet-like puppets into the dreary semblance of life. 'No more

Mulvaney, Ortheris, and Learoyd, an you love us! No more Mrs. Hauksbee, and Strickland, and Mrs. What's-her-name. They are only visible and palpable object-lessons of your inability to create characters!' Such an inability at this present time, when characterization is being more and more recognized as the supreme gift of the writer and artist, is a vital matter. Then, again, although Mr. Kipling is young and full of vigour, what are we left to infer from the undeniable fact that the ascending force in his work is very slight? Nay, we might question its existence. His work has not gone on improving in his successive efforts. He has never excelled 'The Big Drunk Draf', or 'The Drums of the Fore and Aft', or 'At the Pit's Mouth', or 'Gemini', each in their special style, and these (if I do not mistake) are all from his earlier period. There is nothing in any degree better—shall I say there is nothing in any degree so good?—in the whole collection of stories gathered up in *Plain Tales from the Hills* and *Life's Handicap*. Any attempt to classify Mr. Kipling, to give him a place, and his true place, in our modern fiction would be premature. Hope (which, according to the Latin phrase, is 'the expectation of good') clings to this saving clause. But after his next book will this still be so? What should we make of another huge slice of the 'Incarnation of Krishna Mulvaney' style of thing, and 'Namgay Doola', and 'The Lang Men of Larut'?

But, once more, let me not seem to strike the unjust and ungracious note of depreciation and disappointment, especially at the close of my review. We should be thankful for what we have got; but, if we chiefly show our thankfulness by energetically asking for more, let us not fall under the suspicion of want of generosity. The case, we say, for taking Mr. Kipling seriously has surely been made out beyond cavil. His vogue may pass—it seems passing somewhat already—as all vogues pass; but, at least, we shall not be able to declare of it, as of so many of its fellows—and, indeed, of some which seem at this hour to stand above all such changes and chances—that it was won on such inadequate grounds that a total extinction and oblivion were, in mercy to the vileness of the English artistic taste, its most expedient as well as its worthiest fate. That can never be said of the man who could describe Anglo-Indian society as in 'At the Pit's Mouth', who could tell a story like 'The Courtship of Dinah Shadd', who could do a piece of such splendid analytical and dramatic work as 'The Drums of the Fore and Aft'.

21. Henry James's Introduction to *Mine Own People*

1891

Introduction to authorized collection of stories, five of which had been 'pirated' in *The Courting of Dinah Shadd* (1890) with 'A Biographical and Critical Sketch' by Andrew Lang (also 'pirated'). Issued in March 1891 by John W. Lovell Company of New York. James's 'Introduction' occupies pages [vii]–xxvi.

James wrote to his brother a few days later (6 February 1892) that 'Kipling strikes me personally as the most complete man of genius (as distinct from fine intelligence) that I have ever known'. But after 1900 he lost touch both with him and his work. (See above, No. 11.)

It would be difficult to answer the general question whether the books of the world grow, as they multiply, as much better as one might suppose they ought, with such a lesson on wasteful experiment spread perpetually behind them. There is no doubt, however, that in one direction we profit largely by this education: whether or no we have become wiser to fashion, we have certainly become keener to enjoy. We have acquired the sense of a particular quality which is precious beyond all others—so precious as to make us wonder where, at such a rate, our posterity will look for it, and how they will pay for it. After tasting many essences we find freshness the sweetest of all. We yearn for it, we watch for it and lie in wait for it, and when we catch it on the wing (it flits by so fast), we celebrate our capture with extravagance. We feel that after so much has come and gone it is more and more of a feat and a *tour de force* to be fresh. The tormenting part of the phenomenon is that, in any particular key, it can happen but once—by a sad failure of the law that inculcates the repetition of goodness. It is terribly a matter of accident; emulation and imitation have a fatal effect upon it. It is easy to see, therefore, what importance the epicure

159

may attach to the brief moment of its bloom. While that lasts we all are epicures.

This helps to explain, I think, the unmistakable intensity of the general relish for Mr. Rudyard Kipling. His bloom lasts, from month to month, almost surprisingly—by which I mean that he has not worn out even by active exercise the particular property that made us all, more than a year ago, so precipitately drop everything else to attend to him. He has many others which he will doubtless always keep; but a part of the potency attaching to his freshness, what makes it as exciting as a drawing of lots, is our instinctive conviction that he cannot, in the nature of things, keep that; so that our enjoyment of him, so long as the miracle is still wrought, has both the charm of confidence and the charm of suspense. And then there is the further charm, with Mr. Kipling, that this same freshness is such a very strange affair of its kind—so mixed and various and cynical, and, in certain lights, so contradictory of itself. The extreme recentness of his inspiration is as enviable as the tale is startling that his productions tell of his being at home, domesticated and initiated, in this wicked and weary world. At times he strikes us as shockingly precocious, at others as serenely wise. On the whole, he presents himself as a strangely clever youth who has stolen the formidable mask of maturity and rushes about making people jump with the deep sounds, the sportive exaggerations of tone, that issue from its painted lips. He has this mark of a real vocation, that different spectators may like him—must like him, I should almost say—for different things: and this refinement of attraction, that to those who reflect even upon their pleasures he has as much to say as to those who never reflect upon anything. Indeed there is a certain amount of room for surprise in the fact that, being so much the sort of figure that the hardened critic likes to meet, he should also be the sort of figure that inspires the multitude with confidence—for a complicated air is, in general, the last thing that does this.

By the critic who likes to meet such a bristling adventurer as Mr. Kipling I mean of course the critic for whom the happy accident of character, whatever form it may take, is more of a bribe to interest than the promise of some character cherished in theory—the appearance of justifying some foregone conclusion as to what a writer or a book 'ought', in the Ruskinian sense, to be: the critic in a word, who has, *a priori*, no rule for a literary production but that it shall have genuine life. Such a critic (he gets much more out of his opportunities, I think, than the other sort) likes a writer exactly in proportion as he is a challenge, an appeal to interpretation, intelligence, ingenuity, to what is elastic in the critical mind—in proportion indeed as he may be a negation of things familiar and taken for granted. He feels in this case how much more play and sensation there is for himself.

Mr. Kipling, then, has the character that furnishes plenty of play and of vicarious experience—that makes any perceptive reader foresee a rare luxury. He has the great merit of being a compact and convenient illustration of the surest source of interest in any painter of life—that of having an identity as marked as a window-frame. He is one of the illustrations, taken near at hand, that help to clear up the vexed question, in the novel or the tale, of kinds, camps, schools, distinctions, the right way and the wrong way; so very positively does he contribute to the showing that there are just as many kinds, as many ways, as many forms and degrees of the 'right', as there are personal points of view. It is the blessing of the art he practises that it is made up of experience conditioned, infinitely, in this personal way—the sum of the feeling of life as reproduced by innumerable natures; natures that feel through all their differences, testify through their diversities. These differences, which make the identity, are of the individual; they form the channel by which life flows through him, and how much he is able to give us of life—in other words, how much he appeals to us—depends on whether they form it solidly.

This hardness of the conduit, cemented with a rare assurance, is perhaps the most striking idiosyncrasy of Mr. Kipling; and what makes it more remarkable is that accident of his extreme youth which, if we talk about him at all, we cannot affect to ignore. I cannot pretend to give a biography or a chronology of the author of *Soldiers Three*, but I cannot overlook the general, the importunate fact that, confidently as he has caught the trick and habit of this sophisticated world, he has not been long of it. His extreme youth is indeed what I may call his window-bar—the support on which he somewhat rowdily leans while he looks down at the human scene with his pipe in his teeth; just as his other conditions (to mention only some of them), are his prodigious facility, which is only less remarkable than his stiff selection; his unabashed temperament, his flexible talent, his smoking-room manner, his familiar friendship with India—established so rapidly, and so completely under his control; his delight in battle, his 'cheek' about women—and indeed about men and about everything; his determination not to be duped, his 'imperial' fibre, his love of the inside view, the private soldier and the primitive man. I must add further to this

list of attractions the remarkable way in which he makes us aware that
he has been put up to the whole thing directly by life (miraculously,
in his teens), and not by the communications of others. These elements,
and many more, constitute a singularly robust little literary character
(our use of the diminutive is altogether a note of endearment and enjoyment), which, if it has the rattle of high spirits and is in no degree
apologetic or shrinking, yet offers a very liberal pledge in the way
of good faith and immediate performance. Mr. Kipling's performance
comes off before the more circumspect have time to decide whether
they like him or not, and if you have seen it once you will be sure to
return to the show. He makes us prick up our ears to the good news
that in the smoking-room too there may be artists; and indeed to an
intimation still more refined—that the latest development of the
modern also may be, most successfully, for the canny artist to put his
victim off the guard by imitating the amateur (superficially, of course)
to the life.

These, then, are some of the reasons why Mr. Kipling may be dear
to the analyst as well as, M. Renan says, to the simple. The simple
may like him because he is wonderful about India, and India has not
been 'done'; while there is plenty left for the morbid reader in the
surprise of his skill and the *fioriture* of his form, which are so oddly
independent of any distinctively literary note in him, any bookish
association. It is as one of the morbid that the writer of these remarks
(which doubtless only too shamefully betray his character) exposes
himself as most consentingly under the spell. The freshness arising
from a subject that—by a good fortune I do not mean to under-
estimate—has never been 'done', is after all less of an affair to build
upon than the freshness residing in the temper of the artist. Happy
indeed is Mr. Kipling, who can command so much of both kinds.
It is still as one of the morbid, no doubt—that is, as one of those who
are capable of sitting up all night for a new impression of talent, of
scouring the trodden field for one little spot of green—that I find our
young author quite most curious in his air, and not only in his air but
in his evidently very real sense, of knowing his way about life. Curious
in the highest degree and well worth attention is such an idiosyncrasy
as this in a young Anglo-Saxon. We meet it with familiar frequency
in the budding talents of France, and it startles and haunts us for an
hour. After an hour, however, the mystery is apt to fade, for we find
that the wondrous initiation is not in the least general, is only exceedingly special, and is, even with this limitation, very often rather

conventional. In a word, it is with the ladies that the young Frenchman takes his ease, and more particularly with ladies selected expressly to make this attitude convincing. When *they* have let him off, the dimnesses too often encompass him. But for Mr. Kipling there are no dimnesses anywhere, and if the ladies are indeed violently distinct they are only strong notes in a universal loudness. This loudness fills the ears of Mr. Kipling's admirers (it lacks sweetness, no doubt, for those who are not of the number), and there is really only one strain that is absent from it—the voice, as it were, of the civilised man; in whom I of course also include the civilised woman. But this is an element that for the present one does not miss—every other note is so articulate and direct.

It is a part of the satisfaction the author gives us that he can make us speculate as to whether he will be able to complete his picture alto-gether (this is as far as we presume to go in meddling with the question of his future) without bringing in the complicated soul. On the day he does so, if he handles it with anything like the cleverness he has already shown, the expectation of his friends will take a great bound. Meanwhile, at any rate, we have Mulvaney, and Mulvaney is after all tolerably complicated. He is only a six-foot saturated Irish private, but he is a considerable pledge of more to come. Hasn't he, for that matter, the tongue of a hoarse syren, and hasn't he also mysteries and infini-tudes almost Carlylesc? Since I am speaking of him I may as well say that, as an evocation, he has probably led captive those of Mr. Kipling's readers who have most given up resistance. He is a piece of portraiture of the largest, vividest kind, growing and growing on the painter's hands without ever outgrowing them. I can't help regarding him, in a certain sense, as Mr. Kipling's tutelary deity—a landmark in the direction in which it is open to him to look furthest. If the author will only go as far in this direction as Mulvaney is capable of taking him (and the inimitable Irishman is, like Voltaire's Habakkuk, *capable de tout*), he may still discover a treasure and find a reward for the services he has rendered the winner of Dinah Shadd. I hasten to add that the truly appreciative reader should surely have no quarrel with the primitive element in Mr. Kipling's subject-matter, or with what, for want of a better name, I may call his love of low life. What is that but essentially a part of his freshness? And for what part of his fresh-ness are we exactly more thankful than for just this smart jostle that he gives the old stupid superstition that the amiability of a storyteller is the amiability of the people he represents—that their vulgarity, or depravity, or gentility, or fatuity are tantamount to the same qualities in the painter himself? A blow from which, apparently, it will not easily recover is dealt this infantine philosophy by Mr. Howells when, with the most distinguished dexterity and all the detachment of a master, he handles some of the clumsiest, crudest, most human things in life—answering surely thereby the playgoers in the sixpenny gallery who howl at the representative of the villain when he comes before the curtain.

Nothing is more refreshing than this active, disinterested sense of the real; it is doubtless the quality for the want of more of which our English and American fiction has turned so woefully stale. We are ridden by the old conventionalities of type and small proprieties of observance—by the foolish baby-formula (to put it sketchily) of the picture and the subject. Mr. Kipling has all the air of being disposed to lift the whole business off the nursery carpet, and of being perhaps even more affable than he is disposed. One must hasten of course to parenthesise that there is not, intrinsically, a bit more luminosity in treating of low life and of primitive man than of those whom civi-lisation has kneaded to a finer paste: the only luminosity in either case is in the intelligence with which the thing is done. But it so happens that, among ourselves, the frank, capable outlook, when turned upon the vulgar majority, the coarse, receding edges of the social perspective, borrows a charm from being new; such a charm as, for instance, repetition has already despoiled it of among the French—the hapless French who pay the penalty as well as enjoy the glow of living in-tellectually so much faster than we. It is the most inexorable part of our fate that we grow tired of everything, and of course in due time we may grow tired even of what explorers shall come back to tell us about the great grimy condition, or with unprecedented items and details, about the grey middle state which darkens into it. But the explorers, bless them! may have a long day before that; it is early to trouble about reactions, so that we must give them the benefit of every presumption. We are thankful for any boldness and any sharp curiosity, and that is why we are thankful for Mr. Kipling's general spirit and for most of his excursions.

Many of these, certainly, are into a region not to be designated as superficially dim, though indeed the author always reminds us that India is above all the land of mystery. A large part of his high spirits, and of ours, comes doubtless from the amusement of such vivid, heterogeneous material, from the irresistible magic of scorching suns, subject empires, uncanny religions, uneasy garrisons and smothered-up women—from heat and colour and danger and dust. India is a portentous image, and we are duly awed by the familiarities it undergoes at Mr. Kipling's hands and by the fine impunity, the sort of fortune that favours the brave, of *his* want of awe. An abject humility is not his strong point, but he gives us something instead of it—vividness and drollery, the vision and the thrill of many things, the misery and strangeness of most, the personal sense of a hundred queer contacts and risks. And then in the absence of respect he has plenty of knowledge, and if knowledge should fail him he would have plenty of invention. Moreover, if invention should ever fail him, he would still have the lyric string and the patriotic chord, on which he plays admirably; so that it may be said he is a man of resources. What he gives us, above all, is the feeling of the English manner and the English blood in conditions they have made at once so much and so little their own; with manifestations grotesque enough in some of his satiric sketches and deeply impressive in some of his anecdotes of individual responsibility.

His Indian impressions divide themselves into three groups, one of which, I think, very much outshines the others. First to be mentioned are the tales of native life, curious glimpses of custom and superstition, dusky matters not beholden of the many, for which the author has a remarkable flair. Then comes the social, the Anglo-Indian episode, the study of administration and military types and of the wonderful rattling, riding ladies who, at Simla and more desperate stations, look out for husbands and lovers; often, it would seem, the husbands and lovers of others. The most brilliant group is devoted wholly to the common soldier, and of this series it appears to me that too much good is hardly to be said. Here Mr. Kipling, with all his offhandedness, is a master; for we are held not so much by the greater or less oddity of the particular yarn—sometimes it is scarcely a yarn at all, but something much less artificial—as by the robust attitude of the narrator, who never arranges or glosses or falsifies, but makes straight for the common and the characteristic. I have mentioned the great esteem in which I hold Mulvaney—surely a charming man and one qualified to adorn a higher sphere. Mulvaney is a creation to be proud of, and his two comrades stand as firm on their legs. In spite of Mulvaney's social possibilities they are all three finished brutes; but it is precisely in the finish that we delight. Whatever Mr. Kipling may relate about them for ever will encounter readers equally fascinated and unable fully to justify their faith.

Are not those literary pleasures after all the most intense which are the most perverse and whimsical, and even indefensible? There is a logic in them somewhere, but it often lies below the plummet of criticism. The spell may be weak in a writer who has every reasonable and regular claim, and it may be irresistible in one who presents himself with a style corresponding to a bad hat. A good hat is better than a bad one, but a conjurer may wear either. Many a reader will never be able to say what secret human force lays its hand upon him when Private Ortheris, having sworn 'quietly into the blue sky', goes mad with home-sickness by the yellow river and raves for the basest sights and sounds of London. I can scarcely tell why I think 'The Courting of Dinah Shadd' a masterpiece (though, indeed, I can make a shrewd guess at one of the reasons), nor would it be worth while perhaps to attempt to defend the same pretension in regard to 'On Greenhow Hill'—much less to trouble the tolerant reader of these remarks with a statement of how many more performances in the nature of 'The End of the Passage' (quite admitting even that they might not represent Mr. Kipling at his best), I am conscious of a latent relish for. One might as well admit while one is about it that one has wept profusely over 'The Drums of the Fore and Aft', the history of the 'Dutch courage' of two dreadful dirty little boys, who, in the face of Afghans scarcely more dreadful, saved the reputation of their regiment and perished, the least mawkishly in the world, in a squalor of battle incomparably expressed. People who know how peaceful they are themselves and have no bloodshed to reproach themselves with needn't scruple to mention the glamour that Mr. Kipling's intense militarism has for them and how astonishingly contagious they find it, in spite of the unromantic complexion of it—the way it bristles with all sorts of uglinesses and technicalities. Perhaps that is why I go all the way even with *The Gadsbys*—the Gadsbys were so connected (uncomfortably it is true) with the Army. There is fearful fighting—or a fearful danger of it—in 'The Man who would be King': is that the reason we are deeply affected by this extraordinary tale? It is one of them, doubtless, for Mr. Kipling has many reasons, after all, on his side, though they don't equally call aloud to be uttered.

One more of them, at any rate, I must add to these unsystematised remarks—it is the one I spoke of a shrewd guess at in alluding to 'The Courting of Dinah Shadd'. The talent that produces such a tale is a talent eminently in harmony with the short story, and the short story is, on our side of the Channel and of the Atlantic, a mine which will take a great deal of working. Admirable is the clearness with which Mr. Kipling perceives this—perceives what innumerable chances it gives, chances of touching life in a thousand different places, taking it up in innumerable pieces, each a specimen and an illustration. In a word, he appreciates the episode, and there are signs to show that this shrewdness will, in general, have long innings. It will find the detachable, compressible 'case' an admirable, flexible form; the cultivation of which may well add to the mistrust already entertained by Mr. Kipling, if his manner does not betray him, for what is clumsy and tasteless in the time-honoured practice of the 'plot'. It will fortify him in the conviction that the vivid picture has a greater communicative value than the Chinese puzzle. There is little enough plot in such a perfect little piece of hard representation as 'The End of the Passage', to cite again only the most salient of twenty examples.

But I am speaking of our author's future, which is the luxury that I meant to forbid myself—precisely because the subject is so tempting. There is nothing in the world (for the prophet) so charming as to prophesy, and as there is nothing so inconclusive the tendency should be repressed in proportion as the opportunity is good. There is a certain want of courtesy to a peculiarly contemporaneous present even in speculating, with a dozen deferential precautions, on the question of what will become in the later hours of the day of a talent that has got up so early. Mr. Kipling's actual performance is like a tremendous walk before breakfast, making one welcome the idea of the meal, but consider with some alarm the hours still to be traversed. Yet if his breakfast is all to come the indications are that he will be more active than ever after he has had it. Among these indications are the unflagging character of his pace and the excellent form, as they say in athletic circles, in which he gets over the ground. We don't detect him stumbling; on the contrary, he steps out quite as briskly as at first and still more firmly. There is something zealous and craftsman-like in him which shows that he feels both joy and responsibility. A whimsical, wanton reader, haunted by a recollection of all the good things he has seen spoiled; by a sense of the miserable, or, at any rate, the inferior, in so many continuations and endings, is almost capable of perverting poetic justice to the idea that it would be even positively well for so surprising a producer to remain simply the fortunate, suggestive, unconfirmed and unqualified representative of what he has actually done. We can always refer to that.

22. An Open Letter to Rudyard Kipling

1892

From *Letters to Eminent Hands* (1892), pp. 56–61. The book (suggested by Andrew Lang's *Letters to Dead Authors*, 1886) was published over the pseudonym '*i*' [iota], but was later acknowledged by its author. Other living authors addressed included Hardy, George Moore, R. L. Stevenson, Lang, Anstey, Bret Harte, etc.

Gleeson White (1851–1898) was best known as an art critic, his publications including *English Illustration* (1897) and *Master Painters of Britain*, 4 vols. (1897–8). He also edited *Ballads and Rondeaux* (1887), *The Pageant* (1896–7) and other volumes notable in the nineties.

TO RUDYARD KIPLING, ESQ.

Sir,

What is to hinder your fame being 'dispershed most notoriously in sev'ril volumes'? Today under the novel spell of your genius we are all in the uncritical stage of hero-worship. First came the rumour of another new genius 'from the East', after the manner of creeds from time immemorial; next, during a period of ignorant but vicious antagonism, and an inward resolve to stand upon one's dignity, refusing to accept a new genius at any man's bidding, we read a chance thing of yours, and were still more decided to keep a firm attitude of neutrality. Then, alas for our consistency, came *Departmental Ditties*, *Plain Tales from the Hills*, and so on to *Life's Handicap*, compelling an abject down-climb and complete surrender; since when, we have delighted to pass on the badge of servitude to the unenlightened, and be your most obedient and humble servants.

Having thus become converts, it was curious to find 'Cheop's Pyramid' familiar; and it would be interesting to ask how many of its present admirers remember it quoted as from a pamphlet 'in the shape of an official paper, the envelope is the cover', in *The Sign of the Ship*, October 1886. The Indian *vers de société*, by the modest author who did not give his name, were then formally introduced to London, as any doubter may see by reference to his set of *Longman's Magazine*, if he be wise enough to bind those pleasant monthly gossips of men and books.

Now while a nation is grovelling at your feet, will you display an English contempt towards such servile adulation, or the kindly forbearance with a tinge of deeper brotherhood that, we fancy, underlies all your cynicism? For you write of 'niggers' and children with a loving pen—not sentimentally, nor patronisingly, but with the manlier tone of kinship with the least of these, that whined as it may be by specious hypocrites, is yet the noblest truth of our common life.

The gods be thanked that although you are popular you have humour. Can it be that the British public is awakening to that salt of life? After periods of theological meanderings and savage blood-letting, it is good to think that Bret Harte is yet a power and that you are becoming one. On every side, if you look hard for it—in spite of 'fads' and comic papers, in spite of burlesques at the theatres and comic songs—there appears to be a streak of humour lightening the dull grey sky. We have had a serious epoch—gloomy in literature, gloomy in art and in its professionally comic element gloomier than words may say. Is it passing away? Dickens roused the nation to its last hearty laugh. Du Maurier has made us smile; Gilbert has delighted a comparative few; but the whole mass of English people still affect to believe *Ally Sloper* a comic person, instead of a tragedian of some rude power. Ouïda is powerful; but Miss Rhoda Broughton's humour nearly lost her respectability. To be cynical, even though you have humour—as Mr. Lang for instance—is pardoned: to be humorous without much cynicism is not, or was not until lately, permissible. Heaps of people voted *Vice Versa* a dull book. There are those who fail to find the *Bab Ballads* funny, or Mr. Anstey's *Burglar Bill* an uproariously amusing collection. But from the cliques who believe in such things, and the crowd who are—so we hope—about to welcome you, it may be that the English lack of humour will be a reproach out of date soon, and that *Merry England* will no longer indicate an excellent but somewhat obscure magazine, but be a worthy term to apply to our great empire, which knows no sunset and has no name.

To have made India a real place to dwellers in Great Britain is in itself an imperial conquest. *Mr. Isaacs*,[1] *The Dilemma*,[2] and a few other novels awoke English stay-at-homes to the fact that there was an English society in India. Mr. Phil Robinson[3] added the beasts and birds; and now you have thrown in the rank and file of the British Army and a few million natives to complete our mental picture of the great empire that was not officially recognised in *Whitaker's Almanac* as a part of the British Crown until recent years, and is still to most people but an excuse for a party cry, or a useful place to acquire enlarged livers and reduced pensions.

From America comes news of a 'Rudyard Kipling' Society for the study of your works. Philadelphia claims the honour of this somewhat premature attempt to exploit you. Personal paragraphs full of charming detail are already showing the brilliant invention of the Western boys. Will you find them as charming as the dusky Eastern ones, or will you return to the Orient disgusted with our commonplace lot? Yet Anglo-Indian colonels, who proffer much detail of your early life unasked, spin a yarn as colourless and respectable as though you were a person of no genius whatever, and had never lived in a place 'where the best is like the worst—where there aren't no Ten Commandments, an' a man can raise a thirst'.

It is to be hoped that, cleverly as you depict society and its foibles and keenly conscious as you are that even its puppets are men and women with passions, it will not monopolise your pen. The hand that sketched *Soldiers Three* and *Black and White* can do greater work. The studies of native life collected under various titles have importance far beyond their relative size. 'Without Benefit of Clergy', 'The Man who Was', and a dozen others are each told in few pages, and yet fill a space on the shelves of the real library we carry with us wherever we go, entirely beyond the whole series of volumes by many quite respectable authors. 'Danny Deever' alone is a masterpiece hard to parallel. 'Rizpah' with all its grim horror affects us less strongly, for the humour of 'Danny Deever' adds awful force to the tragedy so wonderfully told. Like a clever impressionist your aim is for colour, air and light, with the supreme moment only. Your art is modern in its breadth and classical in its restraint. No words are too mean or common for you to use, but you employ them with the vivid, direct power that is itself proof of mastery. Only those who grope for *the* word, and,

---

[1] [1882. By F. Marion Crawford]
[2] [1876. By Sir George Chesney]
[3] [*In My Indian Garden*, 1878]

failing, have to make shift with a possible synonym, can realise the delight of finding a writer who knows his trade, can handle his tools deftly, and is aware of the enormous wealth of material at hand in the vernacular of the masses hitherto deemed undignified for literary uses.

You show that hybrid monstrosities, Latinised polysyllables or scientific terminology dragged from its lawful place are none of them required to make good honest English. The power of making colloquial prose telling and yet understanded of the people is an enviable gift, and you possess it; and for it we ought all—yourself as well as ourselves—to thank the gods and pray that the example may not be in vain.

You have the daring of youth with the knowledge that comes later. It has been said there was never a 'prodigy' in painting, and rarely in literature; but you are not far off becoming an example of the latter. You dare also to be frank and nearly raise the blush to Mrs. Grundy's cheek. 'The Taking of Lungtungpen', for instance, is a shock to her 'dasincy' as much as to 'Lift'nint Brazenose'. We recall Marryat's open-air humour, or the breezy animal spirits of Fielding and Smollett when such pages appear, and long more than ever for a unanimous and vigorous protest against the societies for the suggestion of pruriency that weigh us down.

The large virtue of Purity we all prize, but the small vice of Prudery should be shocked to death; and there are not wanting signs that you may help to do it. There are many pages of Indian life and manners, no doubt familiar to you, that would terrify a respectable Philistine to hear. Although we are so used to condoning English vices, we have still a shudder left for alien ones; and if it is not within your programme to revive our code of morality, a study of Eastern manners is a good tonic to spur our jaded sensibility to call right and wrong by their proper names, and not confound sins against society with sins against natural morality.

But here creeps in the cant of the day, and all unwittingly you are requested to be a moralist with a mission. For this—ten thousand pardons—the parochial influences will tell after years spent under their sway. The didactic moralising called art criticism, and the sermons in stones, parables in paint, and homilies in marble we have been taught to expect have naturally dulled our love of Art; and cause us even now to forget that in an artist we have no more right to look for a reformer of society than to expect a bishop, say, to know aught of art. If they both chance to stray into the domains of the other, it is, as a rule, the worse for their own kingdoms. So, forbearing all hope that you will do much to convert us, let us thank you for amusing us, for awakening our sense of humour to a new response and touching our hearts in a way not perilous to true manly dignity; and above all for the creation of the undying *Soldiers Three*, and the budget of songs worthy of such heroes. To have spurred the money-grubbing apathy of this prosaic generation to show new interest in its fighting-men is a supreme achievement; for if in the course of events we have suddenly to fight for the honour and existence of Old England as a nation, the spirit aroused in raw recruits by your rollicking songs might be worth more than the addition of a million mercenaries to our little army, and prove, even as the 'Marseillaise' or the 'Watch by the Rhine' has shown before, the overwhelming power of a war-cry that touches the hearts and nerves the sinews of those in battle. Such sentiments as those expressed in 'The Drums of the Fore and Aft', or 'the Young British Soldier'—

> When you're wounded and left on Afghanistan's plains,
> An' the women come out to cut up your remains,
> Just roll to your rifle, an' blow out your brains,
> And go to your Gawd like a soldier—

are worth all the excellent leaflets on temperance, all the plaintive stories of the Hedley Vicars type—nay, may even be more powerful than the graphic summary of the life of a Havelock, in evoking the simple obedience and pagan stoicism which are worth as much today as ever they were in the stern prose of warfare.

From Rudyard Kipling as a writer of short stories to the same author as the saviour of an empire is a far cry; yet precedents exist to show that such a forecast however improbable can hardly be deemed impossible. But whether you become a mythological entity or remain merely a first-rate storyteller, matters little; the love you have won from British hearts is hardly a passing fancy, but a good life-long devotion that will stick to you, and possibly bore you with its indiscriminating laudation for many a long year.

23. Letters from Lafcadio Hearn
1892–8

Extracts quoted from *The Life and Letters of Lafcadio Hearn* (1906) by Elizabeth Bisland.

Lafcadio Hearn (1850–1904), half English and half Greek, was the well-known writer on Japan who married a Japanese girl, took Japanese nationality, and became Professor of English Literature at Tokyo University.

---

1. From Lafcadio Hearn to Ellwood Hendrick: April 1892: '. . . I hate the Jesuit; but he has a particular cleverness of his own indeed. I hate him first because he is insincere, as you suggest; then I hate him because he is morbid, with a priestly morbidness—sickly, cynical, unhealthy. I like Kipling's morbidness, which is manly and full of enormous resolve and defiance in the teeth of God and hell and nature.'
2. From Lafcadio Hearn to Ellwood Hendrick: January 1895: '. . . Kipling is priceless—the single story of Puran Bhagat is worth a kingdom; and the suggestive moral of human life is such a miracle! I can't tell you what pleasure it gave me.'
3. From Lafcadio Hearn to Ellwood Hendrick: February 1897: '. . . Oh! have you ever read those two marvellous things of Kipling's last—"McAndrews' Hymn", and "The Mary Gloster"? Especially the "Mary Gloster"! I have no more qualified ideas about Kipling. He is to my fixed conviction the greatest of living English poets, and greater than all before him in the line he has taken. As for England, he is her modern Saga-man—skald, scôp, whatever you like; lineal descendants of those fellows to whom the Berserker used to say: "Now you just stand right here, and see us fight so that you can make a song about it." '
4. From Lafcadio Hearn to Mitchell McDonald: December 1898: '. . . Ah! I had almost forgotten. I *have* Kipling's "Day's Work" already. It is great—very great. Don't mistake him, even if he seems too colloquial at times. He is the greatest living English poet and English storyteller. Never in this world will I be able to write one page to compare with a page of his. He makes me feel so small, that after reading him I wonder why I am such an ass as to write at all.'

24. Quiller-Couch on Kipling's Verse

1893

From signed article 'Reviews and Reminders. II. On Some Living English Poets' (review of *Barrack-Room Ballads* and eight other volumes of contemporary verse) in the *English Illustrated Magazine*, Vol. X, No. 120, pp. 901-3 (September 1893).

Sir Arthur T. Quiller-Couch (1863–1944), scholar, novelist, appointed Professor of English Literature at Cambridge in 1912. 'Q' lived by his fiction and by journalism until he received the chair at Cambridge, but had already edited *The Oxford Book of English Verse* and contributed literary *causeries* and reviews to the *Pall Mall Magazine* ('From a Cornish Window') and *The Speaker* for periods of several years. He is best remembered for his Cambridge lectures of later years.

. . . 'Is English Poetry Dead?' Well here, in the first place comes Mr. William Ernest Henley, who has truculence enough at any rate to answer that question in Captain Timothy Edward's fashion; and here also comes Mr. Rudyard Kipling to supply plenty more in the very unlikely case of Mr. Henley's running short. I put these two writers together for the moment because their work (in verse) though very different in method and texture, has certain points of resemblance too salient to be ignored. The sudden growth of Mr. Henley's influence among young writers both of verse and prose strikes me as about the most remarkable phenomenon in the recent history of English letters. I believe (though I speak without precise knowledge) that it may be said to date from the summer of 1888, when his *A Book of Verse* was published by Mr. David Nutt. This little volume sounded a clear challenge. Its temper no less than its unusual handling of rhythm bespoke the innovator. And this challenge Mr. Henley repeated in 1890 with his *Views and Reviews*—and again last year with his *Song of the Sword and other Verses*. But the secret of Mr. Henley's influence has been his editorship of the *National* (late the *Scots'*) *Observer*. He stepped into this post at a time when many were disposed to shake their heads over his future and prophesy that his fine stream of originality, missing its proper channel, would waste itself in the sands. But in the nick of time —though he is perhaps too stout to admit this—came the right kind of opportunity; a captaincy for a born fighter and leader of men.

He can count many young men of talent within the circle of his influence, and one at least of genius. For good or ill that was an important day for Mr. Rudyard Kipling when he and Mr. Henley met; and as a poet one must allow that at present he seems immeasurably the better for it. Others may find more than facile vulgarity in *Departmental Ditties*. Having searched once and twice, I do not; save only in the penultimate poem 'The Galley-Slave', which really gave some promise of the splendid work to come. For the *Barrack Room* volume does indeed contain verse for which 'splendid' is the only term—so radiantly it glitters with incrustations of barbaric words. It has genius in it, of course, in the grim effectiveness (for instance) of 'Danny Deever':

[quotes DV. p. 398 (last stanza)]

and in the simple solemnity of the refrain

> Ford, ford, ford o'Kabul river.
> Ford o'Kabul river in the dark!

in every line of 'East and West'—in almost every line of 'The English Flag', and throughout in the stirring 'Envoi', a poem that takes you by the heart and shakes you. But the first reflection to which this volume gives rise is that which Mr. Henley once made upon Dickens. 'He developed into an artist in words . . . but his development was his own work, and it is a fact that should redound eternally to his honour that he began in newspaper English . . . and went on to become an exemplar.' Mr. Kipling suffers and must suffer, the penalty which awaits every writer who wins renown in youth and has henceforward to develop under the public's eye. Because he has originality he will be continually making experiments in his art; and whenever an experiment fails a dozen critics will arise in their seats and announce that this young author is deteriorating. 'Thus and thus,' they say, 'is poetry written'—

> Thus Gods are made
> And who so makes them otherwise shall die.

We may take comfort in the thought that Mr. Kipling is the last man in the world to listen to them.

To set forth, as only art can, the beauty and the joy of living, the beauty and the blessedness of death, the glory of battle and adventure, the nobility of devotion—to a cause, an ideal, a passion even—the dignity, of resistance, the sacred quality of patriotism.

This was Mr. Henley's ambition, as he declares, when he selected and arranged the other day that capital book of verse for boys *Lyra Heroica*; and this, too, would seem to be the aim of his own poetry. It may stand as his artistic creed—his and Mr. Kipling's. But while Mr. Kipling assails us with simple and even vulgar metres and dazzling crudities of speech, Mr. Henley's versification is learned and elaborate, and his language charged with literary feeling. The *Barrack Room Ballads* are just doggerel in apotheosis, doggerel lifted out of its sphere by a touch of genius. *The London Voluntaries* are ripe and well-considered achievements in rhythm. Each poet loves the highly coloured word; but the word which Mr. Henley selects has taken its colour from a score of literary reminiscences . . . Mr. Henley loves life for the romance in it, and has a beautiful word for its romantic associations. Mr. Kipling finds the East enchanting, for instance, by right of having been born there; Mr. Henley by right of having made acquaintance with it in the pages of the *Arabian Nights Entertainments* . . .

[After two more paragraphs on Henley, 'Q' goes on to review volumes by Norman Gale, George Meredith, Richard Le Gallienne, Arthur Symons, James Dryden Hosken, William Watson (three collections) and T. E. Brown.]

25. George Saintsbury on *Many Inventions*

1893

Review from unidentified periodical, reprinted in *A Last Vintage: Essays and Papers by George Saintsbury* (1950), pp. 178–9.

George Saintsbury (1845–1933), after twenty years of journalism, succeeded David Masson as Professor of Rhetoric and English Literature at Edinburgh University from 1895 to 1915. He is remembered for his many scholarly and critical works such as *A Short History of English Literature* (1898), *A History of English Prosody* (1906–21), *A History of English Criticism* (1911) and *The Peace of the Augustans* (1916). His only Dedication was of *Notes on a Cellar Book* (1920) to Kipling, in which he regretted that he had never had the chance of reviewing any of his books—obviously forgetting this short, early estimate.

Many Inventions is not only good, but very good. I am inclined to think it, using words carefully, the best volume that Mr. Kipling has done. It is, of course, unequal; nobody could write fourteen different tales of the widest range of subject and style and not be unequal. Of course one reader will like this better than that, and another that better than this. The stories draw nigh with fitful success to that 'True Romance' which Mr. Kipling has celebrated, in verse as heartfelt if not quite as finished as he has ever written, at the beginning of the book, and has not extolled too much. For what is romance but creation? and what is creation if not divine? As for the separate stories, I confess to being in something like the frame of mind of Miss Snevellicci's papa—'I love 'em every one,' but as a person of taste must speak with graduated affection, I think I like 'My Lord the Elephant' most as a whole, and 'The Children of the Zodiac' least. The 'Finest Story in the World' which is itself a legend of metempsychosis, has affected me in a very strange fashion, for it seems to me that (in another state of existence, of course) I heard Mr. Kipling tell it, and tell it better than here. 'His

Private Honour' is the noblest and most complete; the conclusion of
'Love o' Women' (which seems to me as a whole to suffer from ups
and downs) is the most passionate and accomplished, I am too much of
a Jingo to be quite a fair judge of 'Judson and the Empire' or 'A Conference of Powers', but it is to me a blessed thing to think that Mr.
Kipling, like Kingsley before him, will breed up Jingos by the thousand. *Badalia Herodsfoot,* though excellent, has been done better before
by Dickens and others, with a little less freedom of speech than Mr.
Kipling is nowadays permitted to use. I would not wish for a better
farce than 'Brugglesmith'; (did Mr. Kipling ever dree the more terrible
weird not of being unable to get away from an adhesive drunken man,
but of having to look after an evasive one?) And of the more imaginative and ghostly pieces 'The Lost Legion' seems to me to bear the bell.
But what a jejune enumeration of personal inpressions is this! For the
book is to be read and rejoiced over by the reader, not analysed or even
pronounced on by the critic, 'which is 'is 'abit', as Mr. Kipling's friend
the policeman says.

26. S. R. Crockett 'On Some Tales of Mr. Kipling's'

1895

Signed article from the *Bookman* (London), Vol. VII, pp. 139–40 (February 1895).

Samuel Rutherford Crockett (1860–1914), Scottish minister and novelist, began in the 'Kailyard School' and graduated as an historical romance writer of considerable power, *The Black Douglas* (1899) being his most outstanding work. He is also remembered for his children's story *Sir Toady Lion* (1897).

In a lonely Sussex house a number of men sat together. The cheerful dinner was done, the ingle flamed, and whenever one, rising, chanced to open the cottage door, the freshness of the still and breathing spring night stole in. There were among these men editors, critics, dons, and writers—modest men all, who yet had tried, each within his possible, to do something. There was talk and turmoil—the incidence of liking, the extreme dissidence of dissent. From argument they went to criticism, and in the forecasting of the future, reputations suffered. All the while the great editor sat above them (in a smoking-jacket), as the gods sit, dividing good and evil. Finally they fell upon a new play.

They resolved to write out, each for himself, a list of the best half-dozen of Mr. Kipling's short stories. The papers were folded. They were put into the hat, and the editor, well-accustomed, made out the final result. 'The Man who would be King' stood proudly at the head of every list, followed by 'At the End of the Passage', 'Withour Benefit of Clergy', 'The Drums of the Fore-and-Aft', and I forget what other.

It is a game that anyone can try, and the results may be varied from theirs. But the fact stood clear that men of book and pen read Kipling for their own pleasure; and, what is more, remember him.

Afterward they fell a-talking of the author. They recalled how he

flashed upon the world, various discoverers claiming him—like a new
planet with an Adams and a Leverrier on the staff of every paper.

'In Vishnu-land what Avatar?' cried Browning long ago from among
the tangled bowers of 'Bells and Pomegranates', when Waring took
his wayward forth-going out of the ken of men—to return, not Waring, but merely Alfred Domett, a forgotten New Zealand statesman
with an unmanageable epic. For Kipling, and not Domett, was to be
the Avatar of Vishnu-land.

To myself the Revealer of the East was made plain one day when a
curious-looking book came to me from India, bearing a strange im-
print, as though Charles Dickens had been inventing names for the
publishers of the Orient.[1]

On the sandhills of Colwyn the Elder I lay and read, while a wind
from the sea whipped the leaves. I found a new language. I trod among
unknown allusions. The East, the skirts of which I had trod, spoke to
me for the first time with authentic voice.

For Fortune was good to me. She opened the book at a Jubilee Ode,
which, had a careful eye noted the image and superscription thereof,
would assuredly not have been read. For who in the later eighties
would read Jubilee Odes, compound of the patriotism and the cham-
pagne of the day before yesterday?

But this ran on in other fashion. And small wonder it was that staid
Anglo-Indians marvelled what snake had crept within the robustly
military columns of their favourite journal, and was now hissing at
them with erected crest.

> By the well where the bullocks go,
> Silent and blind and slow,
> By the field where the young corn dies,
> In the face of the sultry skies,
> They have heard as the dull earth hears,
> The sound of the wind of an hour,
> The sound of a great Queen's voice:
> 'My God hath granted me years.
> Hath granted dominion and power,
> And I bid you, O land, rejoice!'
>
> But the ploughman settled the share
> More deep in the grudging clod,
> For he saith, 'The wheat is my care,
> And the rest is the will of God!'

[1] [*Departmental Ditties* (3rd. Edn.), Thacker & Spink: Calcutta, 1888]

Thus the words came grimly, solemnly, laden with sympathy for India's inarticulate millions—hopeless, futureless, undesirous even of speech. It is possible that these words, and others in the same set of verses, are oftener remembered by one to whom they told of a new power beginning to be eloquent in the East, than even by the man who wrote them himself.

And there is something here which Mr. Kipling has never yet given rein to—perhaps the preaching strain in the background of his soul. He 'believes in God and the angels', like Colonel John Hay's prairie pioneer, and still more perhaps in the Law Inexorable which strikes once and no more, And, in that case, the preaching is sure to come.

Then the grey paper books began to pour, and we laughed and fought with the much-enduring Mulvaney, trained 'tarriers and poops' with Jock, longed for London 'and the stinks of her' with the Cockney Ortheris.

And we that were of the heather and the salt water were just as mad as the others. The style? queried the critic, whose duty it was to keep his head among the smother of our admiration. Bah! We did not care for the style. It was great story-telling—bold, free, effortless. And we found a sentence to fling at the critic too: 'And over the bastions of Fort Amara, broke the pitiless day. ' "Better that!" we cried at him.'

And then, as Mr. Kipling himself might say, 'there was a great silence between the howling of the jackals'.

As each succeeding book came to us, it grew clearer that the romance writer of the specialist had come to us. He grasped the mechanism of life—and that not only in the Orient. On the seas he 'knew the ropes'. Down in the engineer's grimy Inferno who but him had been keeping an eye upon the gauges. Doctors said; 'None but a doctor could have known that!' Military men claimed him as a comrade. Mr. Thomas Atkins, private in the line, declared him (with the Adjective) to be a time-expired gentleman-ranker. Newspaper men knew him for one who understood how 'to fake the paper' when moribund royalty will not die, the premier will not resign, or the wires are down in the North.

Clearer than the events of our last year's holiday lived the tale for us. We opened the pages at random, and so that Mr. Kipling told of India, in a trice we were transported. Wet, weariness, and day-worry were forgotten. In a moment there was blown across our nostrils the acrid whiff of wood smoke—the danker smell of rotting leaves, and of rushing hill torrents that flow from the caverns under—the true Himalaya smell—which, as Mr. Kipling says, when once a man smells, he will surely come back even from the ends of the earth to smell it again 'ere he die.

Or, as it may happen, we sweltered in the flaring daylong heats on some God-forsaken Indian embankment. We rode about the pine-woods of Simla and watched the star rise over the glacier.

The compact multifarious Indies pushed and shouldered through the tranced pages—Bengali, Sikh, Pathan, men meek of countenance, ghouls fiendish of eye, ill-favoured and treacherous men with long hair from the hills of the horse thieves on the North-Western frontier. We rode a-foraying with the Zukka Kehl, and knew all the while that the alert police officer on the other side of the frontier was going to catch us every time. In which case we should as surely be hanged for the greater glory of Law and Order. And so it ought to be. For when will ever Mr. Kipling give a chance to the horse that never knew a bridle, and the gipsying blood that will call no man master while the world lasts?

But what a new world it was, and what service and thank we owed to the caravels of the Columbus of the East, who pursued Mr. Bret Harte across the prairies and through the gulches, and bore eastward from the Farthest West the secret of its barbaric saga. The pre-Kipling generation had only to glimpse the word 'Indian' at the head of an article, or upon the title of a book, to retreat with a boredom that verged upon disgust. Just as the Indian Budget, or indeed Indian discussions generally, cleared the benches in the House of Commons, so the Indian tale, suggesting tiger-shooting and blue books with an occasional Mahatma, was left alone, untended, to die on the waste. It was once indeed permitted to Mr. Marion Crawford; but editors told him not to do it again, and he wisely obeyed them. Now Mr. Kipling changed all that, and the tribes of the East spoke to us authentic, every man in his own tongue. And more than all our hearts are stirred for Tommy Atkins, whether he might be hanged, like Danny Deever, high as Haman in the hollow square of the regiment, or whether he might finish his career in the worthiest way, as a commissaire outside the 'Grand Metropole'.

> Give him a letter,
> Can't do no better,
> Late Troop-Sergeant-Major, an'—runs with a letter!
> Think what he's been,
> Think what he's seen,
> Think of his pension an'
> GOD SAVE THE QUEEN.

And the faults? To another be the ungracious task for the drums have begun to roll, and the fever's in the blood.

Mr. Kipling may sometimes be inclined, as Mr. Stevenson says, to the heresy of Cain, in that he would let his brother go to the devil his own way. But I think that oftener he will be ready to square him up, and help him as the friendly private helped Mulvaney, 'to preserve his formation', till he lies down among the long grass for his longer rest. For we are inclined to think less of ourselves as it nears the sundown, and as our feet overpass more of 'The Long Trail—the Trail that is always new'.

If an apprentice at the writing trade may say the word, there are some verses of Mr. Kipling's which have often made him work the willinger and the worthier, so far as work he may.

> If there be good in that I wrought,
>   Thy hand compelled it, Master, Thine;
> Where I have failed to meet Thy thought,
>   I know, through thee, the blame is mine.
>
> One instant's toil to Thee denied,
>   Stands all eternity's offence,
> Of what I did with Thee to guide,
>   To Thee, through Thee, be excellence.
>
> Take not that vision from my ken,
>   O whatso'er may spoil or speed—
> Help me to need no aid from men,
>   That I may help such men as need.

27. Charles Eliot Norton on 'The Poetry of Rudyard Kipling'

1897

Signed article from the *Atlantic Monthly*, Vol. LXXIX, pp. 111-15 (January 1897).

Charles Eliot Norton (1827-1908) was Professor of the History of Art at Harvard 1875-98 and editor of Carlyle's letters and reminiscences (1883 and 1887). 'We are both of us awed, and if the truth be told a little scared at your article in the *Atlantic Monthly*,' wrote Kipling to Norton on 31 December 1896. 'You are the only man except my father and Uncle Ned [Burne-Jones] whose disapproval or advice slays me; and I will say just as one says to one's father when one is little, "I'll try to think and be better next time". But, even now, the notion that *you* should have reviewed me rather makes me gasp.'

During the last two or three years, we have often heard the lament that the Victorian era of poetry was closed: that with the death of Tennyson the last great voice had fallen silent; that only the small harpers with their glees were left, such as Chaucer saw sitting at the feet of the mighty masters of old; or that if one or two who might claim to belong to the band of fame lingered on, they were now old men, and their voices were no longer heard or were faint with age. But the lament was futile, however it might seem to be justified by the verse of the new Poet Laureate. Pye was Poet Laureate at the beginning of the century, as Austin is at its end. But before Pye died Scott and Wordsworth had already secured their seats among the immortals, and England, at the end of the century no less than at the beginning, is still the nursing mother of poets; and though Tennyson and his compeers be dead, her genius, with its eternal youth, is still finding fresh expression for itself, inspired with a novel poetic spirit as genuine as any that has moulded English verse.

This splendid continuous fertility of English genius, this unbroken
poetic expression of English character and life from Chaucer to Rudyard Kipling, is unparalleled in the moral and intellectual history of any
other race. For five full centuries England has had such a succession of
poets as no other land can boast. There is no reason to fear that the
succession will fail. One dynasty may follow another, but the throne
will not lack a king. It is a change of dynasty which we are witnessing
now, and it was the mistaking of this for a break in succession that has
given occasion to the lament that the Victorian era of poetry had ended.

As we look back over the poetry of the century, two main inspiring
motives, exhibiting a natural evolution of poetic doctrine and influence,
are clearly distinguishable. The one, of which Wordsworth is the representative, proceeded direct from external nature in her relations to
man; while the other, with many representatives from Keats to Tennyson, Arnold, Clough and Browning, was derived from human nature,
from man himself in his various relations to the universe and to his
kind. And all these latter poets, however they might differ in their look
upon life, treated it either ideally and romantically, or else as matter
mainly of introspective reflection and sentiment. Poetry with them was
not so much an image of life as, on the one hand a scenic representation
of it, and on the other a criticism of it. In their kind, the finer dramatic
lyrics of Browning, scenic representations of life, may long stand unsurpassed, while for criticism and exposition of life of the intellectual
order Clough and Arnold may have no rivals, as Tennyson may have
none in the field of pure sentiment in exquisite lyrical form.

The poetry inspired by these motives was the adequate expression of
the ideals of the age—of its shifting creeds, its doubts, its moral per-
plexities, its persistent introspection. The mood lasted for full fifty
years, and never did the prevailing mood of the higher life of a people
find nobler or more complete utterance. But meanwhile the process of
mental and spiritual evolution was going on. The mood was gradually
changing; the poets themselves, by uttering it, were exhibiting its
limitations; it was a phase of the spiritual life of man, of which no age
exhibits the full orb. A new generation had been growing up under
these poets, with its own conceptions and aspirations and its new modes
of confronting the conditions of existance. It found the poetic motives
of the earlier part of the century insufficient; neither external nature
nor human nature in any select aspect was what it cared most about.
It had taken to heart the instructions of the poets; it aimed 'to see life
steadily and see it *whole*', or, in Clough's words, 'to look straight out

upon the big plain things that stare one in the face'. It took the whole world for its realm and was moved to depict it in its actual aspect and what was called its reality. The realists of yesterday or to-day are the legitimate offspring of the romanticists and idealists of the mid-century, following, as is often the habit of sons, a different course from that which their fathers pursued. The new spirit showed itself at first in prose fiction. It was weak and often misdirected. It waited for its poet. For realism—the aim to see the world and to depict it as it is—required for the fit performance of its work the highest exercise of the poetic imagination. The outward thing, the actual aspect, is in truth the real thing and the true aspect only when seen by the imaginative vision. To see a thing truly, a man must as Blake says, look *through*, not *with* the eye. The common reporter sees *with* his eye, and, meaning to tell the truth, tells a falsehood. But the imagination has insight, and what it sees is reality.

It is now some six or seven years since *Plain Tales from the Hills* gave proof that a man who saw through his eyes was studying life in India and was able to tell us what he saw. And those who read the scraps of verse prefixed to many of his stories, if they knew what poetry was, learned that their writer was at least potentially a poet, not by virtue of fantasy alone, but by his mastery of lyrical versification. The rhythm of these fragments had swing and ease and variety, and there was one complete little set of verses, at the head of the last story in the book, which made clear the writer's title to the name of poet. We had not then seen *Departmental Ditties and Other Verses*, or *Ballads and Barrack-Room Ballads*: they came to us before long, and showed that the qualities which distinguished Mr. Kipling's stories were not lacking in his poems. There was the same sure touch, the same insight, the same imaginative sympathy with all varieties of life, and the same sense of the moral significance of life even in its crudest, coarsest, and most vulgar aspects. Many of these verses were plainly the work of youth—of a boy full of talent, but not yet fully master of his own capacities, not yet wholly mastered by his own genius. They had a boyish audacity and extravagance; they were exuberant; there was too much talent in them, usurping the place and refusing the control of genius: but underneath their boyishness, and though their manner was not yet wholly subdued to art, there was a vital spirit of fresh and vigorous originality which, combined with extraordinary control of rhythmical expression, gave sure promise of higher manly achievement.

Mr. Kipling's progress as poet has been plain to those who have read the pieces from his hand which have appeared in magazine and newspaper in England and America, or have had their place in his volumes of stories during the last four or five years. A good part of this scattered verse is now gathered into *The Seven Seas*, but this volume is by no means a complete collection, and there are poems omitted from it which the lover of poetry can ill spare, and for which he would readily exchange some of those included in it.

But in spite of omissions and inclusions alike to be regretted, *The Seven Seas* contains a notable addition to the small treasury of enduring English verse, an addition sufficient to establish Mr. Kipling's right to take place in the honourable body of those English poets who have done England service in strengthening the foundations of her influence and of her fame. The dominant tone of his verse is indeed the patriotic; and it is the tone of the new patriotism, that of imperial England, which holds as one all parts of her wide-stretched empire, and binds them close in the indissoluble bond of common motherhood, and with the ties of common convictions, principles, and aims, derived from the teachings and traditions of the motherland, and expressed in the best verses of her poets. It is this passionate, moral, imperial patriotism that inspires the first poem in the book, 'The Song of the English', and which recurs again and again through its pages.

But if this be the dominant tone, easily recognized by every reader, the full scale which includes it and every other tone of Mr. Kipling's verse is that of actual life seen by the imagination intensely and comprehensively, and seen by it always, in all conditions and under all forms, as a moral experience, with the inevitable consequences resulting from the good or evil use of it.

The gift of imagination, with which as a quality Mr. Kipling is endowed as few men have ever been, has quickened and deepened his sympathies with men of every class and race, and given him free entrance to their hearts. He 'draws the thing as he sees it for the God of things as they are;' and the thing as he sees it is the relation of experience and conduct, while the rule of life which he deduces from it is that of 'Law, Duty, Order and Restraint, Obedience, Discipline'. He does not enforce this rule as a preacher from the pulpit, but, as Shakespeare teaches it, by the simple exhibition of life in its multiplicity and apparent confusion.

'What is a poet?' asks Wordsworth, and he answers his question: 'He is a man speaking to men . . . carrying everywhere with him relationship and love . . . He binds together by passion and knowledge the vast empire of human society.' And this vast empire of society includes the mean and the vulgar no less than the noble and the refined, Tommy Atkins and Bill 'Awkins as well as McAndrew and True Thomas. The recklessness, the coarseness, the brutality of Tommy Atkins, the spirit of the beast in man, all appear in the *Barrack-Room Ballads*, but not less his courage, his fidelity, his sense of duty, his obscure but deep-seated sentiment. The gist of all these Ballads is the display of the traits of human nature which makes this semi-savage 'most remarkable like you'. Yet it will not be only the fastidious and the super-refined reader who will find that some of the ballads might well be spared. There is more than one in this last volume which offends the taste by coarseness insufficiently redeemed by humour or by suggestion of virtue obscured by vulgarity, diminishes the charm of the book as a whole, and interferes with the commendation of it which might otherwise be hearty and unqualified. And yet, in condemning these few pieces, and in regretting their association with nobler work, I am reminded of a sentence in the *Apologie of Poetrie* of Sir John Harington, printed in the year 1591, which runs as follows:

But this I say, and I think I say truly: that there are many good lessons to be learned out of these poems, many good uses to be had of them, and that therefore they are not, nor ought not to be, despised by the wiser sort, but so to be studied and employed as was intended by the writer and deviser thereof, which is to soften and polish the hard and rough disposition of men, and make them capable of virtue and good discipline.

But enough of blame and of excuse. From the reek of the barrack-room we come out with delight to the open air and to the fresh breezes of the sea. For the sea has touched Mr. Kipling's imagination with its magic and its mystery, and never are his sympathies keener than with the men who go down upon it, and with the vast relations of human life to the waters that encircle the earth. Here too is manifest his love of England, the mistress of the sea. The ocean is the highway of her sons, and the paths of the ocean which they travel from one end of the earth to the other are paths from one region to another of her imperial dominion.

The passion for the sea, the mastery of its terrors, the confident but distrustful familiarity with it of the English seaman, have never had such expression as Mr. Kipling has given to them. From his splendid paean of 'The English Flag'—'What is the flag of England, winds of the world declare', to 'The Song of the English'—

> We have fed our sea for a thousand years,
>   And she calls us, still unfed,
> Though there's never a wave of all her waves
>   But marks our English dead

—his imagination dwells with vivifying emotion on the heroic com-
bats—now victories, now defeats—of his race with the winds and the
waves from which they draw their strength. All that belongs to the
story of man upon the sea—the line-of-battle ship, the merchantman,
the tramp steamer, the derelict, the little cargo-boats, the lighthouse,
the bell-buoy—has its part in his verse of human experience. And so
vivid are his appreciations of the poetic significance of even the most
modern and practical of the conditions and aspects of sea life that in
'McAndrew's Hymn', a poem of surpassing excellence alike in conception and in execution, Mr. Kipling has sung the song of the marine
steam-engine and all its machinery, from furnace-bars to screw, in such
wise as to convert their clanging beats and throbs into a sublime sym-
phony in accord with the singing of the morning stars. He has thus
fulfilled a fine prophecy of Wordsworth's, that when the time should
come, if it should ever come, when the discoveries and applications of
science shall become

familiarized to men, and shall be ready to put on, as it were, a form of flesh and
blood, the Poet will lend his divine spirit to aid the transfiguration, and will
welcome the Being thus produced as a dear and genuine inmate of the
household of man.

Such a poem as 'McAndrew's Hymn' is a masterpiece of realism in
its clear insight into real significance of common things, and in its
magnificent expression of it. Here Mr. Kipling is at his best, revealing
the admirable quality of his imaginative vision and obeying the true
command of his genius. It is not strange that the insistence of his varied
and vigorous talents should often, during youth, when the exercise of
talents is so delightful and so delusive, have interfered with his perfect
obedience to the higher law of his inward being. And the less strange
is it because of the ready acceptance of the work of talent by the world
and by the critics, and their frequent lack of readiness of appreciation
of the novel modes of genius. Moreover, this age of ours, like every
other age, is full of false and misleading doctrines of art, of which the
fallacies are often to be discovered by the artist only through his own
hard experience. But the interested reader of Mr. Kipling's verse will
not fail to note that almost from the beginning there were indications
of his being possessed by the spirit which, whether it be called realist

or idealist, sees things as they are; delights in their aspect; finds the shows of the earth good, yet recognizes that they all are but veils, concealments, and suggestions of the things better than themselves, of ideals always to be striven after, never to be attained. The dull-eyed man finds life dull and the earth unpoetic. He is McAndrew's 'damned ijjit' who asks: 'Mr. McAndrew, don't you think steam spoils romance at sea?' But the poet finds to-day as entertaining as any day that ever dawned, and man's life as interesting and as romantic as it ever was in old times. Yet he is not satisfied; he reveals this human life to himself as well as to his fellows; he gives to it its form of beauty; but for himself there is a something for which he longs, which he seeks for, and which always eludes him. It is his beloved, it is his ideal; it is what Mr. Kipling, in one of his most beautiful poems, and one in which he gives expression to his deepest self, calls the True Romance. This poem begins:

> Thy face is far from this our war,
>   Our call and counter-cry,
> I shall not find Thee quick and kind,
>   Nor know Thee till I die:
> Enough for me in dreams to see
>   And touch Thy garments' hem;
> Thy feet have trod so near to God
> I may not follow them.

It is this poem which more than any other gives the key to the interpretation of Mr. Kipling's work in general, and displays its controlling aim. And more than this, it gives assurance of better work to come than any which Mr. Kipling has yet achieved. For as with every man who holds to a high ideal, pursuing it steadily, each step is a step in advance, so is it with the poet. The imagination, if it be a genuine faculty, and not a mere quality, is not to be worn out and exhausted by use. Nay, rather, it grows stronger with exercise; it is constantly quickened by each new experience; its insight becomes deeper and more keen. It is the poets in whom imagination is a secondary quality who, as they grow old, fail to equal their youthful selves. But the poets whose imagination is the essence of their being lose nothing, but gain always with advance of years. They are the real idealists.

I have said too little, in what precedes, concerning the gifts possessed by Mr. Kipling which would be matters of chief consideration with a minor poet—gifts subsidiary to his imagination, though dependent on it for their excellence—the frequent perfect mating of word with sentiment, the graphic epithet, the force, freedom, directness, and simplicity of diction, the exquisite movement and flow of rhythm, the felicity of rhyme. It would be easy to illustrate these qualities of his poetry by the selection of verses in which they are displayed; but there is little need to do so, for the poems are already familiar, not only to the readers of poetry, but to many who have hardly read any other verse. The *Barrack-Room Ballads*, set to old tunes, are already sung wherever the British soldier plants his camp. The correspondent of the London *Times*, who accompanied the recent expedition to Dongola, told in one of his letters how, while he was writing, he heard the soldiers outside his tent singing one of Kipling's songs.

The study of the forms of Mr. Kipling's verse must be left for some other occasion. It is enough now gratefully to recognize that he continues the great succession of royal English poets, and to pay to him the homage which is his due.

28. W. D. Howells on 'The Laureate of the Larger England'

1897

Signed review of *The Seven Seas* from *McClure's Magazine*, Vol. VIII, pp. 453–5 (March 1897).

William Dean Howells (1837–1920), famous American novelist and critic, was editor of *Atlantic Monthly* for ten years 'encouraging realism among the contributors' who included Mark Twain, Bret Harte and Henry James. Later he carried on the same policy as a member of the staff of *Harper's Magazine*.

If Mr. Rudyard Kipling should remain the chief poet of his race in his time, his primacy would be the most interesting witness of the imperial potentialities of that race in literature. He was not born English, if that means born in England, but the keynote of his latest volume is a patriotism intense beyond anything expressed by other English poets. He is so intense in the English loyalty which always mystifies us poor Americans, that one has a little difficulty in taking him at his word in it. But he is most serious, and in the presence of the fact one cannot help wondering how far the ties of affection, the sentiment of a merely inherited allegiance, can stretch. If we had not snapped them so summarily a century ago should we be glowing and thrilling at the name of England, which now awakens only a cold disgust in us, or at the notion of an anthropomorphic majesty, which only makes us smile? One cannot read 'A Song of the English' in Mr. Kipling's new book without thinking we might, though as it is we read it without a responsive heart-throb, or any feeling but wonder for its beauty and sincerity.

Its patriotism is not love of the little England, 'encompassed by the inviolate seas' on the west coast of Europe; but the great England whose far-strewn empire feels its mystical unity in every latitude and longitude of the globe. It has its sublimity, that emotion, and its reason, though we cannot share it; and it is only in asking ourselves why a man of any nation, any race, should so glory in its greatness or even its goodness when he has the greatness, the goodness of all humanity to glory in, that we are sensible of the limitations of this outborn Englishman. Possibly when we broke with England we broke more irreparably with tradition than we imagined, and liberated ourselves to a patriotism not less large than humanity. Possibly it has been for much more than we knew that we have made a home here for all mankind, and America is yet to make her own home in the heart of every man. At any rate, it seems certain that if we had not taught England that sharp lesson of a hundred years ago in colonial government, there would be no such imperial England as we see today, and no such poet of the imperial English race to sing her grandeur as he who holds the first place today among English poets.

Upon this hypothesis we may claim Mr. Kipling, whether he likes it or not, as in some sort American. He has, in fact, given us a kind of authority to do so by divining our actual average better than any American I can think of offhand, in this very extraordinary poem, where he supposes the spirit of America to speak at a well-known moment of civic trouble:

[quotes the whole of 'An American' (DV. pp. 184–5)]

The American spirit speaks here as if with the blended voices of Emerson and Ironquil; and it is from no one essentially alien to us that knowledge of us so subtle can come. I am tempted to call the piece the most important thing, intellectually, in Mr. Kipling's new volume of *The Seven Seas*. To me, it gives a sense of his penetration and his grasp that nothing else does, though there are many other things in the book which I like as well and which have the force and charm possible only from the habit of thinking in tones and colors. These things all bear witness to his uncommon quality as a poet, but if it is something more to be a humanist, then the piece I have quoted marks him as a poet with this distinction to his advantage.

Of course the last book of Mr. Kipling does not make the impression of novelty which his earlier verse made. A man can be novel but once, and for the artist in every kind all surprises after the first are to be in the way of greater strength and depth. These are what keep him new; and no mere variety without them can save his novelty from staling. Certain things this poet gave assurance of in the beginning almost in full measure: dramatic instinct, picturesque emotion, and a mighty music as of drums and trumpets. His verse always marched, with the bands playing, and the flags flying; and it marches so still, but not more bravely; that would be difficult. What it could do and does do is to impart the effect of a sort of veteran solidity in its splendors; everything is more perfect; without losing dash or dare, it is steadier and more equal. The years have not passed without enlarging the poet to vaster ranges of feeling, and giving him new light on his own thoughts and experiences. This is all they can do for any of us; when they do it for one of the best of us it is to the common good of all.

In the new *Barrack-Room Ballads* here, there is, to be sure, nothing with the peculiar thrill of 'Danny Deever', nothing with the peculiar homesick, heartsick touch of 'Mandalay', but there are other things as moving and as true, with a plunge of tragedy into depths which were not sounded before, however the surface was troubled. I could allege this or that in proof, but the temper of the whole book is the best proof, and I must let this witness also for something else that I feel strongly in it: the constant individuality, the constant impersonality. No poet has more distinctly made himself felt than this poet who has always merged and hidden himself in his types, his characters. The terms upon which he could do his kind of work at all were purely dramatic. He could never stand for himself alone; he must always stand for some one else too. He must not move us with his melancholy, his rapture, his passion, except as he makes it appear that of another. With all his love of the heroic, he is one of the least romantic of the poets because the least subjective. But when I have said that he is the least subjective, I am in instant doubt of my position, except as it concerns his expression. As concerns his impression, he is one of the most subjective. He has not so much gone out to that imperial England of his as received it into himself, and given it forth again with the color, the stamp of his mind upon it. For the first time in literature that empire is imagined.

It is imagined with pride in 'The Song of the English', and with a certain pain and futile appeal in this lovely poem, which I like much better, and find the tenderest and sweetest in the whole book.

[quotes the whole of 'The Flowers' (DV. pp. 190–1)]

I think the appeal, here, is futile, because it is from the ardor of the younger world to the indifference of the elder, which must grow more and more with age. It is in the nature of exile to turn with unforgetting fondness to home, but the home soon forgets the exile, or if it does not forget, cannot care for him. The inviolate seas that keep the insular England safe cannot keep her alive to the love that glows for her in the far-off lands they sever from her; and it appears to those who are politically of neither the larger nor the lesser England that if ever her mighty empire is to perish, it will die first at the heart. Canada will not grow cold first, nor Africa, nor Australasia, nor India, but England herself. It has happened so with all empires; and it is not material that empires should survive, the English more than the Roman. But it is very material that what is good in English feeling and English thinking should still inherit the earth; that is far better than English fighting or English ruling; and I do not know anything more significant of what may be hereafter than the fact that the English poet who continues the great tradition of English poetry most conspicuously should not be English born, should not have been reared under English skies, or islanded by English seas. I do not forget the beautiful, the exquisite verse of William Watson when I praise that of Rudyard Kipling; but it seems to me I am sensible of a vaster promise, a more assured future in his work; and there is no one else to name with him. He is, by virtue of his great gift, the laureate of that larger England whose wreath it is not for any prime minister to bestow; but wherever the English tongue is written or spoken, those who are native to it may claim a share in his recognition. He stands for the empire of that language which grows more and more the only English empire which has a common history and a common destiny.

29. J. H. Millar: 'The Works of Mr. Kipling'

1898

Anonymous article in *Blackwood's Magazine*, Vol. CLXIV,
pp. 470–82 (October 1898), Authorship confirmed by *Blackwood's Contributors' Book* now in the National Library of Scotland.
(See *Wellesley Index*, p. 10.)

John Hepburn Millar (1864–1929), son of Lord Craighill, became
an Advocate in 1889, was lecturer in Scottish Literature at Glasgow
1911–12 and Professor of Constitutional Law and Constitutional
History at Edinburgh 1909–25. Besides much criticism he wrote
A Literary History of Scotland (1903) and several other volumes on
literature and law.

Literary reputations have often been rapidly won. To wake one morning and find himself famous has been the lot of many a writer besides
the poet, the England of whose time—the England, that is to say, of
the Peninsula and Waterloo—the England of Wellington, Scott, and
Castlereagh—is pronounced by Mr. Stephen Phillips to have been
'for the most part petty and hypocritical'! (See the *Cornhill Magazine*
for January 1898, p. 21.) Our fathers were almost as much on the alert
as ourselves for the appearance of a new genius; but never have men of
letters succeeded in reaching the substantial honour of a 'collected
edition' so early in life as at the present day. That distinction used to
be jealously reserved for veterans. Now it is liberally bestowed upon
authors who (one hopes) have at least as many years of at least as good
work before as behind them. We do not grumble at the innovation.
The old style of 'edition de luxe', whose inconveniences were so
feelingly portrayed by the late Mr. du Maurier, has fortunately gone
out of fashion; and the new style is sure to be convenient for reading
as well as ornamental to the bookshelf. The resources of typography
are freely drawn upon for its production, and the result is something
eminently pleasant to the eye, whether the contents of the volumes

are to be desired to make one wise or the reverse. From our lips, therefore, no word of disparagement shall fall with reference to the edition of Mr. Kipling's works, the publication of which has just been completed. The printing is all that could be desired, though no more than was to be expected from the celebrated house founded by the late Mr. Robert Clark, that 'warrior' and hero of a hundred well-fought golf-matches. Mr. Kipling, too, has done well in refraining from introducing prefaces—a sort of writing which calls for a touch of the Magician's own wand. But were the edition as mean and unworthy in externals as it is handsome and sumptuous, we should none the less welcome it as supplying a convenient pretext for attempting to weigh in the critical balance the productions of the most remarkable writer of his generation.

It is not much more than ten years since the attention of the English public was first attracted to an unknown author (with a name suspiciously like a *nom de guerre*) by the appearance of some spirited prose sketches and of one or two ballads, possessing the genuine ring of poetry, in the pages of a contemporary. The attention so drawn was riveted by certain poems from the same pen in which a new and original note was undoubtedly struck, and which Mr. Henley was the means of introducing to the world in a vivacious weekly periodical. Thenceforward, Mr. Kipling's literary career is matter of common knowledge. It has been his portion to gain the ear of the great non-literary reading public, and at the same time to win the enthusiastic applause of that limited body of men whose pleasure in a work of art is derived from a perception of the means as well as of the end. Such good fortune falls to few. There are writers whose work is keenly appreciated by their literary brethren, but who make little or no impression upon 'the great heart of the people'. Of such, Mr. Stevenson was a typical representative. There are others, again, who sell their tens of thousands, yet whose glaring faults of taste effectually repel the sympathies of the educated minority, the *cachet* of whose approbation, while they profess to despise, they secretly long for. But the critic to whose palate the works of Miss Corelli or Mr. Caine are as ungrateful as a meal of dust and ashes, is well aware that from the point of view of literature neither the lady nor the gentleman exists. Their performances will have as much significance for the competent critic of the future as the *Dagonet Ballads* or Captain Coe's finals. So, too, the reviewer to whose hardened sensibilities the pathos and the humour of the Kailyard alike appeal in vain, has more than a suspicion that Messrs. Crockett and

Maclaren will not enter into the reckoning of our sons' sons. But he knows that Mr. Barrie is certain to count. And even so it is with Mr. Kipling. You may lay your finger on faults real or imaginary; you may find his verse flashy and his prose irritating. But you cannot (being in full possession of your senses) pass him by; you cannot maintain that, in estimating the literary forces and tendencies of our age, it is possible to leave him out of account. As well ignore Dickens in a review of Victorian literature; as well ignore Keene in a review of Victorian art.

Perhaps the most striking feature of Mr. Kipling's work is the wide range over which it expatiates. Subjects the most diverse are handled with the same air of ease and intimacy; and no other writer is so well entitled to repeat with proper pride the most familiar and the most hackneyed of Terentian sentiments, 'For to admire and for to see, for to behold this world so wide'—that is his *métier*; and we may proceed with the quotation and add that 'he can't drop it if he tried'. How or where Mr. Kipling acquired his 'extensive and peculiar' knowledge of the physical world, of the human heart, and of animated nature, is no business of ours. As he himself sings—

'When 'Omer smote 'is blomin' lyre
'Ed 'eard men sing by land an' sea;
An' what 'e thought 'e might require
'E went an' took—the same as me!'

No doubt in 'The Three Musketeers' he allows the world a glimpse of one of his methods of collecting raw material. But there are matters innumerable in his writings for which there is no accounting unless we are prepared to concede to him a full measure of that faculty of divination which is heaven's best gift to a chosen few.

It is a commonplace that Shakespeare was accustomed to handle with astounding felicity and correctness the technical phraseology of the law, of the *manège*, of venery, and of many other departments of human activity. It being, of course, impossible that a Warwickshire yokel, whom we know to have been but imperfectly educated, could have acquired so minute a knowledge of so many complicated subjects, a sapient school of critics has not hesitated to assure us that the author of the Shakespearean plays was not one but many—was a lawyer, a Jehu, a Nimrod, a Papist, a Protestant, a Jesuit, a Puritan—was anything you please, in short, but a man with an unrivalled *flair* for the niceties of language, and an unequalled share of IMAGINATION—that quality of all others most abhorrent to the dunce. Let us adopt this singular fallacy for a moment, and see to what conclusion it leads us in Mr. Kipling's case.

It is plain, to begin with, that Mr. Kipling must have studied long and ardently at all the best schools and universities in the world. How else could he have acquired his thorough acquaintance with zoology (*vide* the *Jungle Books*), with geography, including the use of the globes (*vide* 'The Flag of England' and 'The Children of the Zodiac'), with archaeology (*vide* 'The Story of Ung'), and with botany (*vide* 'The Flowers')? It is equally beyond dispute that he served a long apprenticeship on the sea; and it seems likely that he first gratified his passion for that element by taking service in a Greek galley and afterwards in that of a Viking. He must then have occupied a post on the following vessels in succession—a chinese pig-boat, a Bilbao-tramp, a New England fishing-smack, a British man-of-war, and an Atlantic liner. It was certainly in the engine-room of the last named vessel that he learned those details about machinery which he reproduces so faithfully in 'M'Andrew's Hymn'.

We infer that Mr. Kipling next withdrew for a few years' complete rest to the solitude of the jungle. He there added materially to his knowledge of natural history, and familiarised himself thoroughly with the manners and customs of bird, beast, and reptile. (If he did not, how on earth *could* he have written the *Jungle Books*?) It is also quite obvious that he has held a large number of appointments in the Indian Civil Service; and that he served for a considerable period in the ranks of the army. No sane man can doubt that he took part in several hot engagements, and fought in at least one Soudan campaign. A good many years must also have been passed by Mr. Kipling in disguise among the natives. By no other means could he have become conversant with their habits of thought and ways of life. It is further beyond dispute that he must have slummed in London; that at one time he must have had a studio of his own; and that the inside of a newspaper office must have been during a certain period of his life a place of almost daily resort.

Our chain of reasoning is now almost complete, and we defy any one to snap it. No man can acquire a knowledge of the terminology of soldiering, or sailoring, or tinkering, or tailoring, unless he has been a soldier, or a sailor, or a tinker, or a tailor. But human life is too short for a man to be all four, and, *a fortiori*, for a man to follow fifty occupations. *Argal*, Kipling is but the name of an amanuensis or hack, through whose pen certain eminent soldiers, sailors, tinkers, tailors, etc., have chosen, for some undisclosed reason, to tell their story to the world. Such, without exaggeration, is the reasoning of the dullards who have presumed to tamper with the fame of England's greatest poet.

While Mr. Kipling surveys mankind from China to Peru, he does so not from the dubious point of view of the cosmopolitan but from the firm vantage-ground of a Briton. It is merely his due to attribute to him the chief share among men of letters in that revival of the Imperial sentiment, both in these islands and in our colonies, which has been so striking a phenomenon of recent years. To have reawakened a great people to a sense of its duties and responsibilities, to have fanned the drooping flame of an enlightened but fervent patriotism—these are achievements of which few indeed can boast. It is, we trust, unnecessary to disclaim all intention of disparaging the good work performed by great men in years when the country seemed plunged in a fatal lethargy, and men appeared to have grown indifferent or insensible to England's mission and destiny. Lord Tennyson, for example, has no stronger claim upon the reverence and affection of all generations of his countrymen than the fact that from time to time he set the trumpet to his lips and blew a strain whose echoes will never cease to encourage and to inspire. But old and neglected truths sometimes require to be presented in a new garb; and abstract principles constantly need to be driven home by concrete illustrations. It has been Mr. Kipling's enviable task to bring down patriotism from the closet to the street, and to diffuse its beneficent influence among millions who had hitherto remained untouched.

As so frequently happens, Mr. Kipling's teaching fell upon willing ears. The English nation is patient and long-suffering enough. It is also extraordinarily loyal in its allegiance to its chosen favourites. But the Government which mismanaged the affairs of this country from 1880 to 1885 was kind enough to supply at least two specimens of the application of Liberal principles to foreign politics which can never be forgotten. The shameful peace concluded after our defeat at Majuba Hill—a peace so pregnant with trouble and disaster—was not rendered more palatable to a people which loves honesty and plaindealing by the sanctimonious cant characteristically employed to justify it. The projected relinquishment of a portion of Egypt might, indeed, have passed at the time without exciting the national resentment. But the cold-hearted abandonment of Gordon aroused a storm of indignation which in reality has been the motive-power of that series of laborious yet brilliant operations whose culmination was successfully attained a few weeks ago. The better-informed classes of Englishmen were at the same time aware that, in the East, Lord Ripon had embarked upon a course of policy, the ultimate result, if not the conscious design, of which must be the overthrow of British power in India. Worse, if worse were possible, remained behind. The most audacious and malignant of blows was presently struck at the integrity of the empire by hands the measure of whose evil-doing not even Majuba Hill and Khartoum had sufficed to fill up. The dismemberment of the United Kingdom was solemnly and seriously offered as the price of political support to a faction 'steeped to the lips in treason'. This master-stroke was attended by at least one happy consequence. The nobler elements in the Liberal party were for ever severed from the baser, and became practically fused with the Conservatives. No wonder that men's hearts were longing for an outspoken proclamation on the side of loyalty and empire! No wonder that the Jubilee celebrations of 1887 were hailed as an outward and visible sign of the reawakening of the national spirit! Yet they announced merely the inception of a great movement. It is surely no vain imagination to suppose that the Jubilee rejoicings of last year possessed a deeper significance and were informed with a more exalted spirit than those of ten years before. The soul of the nation seemed to be more profoundly stirred. Ideas and aspirations of a loftier order seemed to have taken root in the nation's heart. And if such indeed were the case, it was to Rudyard Kipling more than to any other writer that the change was due, just as it was he who seized upon the unspoken national thought and enshrined it in imperishable verse. On one Englishman of eminence, and one alone, it is to be feared, did the writings of Mr. Kipling during the last decade fail to produce a perceptible impression. From childhood to old age the more poignant emotions of patriotism and the fine sense of national honour were, unhappily, strangers to the bosom of William Ewart Gladstone.

We make no apology for this apparent digression; for Mr. Kipling's most characteristic work is really saturated with politics—not the politics of Taper or Tadpole, or even of Mr. Rigby, but the politics of true statesmanship. No patriot assuredly can forget the signal service which he rendered to his country, at a moment when the horizon was darker than one now cares to think of, by the publication of 'Cleared'. It is not only one of the most trenchant pieces of rhetoric in any language (Juvenal himself might be proud to claim it for his own), but it furnishes an absolute and conclusive answer to the contemptible sophistries by which men who had once had at least a bowing acquaintance with honesty were fain to palliate their connection and co-operation with ruffians and assassins. But the truth is, that no more formidable attack has been delivered upon Liberalism in the present generation than Mr. Kipling's work, taken as a whole. The shameless lies by which the friends of disaffection and the devotees of so-called philanthropy have never scrupled to fortify their cause, crumble to atoms at the touch of the artist whose highest aspiration it is 'to draw the Thing as he sees It for the God of Things as They are'. The precious time-dishonoured formulae become meaningless when confronted with the very essence of practical experience. Mr. Kipling has taken the pains (in 'The Enlightenments of Padgett, M.P.') to set forth his opinions in direct and almost didactic shape; but a story like 'The Head of the District' is more valuable than many such discourses, and illuminates the situation as with a flash. Here are facts, stubborn facts, which it is the very *raison d'être* of Liberalism to ignore, but the ignoring of which means the end of all government worthy of the name. It is of a piece with his sound and comprehensive view of politics that Mr. Kipling should strike the true note in comparing the relative value and importance of the man of action and the man of letters. He is guiltless of the affectation of depreciating his own calling. But his judgment coincides with that invariably pronounced by Sir Walter Scott. 'A Conference of the Powers' is in many ways by much the least felicitous of the numerous productions of his pen. Nowhere else is his touch so uncertain; nowhere else does the author strike one as being so much of a *poseur*; nowhere else does he come so near to trespassing upon the unconsciously ridiculous. But, despite its manifold imperfections, it teaches lessons which we fear that many journalists and many more pretentious writers have yet to learn.

The particular quarter of the globe in which Mr. Kipling reduces Liberal principles *ad absurdum* is of course India; and, though the universe is his by right of conquest, India is, no question, his particular domain. 'Twas there his earliest triumphs were achieved; and with it the most instructive portion of his work is concerned. Whatever his excellences or defects, it was he and no other who first brought home to the average Englishman something like an adequate conception of what our Indian Empire means. We all knew that there was a subtle and mysterious charm about the East. Those who had read the *Arabian Nights* and *Tancred* had a faint conception of its potency. Those who were fortunate enough to have relatives in the Company's or the Queen's service were, of course, in the enjoyment of a much ampler knowledge. The Mutiny taught us something, though that something was gradually being forgotten. But it was not until Mr. Kipling's arrival on the scene that 'the man on the knife-board' was dumped down, as it were, by the compelling force of an irresistible will among a mass of 'raw, brown, naked humanity'; that he realised the existence of a vast body of fellow subjects to whom his favourite catchwords (such as 'liberty' and 'progress') would have been absolutely unintelligible; and that he was enabled to apprehend, however imperfectly, the magnitude of the work which it has been the privilege of England to initiate and carry on in the East Indies through the instrumentality of a handful of her sons. One of the main secrets, we believe, of the extraordinary vividness with which Mr. Kipling represents scenes so wholly different from anything in the experience of the average Englishman is that he never pauses to make preliminary explanations. His early writings, by a fortunate accident, were addressed to an Anglo-Indian audience upon whom such explanations would have been thrown away. They knew Jakko and Peliti's, and Tara-Devi, and Benmore and Boileaugunge as well as a man-about-town knows Piccadilly or an East-ender Epping Forest. Tonga-bars and rikshaws, dâk-bungalows and saises, pipals and walers, had no mysteries for them. A glossary would have been more of an impertinence and a superfluity for them than a glossary of the dialect of the *Sporting Times* would be to the ordinary middle-aged and middle-class householder. Hence Mr. Kipling grew accustomed to waste no time in commentary, and the sudden plunge into a strange atmosphere and into unfamiliar 'shop' and slang which he compels the English reader to take is eminently bracing and delightful, though it takes away the breath to start with. In his hands we may truly say that new things become familiar and familiar things new. Which (to borrow a form of sentence much affected by himself) is half the battle.

A vivid impression, it is true, is not necessarily a correct one, and it is quite natural that there should be more than one opinion as to the truth of Mr. Kipling's sketches of Anglo-Indian society. Here his detractors (if he any have) will find the most promising material for animadversion. None of his stories, indeed, is wholly outside the region of possibility; while many of them doubtless had a more or less solid 'foundation in fact'. Some of the *Plain Tales* read like nothing so much as a reproduction of the current gossip of a day now dead and gone, with a proper alteration of names, dates, and immaterial surroundings. Human nature, after all, is not vastly different at Simla from human nature elsewhere. Why should jobbery and favouritism, which find a home in every clime, pass India by? In what country have men not been occasionally preferred to high office through the influence of pretty women? Doubtless merit swelters in the plains from time to time, while stupidity and incompetence are promoted to the honours and emoluments which they never earned. 'Tis a mere question of the thermometer. In more temperate zones, '*virtus laudater et—alget*'. Thus most of Mr. Kipling's anecdotes are probably, in one sense, well-authenticated. Chapter and verse could be cited for every one of them; and regarded as a collection of isolated and independent details they may be said to be literally true to life. But when these details come to be considered as parts of a greater whole, when the picture invites criticism as a complete work of art, the matter assumes an entirely different complexion. The Government of India is emphatically *not* conducted at headquarters in obedience to the dictates of intriguing hussies and their unscrupulous hangers-on. No more is the Government of Great Britain. Yet a satirist with the necessary adroitness could present the world with a description of the social and political life of London which would be absolutely horrifying and absolutely misleading, yet of which each individual stroke should have been painfully copied from the living model. He would be able to quote facts in proof of the existence among us of failings and of vices notoriously inconsistent with social or political wellbeing. But if he inferred, for example, universal corruption from the records of the divorce-court, he would be as wide of the mark as if, from a perusal of their light literature, he drew the conclusion that the French attach no sanctity to family life. The analogy we have suggested should put us on our guard against accepting as typical and representative personages or episodes with no claim to being anything of the kind. To hit off the exact proportion in which the component elements in the character of any community are blended is never an easy task, and its difficulty is not diminished for the storyteller by the fact that the baser ingredients lend themselves to his legitimate purposes in proportion as they are pungent and high-flavoured.

There are, to be quite frank, a few of Mr. Kipling's literary offspring which we would throw to the wolves without the least compunction. Mrs. Hauksbee 'won't do'; and no more will the 'boys' who make love to her. What in the rest of Mr. Kipling's work is knowledge degenerates too often into knowingness, a very different quality, when he begins to depict Indian Society. We become conscious of a certain aggressiveness in his touch—of the absence of the tone of true fashion—of more than a hint of that uneasy familiarity which may be frequently observed in the very young or the hopelessly shy. The ladies are not exactly patterns of good breeding, while the men who associate with them have a cheap swagger which Ouïda's guardsmen would despise. So at least some devil's advocate might argue with no little plausibility. There is unquestionably much better stuff in such slight sketches as 'Bubbling Well Road' or 'The Finances of the Gods' than in a thousand elaborate pieces of the type of 'Mrs. Hauksbee Sits Out', which leave behind the disagreeable suspicion that the author deliberately tried to scandalise. Sailing near the wind is a dangerous and undignified past-time for a writer of Mr. Kipling's calibre.

Nothing, indeed, is more extraordinary in this portion of Mr. Kipling's work than the interminglings of good and bad, worthy and base, essential and trifling. Cheek by jowl with smart snip-snap you find something that probes the inmost recesses of your soul. Only a few pages of print separate a specimen of flippant superficiality like 'The Education of Otis Yeere' from a masterpiece of analysis and penetration like 'The Hill of Illusion'. And *The Story of the Gadsbys*—at once the glory and the shame of Mr. Kipling's prose-muse—what is it but a field where wheat and tares grow together in careless and in-extricable confusion? To read that singular drama for the seventh or eighth time is to pass once more from delight to disgust and again to delight—is to marvel that genius which can soar so high should ever be content to stoop so low. At one moment the author discloses some of the deepest secrets of the human heart—secrets which most men take half a lifetime to find out—with a frankness and a simplicity which attest his extreme youth; at another his facetiousness is such as a re-spectable pot-house would reprobate, and his view of life too raffish for even a military lady-novelist to adopt. The most moving pathos alternates with the most brazen-faced vulgarity, and the most vital facts of human existence are handled with the raw cocksureness of an inspired schoolboy. *The Gadsbys* is the most amazing monument of precocity in all literature. Yet who can doubt that its faults, palpable and serious though they be, are upon a general balance outweighed by its merits? Or who would not swallow the opening scene, albeit with a wry face, rather than give up that later episode, where the author's method is so simple yet so telling, and its outcome makes so irresistible an appeal to the primary emotions—we mean the scene of Mrs. Gadsby's illness and delirium? If in none other of his writings he has sinned so grievously, in none has he made so ample an atonement.

In estimating the accuracy of Mr. Kipling's picture of the English in India the critic is entitled to fall back upon his knowledge of the corresponding ranks of society at home; but no such assistance is available when he comes to consider Mr. Kipling's treatment of native life. Its fidelity to the original has never, so far as we are aware, been impugned, and there are few besides Mr. Kipling himself who possess the qualifications necessary for sitting in judgment on this department of his work. For him, as for Strickland, 'the streets and the bazaars and the sounds in them are full of meaning', though he would probably be the first to admit how superficial any European's knowledge of the inner life of the 'black man' must needs be. It is not safe, to be sure, to take Mr. Kipling seriously at all times. Extravaganza is a form of art to which he occasionally condescends with the happiest results. What else are 'The Germ Destroyer' and 'Pig' in the *Plain Tales*? And what is 'The Incarnation of Krishna Mulvaney' but rollicking, incomparable, irresistible farce? But nobody can suppose for a moment that 'In Flood Time' or 'On the City Wall' was written 'with intent to deceive'; and even if a hundred pedants were to suggest a hundred reasons for suspecting the fidelity of his portraiture, we should prefer to maintain the attitude of unshaken faith, and to enjoy what is so admirably calculated to produce enjoyment. For, to tell the truth, the native tales carry their credentials on their very face. Like holograph documents, they must be allowed the privilege of proving themselves; and if work at once so powerful and so exquisite as 'Without Benefit of Clergy' happens not to be true to nature, so much the worse for nature. The description of life at a Rajput King's Court in *The Naulahka* is worth countless blue-books and innumerable tracts as a revelation of the inveterate habits of thought and of the social customs which a beneficent Government must attempt by slow degrees to accommodate as far as possible to the ethical standards of the West.

Mr. Kipling's military stories have probably enjoyed the greatest vogue of all his writings in this country, and not without reason. The subject of everyday life in the British army, though a tempting one, had been practically left untouched, and clamoured for a man of genius to 'exploit' it. We know with what complete success he took it up. 'Who can withstand Mulvaney, Learoyd, and Ortheris? ' 'Tis immortial fame the gentleman's going to give us,' predicted the first-named, and the prophecy bids fair to come true. Since the deathless Pickwick and his faithful band desisted from their wanderings, no group of personages has gained so well-assured a footing in the affections of the public as these same 'soldiers three'. Men do not love them, perhaps, for their own sakes. As studies of character they count for comparatively little. They are not discriminated with any great nicety, and the marked difference in their speech dispenses with all necessity for the finer and more delicate strokes of the brush. We cannot pretend to look upon Mulvaney as a Milesian Prometheus, with the vultures of remorse preying upon his vitals; nor does Learoyd seem to be distinguishable in any particular from our old friend the Yorkshireman of the stage. The claim which the trio really have upon our undying gratitude and regard arises mainly from their being the mouthpiece of the author for a series of stories which hold their own with any in our language in point of variety, humour, spirit, and power. It is unnecessary to expatiate on their merits, though we may call attention to the extraordinary felicity and appropriateness of their respective settings, of which Mulvaney and his comrades are *pars magna*. Nor is it possible to arrange them in order of excellence. Each seems the best until the next is read. We should not quarrel seriously with any one who indicated a special preference for 'The Courting of Dinah Shadd' and 'With the Main Guard', the latter being Mr. Kipling's best war-piece, with the exception of 'The Lost Legion'. But we cannot pass from them without congratulating the British private upon having at last found his *vates sacer*, and the army generally upon having fallen in with a writer who has taught the least imaginative of nations what manful work its soldiers are doing for it. There is a fine healthy ring in all Mr. Kipling's utterances about her Majesty's forces. But his inspiration was curiously anticipated by a writer who in other respects is his very antithesis. Tom Robertson was timid, artificial, and conventional. Mr. Kipling is dashing, original, and bold. Tom Robertson seems hopelessly out of date. Mr. Kipling is essentially *dans le train*. But he must be a rare hand indeed at the splitting of a hair who can detect any appreciable distinction or difference between the tone and sentiment of 'Ours'[1] and those of 'The Big Drunk Draf'', or 'Only a Subaltern', or 'The Man Who Was', or 'His Private Honour'.

The rough classification which, for convenience sake, we have made of Mr. Kipling's short stories is not quite exhaustive. There remain a

---

[1] [A play (1866) by T. W. Robertson, author of *Caste*]

fair number which are not tales of Anglo-Indian society, nor tales of native life, nor yet tales of the British army. There are, for instance, what we may call the tales of physical horror. Among these are 'Bertran and Bimi', 'A Matter of Fact', and 'The Mark of the Beast'; and, without embarking upon the general question whether such topics as they deal with fall within the legitimate sphere of art, we confess that we could have willingly spared them. The stories of the supernatural, on the other hand, like 'At the End of the Passage', we could spare by no possibility whatever. Finally, there is a small class which stands by itself in virtue of possessing in an especial degree the characteristic excellence of its creator's genius. 'The Finest Story in the World' will always stand out as perhaps the most striking illustration of Mr. Kipling's versatility. The deeper problems it suggests may be put on one side; what is of real moment is the snatches from the galley-slave's experience. Here are the same matchless power of presenting a scene and suggesting an atmosphere, the same realistic commemoration of minute details, the same idealistic selection of the relevant and the essential, which distinguished the Indian narratives, and all applied to a state of facts long since passed away. Yet even this miracle of invention and artifice must give place to 'The Man who would be King', which we venture to consider Mr. Kipling's *chef-d'œuvre* in prose. The fable makes considerable drafts on one's credulity at the outset; but the drafts are instantly honoured, and the reader, falling more and more under the master's spell, is whirled along triumphantly to the close. No time to take breath or to reflect, so impetuous and irresistible is the torrent. Those to whom emotions are as daily bread will find there a truly bounteous repast.

Whether a writer of short stories can write long ones and vice versa has often been acrimoniously debated; but one thing is plain, that Mr. Kipling has not yet proved the affirmative. *The Light that Failed* and *The Naulahka* have their moments. They are much more readable than most contemporary novels, and the latter is as thrilling as *Treasure Island*. But to compare them with, say, 'The Drums of the Fore and Aft' would be ridiculous. Perhaps one reason of their failure is the thoroughly uninteresting character of the hero and heroine. Who cares much for Dick and Maisie? Who for Nicholas Tarvin and Kate Sheriff? Better by far the society of Mowgli and the wolves—than whom indeed more agreeable company is not to be found without much seeking. None of Mr. Kipling's works has the same graciousness and charm as the *Jungle Books*, none is so wise, so considerate, so kindly. If, before trying them yourself, you follow the old maxim and 'Try them on the dog', the result is certain to be satisfactory. Children adore them, and add the animals to that menagerie which Robin, Dickie, Flapey and Pecksey[1] used to adorn. And if, fortified by the success of your experiment, you try them on yourself, you will thenceforth use no others. The reader will perhaps forgive an uncontrollable lapse into the dignified phraseology of latter-day criticism.

The peculiar attraction of Mr. Kipling's prose work lies much less in any solicitude for style than in his unique fertility of imagination. He need never beat about the bush, for it disgorges a hare every two minutes; nor has he time to be fastidious in his choice of words. In some of his earlier pieces his manner is almost vicious. It is like 'the picture-writing of a half-civilised people', to borrow an apt metaphor of his own—crude, jerky, flippant. The straining after smartness and sensation is too evident, and the flash epigram is too frequent and favourite an ornament. That these faults have been to a great extent corrected by the maturer taste and sounder discretion of advancing years is perfectly true. But they are not wholly eradicated, and Mr. Kipling has still to vindicate his title to be considered as a model of English style. That he could make it good if he pleased, we have not the least doubt. A descriptive passage like the following proves that he has little to learn:

Over our heads burned the wonderful Indian stars, which are not all pricked in on one plane, but, preserving an orderly perspective, draw the eye through the velvet darkness of the void up to the barred doors of heaven itself. The earth was a grey shadow, more unreal than the sky. We could hear her breathing lightly in the pauses between the howling of the jackals, the movement of the wind in the tamarisks, and the fitful mutter of musketry-fire, leagues away to the left. A native woman from some unseen hut began to sing, the mail-train thundered past on its way to Delhi, and a roosting crow cawed drowsily. Then there was a belt-loosening silence about the fires, and the even breathing of the crowded earth took up the story.

There is no doubt about that as a piece of English; but the great bulk of Mr. Kipling's most vigorous and successful prose-work is not in ordinary English but in dialect. It is in the lingo of the Cockney, the Irishman, or the Yorkshireman; or it is in a tongue specially invented for the use of birds and beasts; or it is in a language designed to reproduce the characteristic nuances of oriental thought and feeling. It is through such a medium that Mr. Kipling's genius seems to find its

[1] [Bird characters in *The Robins* (1786) by Mrs. Trimmer]

most ample and fitting expression; and perhaps it is on that account that his long stories are disappointing. They are necessarily in more or less literary English, for dialect cannot be maintained beyond a certain length of time without fatiguing the reader.

That Mr. Kipling has performed prodigies of ingenuity, and of more than ingenuity, with dialect in verse as well as in prose, is no more than the truth. He has indeed accomplished what, perhaps, was never achieved before. He has selected a *patois* the associations of which were wholly mean, commonplace, ludicrous, and degrading, and has made it the vehicle of poetry characterised by qualities the very reverse of these. But his verse, whether in plain English or in dialect, is superior to his prose in plain English, because poetry is more exacting than prose. It is the paradox of poetry that it permits no synonyms. The poet is in perpetual quest of the one inevitable word, and only the true poet can find it. Now in Mr. Kipling's poetry the right word emerges at the right moment, and no one can doubt that it *is* the right word.

> So it's knock out your pipes an' follow me!
> An' it's finish off your swipes an' follow me!
> Oh, 'ark to the fifes *a-crawlin'*!
> Follow me—follow me 'ome!

Does not the word we have italicised almost make one catch one's breath by its startling appropriateness? But we must not begin to quote, or this article would never end.

The technical difficulties of poetry have no terrors for Mr. Kipling. His command of rhythm and metre is absolute. No measure is too intricate for him to master, and some of the pleasure with which his verse is read is due to the apparent facility with which he handles a complicated scheme of versification. We think we can detect that Mr. Swinburne engaged some portion of Mr. Kipling's youth; but the influence of that master is not obtrusive in his later productions. For pure poetical prestidigitation we never read anything to compare with the stanza prefixed to chapter vii, of *The Naulahka*. Even Mr. Gilbert, in the happiest hours of his plenary Aristophanic inspiration, never equalled that. But luckily there is infinitely more in Mr. Kipling's poetry than mere nimbleness of wit or mechanical dexterity. His highest flights are high indeed, and it is true of his best work, as of all the world's greatest poetry, that it can be read and re-read without losing its freshness. New beauties are ever to be discovered, and the old ones shine with brighter lustre. His record as a poet is one of steady and rapid progress. His very earliest efforts are perhaps scarcely superior to the best verse in *Punch*, when the letterpress of that journal was worth reading. Among all the *Departmental Ditties* there is but one—'Possibilities'—whose original flavour and half-pathetic, half-cynical humour indicate something transcending extreme cleverness. 'The Ballad of East and West' was the first plain manifestation of genius; while in his subsequent volumes—in the *Barrack-room Ballads* and in *The Seven Seas*—there are poems whose authorship not even the greatest of England's singers need be eager to disavow. 'The Flag of England', 'A Song of the English', 'The Last Chantey', 'M'Andrew's Hymn',—these are strains that dwell in the memory and stir the blood. They have a richness and fulness of note very different from the shrill and reedy utterance of many who have attempted to tune their pipe to the pitch of courage and of patriotism. Yet even they sink into comparative insignificance beside that 'Recessional' which fifteen months ago took England by storm, and which seemed to concentrate in itself the glowing patriotism of a Shakespeare, the solemn piety of a Milton, and the measured stateliness of a Dryden. For sheer ingenuity and lightness of touch, indeed, 'The Song of the Banjo' cannot be matched. (Why, by the by, has the fate of 'the younger son' such a fascination for Mr. Kipling's muse?) But we are not prepared to put it in the same rank as the best of the *Barrack-room Ballads*, though what the best are we shall not be rash enough to say. Let the reader make his own selection.

To frame a concise yet exhaustive judgment upon Mr. Kipling is impossible, so various are his gifts, so rich his endowment. A glowing imagination, an inexhaustible invention, a profound knowledge of the human heart—these are three of his choicest possessions. Yet how inadequately does so bald a statement sum up the rich profusion of his talents! How beggarly and feeble seem the resources of language to do justice to his great achievements! It is good to think that in all human probability he will be long with us to continue his work and to enhance his fame. There will never be wanting persons to dissuade from patriotism, and to point out how expensive the exercise of that virtue is apt to be. It is well for us that a great writer should be in our midst strengthening the weak hands and confirming the feeble knees. Much as he has accomplished in the past, there remains much for him to accomplish in the future, and if in the course of providence we should be spared to survey Mr. Kipling's work thirty years hence, we make no doubt that much of priceless value will have been added to its tale. For the constant burden of his song teaches the lesson which it most behoves the younger generation to learn. 'Law, Orrder, Duty, an' Restraint, Obedience, Discipline!'—these are the foundations of a prosperous State. The Laws of the Jungle are the Laws of the Universe, and we shall be fortunate indeed if, when times of stress and peril arrive, we have realised what our fathers learned in sorrow and tribulation and what their sons are too prone to forget—

> But the head and the hoof of the Law
> And the haunch and the hump is—Obey!

30. 'The Madness of Mr. Kipling'

1898

Article signed 'An Admirer' in *Macmillan's Magazine*, Vol. LXXIX, pp. 131-5 (December 1898): credited to Stephen Gwynn by *The Wellesley Index*.

Stephen Lucius Gwynn (1864–1950), Irish poet and critic, author of studies of Swift, Goldsmith, Scott, Tennyson, Thomas Moore, Stevenson and others.

There is no gratitude more sincere than that which is paid to the man who can amuse us; and few of us would be slow to admit that Mr. Kipling has made the world more amusing. He is one of the most agreeable luxuries that we possess, and for what should we be grateful if not for luxuries? But there are times when gratitude sees, like Desdemona, a divided duty. Should it blind us to the shortcomings of a favourite author? Or should it make us indignant when he produces work seriously below his best level? There is a case to be made out for either side, and of course no artist can reasonably be expected to produce nothing but masterpieces. But when one sees a writer wilfully making play in a definitely wrong direction, it is surely permissible to remonstrate. There are a dozen stories in Mr. Kipling's new book, *The Day's Work*; three of them are, as I think it will be generally allowed, in his best manner; half-a-dozen more are no worse than many good things in his earlier work; but the other three, though in their way clever enough, no doubt, like everything else of their author's, do, I must say, awaken a desire to protest. And some of the protests which must be made against them apply partially to the other stories. But let us analyse the volume.

Over 'The Tomb of his Ancestors', which relates the adventures of Lieutenant John Chinn among the Bhils and his hereditary domination, there will surely be no dispute; nor is there likely, I take it, to be much over 'William the Conqueror', a love-story set against a background of Indian famine. Here is a passage I should like to quote before turning Devil's Advocate. One Scott, of the Irrigation Department in the Punjab, has been ordered down to fight the famine in the Madras Presidency, and, since the rice-eating people will sooner starve than eat unfamiliar grains, he has been forced to give the grain to goats and feed perishing babies on their milk. After a month of milking and baby-feeding he returns to the central camp, where 'William', a hard-riding young lady with a preference for men of action, has been busy also.

He had no desire to make any dramatic entry, but an accident of the sunset ordered it that, when he had taken off his helmet to get the evening breeze, the low light should fall across his forehead and he could not see what was before him; while one waiting at the tent door beheld, with new eyes, a young man, beautiful as Paris, a god in a halo of golden dust, walking slowly at the head of his flock, while at his knee ran small naked Cupids.

That is a pretty picture, and tells all the more against the severe realism of its setting.

The other one of the first three is 'The Bridge Builders', which, for my own part, I should put in a class by itself, ranking it higher than anything of its author's except only 'The Man that would be King'. But it is open to certain objections, and not unreasonable ones. Mr. Kipling suffers from a mania, which is really only the perversion of his best quality. His passionate desire for concrete information makes his whole work a storehouse of curious and sometimes very interesting facts; but with the desire to know all about everything goes a desire to be able to call everything by its right name, and this has bred a kind of collector's mania, a craving for strange words. If Mr. Kipling discovers a new term—a technical term for choice, but any flower of American slang will do nearly as well—he is as happy as an entomologist with a new beetle, and as anxious to produce it. Now a story which turns upon a triumph of modern engineering gives great scope to this bent of mind, and the consequence is that the first three or four pages of 'The Bridge Builders' are sprinkled thick with words like 'spile-pier', 'borrow-pit', 'trusses' and 'revetments'. Tastes differ about the result. To myself it appears to convey the atmosphere which Mr. Kipling wants to attain, and certainly the picture of the bridge rises distinct enough; but to many other people it seems a disagreeable pedantry, and indisposes them to follow with proper attention what comes after. About that also there are two opinions; one fervent admirer said to me that the story broke off just at the interesting part, where the flood came down on the unfinished bridge, and went off into a silly dream. But the peculiar bent of the author's mind, while it gives him the keenest interest in the bridge as a bridge, makes him also see in it not merely a bridge but a symbol. The spanning of the Ganges is not merely an engineering achievement; it stands for a type of the losing battle which the old gods of the East fight against new and spiritual forces. Still, in the use of symbols there always lurks a snare, and though I should defend with enthusiasm the symbolism of this story, which lies a good deal nearer to poetry than to prose, I am constrained to admit that it sins by a trifle of obscurity; and in the other stories the use of a figurative method leads the author into errors much worse than obscurity. In short, as Devil's Advocate, I should sum up my indictment by accusing Mr. Kipling first of an abuse of technical jargon, secondly, and this is a more serious matter, of an abuse of symbolism.

The two faults are at their worst when they occur together, and indeed they are traceable back to one source. Everybody felt that there was symbolism, or allegory, involved in the two *Jungle Books*, but nobody resented it, for the stories were fundamentally interesting. The presence of Mowgli added the human link which is needed to bring us into sympathy, and the animals talked credibly. Animals must, and do, talk, and it seems natural that they should talk as Mr. Kipling makes them. But when it comes to engines discoursing on a railway-siding, or the different parts of a ship holding converse, credibility ceases, and, as Horace observes, *incredulus odi*—the incredible is a bore. But the reason why Mr. Kipling falls into this error is sufficiently simple. He has a passion for machinery, and very rightly, since the marine engine, even more than Finlayson's bridge, is to this age what the Parthenon was to Athens. Probably his sincerest aspiration expresses itself in McAndrew's phrase: 'Oh for another Robbie Burns to sing the song of steam.'

Mr. Kipling may live to sing the song of steam yet, but for the present he trails us somewhat heavily at the heels of his hobby. Machines may be alive to him, but they are not alive to us. Nobody would object to his technicalities when they are used so admirably as in the story 'Bread Upon the Waters', a capital yarn with that touch of something more in it that puts Mr. Kipling miles above so excellent a spinner of yarns as Mr. Jacobs. Mr. Jacobs would never have realised that McPhee had a Shekinah in 'the matter o' fair runnin' '. But in that other story of a steamer, 'The Devil and the Deep Sea', I confess that the technicalities overpower me. It was no doubt an admirable thing that Mr. Kipling should have plotted out exactly what would happen in the engine-room if a five-inch shell fractured the bolts that held the connecting-rod to the forward crank; but the description will be worse than Hebrew to the average reader, for it is not merely unintelligible but tantalising. This, however, Mr. Kipling knows well enough, and he takes his chance; for my own part I willingly accept the bewilderment for the subsequent picture of the repairing. I cannot understand what is being done, but I can feel the feverish activity and the sense of amazing resourcefulness. It enlarges one's view of the possibilities in human nature to read of man, stripped to the skin and reduced all but to a state of nature, at grapple desperately and successfully to improvise the most complicated weapons of civilisation.

But what I suspect Mr. Kipling of not knowing is that a symbol has only value when it translates into the concrete something less intelligible in the abstract; and that an allegory is only tolerable when its story is so interesting that one tacitly forgives it for being an allegory. Finlayson's bridge over the Ganges seems to me an excellent symbol, a material incident to show a spiritual conflict; the *Jungle-Book* stories are admirable allegories because there is very little allegory in them; we are haunted by a sense of some further meaning, not knocked over the head with a moral. But the sketch called 'A Walking Delegate' is an allegory naked and not ashamed. Mr. Kipling has a profound antipathy to Socialism, and a profound belief in 'the day's work'; that renders him a valuable prophet, and in one of his cleverest poems, 'An Imperial

Rescript', he put the case against an artificial limitation of man's energy more convincingly than could be done by a legion of blue-books. But he has now chosen to represent the contempt of real work-ers for the idle demagogue in terms of horseflesh, and the result is, to speak plainly, nonsense. These are not the ideas of horses, for the con-ception of combination for a common end is essentially foreign to them; and if Mr. Kipling wanted to write the dialogue it is hard to see why he should not have written it about men. Very probably he would say it amused him to write it in this way; and that is an un-answerable argument when what amuses the writer amuses the reader also. This Walking Delegate is a caricature of a man, but he is not in the least like a horse. The other horses are like horses, but the situation is not one that could conceivably arise among horses. Swift saw the possibilities long ago, and exhausted the dramatic contrast between a man's conventions and the rules of life among decent animals, in circumstances fabulous, of course, but not inconceivable. And I con-fess that even the better features of the story—for instance, the insight into the experiences of a New York tram-horse—are marred to me by the dialect. There may possibly be some fascination about a tongue in which people say 'nope' and 'yep' for 'no' and 'yes', but I do not feel it; and there are surely enough authors already engaged in garnering the rank crop of American vulgarisms. To a certain extent these have infected Mr. Kipling's own style already; we find him talking about 'slugging' a guard, 'cramping' a coupé, and so forth; and before the century is out, he may be writing 'vim' and 'brainy' with the best of them.

'The Ship that Found Herself' is another allegory, or symbol as you choose. If an organisation—a State, for instance—is to be worth its place in the world, all the bits in that organisation have to do their separate work in the best way they can and not mind if their toes are trodden on, because that is inevitable. That is the moral of innumerable tales in Mr. Kipling's work, and a very admirable moral it is. Servants of the State have to realise that they are parts of a machine, the whole of which depends on the loyalty of every part. That is all very well as a metaphor or illustration. But when you come to writing a story to show how all the parts of a ship, the rivets, stringers, garboard-strake, and heaven knows what else, have feelings to be considered and how each learns a common lesson—why then you are very apt to be a bore. And when you bring in the steam as a kind of guardian angel with a ten-dency to be facetious, you approach to being intolerable.

And yet I must admit that I have heard an intelligent man speaking of this book describe 'The Maltese Cat' as the best story in it, and next to that he placed 'The Ship that Found Herself' and '·007'. There are things to interest one, as well as many to annoy one in the story of the ship; it is doubtless a graphic account of the process of adjustment which actually takes place on a first voyage; but '·007' is beyond me. Here all Mr. Kipling's manias break loose at once—there is the madness of American slang, the madness of technical jargon, and the madness of believing that silly talk, chiefly consisting of moral truisms, is amusing because you put it into the mouths of machines, for machines in Mr. Kipling have mouths. Here is a sample:

'I've trouble enough in my own division,' said a lean, light suburban loco with very shiny brake-shoes. 'My commuters wouldn't rest till they got a parlour-car. They've hitched her back of all, and she hauls worse'n a snowplough. I'll snap her off some day sure, and then they'll blame anyone except their fool-selves. They'll be askin' me to haul a vestibuled next.'

Now in this I do not know what 'brake-shoes', 'commuters', or a 'vestibuled' may be, and as Mr. Kipling has already surfeited me with strange knowledge and unfamiliar terms, I would not thank him to tell me. It is enough that he should let loose upon us all the unknown possibilities of our own tongue without borrowing abominations from America. But the pith of my objection is to this silly perversion of symbolism. It is no doubt perfectly true that complicated machines have their idiosyncrasies, their personalities even, if you please; a bicycle can be nearly as annoying as a horse. For once in a way it may be good fun to push the fancy a little further and attribute to them sentient life, but Mr. Kipling has overdone the thing. If we take 'The Ship that Found Herself' seriously, as I believe he means it to be taken, it is an exaggeration—what Mr. Ruskin used to call a pathetic fallacy; and the thing is capable of indefinite and appalling extension. If Mr. Kipling fell ill (which heaven forbid) or had any reason to in-terest himself in the inside of a chemist's shop, we might have the different pills bragging to one another, and tincture of quinine com-paring its function in the universe with that of a black draught. Why not? It is all in 'the day's work'.

In all seriousness, be his faults what they may, Mr. Kipling has something of nearly every virtue that an author can be credited with. His work is obviously wrought up to the last limit of care; he does not produce too much—indeed, we would welcome more; but he does not seem to have a sure critical instinct. This pedantry of technical terms seems to grow on him, and the craze for symbolism, with the accompanying belief that a thing gains by being said round a corner instead of straight out, might very conceivably mar the work of the one man among us from whom our prose literature has much to expect. And not our prose literature only. Years ago, Mr. Kipling spoilt a poem in which there were almost the best verses he ever wrote, 'L'Envoi', with unnecessary and crabbed nautical terms, all the more annoying because in the same poem he had two or three times over got the real poetry of the thing, whose accidental details he wearied us with cataloguing. Clever as it is, this is not poetry:

> See the shaking funnels roar, with the Peter at the fore,
> And the fenders grind and heave,
> And the derricks clack and grate, as the tackle hooks the crate,
> And the fall rope whines through the sheave.

But there can be no mistake about this:

> Then home, get her home, where the drunken rollers comb,
> And the shouting seas drive by,
> And the engines stamp and ring, and the wet bows reel and swing
> And the Southern Cross rides high!

'McAndrew's Hymn' makes interesting reading, no doubt, but it also misses being poetry, because Mr. Kipling is too much set on the detail and cannot hide his knowledge; what he wants to celebrate is the power, and he only shows us the machinery. And the other fault, excessive indulgence in symbolism, which, as I have said, makes even 'The Bridge-Builders' a trifle obscure, renders many of his verses where he feels he is bound to be lucid, as incomprehensible as the wildest rhapsody of Mr. Swinburne. Enough, however, has been said upon all these matters to explain the objection without further illustration; and enough, also, I hope, to convince Mr. Kipling, should he chance to read them, that these are the words of

AN ADMIRER

31. Neil Munro on 'Mr. Rudyard Kipling'

1899

Signed article from *Good Words*, Vol. XL, pp. 261–5 (April 1899).

Neil Munro (1864–1930) was a popular Scottish novelist who did much to encourage the 'Celtic Revival' with his dialect stories, historical novels and Scots poems.

The past month has seen oceans of ink spilled in the recountment of Mr. Kipling's achievements, yet of the myriad commentators who made the novelist's sick-bed inspire their laudatory pens no one seems to have attempted an analysis of the man, and what, in our indispensable phrase, we call his message. It has been iterated to weariness that he writes with the star-gemmed quill of genius and the fiery exaltation of the patriot. These are the more obvious of his qualities, the abstract impressions created by his work, that would of themselves perhaps have left us cold because of their very commonness, for Providence flicks a brain-patch a little out of the normal in one or two skulls in every English Board School (with a double allowance for North Britain), and reverence for the Old Rag, the zest of the glory of going on and of being an Englishman, is thrust, with gas-pipe drill and the manual exercise, into multitudinous Boys' Brigades till pride of country exudes from every pore. The clanging patriotic note we have heard so much about in the past few weeks is, at least in its more arrogant note of Imperialism, by no means the most universally esteemed of Mr. Kipling's characteristics, nor is it new with him. Did not Campbell trumpet to our hearts in the sonorous call that finds its last lingering haunting note in the name of Elsinore; and did not Tennyson and Doyle and Swinburne, eminently among others, strike lustily on Britain's brass-bossed shield generations more or less before the refrains of Atkins and the Adventurers hummed through the century end?

And yet the application of the spectroscope to a star so new and dazzling is no trivial business, for directly of the star itself we have seen but little. We have biographical glimpses of an infant in Bombay, a school-boy at Westward Ho!, a reporter and sub-editor in India, but no intimate details of what went to the making of a personality matured marvellously at the age of twenty-one, and destined to become the most potent influence in English letters in his own generation, so far as it has gone. What we know of Mr. Kipling must be gathered from his work: him the interviewer has followed vainly, and the personal paragrapher has had to dish up for his patrons disappointing and more or less apocryphal scraps. We find revealed in those works a singular physical and mental vitality, 'a very strong man', as he has said himself of Tommy Atkins, with a great and exuberant zest in every aspect of life, with huge self-confidence, humour, irony, curiosity, and stoicism in a wonderful degree. That ever-apparent delight he has in the terminology of crafts, trades, and callings obviously outwith his direct experience, may be accepted as indicative not only of the common artistic appreciation for out-of-the-way and pregnant words or phrases, but of a real love for the teeming interests, the human activities they express. For generations our poets and romancers have cherished the old mechanical plant of their ancestors—loves, seasons, scenery, and (to a lamentable and indecent extent of late) the internals. Mr. Kipling, thrown by the caprice of fortune into a career oscillating between two worlds, began the business of his life by surrendering most of the old conventional inspirations and locutions, and used his eyes to look abroad upon the marvel of the modern world. Cortes and his men (or, more correctly, Balboa) saw from their peak in Darien but an empty, wind-blown ocean; Kipling had a greater cause for wild surmise as perhaps the very first—Whitman out of count—to behold the Seven Seas thrid by the traffic of man, so infinitely romantic, so infinitely eloquent of the irrepressible valour of the race. Lesser men it has left unmoved—unless they were underwriters—him it touched to great emotional issues. It has been so with him on land too. Tommy Atkins and Britain's pioneer work on vexed frontiers have inspired him, not primarily because he was an Englishman, but because he was a man moved profoundly by the persistence of his fellows in a world whose pathos and oft futility he has obviously at the same time understood. Man the artificer, 'the disease of the agglutinate dust, lifting alternate feet', Mr. Kipling has seen in the light of comprehensive humanity and brotherhood. Ships threshing the seas triumphant, armies combating ague, fever, heathendom, and bloody death; railways roaring over continents, hunters boldly venturing upon trails mysterious and forlorn, outposts of progress in raw new lands—the terrific yet magnificent significance of these human enterprises has impressed him. And all that he has observed he has seen with the philosophic eye, he has enveloped his every picture, his very sentiment with stoic calm, that, now we have emerged from the experiments of the problem—novelists and the didactic poets, is essentially the mood in which the century shall go out.

About a dozen books—a book a year for the years of his activity—provide us with the scope of Mr. Kipling's genius. If he wrote no more they were sufficient to establish his reputation as a man marking an epoch in English letters. We could indeed sacrifice some of his work without detracting in the smallest degree from his permanent reputation, though the loss might mean the surrender of many light and cheerful hours. *Under the Deodars*, for instance, that exposure in youthful sarcasm of domestic eccentricities in Anglo-Indian life, so often superficially flippant and smart, reveals nothing of the mature, reflecting Kipling; another generation will probably confess that it would part without a pang with these and other stories where the Hauksbee flourishes. 'Brugglesmith' and *Badalia Herodsfoot*, 'My Sunday at Home', and a few other caprices of his prose muse might also pass into the limbo unwept, unhousel'd, unanel'd. The marvel is that a writer so profuse and versatile should have made mistakes so few. The perfect remainder, speaking comparatively, charm by their novelty, their vitality, their indubitable genius, but most of all because of the man they reveal, as must be the case in all great works of literary art, Mr. Browning's doctrine of reticence to the contrary. In them we find the human affection that inspires good literature, the essential, but not too prominent, touch of pathos, the tolerance that says the charitable word for the weakling, yet bows the head to just punishment, for man is master of his fate. It may be that Mr. Kipling has sought after the artist's impartiality in limning such a portrait as that of Terence Mulvaney, surely one of the most permanent and lovable characters in fiction, but despite himself his personal predilections emerge in the portrait. We have in that erratic representative of our red-coat rule in India the most familiar type of his creator's heroes. Mulvaney borrows some of the black-guardism of d'Artagnan; he is a little of the bully, of the drunkard, the barrack-room Don Juan, with few claims upon our respect as sober Christians and decent citizens. Yet how humorous are his lovable attributes; his camaraderie shines on him like a cuirass, his response to his better man is frequent and convincing. Savagely surrounded, savagely descended, the bitter circumstances of his life conspiring always to show the worst of him, we must be prizing, as his painter does, the occasions when he defies his destiny and laboriously acts the man. What sins are we not half ready to condone in a hero so speckled when, in 'With the Main Guard', having kept his heat-tortured comrades amused through the sleepless night with his story,

'Oh, Terence,' I said, 'it's you that have the tongue.'
He looked at me wearily, his eyes were sunk in his head, and his face was drawn and white. 'Ey, ey,' said he, 'I've blandandhared him through the night somehow, but can thim that hilps others hilp thimselves? Answer me that, sorr.'

Mulvaney is the composite Kipling hero. Unlike the musketeer of Louis XIII, he moves in an atmosphere, not a vacuum tube; we know not only what he is, but why he is what he is; he is a living person, not a marionette. This realism and this atmospheric envelopment distinguish all the best of Mr. Kipling's creations. His women, whether they be camp heroines, dubious ladies of the married quarters, creatures of Simla intrigue, or common wives and mothers, stand upon their legs, move and have their being in their appropriate and native air, a phrase here and there, let slip as if it had no great relation to the matter at issue, telling all the history and ancestry of which the new novelist of heredity must have numerous chapters, doleful and melancholy chapters, to lay bare. Mrs. Hauksbee is not a heroine except to the tolerant artistic eye that beholds her wonderfully human and true to a life that has contradictions and complexities utterly beyond our unravelling. I have said we might part with her without a pang, and yet I doubt if we could; rather I should have said we could let go her attendant train of vapid and caddish followers, and forget the social life of which she is the centre. She herself is Mr. Kipling's strongest female character. He knows her past, he reveals all the ignominy of her present, but, carrying his tolerance further in her than in any other, he betrays what seems an admiration for her powerful personality.

In his first few books Mr. Kipling, with heroes and heroines more or less variant of the two named, made more populous the world about us of unforgettable men and women of the imagination. *Plain Tales from the Hills*, and the half-dozen booklets published first by Wheeler of Allahabad, in grey paper covers that yet to look upon is to experience a sense of boon friendships—these contain the work that

he will find it difficult to improve upon. There we were made acquaint
for the first time with the Terentian philosophy—

> For to admire and for to see
> For to be'old this world so wide;

the British soldier became for the first time something more than a
Surrey-side melodramatic tinpot hero; our little wars with Pathan and
Dacoit jumped into actuality, and were no longer occult suggestions,
remote, far-off, incomprehensible in the brief telegraphic news of the
morning papers. India itself, with its name redolent of romance from
the days of Virgil, found its exponent for the modern man, and we
became of a sudden familiar with a country where nothing had ever
happened before but famines and mutinies; with its heats, its rains, its
colour, its vast spaces, its commingling odours. The hot savage soil
on the fringe of barbarian blackness turned up red to the coulter of
civilisation. Whitechapel and the English areas where zymotic disease
abounds wrestled for our glory with savage Orientals; we were in a
new world, where, luckily, people, as in the days of Scott, were doing
things eternally, and not simply whining at existence.

'The Drums of the Fore and Aft' and 'The Man Who Would Be
King', these notably among the early essays in a new method of fiction
stirred us by the vivid illusion they conveyed, by the vista they suggested of space and action, by the romance with which they were informed in every image, the wholesome manliness that throbbed in
every sentiment. It is in the genre of which they are the best examples that
Mr. Kipling is pre-eminent. In the superficial elements of many of his
other stories there is much imitable though novel and ingenious, in
those named and in the horror of 'The Mark of the Beast' and 'The
End of the Passage', there is in inspiration of a much more rare and
elusive kind, a quality that cannot be repeated by any other writer.

The gods were extravagantly good to Mr. Kipling, for with his
gift of dramatic tale and a career to equip him for its expression, they
gave him the gift of poetry, lacking which prose narrative is soulless
and evanescent. It is the poetic insight that over and over again re-
deems brutal and even vulgar passages in his tales from our indifference
or contempt; there he would have shown the poet if *Departmental
Ditties*, *Barrack-room Ballads*, and *The Seven Seas* had never been written.
But he has in his works of verse justified himself as the laureate of
English endeavour. A brain-weary people, sick of abstruse sermons
played upon dulcimers, have hailed with gladness a song and chorus

accompanied by the banjo. Some of the strenuous young gentlemen who sing in pestilently unmusical and jerky measure of life, time, and early demise have an equipment Mr. Kipling cannot or does not boast of. They rejoice in vocabularies extensive and precious; they have a fastidiousness that keeps them clear of the cheap tune, the vulgar hero, the sentiment of the *Lion Comique*, the dialect that is unheard in drawing-rooms.They can write much that Mr. Kipling could not write to save his soul, but they cannot write so as to be read or listened to, which, cant aside, has been the first ambition of every ballad-maker since the days when Homer smote his lyre. Literature in prose or poetry is saved from eternal perdition by fresh starts; just when the material of conventional verse has been spread out thin to invisibility, and sheer intellect is going to upset our apple-cart, a lark soars into the heavens with a simple song for lesson, a man sheds the cerements of convention, steps back from the choir, and gives his natural voice a trial unafraid. Then, no matter what he sings—weariness and fret, the joy of life, passion, Spring or stars, if a robust individuality, a clean nature, a lyric lilt and cadence be his, we must be listening. His are the airs that the people find haunting; they may be even only temporary in appeal, but permanence is not, in spite of all we say to the contrary, the first and greatest essential of poetry. Wharton boasted that with 'Lillibulero' he had whistled a king out of three kingdoms; we have today forgotten that air that Uncle Toby so constantly dwelt on, but in the final balancing of things that have influenced, who can say that the forgotten 'Lillibulero' is not more weighty than studious measures in classic mould a few rare exclusive souls have sung for centuries?

With material entirely new, with a method novel, Kipling, in *Barrack-room Ballads* and *The Seven Seas*, has captured the general ear and touched the general heart. That, it may be retorted, was done aforetime by the Muse of Mr. Sims. Yet in this instance there is a great difference, though it seems sacrilege to hint the necessity of differentiation. It is not the music-hall audience alone that is impressed by the weird terror of 'Danny Deever', the sentiment of the majestic 'Ballad of East and West', the *élan* of the 'Sons of the Widow', and the cadence and wistfulness of 'Mandalay'. In these measures artists have found the lyric note no way abased. Good as *Barrack-room Ballads* were, the more recent *Seven Seas* was better. There we found Mr. Kipling still with 'the best words in the best order', as Coleridge defined poetry, but more profound in the hearts of man. A wider sweep of interests, a more mature valuation of the phenomena of life, a more opulent and canorous note peals in his lines, the man behind the instrument is more finely revealed. Any claim by any other living man than the author of 'A Song of the English', to be considered the laureate by divine right of English peoples would be ridiculous. But the Imperialism of the book is only one of its impressive features. The age of steam and telegraph, Hotchkiss guns and Saratoga trunks has found its balladist there, and he has found nothing common or unclean. The soldiers of the later military ballads, too, betray an ageing creator; they are still strumming on the banjo, but their songs have lost some of the shallow inspiration of the 'Alls; they lean upon homing bulwarks and reflect upon the sweet futilities that have stayed them here and there upon the sides of 'the 'appy roads that take you o'er the world'. And the seas cry in his work for the first time, not the played-out oceans of dhow and galley and picturesque but unwieldy three-deckers, but of the darting cruiser, the liner spurning leagues a day in every weather, the buffeting of the elements, and the engineer.

There are other works of Mr. Kipling than those I have named. The *Jungle Books* delight by their insight, almost magic, of the untamed wilds and all their residents; *Captains Courageous*, less felicitously inspired but yet original and unique, *Many Inventions* and *The Day's Work*, *Life's Handicap*, *The Light that Failed*, and *The Naulakha* have material fresh and strong. Taking either his prose or poetry in separate parts, testing by ordinary canons, it will happen that the writing seems often to be on a lower plane than the imaginative inspiration, and a sense of something wanting may ensue. But surveying the work of Mr. Kipling as a whole, the most fastidious must be impressed by the greatness of its genius, the scope and variety it displays, the essentially wholesome influence it creates.

32. Two Reviews of *Stalky & Co.*

1899

Anonymous reviews in the *Athenaeum*, No. 3755, pp. 515–16 and the *Academy*, No. 1432, pp. 421–2 (both 14 October 1899).

These are included to show the divergences of critical opinion about this the most controversial of Kipling's books.

I

Most English boys—and most Englishmen who have anything of the boy still in them—will rejoice in *Stalky & Co.* Boys will declare that the book is 'spiffing' and if they read it in school hours—a not impossible feat—will have to keep a handkerchief ready to stuff into their mouths to prevent their laughter attracting the attention of the form-master. Mr. Kipling himself has every reason to feel proud of the success with which he has phonographed the English public-school boy's talk and sentiments.

Mr. Kipling knows his English boy, as he seems to know everything, outside and inside—especially outside. Most men have a vivid memory of their boyhood's days; but with most there is an idealizing halo round them which altogether alters the value of the picture. Mr. Kipling, with that marvellous memory of his, recalls his school days as in themselves they really were. He sees the British boy, with his infinite capacity for fun, his finite capacity for insubordination, his coarseness in word and act, modified by an ultra-sensitive delicacy of feeling in certain directions. *Stalky & Co.* is almost a complete treatise on the strategy and tactics of the British schoolboy—or perhaps one should say the British public-school boy. Reverence for the head authority and contempt for all other authority, respect for most aspects of physical training, and utter indifference towards the training of the intellect, underlie the whole *Stimmung* of the book. Mr. Kipling has taught his public how Matthew Arnold's Barbarians are trained.

Here he not only describes—he defends; the implications of the whole book is a glorification of the public-school method of training character, or perhaps we should qualify, and say training the character of the leading classes. Two of the stories are bracketed together as 'Slaves of the Lamp, I.', and 'Slaves of the Lamp, II.' (the last story of the book—a kind of epilogue), with the seeming intention of showing that the tricks boys play upon their form-masters come in usefully as training in strategy for frontier warfare. In the first of the stories Stalky 'scores off' the best-hated master by leading a drunken carrier to think that the said master had used a catapult against him, where-upon he resorts to reprisals, and the form-master's study is made to suffer. In the last story Stalky, now a lieutenant on the frontier, is defending a fort which is attacked by two native tribes that have for the moment sunk their feuds. Stalky steals out with a detachment to the rear of their encampments, and, when the attack takes place, peppers one of the tribes with shots, seemingly coming from the direction of the other. Result, revival of the feud, and the form-master tribe is attacked by the carrier one. In short, these portions of the book are, in a measure, Mr. Kipling's answer to the question our neighbours are asking, *A quoi tient la supériorité des Anglo-Saxons?*

It is natural to compare *Stalky & Co.* with Mr. Kipling's other boys' book, *Captains Courageous*: one treats of the boy in his native and natural environment, the other of a boy in strange surroundings. Both are eminently didactic in tone, the chief lesson inculcated being that of the good effects of a sound whacking on a boy's character, even if the cane is applied with seemingly 'flagrant injustice'. In both cases the type of boy to be turned out is that of the military or commercial organizer. 'Save he serve, no man may rule'—not perhaps, a very subtle lesson, nor particularly one that needs insisting on, but it is brought home with all Mr. Kipling's astonishing force, and in *Stalky & Co.* is presented with even a certain amount of polemical intention.

Mr. Kipling evidently does not believe in what is known as appealing to a boy's higher feelings. One of the most subtle sections of the book is that entitled 'The Flag of their Country'. A blatant politician gives an address to the school, just after a volunteer cadet corps has been formed, and at the finish unfurls a cheap calico Union Jack, with the result that the corps is immediately disbanded, and, for the only time, Stalky, in the presence of his chums, bursts into tears. Here Mr. Kipling touches upon one of the profoundest traits in the English character, the abhorrence of English boys—and, for the matter of that, of English men—of having their most sacred feelings referred to publicly. Some slight hits (not in the very best taste) at Dr. Farrar's books are doubtless meant to emphasize the same moral. After all, is not the contrast between the military and clerical ideas of life? Mr. Kipling, here as elsewhere, is on the side of Tommy Atkins.

The interest of *Stalky & Co.* for 'grown-ups' will naturally be the pictures of English military school life presented in it, but it would be misleading to accept them as representing all English boarding schools, or even all English public schools. To complete the picture we need a description of the former, which, on the evidence of others, would not present so pleasant an aspect as Westward Ho! And here it may be noted that Westward Ho! is not perhaps a fair representative of English public schools. Mr. Kipling himself indicates as much by the stress he lays on the undesirable portion of the school which has been with the 'crammer' in town. Public-school boys in general will ask in surprise, Why were the assistants so rotten when the Head was so able? And is it usual for school chaplains to smoke in small boys' studies? The 'honour of the House' is satirized; but is it nothing, ought it to be nothing?

There is another aspect of *Stalky & Co.* which will interest all English people—the light it throws on Mr. Kipling's own school career, and the formative influences on his character. He scarcely disguises that he is the 'Beetle' of the story, and that, but for his early spectacles, he would have tried to emulate the deeds of Indian army subalterns which he takes such pleasure in describing. Rarely has a personal defect proved of such national advantage. The hint is also given that Mr. Kipling's journalistic career was due to the discernment of Mr. Cormell Price, the headmaster of the school.

To the students of Mr. Kipling's art his new book affords a number of interesting problems. His greatest skill has hitherto been shown in the *conte*—the rapid presentation of one 'action', with the appropriate characterization, which makes the action artistically inevitable. Here we have a series of school *contes*, but their total result is to work up into a tolerably complete picture of a certain school organism—a military preparatory school in North Devon. We find not only various types of schoolboys delineated (with the significant exception of the 'sap' or 'swot'), but also a tolerably complete series of portraits of assistant masters, including the rather improbable 'Padre', who has the boys' entire confidence; and then, in a class apart, 'the Head', whose penetrating influence throughout the school is most subtly indicated in every story. We have even the relations of the school indicated with the surrounding population, and occasional snapshots of visitors, parents and guardians, and Old Boys. In this way the seemingly disconnected series of stories makes up a tolerably complete picture of the school as an organic whole. This is true artistry, such as had not been displayed by Mr. Kipling in his previous efforts. His very keenness of vision has apparently prevented him from composing his work on a larger canvas.

It is somewhat difficult and misleading to quote specimens of work which thus depends for its higher qualities on general tone and treatment rather than upon details. Perhaps the following will, at any rate, indicate the absolute accuracy with which boys' words and doings are touched off by Mr. Kipling. Stalky & Co. meet a prefect, while out of bounds with permission:

[quotes 'The Last Term' *Stalky, & Co.*, p. 222, line 16, to p. 223, line 30]

Nothing could be more lifelike and convincing. For the manner in which this episode leads up to a disgraceful rout of the whole body of prefects the reader must be referred to the story itself.

The best test of a book of this kind is not to judge it by the canons of high art, but to get a boy to read it. *Stalky & Co.* comes triumphantly past this test, for the experiment has been tried. The boy in question, on being asked to put in order of merit the various stories which had caused him so many guffaws, expressed his preference for 'The Moral Reformers'; it has a touch of cruelty in it which appeals to the savage elements of that age; then came 'An Unsavoury Interlude', again an appeal to the primeval instincts. The two 'Slaves of the Lamp' were bracketed together next—a triumphant compliment to Mr. Kipling's skill; and the total verdict, in which the higher criticism can but acquiesce, was 'Spiffing!'

II

Whether or not Mr. Kipling claims to have set before us the whole boy, or only a special acquaintance of his own, we do not know; but if *Stalky & Co.*, as we half suspect, purports to tell the truth where *Eric*, Dean Farrar's famous story (and Mr. Kipling's bugbear), only romances, we must say at once that it comes short of that ambition. The impression of boy life conveyed by *Eric* is not more false than that given by *Stalky & Co.*, but the two pictures are the poles asunder. Dean Farrar's weakness for sentiment is quite equalled by Mr. Kipling's infatuation for might. One is as wrong as the other. The real boy comes somewhere between the two; you will find more of him in *Tom Brown* and *Tom Sawyer* than anywhere else. Mr. Kipling for once is caught tripping. In his endeavour to capture his youth he has remembered everything but youth's immaturity. The escapades of youth are here, the joy of living, the high spirits; but a cleverness beyond all credence has been superimposed. The attempt to make forcible dialogue and successful strategy has been too much for the author, and fidelity to the fact has gone overboard in the interests of the yarn. We cannot believe that even at Westward Ho!, Mr. Kipling's own school, three boys ever existed with so complete a theory of life, such rapid and accurate powers of deduction, such uncanny sagacity, such unwavering disregard of the feelings of others, and such brutal and unflagging wit, as Stalky, M'Turk, and Beetle. Mr. Kipling is entitled to idealise his puppets if he likes, and yet we have for so long come to look to him for genuine efforts to depict people as they are that it is with difficulty that the mind is adjusted to this new phase. We shall express the matter more clearly, perhaps, by saying that in these narratives of the adventures of three boys for the discomfiture of masters or other enemies, and the glorification of themselves, the thought, the arrangement, and the orderly accomplishment are adult, the conditions and language—and that only approximately—alone being boyish. Now although the child is the father of the man, and all the rest of it, there is yet a vast difference between a boy's ways and a man's ways. Mr. Kipling seems to us to have overlooked that difference altogether.

He has also so overdone the book that it has to be pronounced his least satisfactory work. There is a piling on of youthful brutality beyond all need, a lack of selective skill. Had *Stalky & Co.* been a whole-hearted attempt at realism, a genuine effort to portray the boy, we should make no such objections. But it is nothing of the kind: the whole boy, indeed, would no more bear setting down in black and white than the whole man. Realism being, then, out of the question, it remains that Mr. Kipling might have made a far better book. For the moment his instinct for the best stories has left him: he has let in a very flood of the second best. 'In Ambush' and 'A Little Prep.', the best things here (as good in their kind as one could wish), make some of their companions appear singularly unnecessary. 'An Unsavoury Interlude', 'The Impressionists', 'The Moral Reformers'—no one of these is worth the amount of spirit and literary power which Mr. Kipling has put into them. 'An Unsavoury Interlude' in particular is quite unworthy—a story which relates how the three heroes, having been accused of neglecting to wash themselves, retaliate by hiding a putrid cat in their traducers' house. Boys doubtless do such things, and for an oral yarn the incident would serve; but when a man of genius sits down to elaborate the affair we feel that he is expending himself wantonly. The thing does not matter, is not worth the doing, especially by the same hand that gave us the beautiful gravity of the *Jungle Books*. However, to balance the less worthy or unworthy chapters there are the two that we have named, which are of the first-class of boisterous school story. These, though often unnecessarily exuberant, justify themselves; and, if we had our way, Mr. Kipling's reputation as a delineator of boy life in a military nursery should rest on them alone. We quote from 'In Ambush' the passages describing part of the conversation of the three when confined to their dormitory for a crime they did not commit:

[quotes 'In Ambush', *Stalky & Co.*, p. 28, line 23, to p. 30, line 4, and 'subsequently their visit to the Head'—p. 34, line 25, to p. 35, line 22]

We have used the phrase, boy life in a military nursery, because it must be remembered that that is what Mr. Kipling has set out to paint. *Stalky & Co.* is the book of empire-makers in the making, a fact which must be kept steadily in mind if one is to come through to the last page without qualms, or, indeed, come through to the last page at all. For empires are not made in accordance with the precepts of the fifth chapter of Matthew, or even of the ordinary citizen of the world, and empire-makers are a kind of boy in whom the softer emotions have no place, and in whom any cultivation of the delicacies is discouraged. The qualities which are most needed on our frontiers are the qualities which Mr. Kipling holds up for admiration. It is not so much Young England that is represented here as Young Fighting England, in whom there cannot be too much of quickness of thought and swiftness of decisive action, and who is successful only in so far as he is also merciless, adamant, and domineering. Courageous, too; although, curiously, Mr. Kipling leaves us to form our own conclusions as to his heroes' personal valour. Their victories are for the most part victories of diplomacy and vicarious blows. Stalky, we know from the last story, became a worthy soldier; but at school the three despised cricket with all their hearts, avoided football except under compulsion, and, so far as their historian informs us, fought no fights. On the other hand they once ill-treated a cow (although Mr. Kipling has not included the account of the incident in this volume), and in the course of curing two bullies of bullying their own experiments in that art reached a point of horrible atrocity. Hence, although for soldiers this is one of the most congenial collections of yarns that they are likely to get for some time, and for Volunteers and the military-minded it is hardly less admirable, for the Czar and for peace-loving and all gentle-souled readers it will be well-nigh impossible. Mr. Kipling, as apostle of muscle and aggressive Imperialism, has uttered many battle-cries in his time; but this is his completest incitement to war, his crowning achievement as the supreme Recruiting Sergeant. Particularly so, since *Stalky & Co.* appeals to the young and plastic mind. Parents must please themselves as to whether they add the book to the holiday library; but we can only say that if it is to be read freely by impressionable boys, the sooner the curtain is rung down on the farce of Christianity the better; for there is hardly a precept of the Sermon on the Mount that is not joyously outraged in its pages.

What the book chiefly needs is some humanising relief. Throughout there is the same unerring metallic smartness, with hardly a hint of deeper feelings; the same torrent of brilliant slang. And this reminds us that besides other reasons for not handing this book to a boy, which will occur to every schoolmaster who happens to read it, there is also the objection that imitators of Stalky, M'Turk, and Beetle would be a very noxious race. For the originals we have admiration, albeit tempered by incredulity; but their derivatives will be appalling.

33. Robert Buchanan: 'The Voice of the Hooligan'

1899

Signed article from the *Contemporary Review*, Vol. LXXVI, pp. 774–89 (December 1899), published with Besant's answer and Buchanan's final retort in a small volume by The Tucker Publishing Company, New York, 1900.

Robert Williams Buchanan (1841–1901) was a soured and unsuccessful minor poet, novelist and dramatist, who had already won notoriety for his virulent attack on Rossetti, 'The Fleshly School of Poetry', also published in the *Contemporary Review* (October 1871).

Although some of the present diatribe is general in application, it is included here in its entirety as the first major attack on Kipling for brutality, warmongering and illiberalism—lines soon to be followed by many other so-called critics for reasons almost entirely divorced from literature.

As the years advance which 'bring the philosophic mind', or at least the mind which we fondly flatter ourselves is philosophic—in other words, as men of thought and feeling approach the latter end of their pilgrimage—there is a tendency among them to under-reckon the advance which the world has made in the course of their experience, and to discover in the far-off days of their youth a light which has almost ceased to shine on earthly things.

Laudatores temporis acti, they look askance at all the results of progress, and assert, more or less emphatically that men were wiser and better when they themselves were young. They forget, of course, that distance lends enchantment to the view, and that the very splendour in which the world once appeared came rather from within than from without; and, forgetting this, they do scant justice to the achievements of later generations. A little sober reflection, nevertheless, may convince them that the world *does* advance, though perhaps not so surely and satisfactorily as they would wish to believe; and that, even if there is some occasional retrogression, inevitable under the conditions of human development, it is only, after all, temporary, and due to causes which are inherent in our imperfect human nature. From time to time, however, the momentum towards a higher and more spiritual ideal seems suspended altogether, and we appear to be swept centuries back, by a great back-wave, as it were, in the direction of absolute barbarism.

Such a back-wave, it appears to me, has been at work during the last few decades, and the accompanying phenomena, in public life, in religion, in literature, have been extraordinary enough to fill even a fairly philosophical mind with something like despair. Closer contemplation and profounder meditation, however, may prove that in all possibility the retrogression is less real than superficial, that the advance forward of our civilization has only been hampered, not absolutely and finally hindered, and that in due time we may become stronger and wiser through the very lessons hardly learned during the painful period of delay.

It would be quite beyond the scope of the present article to point out in detail the divers ways in which modern society, in England particularly, has drifted little by little, and day by day, away from those humanitarian traditions which appeared to open up to men, in the time of my own boyhood, the prospect of a new heaven and a new earth. At that time, the influence of the great leaders of modern thought was still felt, both in politics and in literature; the gospel of humanity, as expressed in the language of poets like Wordsworth and Shelley, and in the deeds of men like Wilberforce and Mazzini, had purified the very air men breathed; and down lower, in the humbler spheres of duty and human endeavour, humanists like Dickens were translating the results of religious aspiration into such simple and happy speech as even the lowliest of students could understand. It was a time of immense activity in all departments, but its chief characteristic, perhaps, was the almost universal dominance, among educated men, of the sentiment of *philanthropy*, of belief in the inherent perfectibility of human nature, as well as of faith in ideals which bore at least the semblance of a celestial origin. Not quite in vain, it seemed, had Owen and Fourier laboured, and Hood sung, and John Leech wielded the pencil, and Dickens and Thackeray used the pen. The name of Arnold was still a living force in our English schools, and the name of Mazzini was being whispered in every English home. The first noticeable change came, perhaps, with the criminal crusade of the Crimean war; and from that hour to this, owing in no little degree to the rough-and-ready generalizations of popular science, and the consequent discrediting of all religious sanctions, the enthusiasm of humanity among the masses has gradually, but surely, died away. Sentiment has at last become thoroughly out of fashion, and humanitarianism is left to the care of eccentric and unauthoritative teachers. Thus, while a few despairing thinkers and dreamers have been trying vainly to substitute a new Ethos for the old religious sanctions, the world at large, repudiating the enthusiasm of humanity altogether, and exchanging it for the worship of physical force and commercial success in any and every form, has turned rapturously towards activities which need no sanction whatever, or which, at any rate, can be easily sanctified by the wanton will of the majority. Men no longer, in the great civic centres at least, ask themselves whether a particular course of conduct is right or wrong, but whether it is expedient, profitable, and certain of clamorous approval. Thanks to the newspaper press—that 'mighty engine', as Mr. Morley calls it, for 'keeping the public intelligence on a low level'—they are fed from day to day with hasty news and gossip, and with bogus views of affairs, concocted in the interests of the wealthy classes. Ephemeral and empirical books of all sorts take the place of serious literature; so that, while a great work like Mr. Spencer's *Justice* falls still-born from the press, a sophistical defence of the *status quo* like Mr. Balfour's *Foundations of Belief* is read by thousands. The aristocracy, impoverished by its own idleness and luxury, rushes wildly to join the middle-class in speculations which necessitate new conquests of territory and constant acts of aggression. The mob, promised a merry time by the governing classes, just as the old Roman mob was deluded by bread and pageants —*panem et circenses*—dances merrily to patriotic war-tunes, while that modern monstrosity and anachronism, the conservative working man, exchanges his birthright of freedom and free thought for a pat on the head from any little rump-fed lord that steps his way and spouts the platitudes of cockney patriotism. The established Church, deprived of the conscience which accompanied honest belief, supports nearly every infamy of the moment in the name of the Christianity which it has long ago shifted quietly overboard. [Footnote quoting verses by Archbishop Alexander. See Besant's answer, page 257]

There is an universal scramble for plunder, for excitement, for amusement, for speculation, and, above it all, the flag of a Hooligan

Imperialism is raised, with the proclamation that it is the sole mission of Anglo-Saxon England, forgetful of the task of keeping its own drains in order, to expand and extend its boundaries indefinitely, and, again in the name of the Christianity it has practically abandoned, to conquer and inherit the earth.

It may be replied that this is an exaggerated picture, and I will admit at once that there is justice in the reply, if it is granted at the same time that the picture is true so far as London itself and an enormous majority of Englishmen are concerned. Only if this is granted, can the present relapse back to barbarism of our public life, our society, our literature, be explained. Now that Mr. Gladstone has departed, we possess no politician, with the single exception of Mr. Morley (whose sanity and honesty are unquestionable, though he lacks, unfortunately, the daemonic influence), who demands for the discussion of public affairs any conscientious and unselfish sanction whatever; we possess, instead, a thousand pertinacious counsellors, cynics like Lord Salisbury or trimmers like Lord Rosebery, for whom no one in his heart of hearts feels the slightest respect. Our fashionable society is admittedly so rotten, root and branch, that not even the Queen's commanding influence can impart to it the faintest suggestion of purity, or even decency. As for our popular literature, it has been in many of its manifestations long past praying for; it has run to seed in fiction of the baser sort, seldom or never, with all its cleverness, touching the quick of human conscience; but its most extraordinary feature at this moment is the exaltation to a position of almost unexampled popularity of a writer who in his single person adumbrates, I think, all that is most deplorable, all that is most retrograde and savage, in the restless and uninstructed Hooliganism of the time.

The English public's first knowledge of Mr. Rudyard Kipling was gathered from certain brief anecdotal stories and occasional verses which began to be quoted about a decade ago in England, and which were speedily followed by cheap reprints of the originals, sold on every bookstall. They possessed one not inconsiderable attraction, in so far as they dealt with a naturally romantic country, looming very far off to English readers, and doubly interesting as one of our own great national possessions. We had had many works about India— works of description and works of fiction; and a passionate interest in them, and in all that pertained to things Anglo-Indian, had been awakened by the Mutiny; but few writers had dealt with the ignobler details of military and civilian life, with the gossip of the messroom and the scandal of the governmental departments. Mr. Kipling's little Kodak-glimpses, therefore, seemed unusually fresh and new; nor would it be just to deny them the merits if great liveliness, intimate personal knowledge, and a certain unmistakable, though obviously cockney, humour. Although they dealt almost entirely with the baser aspects of our civilization, being chiefly devoted to the affairs of idle military men, savage soldiers, frisky wives and widows, and flippant civilians, they were indubitably bright and clever, and in the background of them we perceived, faintly but distinctly, the shadow of the great and wonderful national life of India. At any rate, whatever their merits were—and I hold their merits to be indisputable—they became rapidly popular, especially with the newspaper press, which hailed the writer as a new and quite amazing force in literature. So far as the lazy public was concerned, they had the one delightful merit of extreme brevity; he that ran might read them, just as he read *Tit-bits* and the society newspapers, and then treat them like the rose in Browning's poem:

Smell, kiss, wear it—at last throw away!

Two factors contributed to their vogue; first, the utter apathy of general readers, too idle and uninstructed to study works of any length or demanding any contribution of serious thought on the reader's part, and eager for any amusement which did not remind them of the eternal problems which once beset humanity; and, second, the rapid growth in every direction of the military or militant spirit, of the Primrose League, of aggression abroad, and indifference at home to all religious ideals—in a word, of Greater Englandism, or Imperialism. For a considerable time Mr. Kipling poured out a rapid succession of these little tales and smoking-room anecdotes, to the great satisfaction of those who loved to listen to banalities about the English flag, seasoned with strong suggestions of social impropriety, as revealed in camps and barracks and the boudoirs of officers' mistresses and wives. The things seemed harmless enough, if not very elevating or ennobling. Encouraged by his success, the author attempted longer flights, with very indifferent results; though in the *Jungle Books*, for example, he got near to a really imaginative presentment of fine material, and, if he had continued his work in that direction, criticism might have had little or nothing to say against him. But in an unfortunate moment, encouraged by the journalistic praise lavished on certain fragments of verse with which he had ornamented his prose effusions, he elected to

challenge criticism as a poet—as, indeed, the approved and authorita-
tive poet of the British empire; and the first result of this election, or,
as I prefer to call it, this delusion and hallucination, was the publication
of the volume of poems, partly new and partly reprinted, called
Barrack-Room Ballads.

I have said that Mr. Kipling's estimate of himself as a poet was a
delusion; it was no delusion, however, so far as his faith in the public
was concerned. The book was received with instantaneous and clamorous approval; and, once again, let me pause to admit that it contained,
here and there, glimpses of a real verse-making faculty—a faculty
which, had the writer been spiritually and intellectually equipped,
might have led to the production of work entitled to be called 'poetry'.
On the very first page, however, the note of insincerity was struck, in
a dedication addressed to Mr. Wolcott Balestier, but recognized at
once as having done duty for quite a different purpose—resembling
in this respect the famous acrostic of Mr. Slum, which, although
written to fit the name of 'Warren', became at a pinch 'a positive
inspiration for Jarley'. This dedication, with its false feeling and utterly
unsuitable imagery, suggests the remark *en passant* that Mr. Kipling's
muse alternates between two extremes—the lowest cockney vulgarity
and the very height of what Americans call 'high-falutin' '—so that,
when it is not setting the teeth on edge with the vocabulary of the
London Hooligan, it is raving in capital letters about the Seraphim and
the Pit and the Maidens Nine and the Planets.

The *Ballads* thus introduced are twenty-one in number, of which
the majority are descriptive of whatever is basest and most brutal in the
character of the British mercenary. One deals, naturally enough, with
the want of sympathy shown in public-houses to Tommy Atkins in
time of peace, as contrasted with the enthusiasm for him in time of
war; another, entitled 'Cells', begins as follows:

> I've a head like a concertina: I've a tongue like
> a button-stick:
> I've a mouth like an old potato, and I'm more than
> a little sick.
> But I've had my fun with the Corp'ral's Guard: I've
> made the cinders fly,
> And I'm here in the Clink for a thundering drink
> and blacking the Corp'ral's eye;

it is, in fact, the glorification of the familiar episode of 'drunk and

resisting the guard'. In an equally sublime spirit is conceived the ballad
called 'Loot', beginning:

> If you've ever stole a pheasant-egg be'ind the keeper's back
>   If you've ever snigged the washin' from a line;
> If you've ever crammed a gander in your bloomin' 'aversack,
>   You will understand this little song of mine;

and the verses are indeed, with their brutal violence and their hideous
refrain, only too sadly understandable. Worse still, in its horrible
savagery, is the piece called 'Belts', which is the apotheosis of the
soldier who uses his belt in drunken fury to assault civilians in the
streets, and which has this agreeable refrain:

> But it was: 'Belts, belts, belts, an' that's one for you!'
> An' it was 'Belts, belts, belts, an' that's done for you!'
>   O buckle an' tongue
>   Was the song that we sung
> From Harrison's down to the Park!

If it is suggested that the poems I have quoted are only incidental
bits of local colour, interspersed among verses of a very different
character, the reply is that those pieces, although they are certainly the
least defensible, are quite in keeping with the other ballads, scarcely
one of which reaches to the intellectual level of the lowest music-hall
effusions. The best of them is a ballad called 'Mandalay', describing the
feelings of a soldier who regrets the heroine of a little amour out in
India, and it certainly possesses a real melody and a certain pathos. But
in all the ballads, with scarcely an exception, the tone is one of absolute
vulgarity and triviality, unredeemed by a touch of human tenderness
and pity. Even the little piece called 'Soldier, Soldier', which begins
quite naturally and tenderly, ends with the cynical suggestion that the
lady who mourns her old love had better take up at once with the
party who brings the news of his death:

> True love! new love!
> Best take 'im for a new love!
> The dead they cannot rise, an' you'd better dry your eyes,
> An' you'd best take 'im for your true love.

With such touching sweetness and tender verisimilitude are these
ballads of the barrack filled from end to end. Seriously, the picture
they present is one of unmitigated barbarism. The Tommy Atkins
they introduce is a drunken, swearing, coarse-minded Hooligan, for

whom, nevertheless, our sympathy is eagerly entreated. Yet these pieces were accepted on their publication, not as cruel libel on the British soldier, but as a perfect and splendid representation of the red-coated patriot on whom our national security chiefly depended, and who was spreading abroad in every country the glory of our Imperial flag!

That we might be in no doubt about the sort of thinker who was claiming our suffrages, Mr. Kipling printed at the end of his book certain other lyrics not specially devoted to the military. The best of these, the 'Ballad of the *Bolivar*', is put into the mouth of seven drunken sailors, 'rolling down the Ratcliffe Road drunk and raising Cain', and loudly proclaiming, with the true brag and bluster so characteristic of modern British heroism, how 'they took the (water-logged) *Bolivar* across the Bay'. It seems, by the way, a favourite condition with Mr. Kipling, when he celebrates acts of manly daring, that his subjects should be mad drunk, and, at any rate, as drunken in their language as possible. But this ballad may pass, that we may turn to the poem 'Cleared', in which Mr. Kipling spits all the venom of cockney ignorance on the Irish party, apropos of a certain Commission of which we have all heard, and, while saying nothing on the subject of forged letters and cowardly accusations, affirms that Irish patriots are naturally and distinctively murderers, because in the name of patriotism murders have now and then been done. He who loves blood and gore so much, who cannot even follow the soldier home into our streets without celebrating his drunken assaults and savageries, has only hate and loathing for the unhappy nation which has suffered untold wrong, and which, when all is said and done, has struck back so seldom. In the poem which follows, 'An Imperial Rescript', he protests with all his might against any bond of brotherhood among the sons of toil, pledging the strong to work for and help the weak. Here, as elsewhere, he is on the side of all that is ignorant, selfish, base, and brutal in the instincts of humanity.

Before proceeding further to estimate Mr. Kipling's contributions to literature, let me glance for a moment at his second book of verse, *The Seven Seas*, published a year or two ago. It may be granted at once that it was a distinct advance on its predecessor, more restrained, less vulgar, and much more varied; here and there, indeed, as in the opening 'Song of the English', it struck a note of distinct and absolute poetry. But, in spite of its unquestionable picturesqueness, and of a certain swing and lilt in the go-as-you-please rhythms, it was still characterized by the same indefinable quality of brutality and latent baseness. Many of the poems, such as the 'Song of the Banjo', were on the level of the cleverness to be found in the contributions of the poet of the *Sporting Times*, known to the occult as the 'Pink 'Un'. The large majority, indeed, were cockney in spirit, in language, and in inspiration, and one or two, such as 'The Ladies' and 'The Sergeant's Weddin'', with its refrain:

> Cheer for the Sergeant's weddin'—
> Give 'em one cheer more!
> Grey gun-'orses in the lando,
> And a rogue is married to *etc.*,

were frankly and brutally indecent. The army appeared again, in the same ignoble light as before, with the same disregard of all literary luxuries, even of grammar and the aspirate. God, too, loomed largely in these productions, a cockney 'Gawd' again, chiefly requisitioned for purposes of blasphemy and furious emphasis. There was no glimpse anywhere of sober and self-respecting human beings—only a wild carnival of drunken, bragging, boasting Hooligans in red coats and seamen's jackets, shrieking to the sound of the banjo and applauding the English flag.

Faint almost to inaudibility have been the protests awakened by these cockney caricatures in the ranks of the army itself. Here and there a mild voice has been heard, but no military man has declared authoritatively that effusions like those which I have quoted are a libel on the Service, if not on human nature. Are we to assume, then, that there are no refined gentlemen among our officers, and no honest self-respecting human beings among their men? Is the life of a soldier, abroad as at home, a succession of savage escapades, bestial amusements, fuddlings, tipplings, and intrigues with other men's wives, redeemed from time to time by acts of brute courage and of sang-froid in the presence of danger? Is the spirit of Gordon quite forgotten, in the service over which he shed the glory of his illustrious name? If this is really the case, there is surely very little in the Anglo-Saxon military prestige which offers us any security for the stormy times to come. That Englishmen are brave, and capable of brave deeds, is a truism of which we need no longer to be assured; but bravery and brave deeds are not national possessions—they are the prerogative of the militant classes all over the earth. Englishmen in times past were not merely brave, they could be noble and magnanimous; their courage was not only that of the bulldog, but of the patriot, the hero, and even the philanthropist: they had not yet begun to mingle the idea of a national Imperialism with the political game of brag. I am not contending for one moment that the spirit which inspired them then has altogether departed; I am sure, on the contrary, that it is living yet, and living most strongly and influentially in the heart of the army itself; but, if this is admitted and believed, it is certain that the Tommy Atkins of Mr. Rudyard Kipling deserves drumming out of all decent barracks as a monstrosity and a rogue.

The truth is, however, that these lamentable productions were concocted, not for sane men or self-respecting soldiers, not even for those who are merely ignorant and uninstructed, but for the 'mean whites' of our eastern civilization, the idle and loafing men in the street, and for such women, the well-dressed Doll Tearsheets of our cities, as shriek at their heels. Mr. Kipling's very vocabulary is a purely cockney vocabulary, even his Irishmen speaking a dialect which would cause amazement in the Emerald Isle, but is familiar enough in Seven Dials. Turning over the leaves of his poems, one is transported at once to the region of low-drinking dens and gin-palaces, of dirty dissipation and drunken brawls; and the voice we hear is always the voice of the soldier whose God is a cockney 'Gawd', and who is ignorant of the aspirate in either heaven or hell. Are there no Scotchmen in the ranks, no Highlanders, no men from Dublin or Tipperary, no Lancashire or Yorkshire men, no Welshmen, and no men of any kind who speak the Queen's English? It would seem not, if, the poet of 'The Sergeant's Weddin' ' is to be trusted. Nor have our mercenaries, from the ranks upwards, any one thing, except brute courage, to distinguish them from the beasts of the field. This, at least, appears to be Mr. Kipling's contention, and even in the Service itself it seems to be undisputed.

How then, are we to account for the extraordinary popularity of works so contemptible in spirit and so barbarous in execution? In the first place, even fairly educated readers were sick to death of the insincerities and affectations of the professional 'Poets', with one or two familiar exceptions, and, failing the advent of a popular singer like Burns, capable of setting to brisk music the simple joys and sorrows of humanity, they turned eagerly to any writer who wrote verse, doggerel even, which seemed thoroughly alive. They were amused, therefore, by the free-and-easy rattles, the jog-trot tunes, which had hitherto been heard only in the music-halls and read only in the sporting newspapers. In the second place, the spirit abroad today is the spirit of ephemeral journalism, and whatever accords with that spirit—its vulgarity, its flippancy, and its radical unintelligence—is certain to attain tremendous vogue. Anything that demands a moment's thought or a moment's severe attention, anything that is not thoroughly noisy, blatant, cocksure, and self-assertive, is caviare to that man in the street on whom cheap journalism depends, and who, it should be said *en passant*, is often a member of smart society. In the third place, Mr. Kipling had the good, or bad, fortune to come at the very moment when the wave of false Imperialism was cresting most strongly upward, and when even the great organs of opinion, organs which, like *The Times*, subsist entirely on the good or bad passions of the hour, were in sore need of a writer who could express in fairly readable numbers the secret yearnings and sympathies of the baser military and commercial spirit. Mr. Kipling, in a word, although not a poet at all in the true sense of the word, is as near an approach to a poet as can be tolerated by the ephemeral and hasty judgment of the day. His very incapacity of serious thought or deep feeling is in his favour. He represents, with more or less accuracy, what the mob is thinking, and for this very reason he is likely to be forgotten as swiftly and summarily as he has been applauded, nay, to be judged and condemned as mean and insignificant on grounds quite as hasty as those on which he has been hailed as important and high-minded. Savage animalism and ignorant vainglory being in the ascendant, he is hailed at every street-corner and crowned by every newspaper. To-morrow, when the wind changes, and the silly crowd is in another and possibly saner temper, he is certain to fare very differently. The misfortune is that his effusions have no real poetical quality to preserve them when their momentary purpose has been served. Of more than one poet of this generation it has been said that 'he uttered nothing base'. Of Mr. Kipling it may be said, so far at least as his verses are concerned, that he has scarcely on any single occasion uttered anything that does not suggest moral baseness, or hover dangerously near it.

However, that we might not entertain one lingering doubt as to the nature of the spirit which inspires his easy-going Muse, Mr. Kipling himself, with a candour for which we cannot be sufficiently thankful, has recently laid bare, in a prose work, the inmost springs of his inspiration; in other words, he has described to us, with fearless and shameless accuracy, in a record of English boyhood, his ideal of the human character in adolescence. Now, there is nothing which so clearly and absolutely represents the nature of a grown man's intelligence as the manner in which he contemplates, looking backward, the feelings and aspirations of youthful days.

'Heaven lies about us in our infancy,' says the author of the immortal Ode, and heaven is still with us very often as we more closely approach to manhood. In Goethe's reminiscences of his childhood, we discover, faintly developing, all that was wisest and most beautiful in a soul which was distinguished, despite many imperfections, by an inherent love of gentleness and wisdom; the eager intelligence, the vision, the curiosity, are all there, in every thought and act of an extraordinary child. When Dickens, in *David Copperfield*, described under a thin veil of fiction the joys and sorrows of his own boyhood and youth, there welled up out of his great heart a love, a tenderness, a humour which filled the eyes of all humanity with happy tears. When Thackeray touched the same chords, as he did more than once, he was no longer the glorified Jeames of latter-day fiction—he was as kindly, as tender, and as loving as even his great contemporary. Even George Eliot, with imaginative gifts so far inferior, reached the height of her artistic achievement when she went back to the emotions of her early days— when for example, she described the personal relations of Tom and Maggie Tulliver, or when, in the one real poem she ever wrote, she told in sonnet-sequence of the little 'Brother and Sister'. It would be cruel, even brutal, to talk of Mr. Rudyard Kipling in the same breath as fine artists like these; but all writers, great or little, must finally be judged by the same test—that of the truth and beauty, the sanity or the folly, of their representations of our manifold human nature. Mere truth is not sufficient for Art; the truth must be there, but it must be spiritualized and have become beautiful. In *Stalky & Co.* Mr. Kipling obviously aims at verisimilitude; the picture he draws is at any rate repulsive and disgusting enough to be true; yet I trust for England's sake that it is not—that it is, like nearly all his writings with which I am familiar, merely a savage caricature.

Only the spoiled child of an utterly brutalized public could possibly have written *Stalky & Co.* or, having written it, have dared to publish it. These are strong words, but they can be justified. The story ran originally through the pages of a cheap monthly magazine, and contained, I fancy, in its first form, certain passages which the writer himself was compelled in pure shame to suppress. Its purpose, almost openly avowed, is to furnish English readers with an antidote to what Mr. Kipling styles 'Ericism', by which label is meant the kind of 'sentiment' which was once made familiar to schoolboys by Farrar's *Eric, or, Little by Little*; or, to put the matter in other words, the truly ideal schoolboy is not a little sentimentalist, he is simply a little beast. The heroes of this deplorable book are three youths, dwelling in a training school near Westward Ho!; one of them, the Beetle, reads poetry and wears spectacles, the two others, Stalky and M'Turk, are his bosom companions. This trio are leagued together for purposes of offence and defence against their comrades; they join in no honest play or manly sports, they lounge about, they drink, they smoke, they curse and swear, not like boys at all, but like hideous little men. Owing to their determination to obey their own instincts, and their diabolic ingenuity in revenging themselves on any one who meddles with them, they become a terror to the school. It is quietly suggested, however, that the headmaster sympathizes with them, especially in their power to inflict pain wantonly and to bear it stoically, which appears to him the noblest attribute of a human being. It is simply impossible to show by mere quotations the horrible vileness of the book describing the lives of these three small fiends in human likeness; only a perusal of the whole work would convey to the reader its truly repulsive character, and to read the pages through, I fear, would sorely test the stomach of any sensitive reader. The nature of one of the longest and most important episodes may be gathered from the statement that the episode turns on the way in which the three young Hooligans revenge themselves on a number of their schoolmates who have offended them, by means of a dead and putrefying cat. And here is a sample of the dialogue:

[quotes, p. 86, lines 10-30]

Another equally charming episode is the one describing how a certain plebeian called 'Rabbits-Eggs', through the machinations of the trio, wrecked the room of one of the masters, King:

[quotes, p. 58, line 11, to p. 59, line 16]

As I have already said, however, the book cannot be represented by extracts. The vulgarity, the brutality, the savagery, reeks on every page. It may be noted as a minor peculiarity that everything, according to our young Hooligans, is 'beastly', or 'giddy', or 'blooming'; adjectives of this sort cropping up everywhere in their conversation, as in that of the savages of the London slums. And the moral of the book—for, of course, like all such banalities, it professes to have a moral—is that out of materials like these is fashioned the humanity which is to ennoble and preserve our Anglo-Saxon empire! 'India's full of Stalkies,' says the Beetle, 'Cheltenham and Haileybury and Marlborough chaps—that we don't know anything about, and *the surprises will begin when there is really a big row on!*'

Perhaps, after all, I am unjust to Mr. Kipling in forgetting for the moment to credit him with a poet's prophetic vision? For, if *Stalky & Co.* was written before and not after recent political developments, it certainly furnishes a foretaste of what has actually happened! The 'surprises *have* begun', although the 'rows' have not been very 'big' ones, and the souls of Stalky and his companions *have* been looming large in our empire. Studying certain latter-day records, indeed, listening to the voice of the Hooligan in politics, in literature, and journalism, is really very like reading *Stalky & Co.* Some of our battles, even, faithfully reproduce the 'blooming' and 'giddy' orgies of the schoolroom, and in not a few of our public affairs there is a 'stench' like that of 'the dead cat'. Yes, there *must* be Stalkies and M'Turks and Beetles working busily, after all, and representing the new spirit which appears to have begun in the time of Mr. Kipling's boyhood. But whether they really represent the true spirit of our civilization, and make for its salvation, is a question which I will leave my readers to decide.

So much, however, for the voice of the Hooligan, as reverberating in current literature. It is needless to say that it would hardly have been necessary to discuss seriously such literature, if the object was merely to protest on intellectual grounds against its popularity; one might well examine seriously the current contributions to *Answers* and the *Sporting Times*, or hold up to artistic execration the topical songs in a Drury Lane pantomime. But even a straw may indicate the direction in which the wind is blowing, and the vogue of Mr. Kipling, the cheerful acceptance of his banalities by even educated people, is so sure a sign of the times that it deserves and needs a passing consideration. Behind that vogue lies, first and foremost, the influence of the newspaper press, and I cannot do better than quote in this connection some pregnant words contained in a recent work by a writer of undoubted insight, Mr. George Gissing.

'A wise autocrat might well prohibit newspapers altogether, don't you think?' [says one of Mr. Gissing's characters]. 'They have done good, I suppose, but they are just as likely to do harm. When the next great war comes, newspapers will be the chief cause of it. And for mere profit, that's the worst! There are newspaper proprietors in every country who would slaughter half mankind for the pennies of the half who were left, without caring the fraction of a penny whether they had preached war for a truth or a lie.' 'But doesn't a newspaper,' demands another character, 'simply echo the opinions and feelings of the public?' 'I'm afraid,' is the reply, 'it manufactures opinions and stirs up feeling . . . The business of newspapers in general is to give a show of importance to what has no real importance at all, to prevent the world from living quietly, to arouse bitterness, when the natural man would be quite indifferent . . . I suppose I quarrel with them because they have such gigantic power and don't make anything like the best use of it.'

If this statement is accepted as true—and few readers who have studied the recent developments of journalism will be inclined to doubt it—it will be understood at once how the popularity of Mr. Kipling has been accelerated by 'that mighty engine', the newspaper press.

It is no purpose of mine, in the present paper, to touch on political questions, except so far as they illustrate the movements of that back-wave toward barbarism on which, as I have suggested, we are now struggling. I write neither as a Banjo-Imperialist nor as a Little Eng-lander, but simply as a citizen of a great nation, who loves his country, and would gladly see it honoured and respected wherever the English tongue is spoken. It will scarcely be denied, indeed it is frankly ad-mitted by all parties, that the Hooligan spirit of patriotism, the fierce and quasi-savage militant spirit as expressed in many London news-papers and in such literature as the writings of Mr. Kipling, has measurably lowered the affection and respect once felt for us among European nations. Nor will any honest thinker combat the assertion that we have exhibited lately, in our dealings with other nationalities, a greed of gain, a vainglory, a cruelty, and a boastful indifference to the rights of others, of which in days when the old philanthropic spirit was abroad we should simply have been incapable. But it is not here, in the region of politics and militarism, that I wish to linger. My chief object in writing this paper has been to express my sorrow that Hooliganism, not satisfied with invading our newspapers, should already threaten to corrupt the pure springs of our literature. These noisy strains and coarse importations from the music-hall should not be heard where the fountains of intellectual light and beauty once played, where Chaucer and Shakespeare once drank inspiration, and where Wordsworth, Hood, and Shelley found messages for the yearning hearts of men. Anywhere but there; anywhere but in the speech of those who loved and blessed their fellows. And let it be remembered that those fountains are not yet dry. Poets and dreamers are living yet, to resent the pollution. Only a little while ago the one living novelist who inherits the great human tradition tore out his very heart, figuratively speaking, in revolt against the spirit of savagery and cruelty which is abroad; though, when Thomas Hardy wrote *Jude the Obscure*, touching therein the very quick of divine pity, only a coarse laugh from the professional critics greeted his protest. Elsewhere, too, there are voices, not to be silenced by the clamour of the crowd; as near as our own shores, where Herbert Spencer is still dwelling, as far away as South Africa, where Olive Schreiner has sought and found human love in the dominion of dreams; and there are others, shrinking away in shame from the brazen idols of the mart, and praying that this great empire may yet be warned and saved. To one and all of these has been brought home the lesson—'Woe to you when the world speaks well of you!'—and they have elected to let the world speak ill of them, rather than bow down in homage to its calves of gold. For to speak the truth as we see it, to confront the evil and folly of the hour, is as dangerous today as when Socrates drank his hemlock-cup.

I have left myself no space, I find, to draw a final contrast between the coarse and soulless patriotism of the hour and that nobler Imperialism in which all true Englishmen, to whatever political camp they may belong for the time being, must still believe. In the federation of Great Britain and her colonies, and in the slow and sure spread of what is best and purest in our civilization, there was indeed hope and inspiration for our race, and a message of freedom for all the world. But true Imperialism has nothing in common with the mere lust of conquest, with the vulgar idea of mere expansion, or with the increase of the spirit of mercenary militarism; its object is to diffuse light, not to darken the sunshine; to feed the toiling millions, not to immolate them; to free man, not to enslave him; to consecrate, and not to desecrate, the great temple of humanity. Some of its ways, like the ways of nature herself, must inevitably be destructive; the weaker and baser races must sooner or later dissolve away; but the process of dissolution should be made as gentle and merciful as possible, not savage, pitiless, and cruel. True Imperialism should be strong, but the strength should be that of justice, of wisdom, of brotherly love and sympathy; for the power which is bred of a mere multitude equipped with the engines of slaughter will in the long run avail nothing against the eternal law which determines that the righteous only shall inherit the earth. We are a people still, though we seem for the time being to be forgetting the conditions on which we received our charter, and deep in the heart of England survives the sentiment of a world-wide nationality, as expressed in the passionate lines of a modern poet:

> Hands across the Sea!
> Feet on British ground!
> The Motherhood means Brotherhood the whole world round!
> From the parent root,
> Sap, and stem, and fruit
> Grow the same, or soil or name—
> Hands across the Sea!

There sounds the true Imperial feeling, which will survive, I think, long after the repulsive school of patriotism which I have called (for want of a better name) the Hooligan school, is silent and forgotten. Let me at least hope that it may be so—that Englishmen, after their present wild orgy of militant savagery, may become clothed and in their right minds. There is time to pause yet, although they are already paying the penalty, in blood, in tears, in shame. Let them take warning by the fate of France, let them try to remember the old sanctions and the old enthusiasms; for, if they continue to forget them, they are in danger of being swept back into the vortex of barbarism altogether.

34. Sir Walter Besant: 'Is it the Voice of the Hooligan?'

1900

Signed article from the *Contemporary Review*, Vol. LXXVII, pp. 27–39 (January, 1900). The first ten paragraphs are omitted, being taken up with general principles of criticism and literary good manners.

Sir Walter Besant (1836–1901) was a well-known and successful novelist, and the founder of The Society of Authors. Kipling owed much to Besant, both for the encouragement given him during a dark period in India by reading his *All in a Garden Fair* (1883), and for much kindly advice when they met in London at the end of 1889. (See *Something of Myself*, pp. 65–6 and 83–4.)

If a poet or a novelist is not necessarily a critic—is presumably less likely to possess the critical faculty than if he were not a poet—it behoves him to examine himself very carefully before he ventures to pose as the watch-dog of literature, lest he betray his incompetence by barking, and rending the friends, instead of the enemies, of the literary craft.

Mr. Robert Buchanan has thought fit to attack Mr. Rudyard Kipling after the ancient manner. I do not suppose that what he has written will cost the younger poet a single friend; nor do I suppose that anything I may say on the other side will advance his reputation. Nor, again, do I pretend, myself, to be a watch-dog of literature; nor do I profess to be endowed with the critical faculty. But I think that it may be useful to set forth briefly some of the reasons why one among the many millions of Kipling's readers finds him worthy of the deepest admiration, and, in so doing, to express the views and the judgments of a vast following which may not be critical, yet does not with one consent give its admiration and affection except for good and sufficient reasons.

Except in one point, that of the actual situation, I am not concerned to answer Mr. Buchanan. He has his views and has stated them. Very well, I have mine, and I propose to state them. They are exactly opposite to those of Mr. Buchanan. Why that should be the case is a question which needs no answer in this place.

As regards the situation, then. I read with wondering eyes that this generation has drifted away from the humanitarian teaching which forty years ago, or thereabouts 'opened up to men the prospect of a new heaven and a new earth'. Drifted away? Is the writer serious? Is he blind to the present? Why, if there is any characteristic note of the times at all, it is the new and practical application of that very humanitarian teaching of the past. This teaching has sunk deep into the national heart; it is producing fruits unlooked for, beyond all expectation. The exercise of practical charity by personal service which is remarkable everywhere is the natural result of that teaching and the proof that it has gone home. In all directions is visible the working of the most real philanthropic endeavour that the world has ever seen—the nearest approach to practical Christianity that has appeared, I believe, since the foundation of the Christian religion. What else is the meaning of free schools, free libraries, factory Acts, continuation schools, polytechnics? What else is the meaning of the settlements in which scholars and refined women give their whole strength with all their thoughts and all their soul to the help of the people round them? What else is the meaning of Toynbee Hall, of Mansfield Hall, of Browning Hall, or of Oxford House? What else is the meaning of the quickened life in the parishes with the flocking companies of those who work for nothing but the love of humanity? What else is meant by the long list of associations for the benefit and help, in every degree, of those who can be helped? Is it possible to live in such a time as this and to be so utterly out of touch with all that is attempted, as to speak of a 'drifting away' from the old humanitarian teaching? This said, I leave Mr. Buchanan, and proceed to consider those qualities which the world recognizes in Rudyard Kipling, assuming that, as an average man, my own recognitions are those of what we call the world.

The first essential in fiction is reality. The story must be real; the figures must be real; the dialogue must be real; the action must spring naturally from the situation. Affectations; straining after phrase; a style that suggests labour and repeated correction—these things destroy the interest: the story must be told with directness; it must be told with force; it must be told because the storyteller has to tell it—is constrained to tell it. We want to be carried out of our own environment; we are ready to surrender ourselves willingly to the magnetic force of the storyteller; if he has no magnetic power, we turn away; if he has, we allow him to play upon us as he pleases; we are like one who is mesmerized and does what he is told to do—he really feels the emotions that the storyteller puts into his mind; he laughs when his master bids him laugh; he cries when he is told to cry.

These conditions are all found in Kipling's work, and in full measure, without any reservations. He has this magnetic force; he compels us to listen; he tells his story with directness, force, and simplicity. So real is the story, with such an air of reality does he present it, that we see it as we see the moving pictures which the new photography throws upon the canvas.

It is in writing as in drawing. One man produces his effects with many strokes and careful elaboration; another produces the same effect with a single bold stroke or with the least possible curve or deflection of a line. The effect is produced in Kipling's work by the one bold stroke; without apparent effort the right word presents itself; the right phrase, which others seek, and seek in vain, without apparent hesitation takes its place; it belongs to the story.

He also believes his own story; that faith is necessary if he would make his hearers believe it. And because he believes it he is enabled to tell it simply and directly, without seeking to add the artificial stimulus of a laboured style.

These reasons for the popularity of a writer are elementary. Yet they have, in this case, to be set forth, as the best answer to any assailant. Another reason, not so obvious to the ordinary reader, is his enthusiasm for humanity. Probably Kipling never gave it, consciously, so fine a name—is ignorant, perhaps, that this attribute can be found in his work. Yet the thing is there. Always, in every character, he presents a man, not an actor—a man with the passions, emotions, weaknesses, and instincts of humanity. It is perhaps one of the Soldiers Three, or it is the Man who went into the mountains because he would be a King; or the man who sat in the lonely lighthouse till he saw streaks; always the real man whom the reader sees beneath the uniform and behind the drink and the blackguardism. It is the humanity in the writer which makes his voice tremulous at times with unspoken pity and silent sympathy; it is the tremor of his voice which touches the heart of his audience. And it is this power of touching the heart which causes men and women of all classes and of every rank to respond with a greater love for the writer than for any other writer living among us at the present moment.

Mr. Henry James, who is certainly a critic as well as a novelist, has called attention to Kipling's power of attracting all classes. It surprises him that, 'being so much the sort of figure that the hardened critic likes to meet, he should also be the sort of figure that inspires the multitude with confidence; for a complicated air is, in general, the last thing that does this'. Exactly; but it is the special note of genius that it should present men and women who are real to all who read, and so real that they come with a simple 'air' to the simple and un-cultivated mind and with a 'complicated air' to the scholar. It is not the complicated air that the multitude ask or comprehend. For them it is the simple lay, the plain song. To those who, like Mr. Henry James, are practised observers and students, who can read between the lines, the air is as complicated as any study of human nature by Browning or by Meredith.

Going on with his analysis, Mr. Henry James admirably illustrates the different effects produced on different minds by the case of Mul-vaney, the great Mulvaney. He says, speaking for the multitude, that the figure of Mulvaney is 'a piece of portraiture of the largest, vividest kind, growing and growing on the painter's hands without ever outgrowing them'. And, speaking for himself and those like unto himself, he says: 'Hasn't he the tongue of a hoarse siren, and hasn't he also mysteries and infinities almost Carlylese?' Not for the multitude; for them he is only 'a six-foot saturated Irish private'; but so clearly drawn, so strongly drawn, that not the most simple can fail to under-stand him after their own fashion.

Another reason why we who are not critics—the many millions—delight in Kipling is that he gives us short stories. Not that we demand, as has been asserted, everything to be in paragraphs and scraps—that is quite an unfair interpretation of the demand for short stories—it is that the short story affords endless opportunities of touching life—I again quote Henry James—'in a thousand different places, taking it up in innumerable pieces, each a specimen and an illustration'. In the long story we are occupied with one place, one sequence of events, one set of characters; perhaps we read for the sequence of events, perhaps for the study of the character. Within the space occupied by the long story Kipling's volume of short stories gives us twenty situations, twenty scenes, twenty groups, and twenty sets of characters. Mr. James's critical remarks, from which I quote, are written for the volume called *Mine Own People*, which contains, among other things, the stories called respectively 'At the End of the Passage', 'The Incarnation of Krishna Mulvaney', 'The Courting of Dinah Shadd', and 'The Man who Was'. Every one of these stories—characters, situation, and all—is burned into the memory as deeply as if it had been worked up to occupy a volume all to itself. And we would rather have the short story than a long one from our storyteller, because he gives us picture after picture, play after play, dozens of pictures and of plays, in the time generally occupied by one.

But the man who would become a teller of short stories must have a wealth of material which few have the opportunities of collecting. Kipling has had these opportunities; he knows the world—especially the Anglo-Saxon world—the world of our empire and the world of the American republic. He is one of those thrice blessed who have not only received the gifts of observations and of sympathy—the gift of storytelling with the dramatic instinct and the power of selection and grouping—but he has obtained the gift of opportunity; he has lived in lands where there are still adventures and the adventurous, where there are still tribes who love fighting and tribes who murder the Englishman, where there are still unknown mysteries of hills and forests; he has found mines of material diverse and new and marvellous, and he has worked these mines as they have never been worked before. Henry James has instanced the figure of Mulvaney as one of the most remarkable in Kipling's gallery of portraits. We may, perhaps, take the Soldiers Three as illustrating the 'humanity' of which we have spoken. He has the coarsest and the roughest materials to deal with—three private soldiers of the lower type, which is common enough in our army—and in every other army. The men are foul-mouthed and drunken and tricky. All this must be faced and set forth with no shrinking or false colouring. This has been done, and yet, such is the force of reality in fiction, the result is that we see the real men behind their vices, and that we understand Tommy Atkins as we never understood him before. Had the drawing and the colouring been conventional, there would have been found some, no doubt, to call attention to the artistic treatment of the soldier and the finish and polish of his language and his views. They are, however, not in the least conventional, and for the multitude they are real living men, as living as themselves.

I believe that I am not alone in giving the highest praise—at least for 'grip'—to the story of 'The Man who would be King'. While that story was told, there was not heard in the whole of the vast audience a sound, a whisper, a breath. In dead silence it was received; in dead silence it concluded—in dead silence save for the sigh which spoke of a tension almost too great to be borne. Perhaps that sigh might be taken for applause. Perhaps the storyteller himself took it for applause.

Another point. Kipling presents himself with no apologies, no conventional humility, but with a splendid audacity—a confidence in himself and his own powers which in itself commands admiration; he has the gallant bearing of a soldier, he laughs, knowing that we shall respond; he plunges into his story, knowing that we shall listen; he lets us understand that he has come to conquer the world, and that he means to conquer it. The most finished actor could not impose his part upon the theatre more successfully than Kipling imposes his real nature upon his readers.

These are some of the reasons why we—the many millions—follow after Kipling and listen when he speaks. Some there are who think differently; they have not been carried away; for most of us the reasons above indicated seem sufficient to account for the phenomenal admiration which is also almost universal. To the critic—Henry James's 'hardened critic'—we may leave the analysis of methods and style and art.

I have spoken of Kipling's audience. But what an audience it is! The people sit in a theatre of which the front seats are at the story-teller's feet and the farthest tiers are twelve thousand miles away. Never, in the history of literature, has storyteller, in his own lifetime, faced such an audience. Scott and Dickens enjoy, if they can still look on, the posthumous happiness of this unnumbered audience; in their lifetime the theatre was smaller; the people which even then seemed so great a crowd were much less in number than those who come to hear their successor. Other writers speak today to crowded houses, but none to such a house as assembles when Kipling speaks. Saul has followers by the thousand; David, by the hundred thousand: Rudyard Kipling is the first of storytellers to whom it has been granted to speak, while he still lives, to the hundred millions of those who read the Anglo-Saxon tongue. From east and west and north and south, wherever the Union Jack or the Stars and Stripes may float, they flock into the vast theatre to listen spellbound to a single voice, which reaches clear and distinct to the most distant tier where the white faces look up and listen while the story is told.

Let us consider him next as the poet, and especially as the poet of the empire. He is emphatically not a Londoner; he does not seek inspiration in the smoking-room of a West End club: he does not observe in Piccadilly: he does not evolve humanity out of an easy chair with the aid of a cigarette. He is a son of the empire; he has brought home to the understanding of the most parochial of Little Englanders the sense and knowledge of what the British empire means. What Seeley taught scholars, Kipling has taught the multitude. He is the poet of the empire. Not the Jingo rhymer; the poet with the deepest reverence for those who have built up the Empire, the deepest respect for the Empire, the most profound sense of responsibility.

> Fair is our lot. Oh! goodly is our heritage!
> (Humble ye, my people, and be fearful in your mirth!)
>> For the Lord our God most High,
>> He hath made the deep as dry,
> He hath smote for us a pathway to the ends of all the earth!
> Yea, though we sinned—and our rulers went from righteousness—
> Deep in all dishonour though we stained our garments' hem.
>> Oh! be ye not dismayed,
>> Though we stumbled and we strayed,
> We were led by evil counsellors—the Lord shall deal with them!

That is, I suppose, the 'Voice of the Hooligan'. Again, is it the Hooligan who sings of the Last Chantey to the text 'And there was no more sea'?

[quotes stanzas 1, 8 and 13, DV. pp. 160–2]

Again, what kind of poet—'not a poet at all', says his latest critic—is he who could write the following?

> Take up the White Man's Burden—
>> Send forth the best ye breed—
> Go, bind your sons to exile
>> To serve your captives' need:
> To wait in heavy harness,
>> On fluttered folk and wild—
> Your new-caught sullen peoples,
>> Half devil and half child.
>
> Take up the White Man's Burden—
>> No iron rule of kings,
> But toil of serf and sweeper—
>> The tale of common things.

The ports ye shall not enter,
The roads ye shall not tread;
Go, make them with your living,
And mark them with your dead!

It is unnecessary to quote the Recessional Hymn save to remind ourselves of how this poet, alone of poets or preachers, saw, as in a vision of inspiration, the one thing that needed to be said: We were drunk with the pageant of power and of glory. The empire and all it meant was represented in that long procession of 1897. The people, bewildered with pride, were ready to shout they knew not what—to go they knew not whither. And then the poet spoke, and his words rang true. I know of no poem in history so opportune, that so went home to all our hearts—that did its work and delivered its message with so much force.

[quotes stanzas 1, 3 and 4 of 'Recessional', DV. pp. 328–9]

One more note, and I have done. Kipling, in verse and in prose, is one to whom war is an ever-present possibility and an ever-present certainty. There is a time to speak of war and a time to speak of peace. At this moment it is well that some one who has a voice should speak of war. It seems that in the present stage of civilization, just as in the past, there falls upon the nations, from time to time, the restlessness which can only be pacified by war. The French nation, at this moment, seem to be restless to the highest degree under this obsession. We ourselves are in the throes of the biggest war since the Indian Mutiny. Two years ago, the most pacific country in the world, the great republic of North America, was seized with this restlessness, which it is still working off. A time may come when war will not be a necessity —but that time is not yet. For my own part, I entirely agree with Archbishop Alexander in the words quoted by Mr. Buchanan:

And as I note how nobly natures form
Under the war's red rain, I deem it true
That He who made the earthquake and the storm
Perchance made battles too.

There are worse evils than war. There are

—the lust of Gold
And love of a Peace that is full of wrongs and shames.

It is a threadbare commonplace to write that there are worse evils than war, but it must be said over and over again, especially when the horrors of war are upon us. The poisonous weeds that grow rank in times of peace corrupt the national blood; they deaden the sense of honour; they encourage the ruthless company promoter who trades upon the ignorance of the helpless; they lower the standards of honour; they enlarge the slough of indulgence and the unclean life. War does not kill these things, but it may restore the sense of duty, sacrifice, patriotism; it may bring back the nobler ideals; it may teach the world that there are better gods than the idols they have fashioned with their own hands; it may seize on the hearts of the young and preserve their instincts of generosity.

> Though many a light shall darken and many shall weep
> For those that are crushed in the clash of jarring claims . . .
> . . . And many a darkness into light shall leap,
> And shine in the sudden making of splendid names,
> And noble thought be freer under the sun,
> And the heart of the people beat with one desire.

This potency of war, these possibilities, this necessity of war when the cause is just, this ennobling of a people by war, are present in the mind of Kipling as much as in the mind of Tennyson. The time, indeed, has come again when we are called

> To wake to the higher aims
> Of a land that has lost for a little the lust of gold.

It is not on the side of those who are ruled and led by this lust that Kipling stands; nor is it for barbaric conquest and the subjugation of free peoples that he sings.

I have endeavoured to explain and to justify, to a certain extent, the extraordinary affection with which this writer is regarded by millions unnumbered among our own people and our own kin. As was confessed at the outset, nothing that I can say can increase that affection. I leave criticism to those who, being at least scholars, have the right to take upon themselves the work of criticism; it is for them to discuss methods and style. It is enough for me and for those unnumbered millions to know that here is one who has a message to deliver which concerns us all; that he has people to present to us among whom we walk daily, yet have remained hitherto in ignorance of their ways and thoughts and speech; that he has taught the people of the empire what the empire means; that he has shown us below their rough and coarse exterior the manhood of soldier and sailor, of engine-man and lighthouse-man and fisher-man. It is enough for us that he speaks as no other in his generation—these be reasons enough and to spare why he is loved by old and young in every class and in every country where his language is the language of the folk.

35. Edward Dowden on 'The Poetry of Mr. Kipling'

1901

Signed article from the *New Liberal Review*, Vol. xxxviii, pp. 53–61 (February 1901).

Edward Dowden (1843–1913), scholar and critic, Professor of English at Trinity College, Dublin 1867–1913, is best known for his works on Shakespeare. But he also wrote studies of Southey, Shelley, Browning and Montaigne.

Mr. Kipling ought to be pleased with the acoustic properties of our globe; his voice fills the building. To have something to say, no doubt, helps a voice to carry far; people cease from chatter and look up; and Mr. Kipling, especially perhaps in his verse, has things to say; he says them in no halting or hesitating manner, but 'after the use of the English', as he has himself described that use, 'in straight-flung words and few'.

It was long since a morsel of verse constituted an historical event of importance for two hemispheres; but this, without exaggeration, is what certain short poems of Mr. Kipling have been. They have served to evoke or guide the feelings of nations, and to determine action in great affairs. However we may explain it, such is the fact. And of all explanations the least tenable is that which represents Mr. Kipling as a music-hall singer, addressing a vulgar crowd in the vulgar tones which they expect for the coin they pay. La Bruyère has said some-where that the favour of a prince is no evidence of merit, but that also it indicates no deficiency of merit; the statement holds good of the favour of Prince Demos. It is true that Mr. Kipling sometimes twangs the banjo; and with its *tinka-tinka-tinka-tinka-tink* he has not done ignobly; as a satirist he has with it 'jeered the fatted soul of things'; he has with it gallantly mocked defeat, and sung the song of lost endeavour. But he has also touched the solemn organ-stops, and it is precisely to such a poem as 'Recessional', with its old prophetic strain, its warning against vain idols, and folly, and carnal pride, that the deepest response of our race is made.

Mr. Kipling's swift conquest of the people indicates of course that his inspiration is not private and solitary; it means also that he is not the poet of a coterie or *cénacle*. The poet of solitary inspiration may belong to all the world; striking deep into his own heart, he arrives at the common heart of humanity; but it often takes tedious years to bring the world over to his side. His desire is to reach many minds, and, supported by 'faith in the whispers of the lonely muse', after patient waiting he attains his desire. The poet of a coterie is commonly forced to convert his incapacity to move the public into a proof of superiority. Having really nothing to say, he conceals his emptiness by a legerde-main of caprices, a new doctrine in art, a vaporous obscurity, or a clumsy subtlety, which may induce the coterie to wonder with a foolish face of praise. He declares oracularly: 'If you do not understand me, so much the worse for *you*.' Mr. Kipling says: 'If you do not under-stand me, so much the worse for *me*.' For he is a maker of tribal lays, and if they do not speak for and to the tribe the lays fall dumb. The great good fortune of a maker of tribal lays comes when he divines the moment at which some public sentiment of Imperial power is about to announce or disclose itself and when by one hour he anticipates that moment in his song. Or should we not rather say that the gather-ing emotion finds in the poet the most sensitive nerve of the body politic, and through that nerve first thrills and finds expression? The singer then not only anticipates, but assists in the general outbreak; he moulds passions, and creates new combinations of feeling. He is the earliest ray of the rising sun, which falls upon the petals of a bud that is eager to be a blossom.

Such has been the good fortune of Mr. Kipling, and he has put his opportunity to wise uses. The sense of the brotherhood of the blood was stirring in many English hearts before he wrote, but it was one of the native-born who gave it a resonant utterance. His feeling for Empire is characterised by two chief features: first, it is based securely upon concrete fact; and, secondly, it rises at the summit to a solemn and even a religious sense of duty. The strength and volume of Edmund Burke's political passions came in great part from the circumstance that, through virtue of his all-absorbing, all-retaining intellect, and his imaginative grasp, they were fed by a multitude of vivid details. His eloquence, therefore, did not deal in vacuous abstractions, but resumed, under great principles, a mass of real and various things. It is so also with Mr. Kipling's Imperialism. This is not a flourish of rhetoric, nor intoxication with a doctrinaire theory, but is rather a gathering up of his myriad observations into an ideal unity. It has its origin in 'the little things a fellow cares about'; it clings much to kinship and to comradeship; it rises to civic loyalty and pride:

> Surely in toil or fray
> Under an alien sky,
> Comfort it is to say:
> 'Of no mean city am I.'

It passes from the city to the birth-land, knit by closest ties of sonship to the mother-country; it includes the shepherd on his hill, the ploughman drawing his furrow, the miner delving the ore, the white sails and long smoke trails on all the seas, where the swift shuttles of the great loom ply backward and forward; it embraces finally the whole congeries of thought, and dream, and deed which, below the North Star, the Southern Cross, make up the majestic unity of Empire, of which unity the flag serves as emblem; and at every stage of development the emotions are fed by sights, by sounds, by the very scents of East and West, of land-breeze and sea-breeze, by all brave memories and all tender associations.

But Mr. Kipling's feeling of Empire is solemnised by the weight of real things and by a knowledge of the cost of Empire. The 'Song of the English' includes, as part of the cantata, the 'Song of the Dead'. The sea-wife by the Northern Gate, who breeds her roving sons and sends them over sea, is in no mood of shallow exultation; only in the depth of her old heart she is proud that her sons have indeed been men. There is a wail in Tommy's chorus as he tumbles aboard the transport and sees in imagination the large birds of prey on the far horizon, keen-scented and expectant; but none the less Tommy falls in upon the troop-deck. The Widow of Windsor's party is not all cakes and jam, but you can't refuse the card when the Widow gives the party, and the end of the show is satisfactory to the Colonel:

> We broke a King and we built a road—
> A court-house stands where the reg'ment goed,
> And the river's clean where the raw blood flowed
> When the Widow give the party.

The price of admiralty is blood, and 'Lord God, we ha' paid in full'. But the whisper, and the vision that called the dreamers, whose dreams were prophecy, to go forth and leave their bones on the sand-drift, on the veldt-side, in the fern-scrub, still summon our gentleman adventurers, and the dead cry to us:

> Follow after, follow after! We have watered the root,
> And the bud has come to blossom that ripens for fruit.

It is no lust of territory or empty pride of power that can help us to sustain the white man's burden; we bear it because this also is in the day's work appointed for us by the Master of all good workmen:

> Keep ye the Law—be swift in all obedience—
> Clear the land of evil, drive the road and bridge the ford.
> Make ye sure to each his own
> That he reap where he hath sown;
> By the peace among Our peoples let men know we serve the Lord!

Such is the religious feeling for Empire. If the banjo is strummed, it seems as if a Puritan of the old Ironside breed were the minstrel. Cromwell, after the victory of Dunbar, addressed the Speaker in words which go to the same manly tune.

Even in *Departmental Ditties* which may have been a fillip of fun for jaded Anglo-Indians, though now they seem too precociously clever and not agreeably bitter-sweet, the solemn note was struck at least once, in the finest poem of the collection—'The Galley Slave'. The German has not perhaps yet written a treatise on the *Kiplingsche Weltanschauung*, and it may be worth while to show briefly how it is constituted, and how it is essentially a religious conception of things. Mr. Kipling, with his keen and wide perceptions, sees a world that is 'wondrous large', one that holds 'a vast of various kinds of men'; he is not fastidious—sinners male and female, the coward, the bully, the cheat, the brave, the strong, the weak, the cad, the gentleman, the vain pretender, the simple hero—all seem to have a place in this large world, where passion clashes with passion and deed wrestles with deed. Possessing an un-

wearied curiosity, he views this changeful spectacle, infinitely pleased
to observe 'the different ways that different things are done', of which
things, indeed, some are odd—'most awful odd'—yet, upon the whole,
this world is a highly interesting world to the intelligent spectator:

> Gawd bless this world! Whatever she 'ath done—
> Excep' when awful long—I've found it good
> So write before I die, 'E liked it all!

Mr. Kipling is not fastidious, but he does not sophisticate with good
and evil. In a certain transcendental sense he may tell us that 'sin is
vain', and may indulge a little in the amusements of those gallant
gentlemen of the halls of heaven, who, knowing the vanity of sin, can
fearlessly whistle the devil to make them sport. In general his feeling
is the devout one that it is his task to 'draw the Thing as he sees It for
the God of Things as They Are', or as he says with great dignity in
presenting to the Master a completed volume of his tales:

> One stone the more swings to her place
> In that dread Temple of Thy worth—
> It is enough that through Thy grace
> I saw nought common on Thy earth.

Nought common, however much that is unclean.

But above this turmoil of passions, above this scene of shames and
heroisms, of evil doing, weak doing, mean doing, brave doing, rises
the immutable Law; and that is best in life whether it be toil, or suffering, or sorrow, which brings men into obedience to this law, or
rather into active co-operation with it. Even the goose-step is a stage
in the evolution of order, for the young recruit is silly, keeping himself 'awful', much as he does his side-arms; and it is well for him that
he should be hammered: it is well that he should be put in the way of

> Gettin' clear o'dirtiness, gettin' done with mess,
> Gettin' shut o'doin' things rather-more-or-less.

Not Carlyle himself could more sternly condemn the folly of doing
things 'rather-more-or-less' than does Mr. Kipling; and, in the building
of a man, he especially honours *pukka* workmanship. On that awful
day when Tommy ran, squealing for quarter, and the major cursed his
Maker, and the colonel broke his sword, the root of evil lay in the fact
that 'we was never disciplined'; if an order was obeyed it was considered
a favour; every little drummer had his rights and wrongs. And in the
true beat and full power of his engine, with faithfulness in every crank

and rod, M'Andrew reads its lesson and his own: 'Law, Orderr, Duty an' Restraint, Obedience, Discipline!'

The law and order of the world, again, is presided over by the Law-giver, the Maker of men, who is a somewhat Hebraic or Puritanical deity. Not that, at least in a genial fantasy, He may not appear as a good-humoured, and even as an amused Lord God. It is He who, at the tuneful petition of the souls of the jolly, jolly mariners, supported by the afflicted Judas and the stout apostle Paul, gives back their sea to the silly sailor folk, and permits them to hand in, with tarry fingers, the golden fiddles they had somewhat clumsily handled. Jehovah is not always so good-humoured; but He knows how to value an honest workman, and to a strong man whom death has purged of pride—for pride is the special danger of the strong—who has ever walked 'in simpleness and gentleness and honour and clean mirth', He will tell tales of His daily toil and of the new-made Edens. For us, labourers on His earth, He is the great Overseer, who insists on faithful work, giving at the same time strength to the workman, which shall enable him, even amid hunger and drought and hardship, to accomplish the task assigned:

> If there be good in what I wrought
> Thy hand compelled it, Master, Thine;
> Where I have failed to meet Thy thought,
> I know, through Thee, the blame is mine.

All things—even the fall of a rose upon the garden-path—were determined by His will before the worlds came into existence. Such is the lesson of Mr. Kipling's piece of Oriental Calvinism, 'The Answer'; and the battered rose is consoled by the thought that its ruin has been for ever involved in the divine law governing the entire cosmos.

Faust in his study, pondering the words of Scripture, could not accept the sentence, 'In the beginning was the Word,' and he finally emended the text to 'In the beginning was the Act'. Mr. Kipling's emendation would most probably be, 'In the beginning was the Dream,' but with him the dream is essentially a prophecy of the act, or of some word which is itself of the nature of an act. He is a poet not of contemplation but of action, of the emotions arising from, and also held in check by, action, and of the dreams which result in a deed. In *Werther* and in all creations of the Werther school we have studies of emotions sapping in upon the active powers of the soul. The 'reign-ing personage', to borrow Taine's happy expression, of Mr. Kipling's creations, is the man who has done something, of his own initiative (or of God's), if he be a man of genius; and if not a man of genius, then something which he finds, like the brave M'Andrew—and he is almost a man of genius—allotted or assigned to him as duty. Tomlinson, of Berkeley Square, is spurned by Peter from Heaven's Gate because he can only give a shuffling answer to one straight question:

'Ye have read, ye have heard, ye have thought,' he said, 'and the tale is
                                                        yet to run:
By the worth of the body that once ye had, give answer—what ha' ye
                                                        done?'

The devil in hell knows too accurately the price of good pitcoal to waste it on such a whimpering spirit that had not virtue enough to possess one genuine native vice; off with him, therefore, once more to Berkeley Square! And, in truth, compared with Tomlinson, one of the legion of the lost, a gentleman ranker damned from here to eternity, who has gone the pace and gone it blind, is in an enviable position; his lot is piteous but not contemptible.

There are many emotions, such as those arising from the contemplation of beauty, which do not tend to action; though indirectly, in helping to form character, they may influence our deeds. These, speaking generally, do not enter into Mr. Kipling's poetry. Once or twice his man of action is in the contemplative mood; he leans over the ship-side and looks across the sea, remembering all the past, or sits in clink without his boots, and under either set of conditions, neutral or unhappy, can fall to 'admirin' 'ow the world was made':

For to admire an' for to see,
    For to be'old this world so wide—
It never done no good to me,
    But I can't drop it if I tried.

Far more often what Mr. Kipling portrays—and portrays with power—are those hasty escapes of emotion which action cannot wholly suppress; the swift hiss of steam in its jet from the safety-valve indicates better than any rhetoric the pressure within. Such a tune goes manly. Danny must hang, for is he not the disgrace of nine hundred of his country? and yet Files-on-Parade cannot forget that he drank Danny Deever's beer a score of times. It is a tenderly passionate reminiscence. Three rounds blank are all the honours that remain for the dead comrade, and before starting it is as well to finish off the swipes, but—bitter memory!—it was only last week the comrades fought about a dog—

> An' I strook 'im cruel 'ard, an' I wish I 'adn't now,
> Which is just what a man can't do.

Perhaps there is as much pathos in this as in any eloquent 'He who hath bent him o'er the dead'. The driver as he whips the limber across a wounded brother's body to put him out of pain does not wail or beat the breast; he gives a little coughing grunt and swings his horses handsome when the command 'Forward' is given, knowing that if you want to win your battles you must work your guns. But the driver's grunt holds within it all Malcolm's heartening words: 'Dispute it like a man,' and all Macduff's apology: 'I shall do so; but I must also feel it as a man.'

Through reality Mr. Kipling reaches after romance. It may be asserted in a general way that there are two kinds of romance, which, with no touch of disrespect for either, may be distinguished as its masculine and feminine forms. The one flies from all things gross and common; it chooses to gaze at what may be beheld from some magic casement

> opening on the foam
> Of perilous seas, in faery lands forlorn.

Or it finds its natural haunt and home where the elf-girls flood with wings

> Valleys full of plaintive air;
> There breathe perfumes; there in rings
> Whirl the foam-bewildered springs;
> Siren there
> Winds her dizzy hair and sings.

Of course, it may be alleged that the great and abiding realities of the soul are best discovered by a retreat from that part of life which contains much that is drossy and much that is transitory and accidental. In the palace of Art there are many mansions, and romance feminine has a chamber, enriched like Christabel's with fair things 'for a lady's chamber meet', things that are all made out of the carver's brain. The artist, as Mr. Kipling conceives him, is an artist because he sees the fact and the whole fact more exactly than the rest of the tribe; and, seeing exactly, he can scratch on bone his picture of the aurochs or the mammoth which astonishes his fellow-tribesmen, and brings them a joy that must relieve itself by gifts. The primitive tribesman, Ung, is not yet a romanticist; but he is the forefather of the masters of romance masculine, and precisely because he sees things as they are. The French painter, Millet, was in truth one of Ung's children, and in the figure of his 'Sower' he has left an example of art nobly romantic because it is profoundly real. Mr. Kipling cannot often rival the achievement of Millet; too often he relies on a superficial realism, at times heaping on local colour to excess, abusing his mastery of technical terms (which yet affect our ignorance with a mysterious power like that of the blessed word 'Mesopotamia') and using the cheap realism of Tommy's dialect to verify the strangeness of Tommy's romance. A day may come when the bloom of 'bloomin'' will have departed, and though his dialect helps Mr. Kipling, not illegitimately, to certain comic and pathetic effects, a noble romantic poem in standard English, such as 'The Derelict', may better stand the wear and tear of time.

Mr. Kipling's masculine romance does not require any aid from our charming Irish acquaintances, the people of the faery hills. He does not think that romance died with the cave-men or the lake-folk; it is Romance which brings up the nine-fifteen train:

> His hand was on the lever laid,
>   His oil-can soothed the worrying cranks,
> His whistle waked the snowbound grade,
>   His fog-horn cut the reeking banks;
> By dock and deep and mine and mill
> The Boy-god reckless laboured still.

The Viscount loon who questioned M'Andrew as to whether steam did not spoil romance at sea is very summarily dismissed; it is feebleness of imagination which has no sense of the world-lifting joy that still comes to cheer man the artifex, and a dream, not of the past, not of hide-bound coracle or beaked trireme, but of the Perfect Ship still lures him on. Our miracles are those which subdue the waves, and fill with messages of fate the deep-sea levels, and read the storms before they thunder on our coast, and toss the miles aside with crank-throw and tail-rod. 'Gross modern materialism!' sighs the votary of romance feminine; and such it may be for him, but such it is not for those who with masculine imagination and passion can perceive that it is the dream of the artifex which subdues and organises and animates the iron and the steel. We may sell a creel of turf in a sordid and grasping spirit, and we may design a steam-ship with something like the enthusiasm of a poet.

And as with man's instruments and man's work, so with man's character. It is well to nourish our imagination with tales of ancient gods and heroes; but the true romance still lives in the souls of modern men who dream of things to be—who plan, and toil, and incarnate the dream in a deed. The passion for adventure, which drove Defoe's forlorn hero away from hearth and home, still lives in English hearts, and is still at one with Crusoe's practical inventiveness and wholesome temper of self-help. Let anyone who comes across a volume of 1866, *Two Months on the Tobique*, a volume posthumously published, and which deserves to be reprinted, read the vivid pages in which the writer records his experiences in wintry solitude amid Canadian forests, and he will find that Crusoe was alive in the midmost years of the nineteenth century, islanded by voluntary exile in the impenetrable pine-wood and cedar-swamp. Many impressive passages of Mr. Kipling's poetry tell of this fire in the heart of our race—a race old yet ever young, to whom still come the whisper and the vision:

> with the places of the dead quickly filled,
> Through the battle, through defeat, moving yet and never stopping,
> Pioneers! O pioneers!

The romance again of that spell of the immemorial East laid upon the spirit of the West, and the nostalgia of the wanderer who has responded to the invitation of the East, has never been expressed with more of genuine magic than by Mr. Kipling. There is another form of romance, vulgarised indeed by cheap examples yet part of 'the true romance', with which he has dealt successfully—the discovery of some one, hidden, green oasis in a soul turned into desert by the drifted sand and parching winds of a worldly life. John Bunyan's Mr. Badman died 'like a lamb', for sin had wholly indurated his soul, and God's judgement upon him was to leave him alone. Mr. Kipling's 'Sir Anthony Gloster', in his death-bed wanderings, mingles together piteously carnal pride and sensuality with the relics of an iron will; yet he is not wholly lost, for a spot of sea, 'Hundred and eighteen East, remember, and South just three' by the Little Paternosters, is still sacred for him, and it is there, where he dropped the body of the wife of his youth in fourteen fathoms, that his own body must seek the depths. Perhaps the poor romance of the oasis is better than any splendid romance of the mirage.

36. J. H. Millar reviews *Kim*

1901

Anonymous review of 'Recent Fiction' in *Blackwood's Magazine*,
Vol. CLXX, pp. 793–5 (December 1901).

By J. H. Millar (see his full-scale review-article on Kipling in
1898—No. 29 above).

In discussing a few of the novels of the last six months or so, it is right
and proper, on many accounts, which it were superfluous to specify,
that due precedence should be awarded to Mr. Kipling. *Kim* is in some
respects his most ambitious and elaborate work, and having, we confess,
'shied' at *Stalky & Co.*, we fell with a double portion of alacrity upon
a 'new Kipling' which held out hopes of proving equal to the old
ones. Nor have we been disappointed. Mr. Kipling has decidedly
'acquired merit' by this his latest essay. There is fascination, almost
magic, in every page of the delightful volume, whose attractiveness is
enhanced by illustrations of (to our mind) superlative excellence.

Kim, the eponymous hero, is a white boy, a *pukka* sahib: the son, in
short, of Kimball O'Hara, late sergeant in the Mavericks, and his wife,
once a nursery-maid in the colonel's family. Left an orphan at an early
age, he has been brought up in the town of Lahore, nominally by a
native woman of no character at all, and in reality, upon the educational
principles which found so much favour with the elder Mr. Weller and
find so little at the present day with many men less wise than he. Kim
has thus, when we make his acquaintance, acquired a considerable
knowledge of mankind and their ways, in addition to the nickname of
'Friend of all the world'. He is 'hand in glove with men who led lives
stranger than anything Haroun Al Raschid dreamed of: and he lived
in a life wild as that of the Arabian Nights, but missionaries and
secretaries of charitable societies could not see the beauty of it.'

To him enter an aged lama from Tibet, on pilgrimage in quest of
'the river which washes away all taint of sin'. Kim forthwith becomes
his *chela* or attendant (the word may or may not be at bottom identical

with the Highland *gillie*), and they set out together *en route* for Benares, *via* Umballa, where Kim has been charged with a commission to perform by Mahbub Ali, an Afghan horse-dealer, who is in the pay of the Survey Department of the Indian Government. We cannot detail the incidents which mark the journey by rail and road of this singular pair of travellers. We can only note that they separate for a time, after Kim has fallen in with his father's old regiment, the colonel and chaplains of which are bent upon taking charge of him. The lama, however, insists upon paying for Kim's education. 'Education is greatest blessing if of best sorts. Otherwise no earthly use.' Such are his views, as tersely and sensibly expressed by a professional letter-writer, in Baboo English. Accordingly, Kim is sent to the school of St. Francis Xavier at Lucknow, there to accumulate such information as may be useful to him in after-life. For already he is practically destined by the powers that be to the playing of the Great Game—which, being interpreted, means the Secret Service of the Government. His schooling over, he is almost immediately launched upon his career, wherein, at the outset, he acquits himself, 'in a dam-tight place' (as Babu Hurree Chunder Mookerjee expresses it), with such sagacity and discretion as to please 'all the Department'. Having foregathered once more with the lama, he has much wandering in his company among the hills, with many exciting adventures, in which the fascinating Hurree plays a prominent part. The story concludes with Kim's recovery from a serious illness, brought on by over-fatigue, and with the successful issue of the lama's quest. In other words, the venerable priest falls into a brook, while in a brown study, and, having been with difficulty rescued from a watery grave, believes that he has at length been washed in the river of the Arrow which was the object of his search.

The character of Kim is from first to last a masterly conception. As a study of adolescence—of the progress from boyhood to youth, and from youth to early manhood—it is incomparably fresh and true: full of the delight of the artificer in the work of his hands, of the joy that comes from nothing so much as from the sense of successful achievement. The pride of the labourer in a task well performed has always been a congenial and favourite theme with Mr. Kipling; and we know of no other which, once duly appreciated, is likely to do so much for the maintenance of our Empire in all its manifold interests. Over and above Kim, there is a portrait-gallery of unusual extent and interest. Mahbub Ali, the old Ressaldar, the Rajah's widow, and Baboo Hurree, are the chief of those who find a place in it. And in the background there is always the impressive figure of the lama, whose mysterious apophthegms about the Wheel and the most Excellent Law form a deep and solemn accompaniment, as it were, to the music of the whole composition. You do not stop to inquire whether he or any one else is true to life. You *know* they are; you accept them all without question or reservation or cavil. That absolute perfection, however, may not be predicated of his work, Mr. Kipling has been obliging enough to throw in a couple of characters of whom so much cannot be said. Both Mr. Bennett, the Anglican, and Father Victor, the Roman Catholic chaplain, strike us as being conventional and commonplace—just the sort of personages whom we have learned to expect from Mr. Kipling's imitators.

But it is neither in the fable (exciting and ingenious though it be) nor in the portrayal of character (however skilful and convincing) that the charm of *Kim* consists. Its secret lies in the wonderful panorama it unrolls before us of the life of the great Peninsula over whose government England has now presided for more than a century. We despair of giving our readers any adequate conception of the glorious variety of the feast here spread before them. The kaleidoscopic quality, if we may venture so to call it, of Mr. Kipling's genius, has never before been displayed on so extensive a scale or to such great advantage. Turn to the description of the wayfarers on the Grand Trunk Road (too long, unfortunately, for transcription here), and consider for a moment the patient industry, the protracted observation, the thorough knowledge, which go to the making of these three pages. The thought is merely astounding; and one feels inclined in one's bewilderment to fall back upon the convenient and plausible theory that Mr. Kipling knows everything by instinct. That he knew much of native life we were aware already, but how much he knew we had not—perhaps have not yet—fathomed. Take one of the Strickland series of his stories: expand it, strengthen it, add indefinite multiplicity of detail to it; and you have the formula for producing a *Kim*. But let the adventurous aspirant see that his hand is well 'in' before he tries it.

37. A Review of *Just So Stories*

1902

Anonymous review under 'Juvenile Literature' in the *Athenaeum*, No. 3910, pp. 447–8 (4 October 1902).

The *Just So Stories* (Macmillan), in which Mr. Kipling appears both as author and illustrator, should regain the favour which he has lost in some quarters by indifferent verse. Mr. Kipling is, at his best, the most inspired teller of tales that we have; he understands young folk as few writers do, and better than other mysteries which he has attempted to tackle with expert haste. The result is that several of these stories—for instance those concerning the invention of letter-writing and of the alphabet by the daughter of a cave-dweller, the independence of the domestic cat, the reason for the elephant's trunk—are perfect, told once for all so that other tellers need not hope to compete. The stories being for younger folk than the *Jungle Books*, deal a good deal in what is pure nonsense to the child, and clever fooling with ornate words and phrases to the adult—such writing, in fact, as the catalogues of remedies in Kingsley's *Water Babies*. There is, we fancy, a touch too much of this clever stuff in the earlier stories, but the main invention and the delightfully easy exposition, with feats of duplicated onomatopoeic adjectives and the odd little details which children love aptly interfused, carry one on triumphantly. That invention is not always good; Mr. Kipling can do much better when he likes than assure us that the camel got his hump because he said 'humph' instead of working. The pictures show the author's real talent in a new line, though indeed we might expect as much from his father's son. They recall in their style and the elaborately naïve exposition attached to them that genuine piece of nursery lore *Animal Land*,[1] and in their use of dead black the most original of modern illustrators. Some of them are rather messy, but generally they are a distinct aid to the text. The whole forms an outstanding book, which, though not so delightful as the *Jungle Books*, is yet enough to

---

[1] [*Animal Land Where There Are No People*, 1897. By Sybil Corbet (aged 4)]

have made a reputation for a new author. We are eager to read as much more in this vein as Mr. Kipling will give us.

38. G. K. Chesterton reviews *Just So Stories*

1902

Signed review from the *Bookman* (London), Vol. XXIII, pp. 57–8 (November 1902).

Gilbert Keith Chesterton (1874–1936), essayist, novelist and minor poet, best remembered for his Father Brown detective stories, was also a discerning critic and a master of epigram. The religious writings of his later life are only excelled by those of C. S. Lewis.

For his fuller study of Kipling in *Heretics* (1905) see No. 42 below.

Mr. Rudyard Kipling is a most extraordinary and bewildering genius. Some of us have recently had reason to protest against certain phases of his later development, and we protested because they were pert and cockney and cruel, and full of that precocious old age which is the worst thing in this difficult cosmos, a thing which combines the brutality of youth with the disillusionment of antiquity, which is old age without its charity and youth without its hope. This rapidly aging, rapidly cheapening force of modernity is everywhere and in all things, a veritable spiritual evil: it looks out of the starved faces of a million gutter-boys, and its name is Ortheris. And just as we are in the after-glow of a certain indignation against this stale, bitter modernity which had begun to appear in Mr. Kipling's work, we come upon this superb thing, the *Just-So Stories*; a great chronicle of primal fables, which might have been told by Adam to Cain, before murder (that artistic and decadent pastime) was known in the world.

For the character of the *Just-So Stories* is really unique. They are not fairy tales; they are legends. A fairy tale is a tale told in a morbid age to the only remaining sane person, a child. A legend is a fairy tale told to men when men were sane. We grant a child a fairy tale, just as some savage king might grant a missionary permission to wear clothes, not understanding what we give, not knowing that it would be infinitely valuable if we kept it to ourselves, but simply because we are too kind to refuse. The true man will not buy fairy tales because he is kind; he will buy them because he is selfish. If Uncle John who has just bought the *Just-So Stories* for his niece were truly human (which of course Uncle John is not) it is doubtful whether the niece would ever see the book. One of the most lurid and awful marks of human degeneration that the mind can conceive is the fact that it is considered kind to play with children.

But the peculiar splendour, as I say, of these new Kipling stories is the fact that they do not read like fairy tales told to children by the modern fireside, so much as like fairy tales told to men in the morning of the world. They see animals, for instance, as primeval men saw them; not as types and numbers in an elaborate biological scheme of knowledge, but as walking portents, things marked by extravagant and peculiar features. An elephant is a monstrosity with his tail between his eyes; a rhinoceros is a monstrosity with his horn balanced on his nose; a camel, a zebra, a tortoise are fragments of a fantastic dream, to see which is not seeing a scientific species, but like seeing a man with three legs or a bird with three wings, or men as trees walking. The whole opens a very deep question, the question of the relations between the old wonder and the new wonder, between knowledge and science. The hump of the camel is very likely not so much his characteristic from a scientific point of view as the third bone in the joint of his hind leg, but to the eyes of the child and the poet it remains his feature. And it is more important in this sense that it is more direct and certain: there is a relation between the human soul and the hump of a camel, which there is not between the human soul and the bone in his hind leg. The hump still remains and the bone vanishes, if all these physical phenomena are nothing but a grotesque shadow-show, constructed by a paternal deity to amuse an universe of children.

This is the admirable achievement of Kipling, that he has written new legends. We hear in these days of continual worship of old legends, but not of the making of new; which would be the real worship of legends. Just in the same way we hear of the worship of old ceremonies, but never of the making of new ones. If men decided that Mr. Gladstone's hat was to be carried three times round the House of Commons they would have offered the best tribute to the Eleusinian mysteries. That is the tribute which 'How the Whale got his Throat' offers to the story of Sigurd and Hercules.

39. 'Kipling and the Children'

1902

Article first published in *Anglo-American Magazine* (Toronto), Vol. VIII, pp. 14–21 (December 1902) and reprinted in *English Illustrated Magazine*, Vol. XXX, pp. 470–4 (January 1904). By Agnes Deans Cameron (1863–1912).

Kipling has been considered in many aspects—as the Bard of Tommy Atkins, the exponent of Anglo-Indian life, the Laureate of the Empire, the Poet of Wheel and Axle, Lever and Screw, and a most compelling Voice from the Jungle. Not with his soldiers, nor with his animals, nor his engines would we now deal, but with his children.

At the first blush one would not think to discover in Kipling a fertile field for paternal and pedagogical research, to find him bristling with maxims for the training of the young. But send out a town crier, a sort of Pied Piper of Hamelin searching for children through the length and breadth of Kipling-land, and see the following he will get.

Of Kipling's long stories, *Stalky & Co.* deals entirely with children; *Captains Courageous* is in intent the story of a boy, so is *Kim*. *The Light That Failed*, in its first and best chapters, is a study of child-life; while that wondrous thing *The Jungle Book*, stronger than Aesop and with a witchery all its own, what is it but a sustained treatise on the claims of the commonwealth and the development of the individual?

And as the Piper pipes, out from 'somewhere east of Suez', to answer to the roll-call, comes crowding such a goodly company, a feast here for the student of child-life and for the lover of children.

Let us stand aside and watch the procession pass: Wee Willie Winkie, and his Majesty the King; Muhammed Din, poor baby, from his garden of dust and dead leaves; and Tods of the Amendment. Round the corner we stumble upon the little Japs splashing in their half-sunk barrel and trying to hide one behind the other 'in a hundred poses of spankable chubbiness', with the little American monstrosity, 'who, when it has nothing else to do, will answer to the name of Albert'; across the line of vision reel 'The Drums of the Fore and Aft', followed by 'Baa, Baa, Blacksheep', and Strickland, the son of his Father; here comes William the Conqueror's long line of goats with the naked famine babies as running commentary, while out of the shadows mysterious and fascinating of No-Man's Land glides into our ken The Brushwood Boy; at his heels, 'under a man's helmet wid the chin-straps swingin' about her little stummick', Jhansi McKenna staggers, the Child of the Regiment.

Are they not all very human and very lovable? The Pied Piper, who called them forth, turns to us and says, 'Who is the happy man? He that sees in his own home little children crowned with dust, leaping and falling and crying' (Munichandra). A writer's best stories are always in part autobiographical, and to this rule *Kim* and *Stalky & Co.* are no exceptions. 'Master Gigadibs', the festive Beetle—in retreat in his lair among the furze bushes, waiting for the dead cat to begin to twine like a giddy honeysuckle, worshipping the Head, baiting King, and confiding in the Padre—is always and ever Beetle the inimitable. In the light of what Beetle and Bard has since given us we can scarcely regret that his gig-lamps and short-sightedness kept him out of the army.

Stalky & Co. recently formed the bone of contention in a ladies' literary club, and few were the friends it found. One mother objected to the slang, another to the 'absence of ideals', a third abjured it altogether, but said that her son revelled in it and her husband approved. The chief fault of the book lies, perhaps, in the fact that Kipling has portrayed the scrapes of the trio, and has given us no account of the long, arid stretches of dig, grind, and plodding which must have existed in order that those stiff exams should be passed.

For those blessed with a close understanding of the animal 'boy', the slang part has no power to shock. What is it that George Eliot makes Fred Vincy say? 'All choice of words is slang. It marks a class. Correct

English is the slang of prigs who write history and essays. And the strongest slang of all is the slang of poets.'

The second charge, that against the morale of the story, is a more serious one. Is the effect of *Stalky & Co.* on the mind of the schoolboy reader bad? Does it set before him a low moral standard, and is it lacking in ideals? Let us look at the situation fairly. The Three Incomprehensibles, Stalky, Beetle and McTurk, had a creed, to which they adhered with more consistency than we always do to ours. This creed or code of ethics was not angelic, but it was delightfully human. The Head and the Padre treated them openly and trusted them, and in return were to be met always 'on the level'. The House Masters, King and Foxy, neither gave nor asked for confidence; here the wits of the governing and the governed were pitted against each other in open warfare; the boys looked upon the contest as a fair game, and the other side acquiesced.

And at this we, some of us, cavil. Let us be honest. These boys were being trained for what? For just this sort of thing. As British officers they were to go to 'India's sunny clime', and there to do what? To outwit the wily strategy of Britain's foes. And by what means? Was the enemy to be brought to terms by a 'polite letter-writer' effusion presented on a silver salver, or by meeting wile with wile?

Stalky, the man, proved, we are told, a past grand-master in the art of diplomacy. Who were his foils when he studied the rudiments of primeval warfare and learned his trade? Answer, O King and Prout and Foxy.

The finest bit in the book is, perhaps, the Flag scene. The bare idea of 'teaching patriotism' to British boys is sickening. But the schools have patrons and committee-men and trustees, and when these wise ones give advice, what can the poor pedagogue do but squirm? The satisfaction of blandly referring these to 'a most interesting chapter in *Stalky & Co.* dealing with the subject' is great, and for this thanks are due.

There is proof, if proof is needed, that even while Beetle with his *confrères* were scornfully repudiating 'the jelly-bellied flag-flapper' (!) and his spurious oratory, deep down in the heart of the young Imperialist burned thus early the fires of an Empire-wide patriotism, *vide* his poem '*Ave Imperatrix*', written from Westward Ho! College, on the occasion of the last attempt on the life of the great and good Queen, while Beetle was yet unknown to fame:

[quotes '*Ave Imperatrix*', first 5 stanzas: DV. p. 169]

In 'Only a Subaltern', Kipling gives us another Flag incident; it is just a glimpse. The subaltern is Bobby Wick, just gazetted sub-lieutenant of 'The Tyneside Tail-Twisters'.

More than once, too, he came officially into contact with the regimental colours, which looked like the lining of a bricklayer's hat on the end of a chewed stick. Bobby did not kneel and worship them, because British subalterns are not constructed in that manner. Indeed, he condemned them for their weight at the very moment they were filling him with awe and other more noble sentiments.

Peace hath her victories no less renowned than war. This is the Bobby who day by day in the cholera camp 'played the giddy garden goat', and at night fought with Death for dirty Dormer till the grey dawn came, a few days later, to 'go out' himself, dying for all that the Flag stands for: 'Not only to enforce by command but to encourage by example the energetic discharge of duty and the steady endurance of the difficulties and privations inseparable from Military Service' (Bengal Army Regulations).

Kipling's dedication of *Stalky & Co.* to his old head master is among the very finest things he has written:

[quotes stanzas 5, 7, 11, 13 of 'A School Song': DV. pp. 556–8]

'The Head', who had kindliness and wise insight enough ('God's Own Commonsense') to know that a boy may be in mischiefs manifold, the hero of many scrapes, and remain pure, wholesome, and withal very lovable, would not be insensible to this tribute coming 'after many days'.

Kipling believed in public schools. In 'Thrown Away' he has this to say of the 'sheltered life system':

To rear a boy under what parents call the 'sheltered-life system' is, if the boy must go out into the world and fend for himself, not wise. Unless he be one in a thousand, he has certainly to pass through many unnecessary troubles; and may, possibly, come to extreme grief simply from ignorance of the proper proportion of things. Let a puppy eat the soap in the bath-room, or chew a newly-blacked boot. He chews and chuckles until by-and-by he finds out that blacking and old brown Windsor make him very sick; so he argues that soap and boots are not wholesome. Any old dog about the house will soon show him the unwisdom of biting big dog's ears. Being young, he remembers and goes abroad at six months, a well-mannered little beast with a chastened appetite. If he had been kept away from boots and soap and big dogs until he came to the maturity, full-grown, and with developed teeth, consider how fearfully sick and thrashed he would be.

Apply that notion to the sheltered life, and see how it works. As Kipling says, it does not sound pretty; but is it not most terribly true?

In the 'Jungle School', did not Mowgli the 'Man-cub', find a teacher who on Farne's beadroll of Dominies must take a place second only to Froebel and Arnold, and the great of old? Listen to the words of wisdom which fall from the shaggy lips of Baloo, the brown bear, 'Teacher of the Law', to the Seonee wolf-cubs:

> 'There is none like to me!' says the Cub
> in the pride of his earliest kill;
> But the Jungle is large, and the Cub he is
> small. Let him think and be still.

Hathi, the wild elephant, never does anything till the time comes, and that is one of the reasons why he lives so long.

One of the beauties of Jungle Law is that punishment settles all scores. There is no nagging afterwards.

Better he should be bruised from head to foot by me who loves him, than that he should come to harm through ignorance.

(The sheltered-life system found no exponent in old Baloo.)

A brave heart and a courteous tongue, they shall carry thee far through the Jungle, Manling.

> 'Now these are the Laws of the Jungle,
> and many and mighty are they;
> But the head and the hoof of the Law, and
> the haunch and the hump is—OBEY!'

The Seonee Cubs, who passed under Baloo's hard training, had experience of the dogma of 'Life's Handicap':

> Ride with an idle whip, ride with an unused heel,
> But once in a way there will come a day
> When the colt must be taught to feel
> The lash that falls, and the curb that galls,
> and the sting of the rowelled steel.

And yet was there ever the truest tenderness in the Old Bear's teaching.

Kipling, who went forth

> For to admire an' for to see,
> For to be'old this world so wide,

like a greedily-impressionable bit of blotting-paper, soaking up everything on the face of the earth, in 'From Sea to Sea' pays a warm tribute to the American girl:

Sweet and comely are the maidens of Devonshire; delicate and of gracious seeming those who live in the pleasant places of London; fascinating for all their demureness the damsels of France, clinging closely to their mothers, and with large eyes wondering at the wicked world; excellent in her own place, and to those who understand her is the Anglo-Indian 'spin' in her second season; but the girls of America are above and beyond them all. They are clever; they can talk. They are original, and look you between the brows with unabashed eyes as a sister might look at a brother. They are self-possessed without parting with any tenderness that is their sex-right; they are superbly independent; they understand.

A word, too, for the 'long, elastic, well-built California boy':

Him I love because he is devoid of fear, carries himself like a man, and has a heart as big as his boots.

If I were asked to strike the keynote of all Kipling's teachings, I should say it was 'The sacredness, the imperativeness, to each man, of his own day's work'.

A man must throw his whole being into his task, 'gettin' shut o' doin' things rather more or less'; and that man shall 'by the vision splendid, be on his way attended'. It is the Apotheosis of Work. And, surely, has he earned a right to speak on this subject, for, literally, while his companions slept, he was 'toiling upward in the night'.

Kipling, in his own impressionable youth, had the inestimable advantage of living in India just at the time when the old order was giving place to the new. Around him was an empire in making, and he saw the raw edges of the work. For years, out of sight of the English press, did he work like a grub of genius in a remote corner, spinning, in long, hot, dusty days, and in hotter nights, a golden web out of which only stray strands floated into the world's ken. There is a camaraderie, a sort of freemasonry, in work; had he not himself been a worker, it would not have been given to him to meet at first hand all manners of men.

As it is, he gets his facts in days spent in the huts of the hill-country, in the engine-rooms of great liners, in the opium shops of Lahore, in the busy marts of men, far off on lone hillsides and riverways, where men toiling, sweating, planning, fighting, build walls and bridges, lead forlorn hopes, and do things.

And through the best of Kipling's boy-stories shines ever the insistence of the Day's Work. This lesson, though delayed, must be learned (be it by a bear's blows or at the hard hands of a Cape Cod-fisher), and to him who throws himself headlong into his task the reward will not be lacking.

Kim, hugging himself in sheer intoxication with the love of life and of work, would seem to exclaim with Tommy Atkins:

> Gawd bless this world! Whatever she hath done—
> Excep' when awful long—I've found it good,
> So write, before I die, 'E liked it all.

And so it was that, casting aside conventions, with a this-one-thing-I-do intentness, whether hand in hand with Old Lama, childlike seeking The Way, or following 'The Great Game' off his own bat, he caught brief elusive glimpses of the 'light that never was on land or sea'.

Love of energy is the axis of Kipling's mind. But while it is true that he is no dreamer of Arcady, it is also true that one cannot read his child-sketches without discovering in them a sub-current, a minor note of almost womanly tenderness. It is a pathetic touch, and exquisitely delicate. Is there to be found any other 'mere man' who could have written 'Baa, Baa, Blacksheep' or 'His Majesty the King'?

And then there are the child chapters of *The Light that Failed*, and that rare thing 'The Brushwood Boy'. And which of us can follow to the grave (respectfully, and at a distance, that we may not intrude), little Muhammed Din and not gulp hard to keep back the tears? For we, too, have folded baby-fingers that made gardens of dust and dead flowers, and the heart of a child is the same on whichsoever shore of the Seven Seas he builds his sand-houses and to whatsoever grave we carry him.

Kipling knows his children as he knows his soldiers, his animals, his engines; and when he half startles us with a statement like this, 'The reserve of a boy is tenfold deeper than the reserve of a maid,' it is only the ignorant of us who laugh.

'Only women,' he says, 'understand children properly; but if a mere man keeps very quiet and humbles himself properly, and refrains from talking down to his superiors, the children will sometimes be good to him and let him see what they think about the world.'

40. F. York Powell on 'Rudyard Kipling'

1903

Signed article in the *English Illustrated Magazine*, Vol. XXX, pp. 295–8 (December 1903) preceding Bibliographical List—one of a series.

Frederick York Powell (1850–1904), scholar, man of letters, Professor of Modern History at Oxford and outstanding Scandinavian scholar (he edited the *Corpus Poeticum Boreale* in 1881).

Mr. Kipling is a force in politics as in letters. But this makes it harder to judge him fairly. Some of his least artistic work is wholly sound in feeling. 'Pay! Pay! Pay!' is not his best poem, but as an effectual piece of writing it had a deserved success, and helped many that would have fared ill but for such an appeal. For myself, I do not greatly admire his Hymns, and I find the talking ponies and machinery of the kind tiresome, but these Hymns and Animal stories and the less inspired *Just So* tales are favourites with many both young and old, and certainly the moral is excellent. As a teacher, indeed, Mr. Kipling is undeniably effective. I am profoundly grateful for many of his sermons, and gladly acknowledge the practical good he has done. We English cannot help preaching; it is one of our most notable characteristics to the foreigner's eye that we must be eternally giving advice, advice generally unasked. To my mind, Mr. Kipling is very English (if I may differ, as I regret to do, from Mr. Chesterton); he loves the didactic; he dallies gladly with allegory; he has, like Defoe, practical ends. He is an artist born, but also a born preacher, though it is only fair to say that he does not make himself a missionary, and his ministrations are confined to his own countrymen, who have need of his advice. He preaches Faith, Hope, and Charity. He has enforced, again and again, the necessary lesson of sympathy with everything that lives. He has made us feel that there is a common humanity between us and the most inscrutable 'native'. He has made us understand that there is an abiding interest in the thoughts and ways of the plain man and woman doing their daily work and rejoicing in it. He has got very close to the inwardness of the soldier and the sailor, the engineer, the civilian, and the fisherman. The whole life and mind of the newspaper man, whether editor, reporter, correspondent, compositor, or printer's devil, is open to him, and revealed by him to us.

He is a perpetual and patient and swift observer, ever on the look-out for the vital and distinctive among the mass of phenomena that surrounds us all. He has not a little of Maupassant's gift of giving the local colour and the personal impression without waste of words, though he was trained in a far less artistic studio, and was some time before he worked free of the tricks of the school of Dickens and Sala and the Kingsleys, and reached the higher simplicities of finished art. Dumas has influenced him, as he influenced Stevenson, wholly for good, in the spirit and not in the letter. He has the delight Gautier so often expressed for technical detail; he sees its importance; he knows what the engine is to the engineer and the ship to the sailor. He can paint moods by a very different method to that of Henry James, but one as legitimate, and more Meredithian, discovering the instinct by the act, marking the play of incident on the character. It is not his business to endeavour to trace out, according to the miraculous and unique method of the greatest of American novelists, the whole working of the tangled current of will as it is contorted by circumstance. His prose is straightforward, concise, untrammelled by useless ornament and as he develops less and less disturbed by the episodic appeal to the reader which Defoe disdained, but which spoils much of Thackeray's work. His reader is never unfairly dealt with by Mr. Kipling. If he cannot move him by a 'plain tale', he will not strive by such illegitimate efforts to stimulate his stolid brain and dull heart. With a fine descriptive gift, never sliding into the dangerous catalogue style (which, though it was nobly employed by Balzac, was not seldom abused by Zola) he gets his effect by a careful but spontaneous-looking selection of the touches that really tell. I often wonder whether he does not practise in letters the method Phil May used in design, and write into his first sketch much more than he means to have printed, cutting out all but the really significant lines and leaving them to speak out clearly, unhampered by those that would only fill up and dull the impression he has already secured. He can create characters that help to people the world that each of us has in his brain; a world where Falstaff and Mrs. Gamp are as real as one's flesh-and-blood acquaintance. Mrs. Hauksbee and Private Ortheris,

Dick and the red-haired girl, Terence and Dinah, the Engineer's wife and Kim's old bonze, The Infant, Strickland, Torpenhow, Badalia and Judson, Jakin and Dan, are not paper things, but move, and talk, and laugh, and suffer, and breathe, and bleed, as mere puppets never can. For plot and situation he has of course a most rare and singular gift; such tales as 'The Man Who Was', 'The Brushwood Boy', 'The Strange Ride', and a score more that might be named, attest this power to the full. He has had, of course, scores of imitators, and not a few that have been inspired by him to do good work of their own (like Mr. J. London, whose *Call of the Wild* is far the best book Mr. Kipling's beast-tales have brought into existence), but his imitators have not made the originals stale.

For his verse there is much that is imperfect in it. He has let far too many poems be printed and reprinted that do not fairly represent him, that are imperfect, immature, unbalanced, unfinished. He has not yet the heart to prune his verse as he prunes his prose. He is too easily content with labouring and re-labouring inside the same circles of thought and expression. He injured some of his best poems by leaving ugly flaws that could easily be removed, by imperfect rhymes, extra-metrical lines (a bad fault this because it irritates), jarring discords, superfluity of expression and, above all, by labouring the idea over-much as Victor Hugo continually did. This is the sin of Eli, and it is deadly if a man do not repent and forswear it. Prose may be 'let go at that', but not verse; it is not 'playing the game'. But when all is said, Mr. Kipling is a vigorous and sincere poet. His best verse has music in it, and there are wings to his words. He has learnt much from Mr. Swinburne's early work, but it is the more massive qualities of his Master's rhythm rather than the delicacies of his more elaborate crafts-manship that have chiefly pleased him. Mr. Kipling has the essential gift that the poet of children and the crowd must have, the gift of correct time and clear flow, but he has more than that: there is a soul as well as a body in his finer poems; they cling, they haunt the mind, as they satisfy the ear. Some of the scraps of verse set at the heads of chapters are in this kind admirable. He is also, as few modern English poets are, a real song writer: he makes verse that calls for a singer, that demands the barytone and the tinkle of the strings, and the full-mouthed chorus. What he has written in slang is wonderfully good, full of movement, and never commonplace, as so much dialect verse tends to be. These are excellent specimens: 'Piet', 'M.I.', and 'Me' in his last volume. He is exceptionally strong in allegory, a vein rarely touched of late, but which he has worked to purpose. 'The Galley', 'The Three-decker', 'The Truce of the Bear', 'The Dykes', and 'True Thomas', are notable examples. Neither Tennyson nor (as I think) Browning could write a good ballad, but Mr. Kipling can. 'Fisher's Boardinghouse', 'The Bolivar', 'The Last Suttee', and 'Danny Deever', for instance, are real 'little epics'. For the full, rich, rolling verse in which he excels, perhaps the best are: 'The Last Chantey', 'The Dirge of the Dead Sisters', '*Et Dona Ferentes*', 'The Long Trail', 'The Jollies', 'The Anchor Song', though there are a fair number nearly as good in manner or matter. But if these alone existed Mr. Kipling would go down to posterity with 'a full and proper kit of song' to use his own words.

His limitations are obvious, and they are not elastic, but they are the consequence of his peculiar gifts, and we do not look to him to rival the work of thinkers like Mr. Meredith, to walk with the dreamers like Mr. Yeats or A.E., or to touch the poignant personal note of such poets as Mr. Blunt or the best verse of Messrs. Watson and T. E. Brown. Henley's finest work was much more subjective than Mr. Kipling's is or can be. But there are many mansions in the House of Apollo, and to one of these his title is writ clear enough.

It is pleasant to write about good work, but Mr. Kipling's work may safely be left to speak for itself. He is yet young and strong, and in full power; one may hope for more prose and more verse from him. He will never lack subjects. He evidently loves his work and, like the artists in heaven of his 'Envoy', he would do it for the pure pleasure of it were there neither fame nor reward in it. He has deserved well of England, and well of the Empire. He has never hesitated to speak plainly to his countrymen, and some of them, at least, have taken his lesson to heart. He has been faithful to Art also, and his devotion has not been thrown away. He has always been a learner, and though at first one feared that he could be too easily satisfied, the increasing finish of his prose style (for his verse does not improve perceptibly) shows that he has constantly striven for more perfect expression. His leniency towards his past work is, though regrettable, easy to understand.

Perhaps no English man of letters since Byron has seen his ideas and his manner of conveying them so widely welcomed among the reading public of his countrymen. Unlike Byron in most things, he resembles him in this, that he commands the attention of the public because he can be easily understood, because his manner is that which his age admires and recognises, because he has something new to say, which he must say plainly, and does say well.

41. George Moore on 'Kipling and Loti'

1904

Extracts from section five of *Avowals*, first published in *Pall Mall Magazine*, Vol. XXXIII, pp. 374–9 (July 1904); later published in book form 1919.

George Augustus Moore (1852–1933), Irish novelist once highly esteemed but later neglected. Notable for his interest in style and his break with the conventions of previous novelists.

Perhaps even more than railways and steamboats, modern education has thrown art from the general into the particular; every one understands the particular, but abstract sentiments are understood only by a few. The success of a picture or book is in proportion to the number of facts related, and the inferior artist is tempted by money, and popular appreciation and local colour bring him both. That is why there is so little in modern art of that beautiful mediocrity which we find in ancient art. Local colour is proof of education—it proves the painter has travelled: truth of effect raises him almost to the level of the scientist, and historical accuracy testifies that he spent a good deal of his time in a library as well as in his studio. . . . I am not writing in the hope of converting any one. Men will cease to believe in education as soon as it pleases them to do so. But will things be better then, when the educational folly has passed? Not a jot. We shall exchange one folly for another—that will be all. Painters, writers, and musicians who have no hold upon the eternal verities must seize upon local colour to give passing interest to their work; but why should

critics be enthusiastic about local colour? Critics—well, great critics—
can pursue their calling, whatever artistic fashion prevails. Yet local
colour has been the stumbling-block of criticism for one hundred years.
Great and small, every critic is duped; the artist has only to find out
some particular part of the country and to bring back some curious
notes of travel to dupe every one. It would appear that we learn
nothing that we did not know before. I wrote this phrase twenty years
ago in *Confessions of a Young Man*, and I write it again. Notwithstanding
Berlioz's mistake, there was not one critic in London who was not
deceived in the eighties, when Mr. Kipling came with his *Plain Tales
from the Hills*. His stories are filled with hookahs and elephants, parakeets and crocodiles; they are as amusing as the Zoological Gardens
with beer *ad lib*. All the dialects are there—Irish and Scotch and
Cockney. As the name of Beethoven was introduced when *Le Desert*
was being written about, the name of Shakespeare was introduced
apropos of Mr. Kipling. A critical mistake is soon forgotten; no author
can be held responsible for his critic's blunders; and it is to Mr. Kipling's
credit that he seems to have known more about himself than his
critics. We can only convict him of having made one mistake in those
perilous times—he once got off his camel. It was the editor of an
American magazine who persuaded Mr. Kipling to write a story the
greater part of which should be camel-less. There were a few camels
in the beginning of the story, but there were none afterwards—not as
the story appeared in the magazine; but the story was rewritten, and
the second version ended amid herds of camels. The hero of this story
is a special artist, who has done some sketches in the East; these sketches
(done certainly in wash) attracted a great deal of attention when they
were exhibited in England. A dealer wanted to buy up the whole lot,
but the special artist says: 'I know a trick worth two of that,' and he
determines to get a great deal of money for his sketches. The analogy
between Mr. Kipling and the artist is obvious. We think Mr. Kipling
much better than any special artist ever sent out on a war expedition—
we think that Mr. Kipling libelled himself; if so, it was himself who
did it. An attempt is made to show that Dick Heldar is something
more than a journalist; he is represented painting a picture of Melancholia. A poet may disguise himself as a beggar, but not as a special
artist—to do so shows a certain coarseness of fibre, a lack of sensibility;
and to represent him as painting a Melancholia is to make him ridiculous.

The phrase I have attributed to Dick Heldar may not have been used by him, but his whole personality suggests the words, 'I know a trick worth two of that,'—they are in a way an abridgment, a compendium of his attitude towards life; he browses like a horse in tether within the circle of 'I know a trick worth two of that.' 'I know a trick worth two of that' is the keynote of his mind. It is the key in which he always writes; he indulges in some modulations, but the key of 'I know a trick worth two of that' is never quite out of his ear, and if one were so minded one could trace it through all his prose and a good many poems. Nearly the whole of *Kim* is written in this key; now and then he modulates into the world and its shows, the Great Wheel, etc., but one knows that the terrible key 'I know a trick worth two of that' is never far off. And he delights in Kim, just as he delighted in Dick, and his admiration is so spontaneous that it is impossible to read *Kim* without saying to oneself: 'Kim is Mr. Kipling.' Kim is never taken in, and not to be taken in is in Mr. Kipling's eyes a sort of north star whereby one steers the bark of life. Kim is a spy, but spying is called the Great Game, and nothing matters so long as you are not taken in. Mr. Kipling's beast-kind is the same as his mankind: the animals in the *Jungle Books* that we are to admire are those that 'know a trick worth two of that'. He does not venture among godkind, but if he did, his gods would 'know a trick worth two of that'.

Now it is a moot question if an author's mind extend much beyond the characters he creates. Did not Baudelaire say that in Balzac even the porters had genius? Among Mr. Kipling's works there is a book called *The Gadsbys*, and the theme is that if a man wants to get on in the army he should not get married. This will seem to those who admire the book an unfair description of it; but we must not be deceived by the external form—we must, if we would appreciate a writer, take into account his attitude towards life, we must discover if his vision is mean or noble, spiritual or material, narrow or wide; for all things are in the eye that sees, things having no existence in themselves—the earliest and latest philosophy. In the eighties none knew what world Mr. Kipling was about to reveal; but now his world is before us, and 'noble' and 'beautiful' are not the adjectives that any one would choose wherewith to designate the world of Kipling. Rough, harsh, coarse-grained, come into our minds; Mr. Kipling's world is a barrack full of oaths and clatter of sabres; but his language is copious, rich, sonorous. One is tempted to say that none since the Elizabethans has written so copiously. Others have written more beautifully, but no one that I can call to mind at this moment has written so copiously. Shelley and Wordsworth, Landor and Pater, wrote with part of the language; but who else, except Whitman, has written with the whole language since the Elizabethans? 'The flannelled fool at the wicket, the muddied oaf at the goal' is wonderful language. He writes with the eye that appreciates all that the eye can see, but of the heart he knows nothing, for the heart cannot be observed; his characters are therefore external, and they are stationary. At first we are taken by Kim—he is so well seen, so well observed, so well copied; the Lama we can see as if he were before us—an old man in his long habit and his rosary, we hear his continuous mumbling; but very soon we perceive that Kim and the Lama are fixed—we have not read thirty pages before we see that those two will be the same at the end of the book as they were in the beginning.

The Lama has come from Tibet in search of a sacred river, and he meets a street Arab, precocious and vile in his every instinct, at the outset of his journey, and these two go off together. They are but pegs whereon Mr. Kipling intends to hang his descriptions of India. If they are but pegs I would prefer them to be a little plainer—they are a little too much carved; but let the carving be waived—something must be granted to every writer—the object is henceforth to describe India: we shall see how he does this, and Mr. Kipling shall be measured by our standard. Our standard is *how* much life does the writer evoke, and this standard is applicable whether the writer is describing a sunset or an old woman peeling onions, whether he is putting words into the mouth of a tramp or of a philosopher. Whatever the subject may be, our standard is the same—how much of the precious wine do we taste, and in what intensity while reading? This is our standard whether the art under consideration be literature or painting, whether the literature be prose or poetry; and having stated our standard of criticism, we will proceed with the measurement of Mr. Kipling:

They entered the fort-like railway station, black in the end of night; the electrics sizzling over the goods-yard, where they handle the heavy Northern grain-traffic.

How strong the rhythm, lacking perhaps in subtlety, like the tramp of policemen, but a splendid rhythm! And it is Mr. Kipling's own rhythm; he borrows from no man, and it is always a pleasure to read or hear unborrowed literature or music.

A little farther on we find ourselves in the middle of a spacious paragraph, the sentences moving to the same sonorous march measure:

Then it came out that in those wordly days he had been a master-hand at casting horoscopes and nativities, and the family priest led him on to describe his methods, each giving the planets names that the other could not understand, and pointing upwards as the big stars sailed across the dark. The children of the house tugged unrebuked at his rosary; and he clean forgot the Rule which forbids looking at women as he talked of enduring snows, landslips, blocked passes, the remote cliffs where men find sapphires and turquoise, and that wonderful upland road that leads at last into great China itself.

And how finely it ends, that long sentence stretching itself out like the 'upland road that leads at last into great China itself'!

In saying these things we are praising Mr. Kipling's technical excellence, and technical excellence is of no value for us except as a means through which life is revealed.

A few pages farther on we come upon a description of evening; and evening is one of the eternal subjects—men were sensible to the charm and beauty and the tenderness of evening ten thousand years ago, and ten thousand years hence they will be moved in the same way.

By this time the sun was driving broad golden spokes through the lower branches of the mango-trees; the parakeets and doves were coming home in their hundreds; the chattering, grey-backed Seven Sisters, talking over the day's adventures, walked back and forth in twos and threes almost under the feet of the travellers; the shufflings and scufflings in the branches showed that the bats were ready to go out on the night picket. Swiftly the light gathered itself together, painted for an instant the faces and the cartwheels and bullocks' horns as red as blood. Then the night fell, changing the touch of the air, drawing a low, even haze like a gossamer veil of blue across the face of the country, and bringing out, keen and distinct, the smell of wood-smoke and cattle and the good scent of wheaten cakes cooked on ashes. The evening patrol hurried out of the police-station with important coughings and reiterated orders; and a live charcoal ball in the cup of a wayside carter's hookah glowed red while Kim's eyes mechanically watched the last flicker of the sun on the brass tweezers.

No one will deny the perfection of the writing, of the strong masculine rhythm of every sentence, and of the accuracy of every observation. But it seems to us that Mr. Kipling has seen much more than he has felt; and we prefer feeling to seeing; and when we come to analyse the lines we find a touch of local colour not only in every sentence, but in each part, between each semicolon. 'The sun was driving golden spokes through the branches of the *mango* trees', 'the *parakeets*', 'the doves', 'the chattering grey-backed Seven Sisters', 'the bats ready to go out on the *night picket*', 'the *light painting* the faces and the car wheels and the *bullocks' horns'*. At last a sentence that does not carry any local colour: 'then the night fell, changing the touch of the air, drawing a low even haze like a gossamer veil of blue across the face of the country', but after the comma local colour begins again, 'bringing out, keen and distinct, the smell of *wood-smoke* and *cattle*', 'and the *cakes*', etc. Then there is the evening patrol and the live *charcoal ball*, and then Kim's eyes watching the flicker of the sun on the *brass tweezers*.

It would be difficult to find a passage in literature of the same length so profusely touched with local colour. Was it not a shame to observe that slender wistful hour so closely? Mr. Kipling seems to have followed it about like a detective employed in a divorce case—like Kim himself, who is a political spy. We prefer an evening by Pierre Loti; he experiences a sensation and his words transmit the sensation and remind us of many things that we have experienced at sunsetting. Loti's touch is perhaps a little superficial, a little facile, the feeling is perhaps genteel, even trite, but with all there is more wistfulness in Loti than in Kipling, and an evening that is not wistful is not evening.

But evening comes, evening with its magic, and we relinquish ourselves to the charm once more.

About our brave little encampment, about the rough horizon where all danger seems at present asleep, the twilight sky kindles an incomparable rose border, orange, then green, and then, rising by degrees to the zenith, it softens and quenches. It is the hour indecisive and charming, when amid limpidities which are neither day nor night our odorous fires begin to burn clearly, sending up their white smoke to the first stars; our camels, relieved of their burdens and their high saddles, sweep by the thin bushes, browsing on perfumed branches, like great fantastic sheep, of slow inoffensive demeanour. It is the hour when our Bedouins sit in a circle to tell stories and sing; the hour of rest, and the hour of dream, the delicious hour of nomadic life.

The Bedouins and camels tell us that the evening Loti is describing is an Eastern evening, but even these two touches of local colour, which were unavoidable, add nothing to the beauty of the passage; suppress them, turn the Bedouins into gipsies and the camels into horses, and it would be impossible to say whether the evening described had happened in England or Japan. Loti's intention was to describe something that is eternal in the heart of man, something that he has known always, that he knew ten thousand years before Nineveh, and that he will know ten thousand years hence. Mr. Kipling's intention is more ethnological than poetic. We learn from it that the parakeets and doves come home to the woods in the evening, we learn that the sun turns the faces and the bullocks' horns red as blood, and a variety of other things. From Loti's description we have learned nothing, but we have been moved, as we are moved when we look at a portrait by Rembrandt. Not for a moment must it be thought that I compare Loti with Rembrandt, Loti is a painter in water colours, his sentences flow fragile and transparent like flower blooms; but Rembrandt's intention and Loti's intention are the same—the intention is to interest us in things that always have been and always will be. But we envy Mr. Kipling his copious and sonorous vocabulary, especially his neologisms; he writes with the whole language, with the language of the Bible, and with the language of the streets. He can do this, for he possesses the ink-pot which turns the vilest tin idiom into gold. Last night, his description of the hills was for us a cup of mixed admiration and misery, and we repeat our impression that no one has written as well as this since the Elizabethans, since the Bible.

[quotes *Kim*, p. 334 to top of p. 336]

A miserable midnight is often succeeded by a sunny morning. It was a relief to awake forgetful of what I had read overnight. Envy! Of course! We're envious because we admire; the lay reader neither admires nor envies—art is for the artists. I was glad to awake forgetful of Mr. Kipling, thinking of Pierre Loti, of a book I had not seen for months. On looking into *Kim* again I found pages of dialogue, magnificently wrought, hard and breathless; a hardware shop with iron tulips hanging from the rafters and brass forget-me-nots on the counter. Loti is never hard. His attitude towards life is that of a child, of a blond ringleted child with bright blue eyes and hands full of flower-blooms, and a sensibility like that of a perverse child impelled to caresses.

. . . Mr. Kipling's prose goes to a marching rhythm, the trumpet's blare and the fife's shriek; there is the bass clarionet and the great bass tuba that emits a sound like the earth quaking fathoms deep or the cook shovelling coal in the coal-cellar. The band is playing variations: but variations on what theme? The theme will appear presently . . . Listen! There is the theme, the shoddy tune of the average man—'I know a trick worth two of that.'

42. G. K. Chesterton 'On Mr. Rudyard Kipling'

1905

Extract from the essay 'On Mr. Rudyard Kipling and Making the World Small', in *Heretics* (1905), pp. 38–53. The beginning of the essay is too general to include here, and the end wanders again: the extract from p. 42 to p. 51 gives all that Chesterton has to say about Kipling. For his review of *Just So Stories* see No. 38 (pp. 273–5) above.

. . . The first and fairest thing to say about Rudyard Kipling is that he has borne a brilliant part in recovering the lost provinces of poetry. He has not been frightened by that brutal materialistic air which clings only to words; he has pierced through to the romantic, imaginative matter of the things themselves. He has perceived the significance and philosophy of steam and of slang. Steam may be, if you like, a dirty by-product of science. Slang may be, if you like, a dirty by-product of language. But at least he has been among the few who saw the divine parentage of these things, and knew that where there is smoke there is fire—that is, that wherever there is the foulest of things, there also is the purest. Above all, he has had something to say, a definite view of things to utter, and that always means that a man is fearless and faces everything. For the moment we have a view of the universe, we possess it.

Now, the message of Rudyard Kipling, that upon which he has really concentrated, is the only thing worth worrying about in him or in any other man. He has often written bad poetry, like Wordsworth. He has often said silly things, like Plato. He has often given way to mere political hysteria, like Gladstone. But no one can reasonably doubt that he means steadily and sincerely to say something, and the only serious question is, what is that which he has tried to say? Perhaps the best way of stating this fairly will be to begin with that element which has been most insisted by himself and by his opponents—

I mean his interest in militarism. But when we are seeking for the real merits of a man it is unwise to go to his enemies, and much more foolish to go to himself.

Now, Mr. Kipling is certainly wrong in his worship of militarism, but his opponents are, generally speaking, quite as wrong as he. The evil of militarism, is not that it shows certain men to be fierce and haughty and excessively warlike. The evil of militarism is that it shows most men to be tame and timid and excessively peaceable. The professional soldier gains more and more power as the general courage of a community declines. Thus the Pretorian guard became more and more important in Rome as Rome became more and more luxurious and feeble. The military man gains the civil power in proportion as the civilian loses the military virtues. And as it was in ancient Rome so it is in contemporary Europe. There never was a time when nations were more militarist. There never was a time when men were less brave. All ages and all epics have sung of arms and the man; but we have effected simultaneously the deterioration of the man and the fantastic perfection of the arms. Militarism demonstrated the decadence of Rome, and it demonstrates the decadence of Prussia.

And unconsciously Mr. Kipling has proved this, and proved it admirably. For in so far as his work is earnestly understood the military trade does not by any means emerge as the most important or attractive. He has not written so well about soldiers as he has about railway men or bridge builders, or even journalists. The fact is that what attracts Mr. Kipling to militarism is not the idea of courage, but the idea of discipline. There was far more courage to the square mile in the Middle Ages, when no king had a standing army, but every man had a bow or sword. But the fascination of the standing army upon Mr. Kipling is not courage, which scarcely interests him, but discipline, which is, when all is said and done, his primary theme. The modern army is not a miracle of courage; it has not enough opportunities, owing to the cowardice of everybody else. But it is really a miracle of organization, and that is the truly Kiplingite ideal. Kipling's subject is not that valour which properly belongs to war, but that interdependence and efficiency which belongs quite as much to engineers, or sailors, or mules, or railway engines. And thus it is that when he writes of engineers, or sailors, or mules, or steam-engines, he writes at his best. The real poetry, the 'true-romance' which Mr. Kipling has taught, is the romance of the division of labour and the discipline of all the trades. He sings the arts of peace much more accurately than the arts of war. And his main contention is vital and valuable. Everything is military in the sense that everything depends upon obedience. There is no perfectly epicurean corner; there is no perfectly irresponsible place. Everywhere men have made the way for us with sweat and submission. We may fling ourselves into a hammock in a fit of divine carelessness. But we are glad that the net-maker did not make the hammock in a fit of divine carelessness. We may jump upon a child's rocking-horse for a joke. But we are glad that the carpenter did not leave the legs of it unglued for a joke. So far from having merely preached that a soldier cleaning his side-arm is to be adored because he is military, Kipling at his best and clearest has preached that the baker baking loaves and the tailor cutting coats is as military as anybody.

Being devoted to this multitudinous vision of duty, Mr. Kipling is naturally a cosmopolitan. He happens to find his examples in the British Empire, but almost any other empire would do as well, or, indeed, any other highly civilized country. That which he admires in the British Army he would find even more apparent in the German Army; that which he desires in the British police he would find flourishing in the French police. The ideal of discipline is not the whole of life, but it is spread over the whole of the world. And the worship of it tends to confirm in Mr. Kipling a certain note of worldly wisdom, of the experience of the wanderer, which is one of the genuine charms of his best work.

The great gap in his mind is what may be roughly called the lack of patriotism—that is to say, he lacks altogether the faculty of attaching himself to any cause or community finally and tragically; for all finality must be tragic. He admires England, but he does not love her; for we admire things with reasons, but love them without reasons. He admires England because she is strong, not because she is English. There is no harshness in saying this, for, to do him justice, he avows it with his usual picturesque candour. In a very interesting poem, he says that—

If England was what England seems

—that is, weak and inefficient; if England were not what (as he believes) she is—that is, powerful and practical—

How quick we'd chuck 'er! But she ain't!

He admits, that is, that his devotion is the result of a criticism, and this is quite enough to put it in another category altogether from the patriotism of the Boers, whom he hounded down in South Africa. In speaking of the really patriotic peoples, such as the Irish, he has some difficulty in keeping a shrill irritation out of his language. The frame of mind which he really describes with beauty and nobility is the frame of mind of the cosmopolitan man who has seen men and cities.

> For to admire and for to see,
> For to be'old this world so wide.

He is a perfect master of that light melancholy with which a man looks back on having been the citizen of many communities, of that light melancholy with which a man looks back on having been the lover of many women. He is the philanderer of the nations. But a man may have learnt much about women in flirtations, and still be ignorant of first love; a man may have known as many lands as Ulysses, and still be ignorant of patriotism.

Mr. Rudyard Kipling has asked in a celebrated epigram what they can know of England who know England only. It is a far deeper and sharper question to ask: 'What can they know of England who know only the world?' for the world does not include England any more than it includes the Church. The moment we care for anything deeply, the world—that is, all the other miscellaneous interests—becomes our enemy. Christians showed it when they talked of keeping one's self 'unspotted from the world'; but lovers talk of it just as much when they talk of the 'world well lost'. Astronomically speaking, I understand that England is situated on the world; similarly, I suppose that the Church was a part of the world, and even the lovers inhabitants of that orb. But they all felt a certain truth—the truth that the moment you love anything the world becomes your foe. Thus Mr. Kipling does certainly know the world; he is a man of the world, with all the narrowness that belongs to those imprisoned in that planet. He knows England as an intelligent English gentleman knows Venice. He has been to England a great many times; he has stopped there for long visits. But he does not belong to it, or to any place; and the proof of it is this, that he thinks of England as a place. The moment we are rooted in a place the place vanishes. We live like a tree with the whole strength of the universe.

The globe-trotter lives in a smaller world than the peasant. He is always breathing an air of locality. London is a place, to be compared to Chicago; Chicago is a place, to be compared to Timbuctoo. But Timbuctoo is not a place, since there, at least, live men who regard it as the universe, and breathe, not an air of locality, but the winds of the world. The man in the saloon steamer has seen all the races of men, and he is thinking of the things that divide men—diet, dress, decorum, rings in the nose as in Africa, or in the ears as in Europe, blue paint among the ancients, or red paint among the modern Britons. The man in the cabbage field has seen nothing at all; but he is thinking of the things that unite men—hunger and babies, and the beauty of women, and the promise or menace of the sky. Mr. Kipling, with all his merits, is the globe-trotter; he has not the patience to become part of anything. So great and genuine a man is not to be accused of a merely cynical cosmopolitanism; still, his cosmopolitanism is his weakness. That weakness is splendidly expressed in one of his finest poems, 'The Sestina of the Tramp Royal', in which a man declares that he can endure anything in the way of hunger or horror, but not permanent presence in one place. In this there is certainly danger. The more dead and dry and dusty a thing is the more it travels about; dust is like this and the thistledown and the High Commissioner in South Africa. Fertile things are somewhat heavier, like the heavy fruit trees on the pregnant mud of the Nile. In the heated idleness of youth we were all rather inclined to quarrel with the implication of that proverb which says that a rolling stone gathers no moss. We were inclined to ask: 'Who wants to gather moss, except silly old ladies?' But for all that we begin to perceive that the proverb is right. The rolling stone rolls echoing from rock to rock; but the rolling stone is dead. The moss is silent because the moss is alive . . .

43. Alfred Noyes on 'Kipling the Mystic'

1906

Signed review of *Puck of Pook's Hill* in the *Bookman* (London), Vol. XXXI, pp. 81–2 (November 1906).

Alfred Noyes (1880–1958) was a poet of some distinction, now unduly neglected. His *The Flower of Old Japan* (1903) and *The Forest of Wild Thyme* (1905) have been described as 'the finest fairy poetry since the Elizabethans', while several of his lyrics and ballads have become standard anthology pieces. He was Professor of Modern English Literature at Princeton (1914–23), and published a volume of critical essays, *Aspects of Modern Poetry* in 1924.

'Chops, more chops, bloody ones with gristle in them!'—the cry, of the baser sort of Imperialist—has gently subsided into a fat smile, a benevolent radiation of sweetness and light, since it dawned upon the Mafficking patriot that he must pay, pay, pay and yet again pay, for even his most sanguinary and most human chops with his own yellow coin. We have not much belief in the depth of either of these common moods; but we believe there are 'the makings of a blooming soul' somewhere behind them, and that these outward manifestations correspond to merely momentary circumstances. There are men on both sides, however, in whose deep-seated sincerity one is compelled to believe. There were heroes on opposite sides in the *Iliad*. There are heroes on opposite sides to-day. There would be no grandeur in life but for the fact that its opposites are mighty, and that all great sincerities, if they go deep enough, are rooted in imperishable unity. Whether hard words—traitor, card-sharper, brute and ghoul— break bones or not, they never impart one tremor to that steadfast plinth of things. Political hatreds are of the day, of the hour, of the moment. Death smooths out our troubles; Death—and Love. 'In fifty years,' declares the great Norman of Mr. Kipling's new book, as, with a kind of defiant fury, he sanctions the betrothal of a Saxon maid to another Norman, 'in fifty years there will be neither Norman nor

Saxon, but all English'. It will always be the 'plinth of things' with which true patriotic literature is concerned. Brutus falls; and—if only in the poet's dream—the Antony who drove him to his death must mourn over his body: 'This was the noblest Roman of them all.' We have small concern with the little irrelevancies of their mortal feud. If Caesar, *if* Caesar, we say, now lies ill at Highbury, we may be assured that the overwhelming Liberal majority is not altogether of the party of Cassius. It may be true that Caesar was ambitious; but if and if he were Caesar in very truth, then very certainly it must also be true, in nine cases out of ten, that Brutus is an honourable man who, below the surface of politics, loves not Caesar less, but Rome more. 'Many roads thou hast fashioned: all of them lead to the Light!' That is one of the lines in Mr. Kipling's 'Hymn to Mithras' in the Roman portion of his new book; and it is a very significant one. We see, in this book, signs of a great change in Mr. Kipling. It is not, perhaps, his best work; but it looks like the beginning of his best and greatest work. It would certainly be the most interesting of all his writings if it were not for the fact that it illuminates and makes his former work even more arresting than it was when he had 'a voice with which statesmen might have to reckon'. In his last book of poems there was one of great pathos called 'The Palace', which describes how a Master Builder cleared him ground for a house such as a king should build, and how—under the silt—he came on the wreck of another palace built by a forgotten king.

> There was no worth in the fashion—there was no wit in the plan—
> Hither and thither, aimless, the ruined footings ran—
> Masonry, brute, mishandled, but carven on every stone
> After me cometh a Builder. Tell him, I too have known.

So to his own well-planned ground-works he tumbled the old quoins and ashlars, cut and reset them anew, and, as the old builder had risen and pleaded, he strove to understand 'the form of the dream he had followed in the face of the thing he had planned'.

> When I was a King and a Mason—in the open noon of my pride,
> They sent me a Word from the Darkness—they whispered and called me
> aside.
> They said—'The end is forbidden.' They said—'Thy use is fulfilled,
> And thy palace shall stand as that other's—the spoil of a king who shall
> build.'
> I called my men from my trenches, my quarries, my wharves, and my
> shears.
> All I had wrought I abandoned to the faith of the faithless years.

Only I cut on the timber, only I carved on the stone:
After me cometh a Builder. Tell him, I, too, have known.

In *Puck of Pook's Hill* we suspect that Mr. Kipling has for the first
time dug through the silt of modern Imperialism. He has gone back
to the old ground-works and seen the inscription upon them. The
scheme of the book is simple. Some children meet Puck, the fairy,
who introduces them in separate, yet connected stories to Romans,
Normans, Saxons, Picts and Englishmen from different periods of our
history; and the chief of these characters tell their own stories—grim,
humorous and pathetic, in a manner illustrating the respective period
of each; and on each successive period one seems to find inscribed—
After me cometh a Builder! We know no book in the guise of fiction
that gives the pageant of our history with such breadth and nobility
of feeling, and with so sure and easy a touch. There are few passages
in modern fiction more beautiful than that which describes the chivalry
of a Norman to a conquered Saxon woman, whom he falls in love with,
and eventually, though at first she rails against him as an enemy, wins
and weds. There are few passages in modern fiction more stoically
grand than the farewell letter of the doomed Caesar to his two young
captains on the Great Wall. And always the cry is, *After me cometh
a Builder!* It is impossible to say how far we are justified in saying that
Mr. Kipling sees the writing on a certain modern wall; but there
seems to be a note of very deep pathos in the 'Hymn to Mithras':

> Mithras, God of the Noontide, the heather swims in the heat,
> Our helmets scorch our foreheads; our sandals burn our feet.
> Now, in the ungirt hour; now, ere we blink and drowse,
> Mithras, also a soldier, keep us true to our vows!

And also there is an unexpected note of a very noble humility in the
children's final hymn:

> Teach us the strength that cannot seek,
> By deed or thought, to hurt the weak;
> That, under Thee, we may possess
> Man's strength to comfort man's distress.

Mr. Kipling was, at the high tide of popular Imperialism, one of the
very few popular Imperialists who could either have written or echoed
the feeling of his 'Recessional'. His cry to the true Romance was 'Thy
face is far from this our war!' How deep this vein of mysticism goes in
him it is impossible, at present, to judge. But let popular Imperialists

beware of him. The day may come when he will turn and rend them as he turned and rent large masses of his devoted readers in that delightful onslaught which he called 'The Islanders'. Mystics are always dangerous—to materialists, at any rate; and Mr. Kipling has mysticism in his blood and in his bones. He is, moreover, taking much broader and larger views of cities and men than he did when he wrote his verses on Bombay, for instance. It is a far cry from those verses to this, in his *Puck of Pook's Hill*:

> Cities and Thrones and Powers
> Stand in Time's eye
> Almost as long as flowers
> Which daily die:
> But, as new buds put forth
> To glad new men,
> Out of the spent and unconsidered earth
> The Cities rise again.

If Mr. Kipling has really dug through the silt, as we suspect; if he has, indeed, discovered that all roads lead to the Light, and that the greatness of a people depends, eventually, on that finer strength of love, he is indeed at the beginning of his greatest work. He was never more 'the interpreter to the English-speaking peoples' than he is in this book. Puck occasionally drops even into American-isms! Certainly it is one of those works which hasten the fulness of that time when there will be less need to inscribe on our palaces, *After me cometh a builder.*

44. Conan Doyle on 'Kipling's Best Story'

1907

Extract from *Through the Magic Door* (1907), pp. 118–19. Originally published in *Cassell's Magazine* from November 1906 to November 1907. Only the first paragraph of the following extract appeared in the serial (Vol. XLIII, p. 696, April 1907)—the second was added in book form.

Sir Arthur Conan Doyle (1859–1930) was, in his own kind, one of the leading short-story writers of the period. He seldom indulged in literary criticism—but his comments on his own particular kind of literature are interesting. Besides Kipling, he chose stories by Scott, Poe, Stevenson, Lytton, with Hawthorne, Grant Allen, H. G. Wells and Quiller-Couch in a slightly lower class. He considered Poe 'the world's supreme short story writer', and put Maupassant second.

Which are the greatest short stories of the English language? . . . If it be not an impertinence to mention a contemporary I should certainly have a brace from Rudyard Kipling. His power, his compression, his dramatic sense, his way of glowing suddenly into a vivid flame, all mark him as a great master. But which are we to choose from that long and varied collection, many of which have claims to the highest? Speaking from memory, I should say that the stories of his which have impressed me most are 'The Drums of the Fore and Aft', 'The Man Who Would be King', 'The Man who Was', and 'The Brushwood Boy'. Perhaps, on the whole, it is the first two which I should choose to add to my list of masterpieces.

They are stories which invite criticism and yet defy it. The great batsman at cricket is the man who can play an unorthodox game, take every liberty which is denied to inferior players, and yet succeed brilliantly in the face of his disregard of law. So it is here. I should think the model of these stories is the most dangerous that any young writer could follow. There is digression, that most deadly fault in the short narrative; there is incoherence, there is want of proportion which makes the story stand still for pages and bound forward in a few sentences. But genius overrides all that, just as the great cricketer hooks the off ball and glides the straight one to leg. There is a dash, an exuberance, a full-blooded confident mastery which carries everything before it. Yes, no team of immortals would be complete which did not contain at least two representatives of Kipling.

45. Ford Madox Hueffer's 'Critical Attitude'

1911

Extracts from *The Critical Attitude* (1911) by Ford Madox Hueffer; pp. 4, 106 and 177.

Ford Madox Hueffer (1873–1939) later changed his surname to Ford, and became famous as a novelist. Before he changed his name he collaborated in two novels with Joseph Conrad, wrote children's books, and founded the *English Review*.

There is a considerable writer—once he wrote the best short stories that are to be found in English literature, now, alas! *il pontifie*—there is a certain writer who once said that he welcomed the coming of the motor-car because it would make the Englishman think. We confess to having always been unable to get at the inner significance of this phrase. One motor-car might take an Englishman to Brighton, but could ten thousand make him think? Assuredly not, for nothing could make him think; nothing could make him review his thoughts. PAGE 106 The most dismal instance of this last tendency [attempting to become a social reformer, etc.] is Mr. Rudyard Kipling. In him we have a writer of gifts almost as great as gifts could be. To read merely, let us say *Stalky & Co.* is to be almost overwhelmed by the cleverness in handling incident and in suggesting atmosphere. But at a certain stage of his career Mr. Kipling became instinct with the desire to be of importance, with the result that, using his monumental and semi-biblical language, alternating it with his matchless use of colloquialisms, Mr. Kipling set out to attack world problems from the point of view of the journalists' club smoking-room and with the ambitions of a sort of cross between the German Emperor of caricature and a fifth-form public-schoolboy. This is a lamentable record, for in Mr. Kipling we seem to have lost for good a poet of the highest vitality, a writer the most emotionally suggestive.

PAGE 177 There is only one poet living who has ever appealed to the British public with a sort of clarion note such as was the Tennyson's of 'Riflemen Form'. And it is characteristic that this poet, Mr. Kipling, appealed to the same set of emotions. This set of emotions—those of patriotism, of voluntary service, and of simple physical aggression—probably remain dormant and ready to the hand of any writer with sufficient technical skill to awaken them. Mr. Kipling came exceedingly near being a great poet. Moreover, he is so exceedingly near to a supreme verbal skill, and so exceedingly near to the power of using the rhythm of music as only a genius can, that Mr. Kipling may yet—for all I should care to dogmatise—stand out as the representatively national figure amongst a band of singers as numerous, and as intimately satisfactory, as were ever the minor Elizabethans and the early Jacobeans. Mr. Kipling as a poet has never been regarded with very much critical attention, though his popularity was at one time as unboundedly swelling as it now is, rather unreasonably, on the wane. He is to be commended as much for his boldness in the use of the vernacular, as for his skill and his boldness, too, in catching the rhythm of popular music, with its quaint and fascinating irregularities.

But, with the exception of Mr. Kipling, there is no poet today who attempts successfully to sing of patriotism or any of the other eternal verities. And it is characteristic of the age that the poetry upon which Mr. Kipling built the platform for verse of such bland popularity as 'The absent-minded Beggar'—the poetry which put him in a position to become a prophet, was poetry not of a patriotic or of a national character—was poetry not even of a military type, but was the poetry of intimacy. Thus 'On the Road to Mandalay' expressed not heroic resolve, not the determination to die for England, but the nostalgia of an individual.

46. H. G. Wells on Kipling

1911 : 1920

Quotations from (1) *The New Machiavelli* (1911), Book 1, Chap. 4, Section 6, pp. 128–30; and (2) *The Outline of History* (1920), pp. 521–2.

Herbert George Wells (1866–1946), potentially great novelist and writer of scientific fantasy until (in Chesterton's phrase) he 'sold his birthright for a pot of message', veered sharply in his opinion of Kipling when he appointed himself social reformer instead of imaginative writer. In *When the Sleeper Wakes* (1899) he described 'The Man Who Would be King' as 'one of the best stories in the world', but in his *Experiment in Autobiography* (1934) described Kipling as 'the most incomprehensible of my contemporaries, with phases of real largeness and splendour and lapses into the quality of those mucky little sadists *Stalky & Co.*'.

(1) The prevailing force in my undergraduate days was not Socialism but Kiplingism. Our set was quite exceptional in its socialistic professions. And we were all, you must understand, very distinctly Imperialists also, and professed a vivid sense of the 'White Man's Burden'.

It is a little difficult now to get back to the feelings of that period; Kipling has since been so mercilessly and exhaustively mocked, criticized and torn to shreds—never was a man so violently exalted and then, himself assisting, so relentlessly called down. But in the middle nineties this spectacled and moustached little figure with its heavy chin and its general effect of vehement gesticulation, its wild shouts of boyish enthusiasm for effective force, its lyric delight in the sounds and colours, in the very odours of Empire, its wonderful discovery of machinery and cotton waste and the under-officer and the engineer, and 'shop' as a poetic dialect, became almost a national symbol. He got hold of us wonderfully, he filled us with tinkling and haunting quotations, he stirred Britten and myself to futile imitations, he coloured the very idiom of our conversation. He rose to his climax with his 'Recessional', while I was still an undergraduate.

What did he give me exactly?

He helped to broaden my geographical sense immensely, and he provided phrases for just that desire for discipline and devotion and organized effort the Socialism of our time failed to express, that the current socialist movement still fails, I think, to express. The sort of thing that follows, for example, tore something out of my inmost nature and gave it a shape, and I took it back from him shaped and let much of the rest of him, the tumult and the bullying, the hysteria and the impatience, the incoherence and inconsistency, go uncriticized for the sake of it:

> Keep ye the Law—be swift in all obedience
> Clear the land of evil, drive the road and bridge the ford,
> Make ye sure to each his own
> That he reap where he hath sown;
> By the peace among Our peoples let men know we serve the
> Lord!

And then again, and for all our later criticism, this sticks in my mind, sticks there now as quintessential wisdom:

> The 'eathen in 'is blindness bows down to wood an' stone;
> 'E don't obey no orders unless they is 'is own;
> 'E keeps 'is side-arms awful: 'e leaves 'em all about,
> An' then comes up the regiment an' pokes the 'eathen out.
> All along o' dirtiness, all along o' mess,
> All along o' doing things rather-more-or-less,
> All along of *abby-nay, kul,* an *hazar-ho,*
> Mind you keep your rifle an' yourself just so!

It is after all a secondary matter that Kipling, not having been born and brought up in Bromstead and Penge, and the war in South Africa being yet in the womb of time, could quite honestly entertain the now remarkable delusion that England had her side-arms at that time kept anything but 'awful'. He learnt better, and we all learnt with him in the dark years of exasperating and humiliating struggle that followed, and I do not see that we fellow-learners are justified in turning resentfully upon him for a common ignorance and assumption.

(2) . . . It was quite characteristic of the times [the late nineties] that Mr. Kipling should lead the children of the middle and upper-class British public back to the Jungle, to learn 'the law', and that in his

book *Stalky & Co.* he should give an appreciative description of the torture of two boys by three others, who have by a subterfuge tied up their victims helplessly before revealing their hostile intentions.

It is worth while to give a little attention to this incident in *Stalky & Co.*, because it lights up the political psychology of the British Empire at the close of the nineteenth century very vividly. The history of the last half-century is not to be understood without an understanding of the mental twist which this story exemplifies. The two boys who are tortured are 'bullies', that is the excuse of their tormentors, and these latter have further been excited to this orgy by a clergyman. Nothing can restrain the gusto with which they (and Mr. Kipling) set about the job. Before resorting to torture, the teaching seems to be, see that you pump up a little justifiable moral indignation, and all will be well. If you have the authorities on your side, then you cannot be to blame. Such, apparently, is the simple doctrine of this typical imperialist. But every bully has to the best of his ability followed that doctrine since the human animal developed sufficient intelligence to be consciously cruel.

Another point in the story is very significant indeed. The headmaster and his clerical assistant are both represented as being privy to the affair. They want this bullying to occur. Instead of exercising their own authority, they use these boys, who are Mr. Kipling's heroes, to punish the two victims. Headmaster and clergyman turn a deaf ear to the complaints of an indignant mother. All this Mr. Kipling represents as a most desirable state of affairs. In this we have the key to the ugliest, most retrogressive, and finally fatal idea of modern imperialism; the idea of a *tacit conspiracy between the law and illegal violence* . . .

47. Dixon Scott on 'Rudyard Kipling'

1912

Signed article in the *Bookman* (London), Vol. XLIII, pp. 143–6 (December 1912). Later collected in the author's *Men of Letters* (1916), pp. 48–62.

Dixon Scott (1881–1915) was a critic of great promise whose early death cut short his achievement. Many of his reviews were collected after his death in *Men of Letters* (1916)—including this which, as 'The Meekness of Mr. Rudyard Kipling', occupies pages 48–62.

A writer's reputation is often a kind of premature ghost that stalks between him and his audience, blurring their vision; but in Mr. Kipling's case this *doppelgänger* has proved specially pobby and impervious and full of energy. The convincing autobiography it rattles off runs something like this: 'I came out of the East, a youngster of twenty, but wiser than your very oldest men. Life had told me her last secrets, I could do anything I liked with words, and I tossed you tales of twisted deaths and queer adulteries with the nonchalant neatness of a conjurer and an air of indulgent half-contempt. I was an uncanny mixture of bored pierrot and bland priest; and in my splendid insolence (I was only twenty, mind you), I made poetry learn slang and set her serving in canteens. "Born blasé," muttered one of your own writers, maddened—himself reckoned something of a prodigy. I was the cleverest young man of my day.

And then I came West to your dingy, cosy Babylon, and tasted fame and fleshpots: very good. And the brightness died out of my colours and the snap from my tunes. Your snug horizons hemmed me in, I lost my vision, I relied contentedly on tricks I'd learned before. I wrote a bad novel and it made a worse drama. I made money, I made speeches, I spoiled my paints with party politics. And now here I am, sir, the popular favourite—*Vide* Max—Seen the *Post*? 'Save the King!'

Well, the main desire of this article is to denounce all that as perjury

—force aside the phantom—gain a glimpse of the real man behind; to suggest, that, instead of depreciating, the quality of his work has constantly improved, that his technique has never been so amazing as now, nor his artistic integrity more Lútheran;—and that instead of immensely precocious and worldly-wise—'born blasé' as Barrie (it was Barrie) once said—this young poet has always been, far more than Barrie himself, one of those who never grow up, who are never quite at home in the world, but who wander through it, like Hawthorne or Poe, a little alien and wistful, a little elf-like—and that this quality of envy of 'the happy folk in housen', of the practical grown-ups and worldlings, is indeed the essential characteristic of the man and the key to and core of his work.

Now to get the first glimmer of the ghost, to follow this Jekyll-and-Hyding from the outset, it is necessary to go back to the days of the *Ditties*—so swiftly did the severance begin. Many readers, not yet aged, will no doubt still remember the stab and glitter of the first Kipling furore, and the way the critical raptures went rocketing up, breaking into a superior fire of epigrams, eager to announce the discovery. A new star had arisen, a rival to Loti, and the elect were at once in full song. Perhaps the hour was specially apt for such an overture. It was the hour of the eighties, the ineffable, amateur eighties, when a recondite vulgarity was the vogue; and aesthetic London was not at all unanxious to display its capacity for enjoying raw sensation. Hedonism had deserted the Oxford of Pater for 'The Oxford'[1] of Marie Lloyd and Walter Sickert. If you were a poet you were ashamed not to be seen in cabmen's shelters; and a little hashish was considered quite the thing. A superior hour! And so, when the rag-time chords of the *Departmental Ditties* flicked and snapped an introduction to the laconic patter of the *Tales*, and when the *Tales* themselves, with their parakeets and ivory, their barbaric chic and rubricated slang, proved a mixture of Persian print and music-hall, then the 'ten superior persons scattered through the universe', were persuaded that their hour had found its very voice, that they were listening to the last delicious insolence of aesthetics:

> 'Er petticoat was yaller and 'er little cap was green,
> An' 'er name was Supi-yaw-lat—jes' the same as
> Theebaw's queen;
> An' I see 'er first a-smokin' of a whackin' white cheroot,

[1] ['The Oxford' was a London music hall]

An' a-wastin' Christian kisses on an 'eathen idol's foot:
Bloomin' idol made o' mud
Wot they called the great Gawd Budd
Plucky lot she cared for idols when I kissed her where she
stood.

More daring, this, than even lithographs of music-halls: bizarrerie of the best. The youngster was bracketed with Beardsley, was bracketed with 'Max'. Mr. John Lane began to collect his first editions; Mr. Richard Le Gallienne was told off to Bodley Head him. Mr. Gosse (this is perfectly true), Mr. Edmund Gosse spake publicly of 'the troubling thrill, the voluptuous and agitating sentiment', which these tales sent through his system. The little sun-baked books from Allahabad seemed if anything more golden than *The Yellow Book*. The proof of the literary epicure was his palate for the Kipling liqueur.

And then the exasperating fellow became popular.

What do you call the apostles of the Cubists? Cubicles? Very well then. Consider the consternation of the cubicles if the general public began to clamour for Picassos. Think even of Mr. Roger Fry's chagrin if we made a popular favourite of Matisse. A consternation not dissimilar, we may be sure, shuddered through the initiates of the nineties. Absurd, of course, to suggest that the paling of critical approval, the soft extinction of the starrier estimates, was entirely due to the widening blaze of popularity; but even critics are human, and it helped. It was impossible to watch their liqueur being drained like Bass without having doubts about its quality. They felt that the public's enjoyment of Kipling was too true to be good. They grew querulous, they qualified, they discovered defects.

The defects they discovered, the demands which they made, and the effect of all this hedging and shuffling on Mr. Kipling's development, we will consider in a moment. Remark, parenthetically, first, what an entirely wholesome and satisfactory thing that wider popularity was— and is. There is probably no living writer who is regarded, in England, with such widespread and unprompted veneration. It is the nearest thing we have nowadays to the reverence that used to be excited by the great literary figures of last century. It is touching, it is beautiful, it is altogether honest and good. Bank clerks and clerics, doctors, and drapers, journalists, joiners, engineers,—the average sinful jurymen and his usual daughters and wife, all speak of this man and his work much as another kind of people speak of Wagner. Only, honestly.

There is no priggishness about it, nor any desire to impress or be improved; and yet they find beauty in his work, they find magic, they find hints of strange forces and powers and constant reminders of something unimaginable beyond; they experience that delicious commotion of the blood we call romance, and are thrilled and shaken and renewed by it much as others of us are supposed to be renewed and thrilled by poetry. And at the same time, unlike so much of their 'romance', it is never a mere dallying with lotus-land sensations, a coloured refuge from the drudge of day. Its action is always to excite their zest for life, to send them back into reality more exultantly—not (of course) because of any policy it may preach, but because it so crisply handles, names, and sanctifies, the tools of each man's trade. Much has been written of Mr. Kipling's capacity for picking up knowledge from experts; far too little of the lessons the experts have learned from him. He has renewed the workman's pride in his work and restored their mystery to the crafts. He has done more than any man of his time to make the middle-classes less middle-class.

But all this the ten superior ones were in no position to foresee. Said they, *Yellow Book?*—we meant yellow press. Said they—but he *likes* the music-hall? And, to him—these little tales are very neat, very clever; but before we can take you seriously you must produce a full-length novel. This is striking—but is it Art?

And the real Rudyard Kipling? Had been meanwhile moved, one avers, as little by a desire to please the great public as by the desire to *épater* it. Essentially a dreamer, born in exile, he was oddly innocent of all the motives men ascribed to him—and it was an accident of environment, and a streak of sinful pride, and a sort of homely emulation, that really determined his first choice of tone and topic—the violent topics and the casual tone of those *Plain Tales from the Hills.* He had no notion of exalting the common soldier. He wanted rather the soldier to reverence the pen. His spur was the kind of half-resentment from which many writers suffer—the emotion that probably had a good deal to do with the making of 'Don Juan', and that is accountable for Mr. Shaw's affection of ferocity and that perhaps prompted Mr. Maurice Hewlett's early hectics. It is the artist's human retort to that intolerable tolerance with which the workers, doers, men of action, regard his anaemic indoor trade. It was Beetle's way of enforcing respect at Westward Ho! It was young Kipling's way of adjusting things at Simla. He would prove that ink is thicker than blood and the pen more masculine than the sword; and that a certain small spectacled sub-editor fond of poetry was not quite the lamb that he looked. And so he borrowed tales from the bazaars and the barracks, and Bret-Hartened them and pointed them with Poe; and wrote them out, with an infinite cunning, in a hand like an indifferent drawl. One of the ways of out-Heroding Herod is to yawn when the head is brought in. Mr. Kipling's yawn was a masterpiece. His make-up was perfect, the deception complete; the mess-rooms were duly impressed: it was another victory for the pen . . .

But a mask is a dangerous thing; it often moulds the face beneath. Left alone with his soothing Simla success, quietly sheltered behind it, young Kipling might indeed now have softly discarded his make-up and let his instincts find their native expression. But there leapt out upon him from Europe our roar of applause, and that riveted him to his role. Even the dabs of deprecation, the raps from falling rocket sticks, perversely whipped him in the same direction. 'You can write these little tales,' said they, 'but are you knowing enough to write long ones?' He did not know enough: he was never meant to be a novelist—but even less was he adapted for letting taunts slip by unanswered, and so he set his teeth, took up the challenge, and produced *The Light that Failed*. It did fail; and the critics who were really its sponsors had their moment of mean triumph. But by now his pride was in pledge; he would write a brilliant novel if it broke him; and for ten years he fought out fresh perfections of technique, using his convention of violence to hammer out new details of equipment until at length by dint of sheer virtuosity he achieved the protracted tale called *Kim*. He himself, it is said, considers *Kim* his master-work. He might well view it as a second vindication; his work henceforward, if I see it aright, stands for one long attempt on the part of his relieved genius to loosen the bars it had built about itself, and to twist an alien and artificial technique into an instrument for its deeper desires.

For it is the books that followed *Kim*—it is *Traffics and Discoveries*, *Actions and Reactions*, *Puck of Pook's Hill*, *Rewards and Fairies*, and the concurrent verse—that betray to us most clearly this queer subterranean disharmony and feud. If a reader will take these four books and consider them apart; if he will let their characteristics form a picture in his mind, an image of the kind of man who wrote them; and if he will then apply this reagent to the books that came before *Kim*, he will see how it eats out their accidentals. The falsities fade, there is a linking up of lighter touches, certain qualities, unrecognised before, rise glittering like veins. This fundamental filigree, this clear resultant mesh, is a map of Kipling's mind.

Now of this fundamental Kipling the cardinal qualities are three. The first is a passion for definition—a spiritual horror, almost desperate, of vagueness—a hunger for certitude and system. The second is the imaginative instrument of the first: a prodigious mental faculty, namely, for enforcing design, compelling coherence, for stamping dream-stuff into shapes as clean-cut and decisive as minted metal discs. And the third, on the physical plane, is the almost manual counterpart of these: a craftsman's cunning and capacity for fitting these terse units into complex patterns, adjusting them like the works of a watch with an exquisite accuracy, achieving miracles of minute mechanical perfection.

These are the three faculties, often bitted and strained, that form everywhere the sinews. Take, first, because most obvious, the so-called technical elements of his style. 'There is a writer called Stevenson,' he once said, 'who makes the most delicate inlay-work in black-and-white and files out to the fraction of a hair.' Kipling's own work is no less free from fluff or haze or slackness. The rhythms run with a snap from stop to stop; every sentence is as straight as a string; each has its self-contained tune. Prise one of them out of its place and you feel it would fall with a clink, leaving a slot that would never close up as the holes do in woollier work. Replace it, and it locks back like type in a forme, fitting into the paragraph as the paragraph fits into the tale. There are no glides or grace-notes, or blown spray of sound. Most prose that loves rhythm yields its music like a mist, an emanation that forms a bloom on the page, softly blurring the partitions of the periods. Kipling's prose shrinks stiffly from this trustfulness. The rhythms must report themselves promptly, prove their validity, start afresh after the full-stop. Lack of faith, if you like—but, also, constant keenness of craftsmanship.

Turn next to the optical integers—the sudden scenes which stud his page like inlaid stones. '*The leisurely ocean all patterned with peacocks' eyes of foam.*' '*I swung the car to clear the turf, brushed along the edge of the wood, and turned in on the broad stone path to where the fountain-basin lay like one star-sapphire.*' '*When his feet touched that still water, it changed, with a rustle of unrolling maps, to nothing less than a sixth quarter of the globe, with islands coloured yellow and blue, their lettering strung across their faces.*' And these are no mere decorations. These tales are jewelled, as watches are; it is round these tense, irreducible details that the action revolves. What is the emotional axis of 'The Finest

Story in the World?' It is that *'silver wire laid along the bulwarks which I thought was never going to break'*. Are we to know that a man was struck dumb? Then *'just as the lightning shot two tongues that cut the sky into three pieces . . . something wiped his lips of speech as a mother wipes the milky lips of her child'*. The motive of all his tales, as of 'At the End of the Passage', is a picture seen in a lens. Even the shadowy outer influences that brood over Kim's life, the inscrutable Powers that move in its background, come to us first in shapes vivid as heraldry—as a red Bull on a Field, as a House of Many Pillars; and before the close are resolved into the two most definite, clean-cut, and systematic of all earthly organisations: the military mechanism of India and the precise apparatus of Freemasonry. Kipling must have pattern and precision— and he has the power as well as the will. He can crush the sea into a shape as sharp as a crystal, can compress the Himalayas into a little lacquer-like design, has even in 'The Night Mail'—that clean, adroit, contenting piece of craftsmanship—printed a pattern on the empty air. He is primarily a pattern-maker; and the little pieces thus obtained he builds into a larger picture still. As the sentence into the paragraph— as the paragraph into the page—so do these sharp-edged items click together to form a geometrical pattern called the plot.

'The pattern called the plot.' It is here that we come very close to the irony that has ruled and wrenched all his career. Switch this map-making, pattern-making faculty upon the third element in fiction, the element of human nature, and what is the inevitable result? Inevitably, there is the same sudden stiffening and formulation. The characters spring to attention like soldiers on parade; they respond briskly to a certain description; they wear a fixed suit of idiosyncrasies like a uniform. A mind like this must use types and set counters; it feels dissatisfied, unsafe, ineffective, unless it can reduce the fluid waverings of character, its flitting caprices and twilight desires, to some tangible system. His characters will not only be definite; they will be definitions. His heroes will be courage incarnate; his weak men will be unwaveringly weak; and those who are mixed will be mixed mathematically, with all their traits clearly related to and explained by some neat blend of blood and race and caste behind. Is not all this true of Kipling's characters? They are marked by a strange immobility. They strike certain attitudes and retain them. Mulvaney, Ortheris and Learoyd live long but never alter; Kim never grows up. And indeed it is this very fixity that makes the short stories so effective. Their maker took these frozen gestures, rigid faces and tense attitudes, and fitted them together to form his effect; and whilst the inflexibility was exactly what he needed for neat mosaic-work, for making the sudden star called the story, the vividness of the details ('life seen by lightning-flashes' someone called them) seemed to prove the piercing humanity of the writer. It was only when he tried to construct a novel with them that the stiffness of these details turned to obstinacy, and their numbness became a kind of death. A short tale can be told in tableau—but a novel is not a long short tale. The pattern of *The Light that Failed* is as neat as the most successful of the *contes*, but it is the static symmetry of decoration and stained glass. It is applied art—that is to say, misapplied art. Its logic is not that of life. The characters are stowed into the interstices of a design that relies upon their remaining fixed quantities.

Perceive then, the almost maddening position! The very qualities that made the first tales tell, that seemed to prove his supreme capacity for fiction, are exactly the qualities that cut him off from the ability to write novels. The novelist is essentially the explorer, the questioner, the opener of doors; and the only law of human nature he knows is that the exception is the rule. But Mr. Kipling's first word is obedience; he is all for rules and rivets; for regularity and a four-square plan. Born under the sign of the Balance, his emblem is the compass and the square—and it is not with tools like these that men's motives can be measured. His vision of the world, like the Lama's, is a Wheel of Life with a neat niche for the individual; and even his famous militarism, his worship of the apparatus of war, is nothing more, in essence, than a longing for quiet comeliness and order. It is the mind, if you like, of a martinet—incapable therefore of complete imaginative sympathy. Any lapse from efficiency fills his craftsman's nature with disgust, and the only characters he can handle with perfect satisfaction are the Stricklands, the Mowglis, the Kims, as unconquerably capable as machines. His voice indeed is never so tolerant and humane as when he is dealing with heroes and heroines that are not human at all—with beasts and ships and polo-ponies or those odd little half-animals called children. His *Jungle Books* are among his best because here a psychology as elementary as Aesop's serves to convey the sense of an unusual understanding. A like reason gives its race and richness to his dialogue the moment it takes refuge in a dialect. For dialect, in spite of all its air of ragged lawlessness, is wholly impersonal, typical, fixed, the code of a caste, not the voice of an individual. It is when the novelist sets his characters talking King's English that he really puts his sympathy for the unconventional and capricious to the strain. Mr. Kipling's plain conversations are markedly unreal. But honest craftsmanship and an ear for strong rhythms provide him with many suits of dialects. With these he dresses the talk till it seems to surge with character.

And so, in this way and in that, the actual words he wrote joined in the conspiracy to keep him toiling, still hopefully, after that *ignis fatuus* of fiction. Until at length he made his supreme effort, fitted all the lore he had gathered—the sharp-set scenes, the well-cut dialects, the crisp impressions of life—into a single zoetrope, set it whirling on one of the spindles of the Indian machine, the secret spindle called the Great Game, and so created that spirited illusion of a novel which we know as *Kim*.

Thenceforward his work in prose has been a wonderful attempt to make his qualities cure their natural defects—to make sharpness and bright neatness produce their natural opposites—depth and shimmer and bloom. And by dint of an incomparable dexterity he has succeeded. There is no space left me now to trace the process with completeness—but roughly it may be described as an attempt to superimpose, as when you furl a fan, all the elements which in *Kim* had been laid side by side. The best example is perhaps *Rewards and Fairies*. If the reader will turn back to those wise fairy-tales he will see that each is really four-fold; a composite tissue made up of a layer of sunlit story (Dan's and Una's plane), on a layer of moonlit magic (plane of Puck), on a layer of history-stuff (René's plane and Gloriana's), on a last foundation of delicately bedimmed but never doubtful allegory. And he will note, too, the exquisite precision of the correspondences, a kind of practical punning, so that the self-same object plays a different part in every plane. One instance will suffice. Puck kicks a bunch of scarlet toad-stools idly. Why? Simply so that the red colour may stain back through all the textures till it matches, in the third, with the name of Rufus. This is not the mere swagger of virtuosity. The result of these imposi-tions is a very beautiful imposture. It gives the tales an opalescence that had hitherto seemed foreign to his work. It gives them the milki-ness of a magic crystal and makes them the completest symbols of life he has yet produced. These fairy tales for children are far more realistic than the *Plain Tales from the Hills*. For half of life is moonlit, and the image that would copy it exactly must be vague.

Nor is this all. If there be any logic in the lines of effort we have traced it is not here they find their consummation: they leap forward through this magic haze, emerge beyond it strangely clarified; they make it impossible not to believe that this woven obscurity, this new delicate dimness, is indeed but a curtain—a mist—not of dusk, but of dawn—that will dissolve to reveal Kipling carving his true master-work. Released at last from the conventions thrust upon it by pride and accident and the impertinencies of criticism, his system-seeking genius can now openly take up its true task, the task it has hitherto attempted only intermittently, and begin the sustained practice of that colossal kind of craftsmanship for which it is so singularly suited. It will beat out for itself a new form of imaginative prose, as unclogged by characterisation as his verse. The devices of drama it will use no doubt, and some of the tricks of narration; but its true medium will be massed impersonal things—tangles of human effort—the thickets of pheno-mena—the slow movements of industry, so muffled to the average eye—the general surge and litter of sensation. What his genius can do with material of this kind we have already in some sort seen. Driving into the darkness that beleaguers us, swirling and thrusting like a searchlight in a forest, it could bring out the essential structure of events and display the soaring pillars of contemporary achievement. It might not be the perfect definition; it might tend too much to turn the tides into firm floors, the branching constellations into rafters; but it would be enormously exhilarating. It would give toil a con-scious habitation; like actual architecture, like statuary, like all firm material forms, it would create, instead of merely copying, the emo-tions it lacks power to reproduce.

48. Ian Hay on *Stalky & Co.*

1914

Extract from *The Lighter Side of School Life* (1914) by Ian Hay, p. 158.

'Ian Hay'—pseudonym of John Hay Beith (1876–1952) wrote several books about the First World War, and followed them by popular novels and plays of a humorous kind, notably *Housemaster* (1936).

[re School Stories] We have many to choose from—*Stalky*, for instance. *Stalky* has come in for a shower of abuse from certain quarters. He hits the sentimentalist hard. We are told that the book is vulgar, that the famous trio are 'little beasts'. (I think Mr. A. C. Benson said so.) Still, Mr. Kipling never touches any subject which he does not adorn, and in *Stalky* he brings out vividly some of the salient features of modern school life. He has drawn masters as they have never been drawn before: the portraits may be cruel, biassed, not sufficiently representative; but how they live! He has put the case for the unathletic boy with convincing truth. He depicts, too, very faithfully, the curious camaraderie which prevails nowadays between boys and masters, and pokes mordant fun at the sycophancy which this state of things breeds in a certain type of boy—the 'Oh, sir!' and 'No, sir!' and 'Yes, sir!' and 'Please, sir!' brigade—and deals faithfully with the master who takes advantage of out-of-school intimacy to be familiar and offensive in school, addressing boys by their nicknames and making humorous references to extra-scholastic incidents. And above all, Mr. Kipling knows the heart of a boy. He understands, above all men, a boy's intense reserve upon matters that lie deepest within him, and his shrinking from and repugnance to unrestrained and blatant discussion of these things. Do you remember the story of the fat man—'the jelly-bellied flag-flapper'—who came down to lecture to the school on patriotism?

[quotes from 'The Flag of their Country', *Stalky & Co.* pp. 212–13]

It was a Union Jack, you will remember, suddenly unfurled by way of peroration. 'Happy thought! Perhaps he was drunk.' That is true, all through.

49. 'A Diversity of Creatures'

1917

Anonymous review in the *Athenaeum*, No. 4617, p. 240 (May 1917).

If we had any misgivings, strengthened by some recent excursions in journalism, that decadence had set in with Mr. Kipling, this new book puts them to rest. He has never shown himself a greater master of the art of storytelling, never combined creative imagination with more triumphant realism, or handled his own English prose with more ease, economy, and certainty of effect. The first of the fourteen, 'As Easy as A.B.C.', is perhaps the finest short story of the future ever written. A sort of sequel to 'With the Night Mail', it is dated A.D. 2065, and is an historical episode in a world that has passed through the most profound and complete of social revolutions. Politics have ceased. No human being takes any interest in government, for all things run smoothly and in perfect order under a small and unobtrusive Aerial Board of Control, which leaves absolute privacy and security to the individual. 'Transportation is Civilization. Democracy is Disease.' In such a world, crowds and the people are the one source of evil, and a sporadic outbreak of now obsolete and mediaeval democratic agitation in Chicago arouses a storm of agoraphobia, and brings about the events to be narrated. Mr. Kipling does not describe, but makes the reader's imagination vividly realize, the wonders of aerial navigation, the ground-circuits, and the destructive sound-vibrations and withering rays of light, which are the defences and the artillery of the future. He moves among these sensations as if they were the commonplace of existence, as if mankind had been used to them for generations. His is a realism that Swift might have envied.

Some artists excel in giving an air of the marvellous and stupendous to things that really exist. Such is Mr. Pennell in his romantic pictures of colossal buildings, engines, and machinery. Others, like Mr. Muirhead Bone, can make the most incredible structures and implements of war matters of everyday familiarity. Mr. Kipling can do both. He can make the ordinary ultra-romantic; he can let us feel at home in a world where everything is new, strange, and astounding. To him romance is a plaything, which he handles with the skill and ease of a tennis champion brandishing a racket. Though none of the other stories travels into the world of mechanical wonders, several, perhaps most, would in cold analysis seem quite as improbable. In three, 'The Dog Hervey', 'In the Same Boat', and 'Swept and Garnished', occult sympathies, some form of telepathic bond, or a faculty of seeing the invisible, are rendered more than credible by like realistic devices. There are farces, such as 'The Vortex', 'The Horse Marines', and 'The Village that voted the Earth was Flat', which pile situation on ludicrous situation, and climax on climax, long after it seems as if the final limit of extravagance had been reached. The last-named story is a piece of uproarious comedy that exceeds 'The Incarnation of Krishna Mulvaney', and has the advantage of being laid in the home counties, and enacted by local magnates, villagers, city men, and M.P.s such as we all know. The success with which the inventor brings off his daring complications of humorous circumstance is not a whit less amazing than that of his 'Easy as A.B.C.'.

It is, in fact, all as easy as A.B.C. to Mr. Kipling, and that is perhaps what chiefly enthrals the discriminating reader and seizes our admiration. For it is the manner, not the matter, of these latest masterpieces which challenges attention. Mr. Kipling offers nothing conspicuously new. Various as the contents are, we are well acquainted with their different kinds. He set the direction in every instance years ago. The only wonder is that he is able to proceed still farther in every one. True, there is nothing of the same kind of imagination as in 'They' or 'The Brushwood Boy'. This set contains no story having the fundamental seriousness of several earlier ones that cling to memory. But as a craftsman, and something higher than a craftsman, Mr. Kipling has gone on developing. Though he is not a novelist, his character-drawing is substantial enough to last out the different events of many stories. Stalky and Beetle reappear here, and the former has obviously lived. There are also some Sikhs and Goorkhas reminiscent of *Kim* and other Indian stories. Perhaps it is a result of the War that infractions of the sixth commandment are treated with such sang-froid and nonchalance in 'Friendly Brook' and 'The Edge of the Evening'. Each story is followed by a kind of epilogue in verse, which sometimes explains a rather cryptic meaning, or at least enforces its bearing as Mr. Kipling conceives it. 'The Land' is an excellent history of the British peasant, who was there when the Romans came, and still is in real possession, 'For whoever pays the taxes old Mus' Hobden owns the land.' But the average quality of the verse is low; some pieces, such as 'The Children', in spite of a Swinburnian measure and fluent double-rhyming, are merely consecutive lengths of prose.

We should like to have quoted from that charming comedy of schoolboy humours and howlers, *Regulus,* to show what Mr. Kipling can do in the way of Platonic as well as other dialogue. He is first-rate on the teaching of Latin and its effect on living. But to open the book anywhere is to see that he is a supreme master of style, in all its applications.

50. T. S. Eliot's 'Kipling Redivivus'

1919

Signed ('T. S. E.') review of *The Years Between* in the *Athenaeum*
No. 4645, pp. 297–8 (9 May 1919).

Thomas Stearns Eliot (1888–1965), leading poet of his period and
a distinguished critic, later edited *A Choice of Kipling's Verse* (1941)
with a long critical introduction of judicious praise that was prelude to the serious study of Kipling's place in literature which is
now taking place. Eliot balanced this short early appreciation of
Kipling with another forty years later delivered before the
Kipling Society in October 1958 and published in the *Kipling
Journal* number 129 (March 1959) and reprinted in Elliot L.
Gilbert's *Kipling and the Critics* (1965).

Mr. Kipling is a laureate without laurels. He is a neglected celebrity.
The arrival of a new book of his verse is not likely to stir the slightest
ripple on the surface of our conversational intelligentsia. He has not
been crowned by the elder generation; malevolent fate has not even
allowed him to be one of the four or five or six greatest living poets.
A serious contemporary has remarked of the present volume that 'in
nearly all our poetical coteries the poetry of Kipling has long been
anathema, with field sports, Imperialism, and public schools'. This is
wide of the mark. Mr. Kipling is not anathema; he is merely not discussed. Most of our discerning critics have no more an opinion on
Mr. Kipling than they have on the poetry of Mr. John Oxenham. The
mind is not sufficiently curious, sufficiently brave, to examine Mr. Kipling. Yet the admired creator of Bouvard and Pecuchet would not have
overlooked the Kipling *dossier*.

   Mr. Kipling has not been analysed. There are the many to whom he
is a gospel; there are the few to whom he is a shout in the street, or a
whisper in the ear of death, unheard. Both are mistaken. Mr. Kipling
is not without antecedents; he has an affinity to Swinburne, even a

322

likeness. There are, of course, qualities peculiar to Mr. Kipling; but several of the apparent differences are misconceptions, and several can be reduced to superficial differences of environment. Both are men of a few simple ideas, both are preachers, both have marked their styles by an abuse of the English Bible.

They are alike even in a likeness which would strike most people immediately as a difference; they are alike in their use of sound. It is true that Swinburne relies more exclusively upon the power of sound than does Mr. Kipling. But it is the same type of sound, and it is not the sound-value of music. Anyone who thinks so may compare Swinburne's 'songs' with verse which demands the voice and the instrument, with Shelley's 'Music when soft voices die' or Campion's 'Fairy Queen Prosperpina'. What emerges from the comparison is that Swinburne's sound like Mr. Kipling's, has the sound-value of oratory, not of music.

'When the hounds of spring are on winter's traces' arrives at similar effects to Mr. Kipling: ' "What are the bugles blowin' for?" said Files on Parade;' or in the present volume:

> There was no need of a steed nor [sic] a lance to pursue them;
> It was decreed their own deed, and not chance, should undo them.

It is, in fact, the poetry of oratory; it is music just as the words of orator or preacher are music; they persuade, not by reason, but by emphatic sound. Swinburne and Mr. Kipling have, like the public speaker, an idea to impose; and they impose it in the public speaker's way, by turning the idea into sound, and iterating the sound. And, like the public speaker's, their business is not to express, to lay before you, to *state*, but to propel, to impose on you the idea. And, like the orator, they are personal; not by revelation, but by throwing themselves in and gesturing the emotion of the moment. The emotion is not 'there' simply, coldly independent of the author, of the audience, there and for ever like Shakespeare's and Aeschylus' emotions: it is present so long only as the author is on the platform and compels you to feel it.

> I look down at his feet: but that's a fable.
> If that thou be'st a devil, I cannot kill thee

is there, cold and indifferent.

> Nothing is better, I well think
> Than love; the hidden well-water
> Is not so delicate a drink.
> This was well seen of me and her

(to take from one of Swinburne's poems which most nearly resembles
a statement); or

> The end of it's sitting and thinking
> And dreaming hell-fires to see—

these are not statements of emotion, but ways of stimulating a particular
response in the reader.

Both of the poets have a few simple ideas. If we deprecate any
philosophical complications, we may be allowed to call Swinburne's
Liberty and Mr. Kipling's Empire 'ideas'. They are at least abstract, and
not material which emotion can feed long upon. And they are not (in
passing) very dissimilar. Swinburne had the *Risorgimento*, and Gari-
baldi, and Mazzini, and the model of Shelley, and the recoil from
Tennyson, and he produced Liberty. Mr. Kipling, the Anglo-Indian,
had frontier welfare, and rebellions, and Khartoum, and he produced
the Empire. And we remember Swinburne's sentiments toward the
Boers; he wished to intern them all. Swinburne and Mr. Kipling have
these and such concepts; some poets, like Shakespeare or Dante or
Villon, and some novelists, like Mr. Conrad, have, in contrast to ideas
or concepts, points of view, or 'worlds'—what are incorrectly called
'philosophies'. Mr. Conrad is very germane to the question, because he
is in many ways the antithesis of Mr. Kipling. He is, for one thing, the
antithesis of Empire (as well as of democracy); his characters are the
denial of Empire, of Nation, of Race almost, they are fearfully alone
with the Wilderness. Mr. Conrad has no ideas, but he has a point of
view, a world; it can hardly be defined, but it pervades his work and is
unmistakable. It could not be otherwise. Swinburne's and Mr. Kipling's ideas could be otherwise. Had Mr. Kipling taken Liberty and
Swinburne the Empire, the alteration would be unimportant.

And this is why both Swinburne's and Mr. Kipling's verse, in spite
of the positive manner which each presses to his service, appear to
lack cohesion—to be, frankly, immature. There is no point of view to
hold them together. What is the point of view, one man's experience
of life, behind 'Mandalay', and 'Danny Deever', and 'MacAndrew',
and the 'Recessional'? The volume in hand, at least, ought to be consistent with itself: the subjects are in sympathy with each other; they
express Mr. Kipling's attitudes toward various aspects of the war. But
the poems no more hang together than the verses of a schoolboy. This,
in spite of Mr. Kipling's undeniable manner.

The manner itself, indeed, involves no discoveries in syntax or
vocabulary; the structure reveals nothing unusual.

> The banked oars fell an hundred strong,
> And backed and threshed and ground,
> But bitter was the rowers' song
> As they brought the war-boat round.

The construction 'bitter was . . . as . . . ' has a very familiar sound. The old order of words persists, not giving place to new. This is not, however, *the* manner. And we should not be positive that

> The Hun is at the gate! . . .
> Be well assured that on our side
> The abiding oceans fight . . .

(Mr. Conrad would hardly issue this opinion about the oceans) were by Mr. Kipling, though we could not associate them with any equally distinguished name. But when we peruse the following:

> A tinker out of Bedford
> A vagrant oft in quod . . .
> And Bunyan was his name! . . .

> They do not preach that their God will rouse them a little before the nuts
> work loose.
> They do not preach that His Pity allows them to leave their work when
> they damn-well choose . . .

> There is a gland at the back of the jaw
> And an answering lump by the collar-bone . . .

> When the Himalayan peasant meets the he-bear in his pride . . .

in all of these we have the true formula, with its touch of the newspapers, of Billy Sunday, and the Revised Version filtered through Rabbi Zeal-of-the-Land Busy. The Revised Version (substantially the same style as all the versions from Tindal) is excellent prose for its matter. It is often redundant and bombastic in the Prophets, who sometimes fell into these vices, and it is a model of firm and limpid style in the sayings of Jesus. But it is not a style into which any significant modern content can be shoved. Mr. Kipling is one of the Minor Prophets.

There is one more element in the style or manner of Mr. Kipling which demands attention. The eighteenth century was in part cynical and in part sentimental, but it never arrived at complete amalgamation of the two feelings. Whoever makes a study of the sentimentalism of the nineteenth and twentieth centuries will not neglect the peculiar cynical sentiment of Mr. Kipling. In a poem like Mr. Kipling's 'The Ladies' the fusion is triumphant. The sentiment of Tennyson and Mrs. Browning is obsolete, it is no longer a living force; it is superseded by Mr. Kipling's. Tennyson, we must insist, could never have written

> Love at first sight was her trouble,
> She didn't know what it were;
> But I wouldn't do such, 'cause I liked her too much—
> And I learned about women from 'er;

nor could he have written

> Gentlemen-rankers off on a spree,
> Damned from here to eternity.
> O God, have mercy on such as we:
> Ba Ba Ba.

Mr. Kipling may have winked at Tennyson down the road. But Tennyson did not wink back.

And yet Mr. Kipling is very nearly a great writer. There is an unconsciousness about him which, while it is one of the reasons why he is not an artist, is a kind of salvation. There is an echo of greatness in his naïve appeal to so large an audience as he addresses; something which makes him, like one or two other writers who are not or hardly artists, a lonely figure. And in *Plain Tales from the Hills* he has given the one perfect picture of a society of English, narrow, snobbish, spiteful, ignorant and vulgar, set down absurdly in a continent of which they are unconscious. What Mirza Murad Ali Beg's book[1] is to all other books of native life, so is Mr. Kipling's to all other books of Anglo-Indian life. It is wrong, of course, of Mr. Kipling to address a large audience; but it is a better thing than to address a small one. The only better thing is to address the one hypothetical Intelligent Man who does not exist and who is the audience of the Artist.

[1] [*Lalun the Beragun*, Bombay 1884. See *Plain Tales*, p. 333]

51. Richard Le Gallienne on 'Kipling's Place in Literature'

1919

Signed article in *Munsey's Magazine*, Vol. LXVIII, pp. 238-46 (November 1919), reprinted in *Around the World with Kipling* (New York, 1926), pp. 45-51.

Richard Le Gallienne (1866-1947), minor poet and essayist, is remembered best for *The Quest of the Golden Girl* (1896) and *The Romantic Nineties* (1926). He also wrote studies of Meredith (1890), Whitman (1898), and Kipling (1900)—the last, echoing the contemporary attack on Kipling for 'hooliganism', is in a very different vein from the more balanced and considered judgment of the following essay.

Henry James, in an early appreciation of Rudyard Kipling's writings, which was a striking illustration of his own literary catholicity, referred to 'the particular property that made us all so precipitately drop everything else to attend to him'. The phrase is vividly and truthfully descriptive of the manner in which, so to say, Mr. Kipling first hit literary London; for his sudden and swift arrival was a very unmistakable jolt to the literary fashions then prevailing.

The times were decidedly 'precious'. We were in the midst of a rather hectic aftermath of pre-Raphaelitism and the 'esthetic' movement. The labels 'decadent' and '*fin-de-siècle*' were the prevailing catchwords, and 'strange sins', and peculiar 'soul-states', and 'artistic temperaments' were in vogue. It was the heyday of Oscar Wilde and Aubrey Beardsley, of Paterian and Stevensonian prose. 'Style' and 'distinction' were our only wear. Also the cults of the poster, the music-hall, and the short story were at their height. *The Yellow Book* was being published in Vigo Street, and the Rhymers' Club was meeting at the Cheshire Cheese. In short, it was the eighteen-nineties.

It is not necessary to depreciate those stirring times, as surely I would be the last to do, in order to emphasize the singularity of Mr. Kipling's paradoxical arrival among them. There was a genuine artistic vitality in them, which has not only left behind some notable work, becoming more seriously recognized as time goes on, and the picturesque memories of certain ill-starred men of talent, if not genius, but which is, at the moment, perhaps too potently alive and influential in that new wave of 'preciousness' wherein we are at present engulfed. Indeed, the despised and rejected of the eighteen-nineties have become, it is to be feared, almost too much the chief corner-stones of contemporary movements and manifestoes.

However, 'that', as Mr. Kipling first taught us to say, 'is another story'. Mr. Kipling's influence has had a long innings. If those influences which he temporarily overwhelmed are now to have theirs—well, it takes all sorts to make a world. Of one thing we may be gladly certain—the iron and quinine with which he has so plentifully dosed us will remain in the blood of the younger generation, and will serve to correct any threatened fevers of luxurious 'hedonism'. No recent writer can so confidently apply Whitman's words to himself, in addressing his contemporaries, and say:

> You will hardly know who I am or what I mean,
> But I will be good health to you, nevertheless,
> And filter and fibre your blood.

Leaving artistic considerations aside for a moment, Mr. Kipling's moral influence on his day and generation has been of an importance which it is scarcely an exaggeration to call prophetic. Few writers have ever come so precisely in the nick of time. If a voice crying 'England hath need of thee' had summoned him, he could not have been more pat to the occasion. Wordsworth's 'stern daughter of the voice of God' has seldom been in greater need of a candid friend and servant. But how whimsically characteristic of the times it was, too, that that mouthpiece of the ancient verities should come in the guise of an Anglo-Indian teller of tales, the banjo-minstrel of Tommy Atkins and *Supi-yaw-lat!*

And surely, at first, no one dreamed what this cock-sure *enfant terrible* was to mean to the British Empire in particular, and to the morale of the world in general. His guise was certainly anything but prophetic, and his accents anything but reverential. Other-world-liness—of which he has essentially a great deal—was the last quality

you would attribute to him. On the contrary, a queerly acrid world-
liness, an omniscient cynicism, and a jarring brutality, made the peculiar
tang of this strange, new fruit from the Tree of Knowledge. One's first
reading of him was like one's first experience with olives. Some people
never learn to like olives, and some people—lovers, too, of the best in
literature—have never quite learned to like Rudyard Kipling. There is
something in him that still frightens them.

But the fruit that Mr. Kipling brought us, even in that first astonishing volume of *Plain Tales from the Hills*, was more subtly blended in
flavor than any olive. It had, indeed, every kind of flavor, and was not
without an odd touch of the nectarine. Among all his other experiences,
its author had not missed the honey of pre-Raphaelitism, was not
unacquainted with the Lady Lilith, and could put Rossetti's 'Song of
the Bower' into the mouth of his drunken acquaintance, McIntosh
Jellaludin. And, while on one page we would find him lyrically celebrating 'the hunting of man', what exquisite tenderness we would find
on another—lover-tenderness, mother-tenderness—and what noble
and touching pity for the sorrows and frailties of his fellows! With
all his uncanny and precocious knowledge of the world—so many
different worlds—his somewhat overdone and distasteful knowingness,
and along with his apparent cold-bloodedness of observation and
accent, there went, in unaccustomed association, so deep a sense of the
tears in mortal things that one soon realized that here was something
more than a diabolically clever teller of tales, and that, in fact, we were
safe in the hands of a deep and serious poet.

It need hardly be said that one of the first notes to be struck by Mr.
Kipling, a note that has reverberated as from an iron string through
all his subsequent writings, has been that an Englishman's first duty is
his duty to England. 'Keep we the faith!' From first to last he has been
an incorrigible Britisher, and in his case there seems never to have been
a shadow of those Gilbertian temptations to belong to other nations.
Least of all has he ever shown the smallest inclination to be an inter-
nationalist. In that famous envoi to *The Seven Seas*, in which he
expresses his creed as an artist, he has told us that in the happy hereafter
for artists, 'when the oldest colors have faded and the youngest critic
has died'—

> . . . Only the Master shall praise us, and only
> the Master shall blame;
> And no one shall work for money, and no one
> shall work for fame;

But each for the joy of the working, and each,
in his separate star,
Shall draw the Thing as he sees It for the God
of Things as They Are!

From first to last the God he has served, with a prayerful devotion which gives all his work a curious seriousness, even solemnity, has been the God of Things as They Are; and, when you come to think of it, what other god is there? Under another name, such was the deity of another modern writer who seems very different from Mr. Kipling, but from whom, I conjecture, he has drawn no little inspiration—George Meredith. 'Sacred Reality', Meredith called his divinity. 'Smite, Sacred Reality,' he cries in the anguish of *A Faith on Trial*; and when we can say that in sincerity, he adds, 'we have come of our faith's ordeal'. Meredith and Mr. Kipling alike are fiercely impatient, of sentimental evasions of the facts of existence, and though, perhaps, far from agreement on details, are alike intolerant of half-baked social and political panaceas, both having gone to school to that wise spirit which teaches us to discriminate between true idealism and its spurious, sophomoric imitations.

For this reason Mr. Kipling is by many regarded as a reactionary—a label, it is to be feared, which must be patiently accepted by all such who do not swallow wholesale those nostrums of contemporary lawlessness and disorder which parade variously under the names of progress and revolution.

Mr. Kipling has an old-fashioned belief in duty, and in the discipline which enforces it, and makes it second nature. 'He did not know,' he says of his Brushwood Boy, 'that he bore with him from school and college a character worth much fine gold.' Character—that is the old-fashioned quality which again and again he holds up for our admiration in his mute, inglorious heroes, and possibly he writes sometimes a little too much as if it were an exclusively British possession.

For, in spite of his having, in Barrie's phrase, swaggered in bad company over so many continents, he is the least cosmopolitan of writers. He is nothing if not patriotic—that antique virtue which our internationalists are doing their best to ridicule and destroy. It was already, in many intellectual quarters, being superciliously depreciated as insularity, and so forth, when Mr. Kipling first 'smote 'is bloomin' lyre'. Perhaps, for some, the recent war, with its fearful menace, may point an old-fashioned moral in Mr. Kipling's favor; and those who study it, and who are following, too, the recent developments among the various new peace-born nations, may hesitate before exchanging it for the blessings of the 'inter-nation'.

In fact, Mr. Kipling is, both by temperament and by conviction, a Tory. But it is not necessary to agree with the whole of a writer to be glad of him, and this is especially true of Mr. Kipling. One may, indeed, often violently, disagree with him, for his work is very much of a challenge to his time, yet admire and give thanks for him all the same. Perhaps as one grows older and better acquainted with the works and ways of his God of Things as They Are, one is inclined to agree with him more rather than less; nor need the doing so imply our senectitude, for we must recall that Mr. Kipling thought the same at twenty as he does now, that his young shoulders were born with a strangely old Tory head upon them. He saw the Thing as It Is from a very early age; and, when we say that, we must not forget that it was far from being only the seamy side of it that he saw. He saw that, indeed, with strangely precocious eyes, but it was as nothing in his vision compared with the power and the glory, the wonder and the mystery, which he also saw, and which no man of our time has seen with clearer, more passionate, or more worshipful seeing.

52. Edmund Blunden: Review of
The Irish Guards

1923

Extract from review of *The Irish Guards in the Great War* headed 'Mr. Kipling Reconstructs' published in the *Nation and Athenaeum*, Vol. XXXIII, pp. 122–3 (28 April 1923). The rest of the article deals generally with histories and descriptions of the War, and only the last paragraph is concerned directly with Kipling's book.

Edmund Charles Blunden (1896–   ) one of the leading poets and critics of his generation is also the author of the best volume of First War memories, *Undertones of War* (1929). He succeeded Kipling as literary adviser to the War Graves Commission.

The fact is that Mr. Kipling appears not perfectly to understand the pandemonium and nerve-strain of war; it seldom surges up in his pages of that appalling misery which brought seasoned men down in the shell holes beyond Thiepval, as they went up to relieve the Schwaben Redoubt, crying, and 'whacked to the wide'. He makes constant stern attempts at actuality; he constantly falls short, in expressions merely strained, in sheer want of comprehension. To those who were in the line, his technical phraseology will seem incongruous now and then; but the deeper defects may be exemplified by such expressions as—touching pill-box warfare—'the annoying fights and checks rounded the concreted machine gun posts'; or 'While they watched drowsily the descent and thickening of a fresh German shell-storm, preluding fresh infantry attacks . . .'; or again, 'what had been a Brigade ceased to exist—had soaked horribly into the ground'. Here mere languidness, these exaggerations, conflicts with memory; the Irish Guards have been chronicled with decision and skill, but as to the multitudinous enigma of war atmosphere, Mr. Kipling has not written much that convinces us.

53. Christopher Morley on 'Horace, Book Five'

1926

Signed review of 'Horace, Book Five' (and *Debits and Credits*) published in the *Saturday Review of Literature* (New York), Vol. III, p. 155 (2 October 1926).

Christopher Morley (1890–1957) was a well-known American novelist and essayist, highly regarded for his reviews. He is best remembered for *Thunder on the Left* (1925) and *The Seacoast of Bohemia* (1929).

With gay instinct for the painful and irrelevant, the editorial writers mostly agreed to pick upon the least important poem in Rudyard Kipling's new book, and wrote ponderous grievance about it. As a matter of fact not one but three of the poems are pretty straightly barbed against America; but the other two are too subtly led to be readily observable. The one on Prohibition would have been the one to quote, for an editor with a nostril for News.

But I did have to blink my eyes a little, finding in our gravest journals such remarks as this: 'The numerous poems which adorn *Debits and Credits* do not compel one to much comment . . . Frankness compels one to state that the original pieces composed for the present volume do not measure up.' What, do four new 'translations' from the Fifth Book of Horace's Odes compel no comment? Or are we to suppose that our reviewers don't know the joke about Horace's Fifth Book? I was brooding a bit morosely on this matter when, just in time to gruntle my heart somewhat, I met F.P.A.[1] coming out of the subway. It was a jocund coincidence, for he had under his arm the rare little *Carminum Liber Quintus* (*a Rudyardo Kipling et Carolo Graves Anglice Redditus*) which is also one of my treasures. We stood prating

---

[1] [Franklin Pierce Adams, popular American columnist and author, generally known by his initials, with which he signed his work.]

together in City Hall Park, two happy casuals, our erring bosoms full of homage to the man who, after nineteen centuries, recaptures the very voice.

The huge paradox of Kipling is never more apparent than when you read the reviews of a new book of his. This extraordinary writer, whom we are accustomed to see billed as speaking to the world's hugest fiction audience, is really the subtlest of highbrows. His finest things would bore the slackwit reader just as Shakespeare does. He would have been the greatest professor of English Literature that our tongue has ever known, because he has the violent and tragic sense of literature as the very perspiration on the brow of life. He writes a story ostensibly about big howitzers, and it is really a lover's tribute to Jane Austen. He writes a story apparently about wireless, and it means nothing save to a student of Keats. In this new volume the two Stalkies and the Jane Austen story coruscate with literary allusion and esoteric jape. 'The Propagation of Knowledge' might have been written specially to wring the withers of the Modern Language Association. His fragment on 'How Shakespeare Came to Write *The Tempest*', written in 1898 as a letter to the London *Spectator*, like all his marvellous side-glances into Elizabethan doings (have a look at his old poem 'The Craftsman') shows his understanding of how and where poetry is born. Only learned students, packed with curious and private lore, could properly trace the wild chameleon variation of his mind. How, with a hundred tints and shadings he has been able to take at will the color of any man from Horace to Mulvaney—and yet, in the core of the crystal, we see ever the identity of the egregious Beetle. When was there a more vast, wanton, irrepressible, furious, grotesque, and impossible fecundity? It is a silly thing to say—yet how much of literature consists in saying the silliest things possible—there is perhaps more of the specific and technical Shakespeare-gift in our well-loved Beetle than in any other man these times have seen. At his worst, God knows, he is as bad as Shakespeare ever was. At his best, he has looked upon pure flame. Those who know the color of naked fire will recognize it when they see,

> Rubies of every heat, where through we scan
> The fiercer and more fiery heart of man.

It was odd that 'The United Idolaters', perhaps the charmingest tribute of love ever paid to an American sanctity—Uncle Remus— hasn't been mentioned in the editorials. But that is not what editorials are for. They must leap upon the verses in which a man with tragedy in his heart ventures to say, and with mannerly disguise, some words that seem to him bitterly true. There are others in which the soul is opened so plainly that one keeps decent silence. And here and there, if you are on the air for these things, is that specific wavelength of Kipling genius, that is not always relished or understood but is uniquely itself. If anyone ever tells you it is a genius available for the million, I think you will be safe to contradict. I haven't yet read all the stories, but I didn't let the sun go down on any unread poems. With no right or permission whatever I'm going to quote from the addenda to Horace—

TO THE COMPANIONS
Horace, Ode 17, Bk. V

How comes it that, at even-tide,
    When level beams should show most truth,
Man, failing, takes unfailing pride
    In memories of his frolic youth?

Venus and Liber fill their hour,
    The games engage, the law-courts prove,
Till hardened life breeds love of power
    Or Avarice, Age's final love.

Yet at the end, these comfort not—
    Nor any triumph Fate decrees—
Compared with glorious, unforgot—
    ten innocent enormities

Of frontless days before the beard,
    When, instant on the casual jest,
The God Himself of Mirth appeared
    And snatched us to His heaving breast.

And we—not caring who He was
    But certain He would come again—
Accepted all He brought to pass
    As Gods accept the lives of men.

Then He withdrew from sight and speech,
    Nor left a shrine. How comes it now
While Charon's keel grates on the beach,
    He calls so clear: 'Rememberest thou?'

I've been interested to see that the *Literary Review* is conducting a symposium on whether authors care what the critics say about their work, and perhaps that topic is akin to the present matter. If any writer says he is not interested in the critics' comments he is probably either a liar or a genius. But as to reviews having any real effect, turning any of his inward valves, it seems to me inconceivable.

Long before a book reaches the reviewers, its author has made up his own mind about it. He knows bitterly well how nearly it represents his intentions. Praise from those he respects probably shames him and makes him eager to do better. Reproach usually stiffens his neck. But in his core and gizzard he is totally unmoved. I am told that some writers actually subscribe to clipping bureaus so as not to miss any of their 'notices'. The idea is incredible.

For printers' ink, chucked about at random, is so murderous to the finer delicacies that one is soon cured of any appetite for mere publicity. And if you ever had a notion to deal, a bit savagely, with some of the central realities and joys and horrors, you would probably be told that you are pleasantly whimsical. Also there will always be those who resent any man saying what he exactly thinks. To such resentment there can be no answer. Horace suggested in the Fifth Book—since he didn't write it—that silence is best.

54. Brander Matthews on 'Kipling's Deeper Note'

1926

Signed review of *Debits and Credits* in *Literary Digest International Book Review* (U.S.A.), Vol. IX, pp. 745–6 (November 1926) headed 'Mr. Kipling Strikes a Deeper Note'.

Brander Matthews (1852–1929) was a notable American essayist and dramatic critic of his period. He held Chairs in Literature at Columbia University from 1892 to 1924, and wrote more than forty books ranging from literary essays such as *Pen and Ink* (1888) and short stories such as *Tales of Fantasy and Fact* (1896) to such scholarly works as *Molière* (1910) and *Principles of Playmaking* (1919).

It is pleasant to welcome this new collection of Rudyard Kipling's short stories, the first in ten years; and it is pleasant to know that his popularity is attested by the steady sale of his many volumes. His earliest books, those which gave him his sudden fame, *Plain Tales from the Hills*, *Soldiers Three*, and their companions, were not protected by copyright in this country when they first appeared; they were pirated by half-a-dozen publishers; and they were sold by tens of thousands. The international copyright act went into effect on the first of July, 1891; and Kipling has been able to profit by the books he has written in the past thirty-five years. To the courtesy of the publishers who have just issued *Debits and Credits*, I am indebted for the privilege of stating that since they took over the publication of Kipling's books they have sold more than two and a half million volumes. *Kim* and *Just So Stories* have each attained to a circulation of more than 150,000; and *The Day's Work* is not far behind.

There are signs, it is true, that Kipling is not now held in high esteem by the Little Group of Serious Thinkers, who are proud to style themselves 'Young Intellectuals'—altho' they are certainly not as juvenile as they act, and probably not as intellectual as they believe; Their dislike for the foremost figure in the contemporary literature of our language is easily explicable; they are vociferous in vaunting their revolt from all the conventions, all the traditions, and all the inheritances from the past; they assert with persistent violence the right of every man to 'express himself' and to 'live his own life' more or less regardless of the rights of every other man; and, therefore, they can not but be annoyed by Kipling's sobriety and sanity, by his regard for form, by his resolute self-control, by his freedom from freakishness, and by his insistence in holding fast to that which is true and of good report. Altho' he never preaches, there is a moral implicit in all his work. When I once exprest to him my appreciation of the Mowgli stories, he explained that they were easy enough: 'When I had once found the Law of the Jungle,' he said, 'then all the rest followed as a matter of course.' Obey the law, do your duty, play the game, be a man, and do the day's work—that is the moral which underlies the *Jungle Book* and *Captains Courageous* and *Kim* and the rest of that noble company. Perhaps it is in 'If' that this ethical code is most resonantly exprest; and probably there are few lyrics more distasteful than this to the Young Intellectuals, be the same more or less. As Mr. Paul Elmer More pointed out a few years ago, Mr. Kipling's sense of order and obedience 'rises into a pure feeling for righteousness that reminds one of the Hebrew prophets'—and yet he never goes up into the pulpit to inculcate a moral. If there are sermons in his songs and in his stories, the reader, young or old, must find them for himself.

Kipling is the only man of letters in our time who is equally esteemed as a singer of ballads in rime and as a teller of tales in prose. He is the only man of letters in our time who is revered by young and old alike. Only the mature, who have come to an understanding of life, can fully appreciate *Kim*, that prose Odyssey of Hindustan; and only they have experience enough to relish the rich savor of *Puck of Pook's Hill* and *Rewards and Fairies*, that incomparable pair of volumes in which Kipling (as Barrett Wendell put it) 'makes the past of English history live with such implicit learning as is the wonder of historians and such imaginative truth as is paralleled in literature only by the splendidly vagrant chronicle-histories of Shakespeare'. These books, ripe in wisdom, are for the elders; and the *Just So Stories* and the *Jungle Books*, equally beloved by the old, are more particularly for the youngsters. They have taken their place by the side of *Alice in Wonderland* and *Uncle Remus* as permanent additions to the books not to be denied to youth. If a boy or girl is not made familiar with them at the age when they are most appealing, he has been deprived of his heritage.

That Kipling is one of the supreme masters of the short story is, I take it, admitted by all who have dealt with the theory and the practise of that form of fiction. There are some, and they are not a few, who are tempted at times to declare that in some respects at least Kipling is more accomplished than any of his rivals in his art. And who are these rivals? Who are the short-story writers worthy to be set by his side? They are not many, a scant half-dozen at the most—Hawthorne and Poe, at the beginning of the list, Maupassant and Stevenson at the end. It is futile to attempt to set these makers of myths in the serried order of their achievement. Beyond all question, each of them is a master in his own fashion and in spite of his limitations. But it would not be presumptuous to maintain that Kipling, whatever his ultimate rank among them, is obviously more various and more multifarious. He has more masterpieces to his credit than any of these competitors; and these masterpieces of his are of more different kinds.

Hawthorne (and I yield to no one in acknowledging the value of his best work), has less than half-a-score of truly great short stories; and a few of his other tales are rather pallid apologs. Poe, in his turn, is purely intellectual; as Lowell said: 'the heart is squeezed out by the mind'; he lacks 'the ruddy drop of human blood'; and his marvelous narratives are not peopled by men and women like unto ourselves. Stevenson has left us one indisputable and (in its kind) incomparable short story, 'Markheim', in which we behold the insatiable artist (which Stevenson was) working in partnership with the Shorter Catechist (which Stevenson was also); but in most of his other short stories even his most ardent admirers admit a lack of ease and an ill-concealed artificiality; these tales are 'not inevitable enough'. Remains Maupassant, whose ease is almost his most evident quality; but he is—in his earlier short stories at least—unsympathetic, devoid of sentiment, hard and heartless. That most perfect specimen of narration, 'The Necklace', is cruel in its frigidity, not to call it inhuman. It is true that in his later novels Maupassant softened into sentiment, and lost that cold contempt for all mankind which is paraded in his earlier and briefer tales.

Kipling has a far wider range than any of his rivals. His masterpieces —and they are at least as many as any of these competitors can boast —are of many different kinds. Take 'Without Benefit of Clergy' (that simplest of stories, with a pathos as unforced as it is poignant), and set this by the side of 'An Habitation Enforced' (that lovely idyll of married life, exquisite in its unparaded sentiment). Take 'The Man Who Was' (that brief tenth act in an untold tragedy), and set this over against 'The Brushwood Boy' (one of the most perfect of love stories, as it is one of the most original in its invention and in its imagination). Compare 'They' (with its sheer poetry and its mystic penumbra) with the robust 'Courting of Dinah Shadd'. Once more, compare 'The Children of the Zodiac' (that cosmic fantasy, which is intensely and eternally human, altho' it seems to transcend time and space)—compare this with 'The Centurion on the Wall' (that martial tale which marches straight forward, keeping step boldly with the blare of the trumpets). Nor must we overlook the kaleidoscopic color of 'Krishna Mulvaney' or the rapid-fire action of any one of a dozen other adventures of *Soldiers Three*.

'When an author is yet living,' said Dr. Johnson, 'we estimate his powers by his worst performance, and when he is dead, by his best.' This seems to me an overstatement. I doubt if we really estimate a living writer by his worst performance; but we tend to judge him by his latest. Here, in *Debits and Credits*, we have Kipling's latest performance; and what is our estimate of it? Of course, the fourteen tales it contains are not equal in merit—a statement which might be made of any volume by any other writer of short stories. That is to say, some of these narratives are better than others; and it must be noted at once that several of them are very good indeed, even if no one of them is as indisputably supreme as 'They' or 'The Brushwood Boy' or 'An Habitation Enforced'. It needs to be said also that, taken as a whole, the collection is completely characteristic. There are here three or four tales that no other living writer could equal.

In his *Philosophy of Art*, Taine tells us that there is a certain quality in the work of a great artist which we may adorn with beautiful names:

we may call it genius or inspiration, which is right and proper; but if you wish to define it precisely, you must always verify therein the vivid, spontaneous suggestion which groups together the train of accessory ideas, and which masters them, fashions them, metamorphoses them and employs them in order to make itself manifest.

And in nearly every one of these new stories Kipling has given us this 'vivid, spontaneous suggestion'. He here delights us with the old mastery; he charms us with the old craftsmanship; and he moves us with the old magic. And it is magic, this essential quality of his. There is no other word for it—a magic made up of insight and understanding and imagination.

Two of the fourteen tales are, as it were, omitted chapters from *Stalky & Co.*, that intimate study of a boy's school, in which Kipling recovers the days of his youth, just as Mark Twain did when he wrote *Tom Sawyer*. Two others, 'Enemies to Each Other' and 'On the Gate', are fantasies not unrelated to 'The Children of the Zodiac'. A fifth, 'The Eye of Allah', is a resuscitation of the remote past with Roger Bacon for the central figure—a resuscitation which might easily have been included in *Puck of Pook's Hill* or *Rewards and Fairies*, and which is worthy of that companionship. A sixth, 'The Bull that Thought', is to be set by the side of 'The Maltese Cat', in that this new tale pictures for us a bull-fight as the earlier story presents a polo match; and the adventure of the thinking bull is richer in content and deeper in meaning than the exciting narrative wherein the quick-witted polo pony is the protagonist.

Half-a-dozen of the other tales have to do with the War, as the War was seen in retrospect by certain of the surviving combatants; and I know no other visions of actual fighting more illuminating than two or three of these, in which we are made to see the ghastly horrors of the days in the trenches and also to catch a glimpse—and often more than a glimpse—of the joy of the combat, the fleeting ecstasy of battle, the glorious hour of strife, which seemed for the moment to make fighting eternally worth while. One of the sequels to war's alarms, 'The Gardener', is a beautiful tale beautifully told; and in its spirit it is akin to 'They', as it has something of the same misty mysticism at the end, which leaves us wondering exactly what had happened and who the mysterious gardener might be. But those will pierce the veil who recall the memorable meeting of Mary Magdalen with 'one in the likeness of a gardener'.

In two of the tales, 'The Wish-House' and 'The Madonna of the Trenches', both stories of love enduring through life and even after death, I have been surprised to find a new note—the note of passion, of deep and dominating passion, not debased by the puerile salacity which is paraded in certain contemporary fictions falsely acclaimed as 'frank' and 'daring'. In these two stories of Kipling there is no leering lewdness, there is true passion, presented with manly reticence, but burning none the less and all the more fiercely because it is an inward fire, which never comes to the surface.

55. Bonamy Dobrée: 'Rudyard Kipling'

1927

Signed article from the *Monthly Criterion*, Vol. VI, pp. 499–515 (December 1927). This is the original article, which Professor Dobrée later rewrote and expanded in his *The Lamp and the Lute* (1929 and 1964)—and completely superseded by his admirable study *Rudyard Kipling : Realist and Fabulist* (1967).

Bonamy Dobrée, O.B.E. (1891–   ) was Professor of English Literature at Cairo 1926–9, and at the University of Leeds 1936–55. He is a leading authority on the literature of the Restoration and Augustan periods, and contributed the volume on *English Literature in The Early Eighteenth Century, 1700–1740* to the Oxford History of English Literature in 1959. He has written reviews and literary criticism for the *Criterion, Spectator, TLS* and other periodicals.

Mr. Kipling has so scrupulously winnowed the elements of his art, that his candour has deceived many into thinking him too near a simpleton to yield much that can be of use to them in exploring life. They are inclined to take too literally Mr. Max Beerbohm's vision of him dancing a jig with Britannia upon Hampstead Heath, and have thought her as much belittled by his hat, as he is made ridiculous by her helmet. Really it is only the high finish of his art which has made him seem to lack subtlety, for he does not display the workings of his mind, his doubts, and his gropings. He drives his thought to a conclusion, and only when it has reached the force of an intuition, of an assent in Newman's sense of the word, does he clothe it in symbols.

He is, perhaps, romantic by impulse, but he tries his romance seven times in the fire of actuality, and brings it to crystal clearness. Romance, for him, does not lie in yearning, but in fruition; it is not a vague beacon floating in a distant void. It may be

> A veil to draw 'twixt God his Law
> And Man's infirmity:

342

but that throwing up of the sponge, that beglamouring of facts, is not
really to his taste. What is more to the credit of romance is that it
brings up the nine-fifteen. Yet, if that were the end, romance itself
would be a trivial thing to make such a pother about, even if bringing
up the nine-fifteen stands also for building cities and conquering
continents. For even these things are not, in themselves, of vast worth
to Mr. Kipling; they are of value only in so far as they are the mechanism which brings action into play. For action is, on this scheme of
things, of the first and final importance, since nothing else can make
real for man what is no more than a dream in the mind of Brahma.
So small a matter as

> . . . the everyday affair of business, meals and clothing
> Builds a Bulkhead 'twixt Despair and the Edge of Nothing,

for man is playing a Great Game of 'To be or not to be' in the face of
an indifferent universe. Man must work, since, 'For the pain of the
soul there is, outside God's Grace, but one drug; and that is a man's
craft, learning, or other helpful motion of his own mind,' and by the
last Mr. Kipling means action, because it is only through doing that
thought is brought to completion.

The story, 'The Children of the Zodiac', seems most wholly to
express Mr. Kipling's view; and there we read 'You cannot pull a
plough,' said the bull, with a little touch of contempt. 'I can, and that
prevents me thinking of the Scorpion,' namely death. But that is not
running away from thinking, it is identifying oneself with the material
of thought. But even so the problem is not so clear and shallow as to
be solved so easily, for disillusion lurks even behind useful action, and
the void may still be there:

> As Adam was a-working outside of Eden-Wall,
> He used the Earth, he used the Seas, he used the Air and all;
> And out of black disaster
> He arose to be the master
> Of Earth and Water, Air and Fire,
> But never reached his heart's desire!
> (The Apple Tree's cut down!)

It is plain that this disillusion must also be warded off, otherwise work
will not take place; and the Children of the Zodiac did not succeed
in warding it off until they had learnt to laugh. Therefore Mr. Kipling
also laughs, sometimes to ease his bitterness in this way, but more often
to do more than this, and he laughs, not the Bergsonian laughter of

social adjustment, but the impassioned, defiant laughter of Nietzsche; not the rectifying laughter of comedy, but the healing laughter of farce. Whence 'Brugglesmith', 'The Village that Voted the Earth was Flat', and the immortal, the Puck-like Pyecroft. Man must laugh lest he perish, just as he must work if he is to exist at all.

Yet it must not be thought that by work Mr. Kipling means fuss and hurry; he will have nothing of 'indecent restlessness'. As to the battle of life, 'The God who sees us all die knows that there is far too much of that battle', and the man who created Kim's Lama is not blind to the possible vanity of his own means of defeating emptiness and evading the fear of death. There is a small rift somewhere, and Ganesh in *The Bridge Builders* may after all be right in regarding the toil of men but as 'dirt digging in the dirt'. There must then be something behind action, something which justifies it, and it is with a love of loyalty that Mr. Kipling reinforces his philosophy of action. First of all there is that of man to man, a loyalty born through understanding of a man's work, and the wholeness of his character. But personal loyalty, if infinitely valuable, is also horribly rare, and Mr. Kipling has not too great faith in it; he has come not to hope overmuch of man. 'The raw fact of life,' Pharaoh Akhenaton told him (why did he choose that particularly nauseating, pot-bellied king?), 'is that mankind is just a little lower than the angels, but if you begin by the convention that men are angels, they will assuredly become bigger beasts than ever.' And loyalty is an angelic quality.

This, we see, takes us a long way from the 'personal relation', the establishment of which figures so large in recent literature; and indeed, what distinguishes Mr. Kipling from so many present-day writers, is precisely that he does not attempt to break down man's loneliness, seeing only futility in the balm of the 'personal relation':

> Chase not with undesired largesse
> Of sympathy the heart
> Which, knowing her own bitterness
> Presumes to dwell apart.

That is why, when Mulvaney told him the story of 'The Courting of Dinah Shadd', Mr. Kipling said nothing; he gave him a hand, which can help, but not heal, for at the moment when a man's black hour descends upon him he has to fight it out alone. 'When I woke I saw Mulvaney, the night dew-gemming his moustache, leaning on his rifle at picket, lonely as Prometheus on his rock, with I know not what vultures tearing his liver.'

But since man is thus unavoidably lonely among men, there is another loyalty to serve as a spring of action, and this is a devotion to something each man must conceive of as bigger than himself. Power man has, yet

> It is not given
> For goods or gear,
> But for the Thing,

whatever the Thing may be. Mr. Kipling does not even admit the last infirmity of noble mind, for fame does not count. Thus more than sympathy, admiration and love, go out from him to obscure men with whom 'heroism, failure, doubt, despair, and self-abnegation' are daily matters, and about whom the official reports are silent. His heart is given at once to any person who strives to do a thing well, not for praise, but through sheer love of the craftsman. For him, as for Parolles, self-love is 'the most inhibited sin in the canon', and, after all, 'one must always risk one's life or one's soul, or one's peace—or some little thing'.

Here, already, we see the scale of Mr. Kipling's values. First it is essential to accept the world for what it is, to play the man while the odds are eternally and crushingly against you. It is hopeless to try to alter the world. Even if you are capable of adding to it, if yours is not the appointed time, your work will be sacrificed, as the priest in *Debits and Credits* had to smash his microscope, and the seaman in *Rewards and Fairies* had to abandon his idea of iron ships: the time was not yet. But man must not complain, nor ask for life's handicap to be reduced. 'My right!' Ortheris answered with deep scorn. 'My right! I ain't a recruity to go whining about my rights to this and my rights to that, just as if I couldn't look after myself. My rights! 'Strewth A'mighty! I'm a man.' It is that kind of individuality, that kind of integrity, proud and secure in its own fortress, which constitutes the aristocracy which alone is worth while, which alone can play the Great Game of actuality.

An aristocrat is, for Mr. Kipling, one who, of whatever race or caste or creed, has a full man within him: Ortheris, Tallantire of the frontier district, Mahbub Ali, M'Andrew—a whole host of them—all are aristocrats, as is Hobden the labourer, with his sardonic smile at the changes of landlords, and the unchangeableness of the world. They are aristocrats because they care little for themselves in comparison with what they stand for, because they are generous, and play the Great Game with laughter on their lips, seeking nobody's help, and claiming no reward. 'First a man must suffer, then he must learn his work, and the self-respect that that knowledge brings.' Never mind if he is a failure, a tramp or a drunkard, he may yet be an aristocrat if he keeps himself whole, and does not set an undue value upon his feelings. This band of chosen naturally hates the intriguers of Simla, or the Tomlinsons, who when they die in their houses in Berkeley Square, deserve neither heaven nor hell. It despises the self-styled 'intellectuals' who 'deal with people's insides from the point of view of men who have no stomachs'. It loathes the rabble which whimpers, and the elements which ruin the industrious hive, crying to the workers, 'Come here, you dear downy duck, and tell us all about your feelings.' The mob which denies the loneliness of man is hateful to it, for it has accomplished nothing, and always defiles what it does not understand. Thus Mr. Kipling's Utopia is one where privacy must not be violated, and where men slink away when they find themselves part of a crowd, loathing the claims of 'the People', who can be crueller than kings. Moreover, Mr. Kipling has only contempt for those who would marshal and pigeon-hole mankind, making it nicely tidy and neat; he feels they are ignorant of men, shallow in their analysis of motives, 'since the real reasons which make or break a man are too absurd or too obscene to be reached from outside'. For him 'social reform' is the selfish game of the idle.

And with this aristocratic preference there goes, as so often, a sense of some Divine Ruler, for to whom else is man to dedicate his work? But Mr. Kipling has no especial choice, he is no sectarian, believing that 'when a man has come to the turnstiles of Night, all the creeds in the world seem to him wonderfully alike and colourless'. He asks of a creed only that it shall give a man the virtues he admires. 'I tell you now that the faith that takes care that every man shall keep faith, even though he may save his soul by breaking faith, is the faith for a man to believe in.' He has small opinion of Christianity because it has not eliminated the fear of the end, so that the Western world 'clings to the dread of death more closely than to the hope of life'. However, he is very tender to other people's beliefs, for men, after all, need a respite. 'Those that faced the figures prayed more zealously than the others, so I judged that their troubles were the greater.' For when all has been written and acted, his own faith also may be subject to disillusion; with perfect consistency he can urge us 'be gentle while the heathen pray to Buddha at Kamakura'.

This, oddly enough, brings us back to Hampstead Heath, for once we speak of Mr. Kipling's religion, we speak of the British Empire. Mr. Beerbohm was cruel in his caricature, but also wittier than appears at first sight, for he made Mr. Kipling look a little unhappy at having thus blatantly to parade the lady of his homage. Yet one must agree that Mr. Kipling cannot be dissociated from the British Empire. It would almost seem that his mission was to bind it together in one blood-brotherhood, a purposive masonic lodge, whose business it is to clear the world of shoddy. Nor can he altogether escape the suspicion of being dazzled by it. He is enraptured by the vision of men clean of mind and thew, clear of eye and inward sight, spreading out over the earth, their lands bound by the ships which fly over the sea like shuttles, weaving the clan together. His is no mere picture of red on the map, since Britannia for him is a goddess. Not only is she a goddess by the fact of her being, but in her nature, for she exacts much toil from her votaries, much of the silent endurance, abnegation and loyalty that he loves. The Empire then is to be cherished, not so much because it is in itself an achievement, but because, like old Rome, it is the most superb instrument to enable man to outface the universe, assert himself against vacancy. Since it unifies the impulses needed to do this, it is Mr. Kipling's Catholic Church.

These things being, apparently, the basis of Mr. Kipling's thought (though the Empire is, strictly speaking, only an accident, an expression rather than a necessity), we may now ask ourselves, honestly facing the risk of being impudent and unduly probing, of what impulses this thought is the satisfaction. And at the foundation of his philosophic love of action we are tempted to find that pining for action men often have when, for one reason or another, it is denied them. He sometimes comes near to blaspheming his art, echoing James Thomson's

Singing is sweet, but be sure of this;
Lips only sing when they cannot kiss,

as though the mere act of writing were itself proof of impotence and frustration. This is not a final attitude, but it indicates what may lie behind Mr. Kipling's adoration of perfectly insufferable and not altogether real subalterns, and others who, in various degrees (so long as it is not from offices), handle the affairs of the world.

Yet, ultimately, he is far too good a craftsman, too whole an artist, not to see that God, or whatever other name He may be known by, is to be praised in more ways than the obvious. Nevertheless he now and then reaches out for support to the knowledge that he also is

347

playing the great game, if not of the universe, at least of the world, and is as worthy of a number as Kim, Mahbub Ali, or Hurree Babu:

> Who once hath dealt in the widest game
>   That all of a man can play,
> No later love, no larger fame
>   Will lure him long away.
> As the war-horse smelleth the battle afar,
>   The entered Soul, no less
> He saith: 'Ha! Ha!' where the trumpets are
>   And the thunders of the Press.

Such an attitude permanently held would be much too jejune to produce the real intensity of vision we get from Mr. Kipling; and luckily for us he has at bottom that worship of his own craft he so much admires in others. Addressing his God, his subtilized Jehovah, who judges man by his deeds, he says:

> Who lest all thought of Eden fade
>   Bring'st Eden to the craftsman's brain,
> God-like to muse on his own trade
>   And Man-like stand with God again.

There he is the priest of the Mysterious Will, who causes all things to come in their own time, but one feels he sometimes needs to justify his work to himself. He finds it necessary to make plain that his stories are all parables. Thus:

> When all the world would have a matter hid,
>   Since Truth is seldom friend to any crowd,
> Men write in fable, as old Aesop did,
>   Jesting at that which none will name aloud.
> And this they needs must do, or it will fall
> Unless they please they are not heard at all.

It is plain that art, for Mr. Kipling, is not an escape: it is a precision of bare facts, which his art must make palatable.

Further, since the choice of a goddess does not altogether lie within a man's mental scope, we may seek in Mr. Kipling's impulses the reason for his profound satisfaction in the Empire, his need to assert it. Perhaps the most important of these is his desire to belong to something, a love, not of the 'little platoon', to use Burke's phrase, but of the large regiment. 'It must be pleasant to have a country of one's own to show off,' he remarks. Indeed, his craving for roots makes even the

deck of a P. and O. British soil; British, because he is a citizen of the
Empire, not of England alone, for if it were essential to be the latter,
he would be partly dispossessed. Having spent so many of his early
years in India, he is not wholly of England: indeed India is the place
where he really belongs. When, for instance, in 1913 he visited Cairo,
he wrote:

It is true that the call to prayer, the cadence of some of the street cries, and the
cut of some of the garments differed a little from what I had been brought up
to; but for the rest, the shadow on the dial had turned back twenty degrees for
me, and I found myself saying, as perhaps the dead say when they have recovered
their wits, 'This is my real world again!'

But he is not an Indian, he is an Englishman; therefore, to be an
integral whole, he must at all costs make England and the Empire one.

Mr. Kipling's love of the Empire and his admiration for those
virtues it brings out in men, make him apt to find qualities in Englishmen only, which really exist in all races, and this is part of the deforma-
tion Mr. Kipling the artist has at times undergone at the hands of Mr.
Kipling the man of action, who found his weapon in the press and his
altar in the British Empire. If there had been no daily, or weekly, or
monthly papers he might have remained a priest; but in his middle days
he fell into the encouraging hands of W. E. Henley, then, in 1893,
editing the *National Observer*. Though this gave his talent scope, it
meant that instead of speaking only to those who would understand
his very special philosophy, he began to proselytise, and shout too loud
into the deaf ear of Demos. His work suffered by the accidents of time
and circumstance, by the mischance that he was born into an age of
magazines and newspapers, when the listeners are the many, and not
the aristocrats to whom he truly belongs. It took him, with his slightly
unhappy expression, on to Hampstead Heath. A change came over
his work, and the echo of the voice of Henley 'throwing a chest'
(another man of action to whom action was denied) is ever and anon
heard between the lines. In 1893 he published *Many Inventions*, a rich,
varied and mature work, which might be singled out as the best
volume of his stories, unless *Life's Handicap* be preferred: but from the
year he joined Henley his writing took on a more obvious and didactic
hue, and we have *The Day's Work*, such parables as 'A Walking
Delegate', that tale of perfectly dutiful horses kicking the Trades-
Union-Agitator horse, and later, the terrible jingo outbursts of the
Boer War. In 1887, or thereabouts, he was writing those delightful

Letters of Marque, with their profound tolerance of India: in 1907 he wrote for the *Morning Post* those clangorous *Letters to the Family*. The man who had in earlier days remarked: 'He began to understand why Boondi does not encourage Englishmen,' could now complain 'Yet South Africa could even now be made a tourists' place—if only the railroad and steamship lines had faith.' That is shocking. It is true that he had always loved the Empire, but he had not loved it in the Hampstead Heath way; and surely it was the exigencies of this later didactic journalism which turned him from a priest into an advance-booking agent, and forced him into a too extravagant statement of 'British' qualities. He does not, however, in all his work feel that these are the monopoly of the British, for he awards his due to the Frenchman and the Sikh, and even to the Bengali, when he really gives rein to his profound instincts, and forgets the thunders of the press. Therefore the distortion does not matter in the long run, for time and again he gives us things of a breadth and a peculiar grip we get from no other writer of his generation.

The accidents, then, of Mr. Kipling's attitude may be dismissed, to allow us to return to his intuitions, and proceed to the next step in our analysis, namely a consideration of what symbols he has chosen to clothe his intuitions with. He has usually chosen men and women to body forth his notions, and his people, as is always the case in really creative art, are symbols of something else. They are not merely vehicles for an idle tale. Where he has chosen other material, as in 'The Mother Hive' or 'The Ship that Found Herself', he has failed, as anyone is bound to do. An apologue always smacks of the schoolroom, and it is worth noticing that these stories belong to his most didactic period. There he is not quite at his ease, his assent is a little forced, but where his intuition was whole, as in *Kim*, in which the artist conquers the moralist and buries him deep underground, he is nothing short of superb: his symbols clothe his intuition so that we take it for flesh and blood. That is, we work from life to the thought that created it, and not from the thought to life, as we do with lesser artists, who have ideas they wish to impose on life. Mr. Kipling's failures occur either when his shallower, demagogue nature takes charge, and we are conscious of didacticism; or where the intuition is uncompleted. It is uncompleted in two sets of circumstances: the first where women are concerned, whence Mrs. Hauksbee, Mrs. Gadsby and others, where the symbols are vulgar because the intuition is false (there is a reservation to be made in the case of the woman in

the last story in *Debits and Credits*); the second is in the mysterious
world of unreality which he feels about him, but which he has not
resolved within himself: hence such failures—one must here defy
popular opinion—as 'They' and 'The Brushwood Boy'. There the
symbols are sentimental because the intuition is feeble.

So far an attempt has been made to define Mr. Kipling's philosophic
apparatus; but without delight, a living sympathy, and perhaps an
attitude of praise, there can be no great art in the grand manner, and
these he has abundantly. *A Diversity of Creatures*; that is not only the
title of a book, it is a phrase continually occurring in other of his
volumes, and he often thanks God for the variety of His beings. He is
an apt illustration of those who claim that only by adoring what is can
one add to life. He revels in men so long as they are positive, since it is
only by his deeds that a man can exist. Also, with a generous sensuality
which rejects no physical sensation, he loves the 'good brown earth',
especially the smells that it produces, West or East. With all these likes
and keen senses, this recognition of adventures in life and his feeling
for romance in works, his zestful following of men on their occasions
lawful and unlawful, he has God's plenty within him.

Thus it is that his best symbols also have God's plenty within them.
It is noticeable that they are not those of Tchekov, say, or Henry
James, since different symbols correspond to different intuitions, and
his are not theirs. Mr. Kipling's live close to the ground, and he has
frequented the more primitive sort of men because 'all the earth is full
of tales to him who listens and does not drive away the poor from his
door. The poor are the best of tale-tellers, for they must lay their ear
to the ground every night.' He met a hundred men on the road to
Delhi, and they were all his brothers, since they were close to the earth,
that is, to the actuality that can be handled. There were the people in
Kim, there were Peachey Carnehan and Daniel Dravot ('The Man
Who Would Be King'); there were forgotten toilers in out-stations;
and above all there were Mulvaney, Ortheris, and Learoyd. Nor must
it pass unnoticed that all his three soldiers had trodden paths of bitterness, and were at times subject to an overwhelming sorrow akin to
madness, the sorrow of disillusion. They are of value as symbols
precisely because they have outfaced much. They were none of them
obviously successful, for Mr. Kipling despises success except that
which consists in keeping one's soul intact. Whence his sympathy for
those who are broken because they are too positive, such as the sometime Fellow of an Oxford college who had passed 'outside the pale',

for the lighthouse man who went mad from the infernal streakiness of the tides, and even for Love o' Women. In such cases, where human beings seem wholly to live the life of the symbol, to exist as a quality, Mr. Kipling is content that men, himself included, should be no more than part of the earth; he is happy to be their interpreter, and give them their place as players of the Great Game.

If, at this point, we try to mark what it is that most distinguishes Mr. Kipling from the other writers to be treated of in this enquiry, we find that he shares with most the despondency of the day, but not its optimism as regards panaceas, and that his delight in the actuality of men, their proven virtues, gives him values instead of vague hopes. In his metaphysical scepticism, his belief in the void which surrounds existence, he is a child of his time, as modern as any of our literary nihilists who see, in Mr. Housman's phrase that, 'when men think they fasten their hands upon their hearts'. It is safe to say that at no modern period has the world seemed so empty a thing, the universe so indifferent, our values so factitious: and as we look back upon the centuries we can see that this attitude has been fatefully coming upon us. Yet, though Mr. Kipling manifests this attitude, he differs from his contemporaries, and it is because of his difference that he already seems to survive them. He is more enduring because something of the past three centuries clings to him.

For the Elizabethans and Jacobeans life gained its glamour largely from its nearness to the plague-pit; its values were determined and heightened by the vigorously expressed dogmas of a Church, which, for pulpit purposes at least, believed in hell; the metaphysical void was filled by the sense that life was given to man as a discipline and an adventure: this is still part of Mr. Kipling's belief. Indeed, if one were to have to choose one man from whom he descends rather than from another, one would say it was Jeremy Taylor. In *Holy Dying* we read:

Softness is for slaves and beasts, for minstrels, and useless persons, for such who cannot ascend higher than the state of a fair ox, or a servant entertained for vainer offices: but the man that designs his son for noble employments, to honours and to triumphs, to consular dignities and presidencies of councils, loves to see him pale with study, or panting with labour, hardened with sufferance, or eminent by dangers. And so God dresses us for heaven.

And in *Letters of Travel*:

I wonder sometimes whether any eminent novelist, philosopher, dramatist, or divine of today has to exercise half the pure imagination, not to mention insight, endurance and self-restraint, which is accepted without comment in what is called 'the material exploitation' of a new country. Take only the question of creating a new city at the juncture of two lines—all three in the air. The mere drama of it, the play of the human virtues, would fill a book. And when the work is finished, when the city is, when the new lines embrace a new belt of farms, and the tide of wheat has rolled North another unexpected degree, the men who did it break off, without compliments, to repeat the joke elsewhere.

The mind is the same, the matter only the difference of the centuries.

Then, with the advance of science and the retreat of the plague, man grew less concerned with himself, and more interested in the outer world, its marvels, its emerging order. Coupled with a somewhat flabby Deism, believing at the most in only a lukewarm hell, was the attitude of mind, best typified by John Evelyn, who, like Mr. Kipling, found naught common on the earth. Here Mr. Kipling largely stays, and with the introspective movement ushered in by Rousseau, with the hysterical subjective idealists whose only reality is their emotion, he will have nothing to do, and it is probable that Proust seems a dreary waste to him. He cannot away with men and women intent upon saving their souls, or who believe, even, that they have souls to save: it is typical that he should have described a man he disliked as 'fearing physical pain as some men fear sin'.

Yet the solipsist attitude still further weakened the idea of future punishment, and we are not surprised that in the century and a half which saw its development, an English Chief Justice, Lord Westbury, should, in a famous judgment, have 'dismissed Hell with costs, and taken away from orthodox members of the Church of England their last hope of everlasting damnation'. This was to have its effect, but habits of impulse do not change so fast, and if there was to be no hell, there was still to be service to God, and of this sense again Mr. Kipling has something, since, for the meaning alone, it might have been Browning who wrote:

> One instant's toil to Thee denied
> Stands all eternity's offence.

But soon it was realized that if there was to be no hell, the only heaven would have to be on earth, and if social reform began at least as early as Shaftesbury, not to go back to Shelburne, it is chiefly characteristic of the Edwardian period. Mr. Kipling, however, who cannot bear the flaccidity of social reform, still has a hope of hell, and agreeing that this world is sufficient for man, he places his hell upon earth. Thus he cannot accept our modern Utopias, so clean and hygienic, so free from temptation and sin and suffering—except, for him, the suffering of being forever in a crowd. Utopian perfection would be insipid and loathsome, and we may surmise that the final reason why the British Empire satisfies him is that it can contain both heaven and hell, at least as much as is good for any man.

Apart from delight, an important reservation, it is doubtful if the real value of any writer is apparent to his close contemporaries: his equals in age are more likely to seize upon what they already share with him, and with mankind's aversion for what is new in ideas, will reject what the next generation eagerly clutches at. As far as can be judged, the elements in Mr. Kipling's writings which have won him popularity, are the least important, the most ephemeral. It will only be possible to give him his rightful place when the political heats of his day have become coldly historical. But to us, the successive generation, he has a value that may well be permanent, apart from his language, which in itself deserves to live. He has indicated an attitude towards life, which to us, groping for a solid basis, may serve, if not for that basis itself, at least as a point of disagreement. He deals, after all, with the enduring problems of humanity, the problems out of which all religion, all real poetry, must arise. Moreover, he provides a solution, which those of his own cast of mind—and they are many, though most may be unaware of it—will greet with satisfaction, and even with that sense of glamour, of invigoration, which it is partly the function of literature to give.

56. R. Ellis Roberts: 'Rudyard Kipling'

1928

Signed article from the *Empire Review*, Vol. XLVII, pp. 184–93 (March 1928). Also collected in the author's *Reading for Pleasure, and Other Essays* (1928).

Richard Ellis Roberts (1879–1953), well-known critic and reviewer of the twenties and thirties.

We all know that Mr. Kipling began his career as a journalist. Some critics have realized that he was that rare thing, a great journalist. But I do not think anyone has realized how extraordinarily he has retained the great journalist's attitude to life. That attitude, like all attitudes of any value or truth, involves an apparent contradiction and a balance of opposites. The great journalist knows that almost nothing is really important, and that almost anything is news. He knows that just as a man forgets the contents of yesterday's paper, so the world forgets the events of last century; and he knows that something is always remembered, and that it is his business, if he wishes to be a good journalist, to learn how to 'spot' the events and the people which will be remembered. A good journalist always keeps his sense of proportion, and always appears to lose it; he must write of all news as if it were the most vital and exciting thing that has ever happened, and yet know in his heart that its interest is evanescent. Yet he must never be indifferent (cynicism is not indifference)—he must be excited about the transient; and the more deeply he believes that everything is transient the more eagerly and simply will he welcome the eternal news if it ever comes his way. The curse of the journalist is over-emphasis, adopted to impress both himself and others; his blessing is that he never suffers, as do the rest of the world, from that dreadful boredom which is the beginning of spiritual death. At the first symptom of accidie in his soul, the good journalist will start to analyse it; and he will make fresh news, late-press news out of the mere monotony of a repetitive universe.

How well Mr. Kipling has retained the great journalist's mind can be seen in the address he made when he was presented with the Gold Medal of the Royal Society of Literature in 1926. He spoke about the art of the novelist and literary fame:

All men are interested in reflections of themselves and their surroundings, whether in the pure heart of a crystal or in a muddy pool, and nearly every writer who supplies a reflection secretly desires a share of immortality for the pains he has been at in holding up the mirror—which also reflects himself. He may get his desire. Quite a dozen writers have achieved immortality in the past 2,500 years. From a bookmaker's—a real bookmaker's—point of view the odds are not attractive, but fiction is built on fiction. That is where it differs from the other arts.

Most of the arts admit the truth that it is not expedient to tell everyone everything. Fiction recognizes no such bar. There is no human emotion or mood which it is forbidden to assault—there is no canon of reserve or pity that need be respected—in fiction. Why should there be? The man, after all, is not telling the truth. He is only writing fiction. While he writes it, his world will extract from it just so much truth or pleasure as it requires for the moment. In time a little more, or much less, of the residue may be carried forward to the general account, and there, perhaps, diverted to ends of which the writer never dreamed.

Take a well-known instance. A man of overwhelming intellect and power goes scourged through life between the dread of insanity and the wrath of his own soul warring with a brutal age. He exhausts mind, heart, and brain in that battle; he consumes himself and perishes in utter desolation. Out of all his agony remains one little book, his dreadful testament against his fellow-kind, which today serves as a pleasant tale for the young under the title of *Gulliver's Travels*. That, and a faint recollection of some baby-talk in some love-letters, is as much as the world has chosen to retain of Jonathan Swift, Master of Irony. Think of it! It is like turning down the glare of a volcano to light a child to bed.

Mr. Kipling exhibits the traits of the great journalist which have served to make him the most popular, the most widely-read, the best-known of all living English authors who are also ranked high by the critics of literature. It is an odd accusation to make against the man who astonished us in the nineties by the *Barrack Room Ballads*, the *Plain Tales from the Hills*, and the collection of army and Indian stories —but I accuse Mr. Kipling, first, of modesty. All good journalists must be modest—they must believe, that is, that what they have to say, what they write about, is more important than themselves. There were many reasons for Mr. Kipling's extreme success; but it was really his modesty, in that age, which was mainly responsible.

He began to write at a time when authors all over Europe were bitten with the heresy of art for art's sake—a doctrine which soon resolves itself into art for the artist's sake. Two great schools had given support to this thesis. There was the aesthetic school, of which the head in England was not Wilde but Walter Pater, who found almost all the interest of their material in its effect on the personality of the artist. It was his nature, his temperament, his moods, his opinions which were of supreme importance: the world of experience only had such value as was given it by the artist's reactions and reflections. Secondly, there was the school—to which in a sense much of Mr. Kipling's earlier work in prose belonged—that followed the teachings of the great French naturalists. Zola, the Goncourts, Maupassant, the early Huysmans professed that the art of the novelist was the art of objective recording; and these men forgot that objectivity was in itself a subjective thing—or, in the modern cant, that extroversion is only a very limited kind of introversion—and that, could he do it, the novelist who did not select at all was, by his very refusal to select, exercising a choice as personal and arbitrary as the most eclectic writer. Both schools, then, attached an undue value to the will and the judgment of the novelist. Now Mr. Kipling, who began writing from a mind exceptionally well-stored from boyhood with many kinds of literature was, except in the matter of style, entirely free from literary *snobisme*. It is the secret of his popularity with men who care little for other modern books (except Mark Twain's, also very free from this weakness), engineers, travellers, businessmen, sailors, and others; and it is the reason why critics who can divest themselves of the fallacy that literature and the other arts are admittedly more important than any other avocations find Mr. Kipling's work some of the most tonic and delightful of our time.

In reading the bulk of Mr. Kipling's work in verse or prose two impressions are immediate and remain constant. The author is avidly curious of all aspects of life, and he has the power to see in any person or incident that unique value which does properly belong to it. In method and superficial manner his debt to Maupassant is evident in his early stories; but he has not Maupassant's deep-seated infidelity. Maupassant could be at times a little sentimental and slightly romantic; but we never believe in his romance nor his sentimentalism as we do in his cynicism and his realism. For Kipling the world of Mrs. Hauksbee, of the people in 'False Dawn', of the Gadsbys is as real as he makes it for us; but it is not more real than the world of 'Wee Willie Winkie', of 'The Brushwood Boy', and of 'They'. Kipling's place as an imaginative reporter is a greater than Maupassant's; no author since Robert

Browning has had quite so great an inquisitiveness into different kinds
of life, quite so great a power of finding out the facts, or quite such a
genius for telling us about the things he discovers. The early critics were
so charmed or terrified by the young Kipling's diabolical cleverness,
by his smartness, his air of cocksureness that they ignored his plain
traditionalism. Really, as I said, Mr. Kipling is a modest author. He
had, and still has at times, a cocksure, positive manner; but actually he
is much less arrogant than such an author as Stevenson. For Mr.
Kipling is cocksure not about what he thinks, nor what he believes,
but about what he has been told. He annoys many people precisely
because of the breadth of his interest, and here again he resembles
Browning. Many people who are too mentally and imaginatively
fatigued to read Browning sweep him aside because he makes them
feel small and limited. Now that Mr. Kipling's smartness is not fresh,
his manner no longer unfamiliar, we can ignore them and we find, if
we read his work sympathetically, that what excites and pleases us is
the author's excitement and pleasure in so many different kinds of
people, in so dazzling a variety of scene as this world affords. We can
apply to Kipling the lines Landor wrote to Robert Browning:

> Since Chaucer was alive and hale,
> No man hath walk'd along our roads with step
> So active, so inquiring eye, or tongue
> So varied in discourse.

This acute criticism of Browning is valuable because it recognizes
the existence of a kind of artist too often confused with another class.
Shakespeare, Dickens, Balzac, Tolstoy are men of great creative
imagination; they do not only observe, they make—their people are
often more real, that is nearer in our judgment to the truth of life, than
the characters we meet. Chaucer, Browning, Kipling are not of that
company. They are men of great invention and observant imagination.
Their figures rarely—this is not true of Pompilia or the Pope in *The
Ring and the Book*—have any reality greater than that of actual life, and
they exist in the circumstances and conditions their creators make for
them, and not outside these conditions. Take one of Mr. Kipling's best
and most heartrending stories *The Record of Badalia Herodsfoot*. Badalia
is dreadfully, poignantly alive. She is solid and three-dimensional. Mr.
Kipling knows her every action, almost her every thought and aspiration, and can show them to us with a precision which not even Maupassant could excel. Badalia, Tom, and Jenny are as vivid as an author
of genius can make them. How the speech of the 'second comforter'

expresses the whole life of a woman in slum-land, if she lives with a blackguard:

Let 'er go an' dig for her bloomin' self. A man wears 'isself out to 'is bones shovin' meat down their mouths, while they sit at 'ome easy all day; an' the very fust time, mark you, you 'as a bit of a difference, an' very proper, too, for man as *is* a man, she ups an' 'as you out into the street, callin' you Gawd knows what all. What's the good o' that, I arx you?

It is the best story of slum-life in English, and it set a fashion both in England and America. Yet, if you turn from these three consummately drawn people, with every action and gesture right, to Charles Dickens' Bill Sikes and Nancy you are aware that you have passed into a higher realm of reality. Kipling's people are the more accurate, the more credible, far less tied to their creator's writing-table; but yet Bill and Nancy are more real. While Badalia, Jenny, and Tom are three-dimensional, Bill Sikes and Nancy and even the bull-terrier are four-dimensional. They exist outside the conditions of the story called *Oliver Twist*. They are free, and not determined. They are more 'types' than Mr. Kipling's people, and yet they are more individuals just because they are more typical. In the last part of Mr. Shaw's *Back to Methuselah*, Pygmalion makes two automata who are as human as human beings of today, though the people of A.D. 31,730 believe they are only dolls. They are consummately made, completely perfect, beautiful, splendid, and are, indeed, alive; they move and speak and feel. Then one of the Ancients touches them, and faintly into them flows the stream of that higher life after which it is man's destiny to strive. There is the difference between the works of the creative imagination and the inventive imagination. The creatures of the creative imagination may be clumsier, more ill-shaped, absurder, less lifelike than those of the inventive imagination; but they belong to a higher realm of reality. This distinction is to be found in all the arts—it is even clearer in painting, perhaps, than in literature—it separates Holbein from Rembrandt, Manet from Van Gogh, Hals from Velasquez, Raphael from Michaelangelo. It is not, let me insist again, that the creatures of the inventive imagination do not live, but they live on another level.

And on that level how alive they are, and what enormous pleasure they can give us. I am sorry for those who cannot appreciate the great company of artists whose work has this proximate reality. Sometimes their sheer craft is so great that their work passes into the other kind—

d'Artagnan sometimes, I think, goes riding with Falstaff, and I believe Mr. Pickwick watched, a little shocked, perhaps, as a certain police stretcher was pushed through the night and dawn to Brook Green, Hammersmith. But I neither understand nor respect the aesthetic Puritanism which will not allow us to enjoy any art which has not an immediate symbolic value. All the world's literatures contain specimens of the pure storyteller's art, and the man who is indifferent to the suggestion of the village fire, or the road to Canterbury, or that low room in which Scheherazade night after night postponed her death-sentence, seems to me to have mistaken his vocation if he writes, or, indeed, concerns himself about literature. There is, I believe, a moral and intellectual cowardice in his attitude. For the supreme storytellers, if they do not give us life as it is lived in the secret places of the heart, as it is in the dreams of the emancipated spirit, give us something inalienable and irreplaceable. They give us the spectacle of life. They give to those of us who cannot, through circumstance or character, have those adventures of the body and mind by the enduring of which man has learnt to desire the adventures of the imagination and the soul, a chance of experiencing what those pioneers experienced. To refuse to listen to them is to try to skip a step in our mental development. The man who despises those hazards which belong to the characters in the art of invention is never fit for those higher and more perilous hazards for the sake of which he pretends to belittle the others. Finally, if we are deaf to the cry of 'Let's pretend!' and 'Once upon a time', we are refusing to listen to an appeal on the response to which depended the very existence of that other art we profess so to value.

Of Mr. Kipling's supremacy of the story of invention I do not think there can be any question. Even Mr. Bennett's virtuosity, even Mr. Wells' intelligence seem a shade too careful, too considered beside Mr. Kipling's cool, unhurried, foolproof ease and skill. It is not possible to say in which tales the normal genius of Mr. Kipling is most obvious; there are too many which are so completely satisfying that they could not be altered without damage. 'The Finest Story in the World' is, perhaps, one in which may be seen at their highest the many and various aspects of his talent; but a critic would choose something less ambitious if he wished to expatiate on the direct force of Mr. Kipling's genius. Wonderful as are *Many Inventions* and *Life's Handicap*, I am not sure that it is not in *The Day's Work* that one can find the stories which display at its height the normal Kipling. 'William the Conqueror' and 'The Tomb of His Ancestors' have a mature mastery which it is difficult to match. If we add to these 'Without Benefit of Clergy' from *Life's Handicap*, 'An Habitation Enforced' from *Actions and Reactions*, we have then, I think, the tales by which an anthologist would represent Kipling's gift at its most characteristic.

'Then there is the other Kipling. Some among the great artists of invention and imagination never seem aware of that other kingdom in which they are not masters. There is no hint in Dumas or in Rubens of a desire for any other world than that which they can control and so magnificently present. They are content that their art should be perfect, unheeding apparently the truth that perfection is something less as well as something more than human. Others, Chaucer is a notable instance, by sheer style carry us into that other country. Browning reached it in some poems by a power of sympathy as strong and more usual than the creative imagination of Keats or of Shelley. In his way, though one would not put him on a level with those poets, a similar event overcomes Mr. Kipling. If I may mis-apply the last sentence of 'The Brushwood Boy', it will stand as Mr. Kipling's question to himself as he records the spectacle of life. 'But—what shall I do when I see you in the light?' His question to himself is 'What shall I do when I see you in my dreams, in the night?' Very early the problem haunted him, often in grim and uncomfortable forms that resulted in stories of horror unequalled outside Poe, but often, especially in his later work, in stories of beauty and longing and a tender reverence which are not the less lovely for his boyishness of spirit. A great journalist, Mr. Kipling knows that there are countries the journalist cannot enter—that is the last lesson of journalism and is very rarely learnt; and so, when he is taken there by his spirit of love and curiosity, he abandons the journalist's method, even if he sometimes keeps the manner. He has stated his own attitude in a poem which is unfairly neglected by those who acclaim him as a party verse-maker, and a defender of the West against the East. Long before, in a brief chapter heading in *The Naulahka*, he had shown that he had, above most men, 'two different sides to his head'. It was no ignorant applauder of the *sahib* who wrote the damaging quatrain:

> Now, it is not good for the Christian's health to hustle the Aryan brown,
> For the Christian riles, and the Aryan smiles, and he weareth the Christian
> down;
> And the end of the fight is a tombstone white, with the name of the late
> deceased,
> And the epitaph drear: 'A fool lies here who tried to hustle the East.'

And it is the same spirit which is alive in that challenging verse:

> I'd not give way for an Emperor,
> I'd hold my road for a King—
> To the Triple Crown I would not bow down—
> But this is a different thing.
> I'll not fight with the Powers of the Air,
> Sentry, pass him through!
> Drawbridge let fall, 'tis the Lord of us all,
> The Dreamer whose dreams come true!

It is that Kipling who wrote a few poems of exquisite loveliness, certain stories of the beyond, and those strange tales of a further reality which force us to reconsider a classification which puts Kipling with those authors for whom the visible world and its inhabitants most supremely exist. 'The Brushwood Boy', 'The Miracle of Puran Bhagat'; most of *Kim*, 'Wireless', 'In the Same Boat', 'The Finest Story in the World', and 'They'—all these stories take me, at least, into the fourth dimension; so does most of the two *Jungle Books*, and at least one of Mr. Kipling's stupendous comedies. 'The Village that Voted the Earth was Flat', though it has in it a rather detestable taint of cruelty, is comedy of a kind which has not been written since Dickens. It has obvious affinities with that side of Mr. Wells' genius which gave us *Kipps* and *Mr. Polly*; it might be compared to some of Mr. Bennett's fantastic effects, but it has an unearthliness, a proper Aristophanic Rabelaisian quality which we cannot find in any other modern author, and only this time in Mr. Kipling. There is not a little of Mr. Kipling's work which shows how well acquainted he is with the men and manners of past time. In *Rewards and Fairies*, in *Puck of Pook's Hill*, I feel not that he has read about the remote days of the Roman occupation, nor of the days of Elizabeth, but that he has been there and comes back to tell us of them. So in 'The Eye of Allah' he writes with an ease which Miss Waddell might envy of the lore and the science of the Middle Ages. He is a supreme interviewer, for he asks his questions with that degree of sympathetic imagination which makes an answer inevitably right. And this gift which in his youth he applied chiefly to the men and women of today he has in later days exercised on the men and women of the past. In 'The Eye of Allah' the talk of the monks about medicine and science and art has a tang that brings the men back to their cloisters; and the final speech of the Abbot has, in brief, the same wry wisdom which Mr. Shaw found in the mediaeval scholastics who condemned St. Joan. In the same terms, for the same reason, the Abbot smashes the microscope and pronounces it idolatry:

He unscrewed the metal cylinder, laid it on the table, and with the dagger's hilt smashed some crystal to sparkling dust which he swept into a scooped hand and cast behind the hearth.

'It would seem,' he said, 'the choice lies between two sins. To deny the world a Light which is under our hand, or to enlighten the world before her time. What you have seen, I saw long since among the physicians of Cairo. And I know what doctrine they drew from it. Hast *thou* dreamed, Thomas? I also— with fuller knowledge. But this birth, my sons, is untimely. It will be but the mother of more death, more torture, more division, and greater darkness in this dark age. Therefore, I, who know both my world and the Church, take this Choice on my conscience. Go! It is finished.'

He thrust the wooden part of the compasses deep among the beech logs till all was burned.

But it is not this story which is the gem of his last volume. The primacy rests with 'the tale of 1916' called 'On the Gate'. It is a tale of the invasion of heaven by those who fell on the field of battle. All the characters are supernatural beings, or the souls of the great dead now in paradise, or the souls of the recently slain. I know no modern story in any language, not even in Russian, in which sacred and deeply moving things are handled at once with such daring and such reverence. I know no story in which Mr. Kipling's deep underlying pity, so often obscured by his cleverness of manner, is so well employed. The guardians of the gate are overworked and call in others to help against the angels of the pit who strive for the souls of the dead at the very bar of heaven. The extra pickets include Joan of Arc, Charles Bradlaugh, John Bunyan, John Calvin, Judas Iscariot, and William Shakespeare. Only a long quotation can do justice to the force and vision of the great scene of struggle:

[quotes *Debits and Credits*, p. 350, line 13, to p. 351, line 27—'Meantime, a sunken eyed Scots officer' to 'and compared notes']

I suppose the conventionally orthodox may be disturbed at Mr. Kipling's vision of the other world: it is not the mythology of the Middle Ages, for here Judas is out of hell and, with a bold return to the eschatology of Origen and the earlier Christian tradition, there is hope for the 'Lower Establishment'. I shall not be surprised if in the years to come this story may not be one of the greatest influences towards popularizing the modern idea of the meaning of eternity. The eternity of hell is not a matter of duration but of intensity; hell can be entered in this life, and its pains are eternal—that is, they have the same blazing quality of reality as the happiness of heaven. They touch all that is permanent and indestructible in the soul of man. And, just because they do that, they cannot be everlasting unless and except any soul insists for ever in remaining obdurate to all the pleadings of God within and without. 'On the Gate' has a wider scope, a deeper beauty than any other of Mr. Kipling's stories of the other world, and in it he justifies all his previous essays, whether in prose or verse, to snatch for a moment the veil from actual things and show to us the reality that alone supports and informs them.

57. Gilbert Frankau on Kipling

1928

Extract from signed article 'Rudyard Kipling' in the *London Magazine*, Vol. LXI, pp. 130–4 (August 1928).

Gilbert Frankau (1884–1952) was a popular novelist of the twenties, best known for *Peter Jackson, Cigar Merchant* (1919). He served in the Royal Field Artillery throughout the First World War, and wrote some of its best poetry in the form of ballads—following, but not imitating Kipling—in *The City of Fear, and Other Poems* (1917). His views on Kipling's work are typical of the general, unacademic appreciation of the period.

... All that I have in me of literary hero-worship was long ago given to the supreme present-day craftsman, and there remains.

I refer to Rudyard Kipling. And when I call him the supreme present-day craftsman, I do so in the perfect awareness that many a tight-lipped highbrow will rise up and disagree. For Rudyard Kipling has never pandered to the highbrow, and therein lies his main power. Nor—and may whatever gods there be bless him for it—has he ever pandered to Woman, who is the burden laid upon the shoulders of every mere novelist, and haunts him in his dreams.

We, the mere novelists of nowadays, are nearly all of us woman-ridden. The female reader with the library subscription (no English women *buy* books) either makes us or mars. And if we depict woman as the average male thinks of her, or talks of her in that which was once called 'the smoking-room', the marring is done swiftly. Thumbs down to the library girl! 'No; I don't think I'll take *that*, thank you, Miss Mudie. Haven't you got the new Marcel Harlene? Only for guaranteed subscribers? Oh dear; now isn't that too bad?'

But Kipling's women are—just women. From Mrs. Bathurst, who had 'It'—the phrase is R.K.'s, written twenty years ago, and whether Elinor Glyn stole 'It' or no is only Elinor Glyn's business—down to Badalia Herodsfoot, who loved the 'curick' and was kicked to death with 'the deadly intelligence born of whisky'. Kipling puts women in their place, whether the kitchen or the drawing-room. And because he does so, the woman who appreciates any but his stories of children is a rarity, to be either married or made a pal of, according to your temperament, as soon as found. Moreover, when Kipling, also the inconsequent, departs from this clear-eyed vision of the 'female of the species', he is apt to stumble, as even the best of craftsmen stumble, by the literary way.

Give Kipling a woman who is nurse, mate, mother, or old wife by the fireside, garrulous about lovers who are dead, and his picture comes away perfect, a marvel of pen-work, not to be denied. Give him woman as the women who read novels like to imagine themselves; that is to say creatures of romance, perpetually adored by perpetual Valentinos in an atmosphere which is one-third amorous excitement, one-third financial extravagance, and the rest sofa cushions—and Kipling jibs at her, as a wise horse jibs at a fence known too high. For Kipling, even as the good horse, knows his limitations. And the craftsman who has not learned that lesson, has not yet learned the rudiments of his craft.

He has other limitations, too, being as human as the rest of us. He can hate—which is no literary virtue. And his opponents' point of view is frequently anathema to him. But on the whole—compare him, let us say, with Galsworthy—his range is as wide as that Empire he loves with a devotion as rare, in these days of shoddy thought, shoddy sentences, and shoddy internationalism, as a poor tailor, or a rich journalist, or a man who won't take legal advantage of his Majesty's income-tax collectors if he gets the chance.

58. Harvey Darton on
'Kipling's Children's Books'

1932

Pp. 309–10 and 314–16 of F. J. Harvey Darton's *Children's Books in England* (1932).

F. J. Harvey Darton (1878–1936), a member of the family and firm that has published children's books for over two centuries, was a literary scholar and bibliographer, besides himself writing books for children. His *Children's Books in England* was the first, and still remains the greatest, work on the subject—though he gave relatively little space to the Golden Age of children's books in the reigns of Victoria and Edward VII. The paragraphs on Kipling show, however, the high and immediate place he took in this branch of Literature.

PAGES 309–10   The school story, however, bore in its very subject the explosive contradiction which was to kill it, or at least to blow away its layer of older readers. That contradiction was that its gradual perfection as a story took away any truth it had in relation to schools. The various kinds of boy, the obvious masters, the school servant, the townee friend or enemy, became all too soon stock actors. There was a mechanization like that of the earlier stage, when Congreve and Sheridan became Foote and Colman, and worse. It had come upon adult literature also, as writers once thought revolutionary perceived in the nineties. *Jude the Obscure*, *Plain Tales from the Hills*, *The Heavenly Twins*, *The Woman who Did*, to jumble a few names, were all books of the Diamond Jubilee decade; and the difference between *Erewhon* (1872) and *Erewhon Revisited* (1901) is more than a difference in the years of one man's life.

But the schoolboy readers, or those who chose books for them, were not conscious of this change in the national intellect. They overlooked the significance of the sub-title of F. Anstey's *Vice Versa* (1882)—

'A Lesson for Fathers'. A great part of that lesson was that many boys are by nature nasty little beasts (in the schoolboy sense), and that life in schools did not stand still, rooted in parental tradition. *Tom Brown* had become a lonely deserted rock in the distance. *Eric* was a kind of immovable moral jelly-fish left behind by the tide. Baines Reed and his imitators were the regular ripples in a smooth sea. No wonder that when *Stalky & Co.* appeared in 1899 there was an outcry. High—the highest —traditions seemed to be flouted and defiled by it. The academy represented—Westward Ho!, which there is reason to believe felt about the book much as King William's College felt about *Eric*—was said by unsympathetic persons not to be a public school at all, but an inferior place for inferior people, who not only spoke the wrong language, as all 'foreigners' do, but had the wrong code of life. It was not easily perceived that the code itself was under scrutiny, and that 'Beetle' was not meant to fit in with Tom Brown and Eric.

The book had in time many repercussions. It was read as general fiction, not only as a story for and about boys. The truth of its picture, in detail, though a matter of interest to persons immediately concerned is not here a question of importance. The significant thing is the absence of the old standards, on the one hand, and the merging of boy-and-man interests on the other. The masters are not stock types, any more than the pupils. Moral issues are largely ignored. The good or evil effect of the events described upon the characters is as irrelevant as the good or evil effect of the book upon the reader. The reader, in fact, was the reader of the average novel; and he was now son as well as father. The 'school story', for any 'young' public over about four-teen years of age, was dead, the public having grown up.

Stalky & Co. in that respect, became a precedent in adult fiction. It was the first of a number of school-life novels for the full-grown reader; later on, perhaps, for the full-blown. In the twentieth century these became common. Retaliation for *Stalky* came and was in turn retaliated upon. H. A. Vachell's *The Hill* (1905), produced in the stock form of a (then) six-shilling novel for the regular circulating library public, provoked the counterblast of Arnold Lunn's *The Harrovians* (1913). Much later, in 1917, Alec Waugh's *The Loom of Youth*, written when its author himself was only just out of school, set a second supply going, until it almost became a distinction for a public school not to have a novel all about itself under a thin disguise.

PAGES 314–16 The upper division of children, then, began in the last quarter of Victoria's reign to experience rapid 'materialistic' growth. Its temper of mind, the sum of little reflections from daily life which grow into an habitual outlook, was perceptibly affected by the mutations of practical progress. Whether there was an equally profound spiritual metabolism at work it is probably not yet time to say. We are still too near the World War and its emetic effects to be confident as to which new thing is symptom, which essence, which mere accident; and in that War many children of the nineties perished.

But in the world of younger children something very like a change of mental outlook was also becoming visible. 'Children', as now distinct from 'boys' and 'girls', were clearly unbabyish: old-fashioned people said more precocious. The simplicities and unquestioned make-believe of folk-lore were no longer quite adequate: even the youngest horizon was not the nursery wall. Rudyard Kipling, though not so devastating in this sphere, is once more a valuable index to what was happening. *Stalky* had been preceded by the two *Jungle Books* (1894 and 1895). Obviously animal study and human sociability for beasts was no new thing. The nurture of Mowgli had a legendary precedent in Roman history, and a vaguely historical one hinted at in the history of Peter the Wild Boy; while the philosophy of Uncle Remus now and then flickers up in gnomic comments on life. But the freshness of style, colour and vision was unmistakable. Even the occasional stridency of emphasis was a novel virtue. As for moral qualities, the Jungle Law was not an unfolding of the wonderful ways of Providence. It was what Life had reached by Social Evolution. Its results were a code of honour based on hard facts, with tooth and claw for its practical sanctions, but with a consciousness of responsibility which the Breed (white bipeds preferably English) felt even more exaltedly. Courage, endurance, observation, good faith, dexterity, physical and mental fitness—all these were transmuted from routine virtues into an eager inspiration. The *Jungle Books* were not romance, not fiction, even; they were young life conscious of itself and its extraordinarily stimulating world. And, while boys, girls and grown-ups could enjoy them, still younger readers could find them, after a little practice in the language (as *Uncle Remus* also had needed), enchanting fairy-tales. The two volumes were and are genuinely a modern children's book, with no predecessors in their kind.

Kim (1901, two years after *Stalky*) was more of a boys' and girls' book, in the new age-ratings, though, as it is the most serenely impersonal of all its author's longer stories, it is for all ages, like *Treasure*

Island and *King Solomon's Mines*. But unlike them, it is almost epic, and it is also instinct with a maturer wisdom. It comes nearest, perhaps, of all modern books in the form of fiction, to an intimacy with the strange association of East and West in India: to the sympathetic sensitiveness of good Imperialism. But it is all about a boy.

Similarly, though not quite so gently, the two 'Puck' books—*Puck of Pook's Hill* (1906) and *Rewards and Fairies* (1910)—come very near to an intimacy with England itself; the England of Bishop Corbet and William Churne of Staffordshire, 'Merlin's Isle of Gramarye'. They are good history and good fiction, both of a kind not common in 1906. Contrast them with the allegorical scraps of history in *The Water-Babies* or with the historical fiction of Harrison Ainsworth, or of Kingsley himself. It is a different voice speaking—it would have to be that, obviously; but it is speaking almost to a different race. The children of the stories, whom one can accept readily enough as true young contemporaries, are not like any that any earlier author had deliberately addressed; though you can conceive that Lewis Carroll really knew their language, and Catherine Sinclair a few words of it, and Stevenson a few more words, and that Shakespeare had heard both Autolycus and Mamilius using it to Puck.

And then in the crude avuncularity of the *Just-So Stories* (1902), the same author is observed to be after all only a conventional 'Victorian' brought up to date, with rather more insight in his jocularity than his grandfathers would usually have shown, but still only pretending to be young, like them: a performer for the occasion.

He is, at any rate, a writer who has influenced adult literature. In children's books he has been both symptomatic and an influence. His effect on the school story has been dealt with. The effect of the *Just-So Stories* has probably been infinitesimal, beyond the crystallizing of some animal attributes. But the other five volumes all contain two elements which have grown strong in the younger juvenile literature of the last thirty years—the qualities of unlimited range for the imagination (very evident in *Kim* and in isolated scenes in the others), and of packed comprehensive thoughtfulness. Mowgli and Kim are thinking hard and vitally throughout; and Puck is thinking for those to whom he is showing all the majesty and littleness of England. The children's story has got right outside its own self, and yet has preserved its identity. The author and the reader are as nearly as possible the same person, but infinitely more capacious—more prehensile and assimilative, perhaps—than ever before. Man and boy, woman and girl, can lawfully try, even hope, to comprehend anything and everything. Nature-study has become a kind of intimate romance, because man, the paragon of animals *is* Nature. The brute creation has been elevated to companionship with flowers and the stars and ourselves. We learn very early now that

> in a moment clouds may be
> Dead, and instinct with deity.

Those words were written before the Diamond Jubilee, nevertheless.

59. 'Stalky' on 'Kipling's India'

1933

Paper read to the Kipling Society on 20 June 1933 by L. C. Dunsterville and published in the *Kipling Journal*, No. 26, pp. 49–55 (June 1933).

Major-General Lionel Charles Dunsterville, C.B., C.S.I., I.A. (1865–1946) was the original of 'Stalky'. Kipling kept up his friendship throughout life, and his belief in Stalky's powers were triumphantly justified during the First World War when he led 'Dunster Force' through Persia. Dunsterville, the author of several books, is an excellent example of the well-read, thoughtful Regular Army Officer of the time—and this Paper is an epitome of the opinions of such a man speaking with the knowledge of one who had served in India throughout Kipling's period. Dunsterville was first President of The Kipling Society (founded 1927), and his paper was read to a gathering of more than 100 members —some of whose remarks are included in the brief note of the Discussion which followed it.

At the outset let me say that I recognise the Society as being divided into two distinct groups: (a) Those who read, enjoy, and admire the words of our great writer; (b) those who, in addition to the above, may justly be regarded as students of Kipling. The latter obviously get a double value out of their membership and might be asked for an enhanced subscription. I hasten to add that I belong to the former category. I feel sure that I can speak for Mr. Kipling, when I say that he likes my lot the better of the two. He doubtless fully appreciates the homage done to his genius by those who study, as well as merely enjoy, his works, but I gather that writers are a little shy of people who ask: 'What did he mean when he wrote so-and-so?' It is possible that if he ever replied—which he does not—to any such question, he would either say (a) 'I often wonder myself,' or (b) 'I meant what I said and there is no paraphrase.' Genius hits off a beautiful line in prose or poetry that is too unique to be capable of paraphrase. The writer knows what he means and can tell you no more. The inner circle of understanding readers also know what he means, but cannot tell the others. This is obviously true of all higher flights of genius.

Mr. Kipling rather looks askance at me in my capacity of Principal Operating Surgeon in the probings of the Kipling Society. He ought not to, because I am very careful and always say, like the dentist, 'Tell me if I'm hurting you'. But he should certainly bestow on me some mark of his favour because I am the only reader of his works who has not written either to him or to the papers to enquire how the 'old Moulmein Pagoda' looked 'eastward to the sea' and I am the only one who knows the answer, which in the author's own words might be, 'I never said it did. You can't read straight.' And now perhaps it is time I begin to tackle the subject announced in my paper.

Kipling, like all powerful writers, has had a great deal of adverse criticism. He has been such an unswerving advocate of what we call, for want of a better word, Imperialism, that every little-englander— and there are lots of them, I'm afraid—naturally rushes to the attack. The noble form of Kipling's Imperialism is distorted by these critics into 'Jingoism', a most foolish and unjust line of attack on the writer of 'Recessional'. He can, however, console himself by quoting his own lines—

> If you can bear to hear the truth you've spoken
> Twisted by knaves to make a trap for fools.

Among many modern critics it is usual to attack his outlook on Indians and Indian problems. His views may have passed muster in the days when his early works were appearing, over forty years ago, but they give us quite a false outlook at the present time. The 'Ballad of East and West' begins: 'Oh, East is East, and West is West, and never the twain shall meet'. But we are told that this is quite wrong; the East and West have met. A few Indian undergraduates at our universities walking arm-in-arm with their English friends proves to the eye the fact of East and West meeting.

So Kipling, you see, was wrong. Although the meeting of East and West is only typified by a hundred or so cases like the above, and the population of India is about 350,000,000, we must allow this fraction of one out of $3\frac{1}{2}$ millions to convince us of this 'meeting' of the races. There is no doubt about their having met, but one can meet in several different ways. You can meet by running up alongside, which sets up no disturbance, or you can meet head on, in the form of a collision. That is just how East and West do meet. Every single idea, every thread of heredity, of the oriental is—and it is right that it should be—diametrically opposed to the occidental mentality and heredity. The Indian way of thinking is perhaps—Mr. Gandhi thinks so—best for the Indians; whether it is best or not doesn't really matter—the fundamental difference is there and nothing will ever alter it. And this unalterable foundation of thought and character is utterly ignored by our politicians when they try to force on India a form of government adapted solely to our purely British and insular evolution. I wonder how the word 'constitution' is translated into Urdu; an assembly of the elders in a Punjab village discussing it would make a splendid theme for our great writer—on the lines of his earlier poems. The fundamental differences of East and West are never to be altered, and none can say that our Western culture is superior to that of the East—no comparison is possible between two opposites. In forcing our ideas on them we do both them and ourselves great harm. Because a certain system has been found to suit us, that is no reason why we should run about the world pressing our great gift on people who think that they are already in possession of something much better. We are like a man suffering from heart disease who says to another suffering from corns: 'This stuff has done my heart a lot of good; you must let me try it on your corns.'

Please do not think that I am trying to make a political speech. All this is merely to prove that the real India has not changed since the days when Kipling wrote, and that nothing can be more literally true than his line: 'Oh, East is East, and West is West, and never the twain shall meet.' I have not had time to analyse all Kipling's prose dealing with India, but have confined myself to his poems alone. He had not served for the best years of his life on the North-West frontier, of India, as many in this room have done. He was only twenty-four years old when he wrote this, and after schooldays most of his time had been spent in the office of a daily paper; yet he pens in these few lines the exact feeling that lies between frontier officers and the marauding tribes from whom they enlist their best soldiers. I could have expressed the same idea inadequately myself in prose, and it would have taken me much paper.

British rule in India may be an 'alien' rule, but India has had alien rulers throughout her long and bloody history. The Aryan rulers were alien invaders from the north, and the Moguls were equally 'alien', both to the Aryans and the aborigines. The only difference between our alien rule and that of our alien predecessors lies in the sense of responsibility which we feel and acknowledge towards the peoples we govern. This sense of responsibility is very hampering in the measures we pass for what we honestly believe to be the betterment of life conditions of the people we rule over. They don't thank us for it, but it is part of our make-up and we can rule in no other way. I can imagine an Indian peasant saying today: 'Not so much talk, please, about doing me good. This generally ends in doing me bad. Please just govern me and leave it at that. I don't want to be done good to. Let me understand that you really do rule me, that your orders are orders, that you mean what you say, and that you mean to be obeyed, and let me get on with my farming. And when you mean what you say, say something that means something. "Constitution" is a word I cannot pronounce and I shall never know what it means, so please don't worry me about it any more, and let's be friends as we used to be before you began all this *tamasha* about reforms.'

This underlying sense of responsibility towards the governed is splendidly expressed in *The White Man's Burden* written 34 years ago. The work we have done in India may have been to the ultimate gain of the Empire and its commercial interests, but the officers of the Executive, both Civil and Military, have reaped nothing, and have desired to reap nothing, of these benefits. I claim for them the honour of working for the love of the work and of the people among whom their lot is cast. When we are dead and gone, and history is written with a true perspective, generations not yet born—both Indians and British, but especially the former—will acclaim the nobility of our share in the evolution of this land of tangled races, religions and languages. If Kipling is out of date in his supposition that East and West can never meet—that is, on the mental and moral plane—then he was wrong when he wrote in 'One Viceroy Resigns':

> You'll never plumb the Oriental mind,
> And if you did it isn't worth the toil.
> Think of a sleek French priest in Canada;
> Divide by twenty half-breeds. Multiply
> By twice the Sphinx's silence. There's your East,
> And you're as wise as ever. So am I.

I can imagine no more lucid exposition of the way in which the Oriental mind works on lines that must forever baffle the Westerner—

that is, the Oriental mind as I knew it during my long service in India. But, like Kipling, I am out of date. I left India thirteen years ago and in those thirteen years the inherited mentality of the Indian family of Orientals has, after 4,000 years of petrifaction, undergone a complete change. At least so we are told. But what exactly will happen when complete freedom is bestowed on this unfortunate country, is prophetically narrated by Kipling in one of his early poems, 'What Happened'.

To sum up the chief points of Kipling's picture of the Indian: he portrays him as a loyal and devoted servant (Gunga Din), a brave soldier in some races, unreasoning and easily aroused by propaganda. Truth and impartiality are foreign to his nature. Sanitation and a regard for the underdog are repugnant to him. Before I leave this subject I must defend myself against a possible charge of blackening the Indian character. In regard to this I can say with truth that there is nothing that may be regarded as insulting to the Indian character in the above remarks that I have not heard from the lips of Indians themselves. And we may credit them with many virtues that we do not possess.

Now let us consider another charge frequently brought against Kipling: the types of the British soldier in *Soldiers Three* and *Barrack-Room Ballads* are untrue to life—there are no soldiers of this type and there never were. When the former was written, about 1887, Kipling was on the staff of the *Civil and Military Gazette* in Lahore, and was acquiring an intimate knowledge of the rank-and-file of the Northumberland Fusiliers and Royal Artillery who formed part of the Mian Mir garrison. We saw each other at intervals, but I never followed to see what he was up to, so I can give you no first-hand information as to what steps he took to ingratiate himself with the men, getting his unequalled insight into the character of the British soldier; it may be taken as a fact that the fiction that resulted from his researches is as near as the human mind can get to fact. As I had at that time more than the average knowledge of the soldier's character, I can speak with authority when I say that Kipling's types are literally men whom I have known in the flesh, and the language my men spoke was nearly word for word the language of his men.

As to the change between the men of those days and today, that is another matter. In those fifty years great changes have taken place; our soldiers were almost illiterate and were altogether a tough lot. Soldiers of today are men of considerable education and the Army attracts a less rough type of man. Crime and drunkenness have diminished, and language has been slightly sweetened. But the change is not really a very considerable one. I do a good deal of travelling by rail (third class and in a tweed suit that has seen better days, so there is little to distinguish me from any other citizen in the humbler walks of life); conversation reveals that 'I did my bit' in the war, so talk flows freely, and really I do not find the vocabulary and mode of expression of the soldier today differing greatly from what you will find in Kipling's early works. The hints on life in those most wise verses, 'The Young British Soldier', are not needed, we are told, by the present type. In this poem the young soldier gets advice from Kipling—a civilian aged about twenty-five—that might have come from an old soldier whose time was up, warning against insidious grog-sellers, the avoidance of cholera and sunstroke, guide to matrimony, treatment of an unfaithful wife, behaviour under fire, how to treat your rifle, what to fire at, how to act when all the odds are against you and when left wounded on the frontier—truly a comprehensive list and full of simple wisdom.

I could continue to quote from *Barrack-Room Ballads*, and repeat *ad nauseam* the question, 'Can it be that things are no longer like this?'— but you yourselves love the poems and many know them better than I do, so I will say no more. I hope at some later date that the Secretary will arrange for a converse to this Paper—a discussion on Kipling's India and the possibility of its having changed; and on the British soldier and his suggested tendency to ultra-refinement of deportment and language, written by an officer of about six years' service, in touch with India and the British soldier of today.

DISCUSSION

When inviting discussion on the lecture the Chairman called attention to its title and suggested that speakers should concentrate on Kipling's India and not be too political, however much they would like to be.

Mr. Bazley pleaded guilty to repeating something he had said at the previous meeting when there had also been some mention of India. General Dunsterville had quoted the poems, but he thought that the strongest testimony to British rule in India was found in 'On the City Wall', where it is shown how, 'year by year, England sends out fresh drafts for the first fighting line, which is officially called the Indian Civil Service; of these men, some die from overwork or worry, while some are killed; if all goes well, the native is praised—'if a failure occurs the Englishmen step forward and take the blame'. This extract presented the same idea as *The White Man's Burden* and these lines from the poem in *Stalky & Co*.

> Set to serve the lands they rule,
> (Save he serve no man may rule),
> Serve and love the lands they rule;
> Seeking praise nor guerdon.

Mr. J. O. Tyler raised the question as to whether or not *The White Man's Burden* had been addressed to the Americans in respect to the Philippine Islands as an exhortation to them to go and do there what the British had done in India, to which an affirmative answer was given.

Mr. J. H. C. Brooking (Founder) thought that, in regard to the question of India and this island, we ought to consider the parallel of Rome and England, which was then a pretty miserable country, and gave it some 500 years of happy rule; but after they left, panic and terror ensued for several hundred years. India now stood in danger; if we let go of her, she would go to the same depths of chaos. The Chairman was in complete agreement with this, and invited the original of 'McTurk' to speak.

Mr. G. C. Beresford began by citing a characteristic of the native villager which he had noticed during a two years' stay. He was always changing from a pro-British to an anti-British attitude, and back again, according as hurt pride or a realisation of the justice and even-handedness of British rule directed. He thought that a point that required emphasis at present was that we didn't (as was said) force our western institutions on the natives; the natives clamoured for them. Vocal India would willingly set aside all traditions; they clamoured for a dose of western medicine and we wouldn't give them a dose. To this point General Dunsterville agreed that 'vocal India does clamour', adding 'that is to say, one voice out of every million clamours!'

60. André Maurois:
'A French View of Kipling'

1934

Paper entitled 'Kipling and His Works from a French Point of View' by André Maurois, read before the Kipling Society on 18 April 1934 and published in the *Kipling Journal*, No. 30, pp. 42–7 (June 1934).

André Maurois, C.B.E., M.C. (1885–1967) [pseudonym of Emile Herzog] was a famous French novelist, essayist and biographer. He is best known in England for his *Ariel* (1923), a biography of Shelley and his *Prophets and Poets* (1935). He also wrote biographies of Byron, Disraeli, George Sand, Victor Hugo, Dumas and others.

He was an Honorary Vice-President of The Kipling Society before whom this paper was read to an audience of over 150, some of whose questions, with his answers are quoted from the Discussion which followed.

When I was asked to speak before you, I replied that my admiration for Kipling was such that I could not refuse, but that unfortunately I was quite unable to lecture in English and that the lecture would be in French. Colonel Bailey said that he thought the lecture would be more generally understood if it was in English; I was not quite so sure about that. I once gave in England a lecture in French which began with a quotation from Shakespeare in English; at the end of the lecture, the Chairman came to me and said: 'Well, your French is much better than I thought; I understood every word you said—except the first sentence!' So, from that day, I decided never to inflict again upon an English audience, a language which is not mine and which is not their own either!

Of course, I cannot possibly pretend to bring before the Kipling Society any new facts about Kipling, but I should like to try and show you, by recalling the memory of my childhood and youth, what Kipling's influence can be on young men who are not Englishmen. It has often been said of Kipling, that he is above all the poet of the British Empire, and it may seem strange at first, that he has given spiritual food to so many young Frenchmen. It is, however, a fact. When I was sixteen or seventeen, I read Kipling's tales of India, and *Kim* affected me more than any other book. I find that this is just as true today on questioning the generation of my sons, who are now 11 and 12. I should like tonight to say what it is that attracts the youth of all countries to Kipling. I think the reason is that they find in his books an heroic idea of life and it is of this idea that I am going to speak to you first—but in French.

[*Translation*] Kipling's heroic conception of life is not the peculiarity either of a country or of one set period of time. Nearly all men who have fought in wars, who have been leaders, who have done something worth doing, have held practically the same view, whether they were fine soldiers in the Trojan War, or fine soldiers in the Great War.

In human life, whatever the country or the century, men seem to have passed through three periods of similar type. First comes the time for the heroes—the big men who dominate their passions—constructors who lay the foundations for social life. Then follows the political period, when administrative methods maintain what has been created by the heroes. After this, when order has been firmly established, men always have the idea that virtues have ceased to be useful; they criticise what has been done and finally destroy society—and it begins all over again.

Kipling covers the three classes of men. The first type is to be found everywhere in his books; he had seen them in India; the men who lay the foundations. Sometimes they are officers, sometimes cotton-planters, but they are always men of very simple character who, during their work, think of nothing else but that work, and not of love or family ties. This kind of man has no confidence in any one replacing him, unless it be a man of his own type. Men of this type, men of action but younger than he, he treats as sons and works like slaves (but who work no harder than he himself); boys who must take his place later, but who would be horror-stricken if such a thing were suggested to them.

These men soon learn that action is not easy and that man is always having fierce struggles. The designing of a bridge is easy; the building very difficult. All kinds of opposition are to be met with: the river itself, the current of the river, weather conditions, and the wrath of the gods. 'What is man against the wrath of Gods?' And this is never absent, for the Gods detest man's victories.

The true hero does not work for wealth or honour, but for love of service. I like so much the portrait of Scott who 'counted eight years' service in the Irrigation Department, and drew eight hundred rupees a month on the understanding that if he served the State faithfully for another twenty-two years, he could retire on a pension of some four hundred rupees a month.' It is the usual thing for such a man to learn, on completing an arduous duty, and at the moment of success, that another is to replace him.

In this same class, but after the leader, comes the subaltern, the young man who is destined one day to command, who is loved and worked hard by his chief. Then comes the sergeant, for whom the chief has a strong admiration (which I share) who rules because of his technical qualities, even as the hero rules because of his heroic qualities. At the bottom of the scale, lowest in rank but the most useful in emergency, follows the private—the worker. More than any other writer, Kipling understands his importance. To illustrate this point, I shall now ask the Baroness Van Heemstra to read Kipling's poem 'The Sons of Martha'. [DV. pp. 382-3.]

When the man who talks claims to control the man who *does*, Kipling becomes fiercely satirical, as in the case of Pagett, M.P., who talks lovingly, with tears in his eyes, of his home; who cannot appreciate any methods of doing which are not strictly of the administrative kind.

Sentimental talk and its consequences is seen in the story, 'The Mother Hive'. The young bees become contemptuous of the other bees who respect the Law, feed the Queen Bee and have a healthy fear of the Wax-moth. All this ends in the loss of the stored honey and the ruin of the hive. But it would be inaccurate to say that Kipling is anti-liberal minded. For him, liberty is essentially the daughter of Discipline and Law. The animals respect the Law; when the wolves forsook it because of the tiger, they met with disaster and begged for leadership again. The Law is the product of hundreds and thousands of years, and can only be changed by the wise and the strong; this view can be seen in 'As Easy as A.B.C.' and 'The Village That Voted the Earth was Flat'.

I must now make a few remarks on Kipling's work in respect to women. In the story of the two men who sought to be kings, all went well until the better of the two broke the contract made between them, and looked upon a woman. According to Kipling, woman kills the man of action and also the action itself. Captain Gadsby is thoroughly put out by his wife; and when Charlie Mears, who could reconstruct the life of pirates and re-live the past, placed before his friend the 'photograph of a girl with a curly head, and foolish slack mouth' it meant that he would write no more. Woman's disastrous effect on man's work is also shown in *The Light that Failed*.

But in contrast to this evil side of woman's sphere in the world, enters also the true wife of an heroic leader, who, like him, thinks of action and helps him to succeed in it. Thus is 'William the Conqueror', she who dealt with a famine, who can combine love and work; Kipling appreciates the wife of the soldier, who can tend the wounded, who knows how to wait and to be resigned. Nevertheless, even when admiring woman, Kipling cannot help thinking that they are mysterious and dangerous at bottom and have a sort of understanding between them, as in 'The Ladies'. [DV. pp. 442–3.]

I come to the question of the place accorded by this great artist in this world of heroes to artists. In my opinion, a writer who likes describing men of action is, to a great extent, a man of action who was frustrated and who feels of less account than the type he describes, even as Cleever felt touched and amazed at the admiration vouchsafed him by young boys who had seen 'dead men, and war, and power, and responsibility'. Did it ever arise that Kipling blasphemed his own Art, to be sorry for it in the morning, as did Cleever?

Kipling has no place in his world for the man who does not act; the wretched Tomlinson was refused place in both Heaven and Hell, because his sins were miserable crimes of which he had read and so non-existent. This does not mean that there is no hope for the artist. Kipling's view is that an artist can be a man of action without even moving from his own sphere but in this case his art must be treated as real work to be done in austere fashion—the technique thereof to be learned even as that of any other craft; he must respect his art—learn it conscientiously before attempting to express mere personal sentiments and, by talking of beauty, lose it.

[*Here the lecture was continued in English*] I promised to end as I began—with a few words in English. I wish to sum up my remarks as follows: Literary talent is very widely spread in the world. I have met in my life hundreds of talented men, but the impression of being face to face with genius is extremely unusual. What does it consist of? It is difficult to analyse. We find ourselves in the presence of a man, and we suddenly feel that he surpasses all others. He has a power of contact with nature, a wealth of invention, a sort of eternal youth that makes him entirely different.

I have had this strong impression only three times in my life. Once at school in the presence of one of my masters, a French philosopher, who, although quite unknown today, will sometime be as well-known as Socrates or Plato. Once in the presence of a soldier—Maréchal Lyautey—whom I saw create a new country. The third time was in the presence of a writer. That writer was Rudyard Kipling.

Of course, I would not use the word 'genius' if Kipling himself were present. I can imagine him stopping me and saying, 'You must not say these things,' but, as he is not present I dare make a prediction that in a thousand years, or in two thousand years, men will still be reading Kipling and will find him still young. That is why your Society in devoting itself to this great writer, has chosen well and chosen the greatest. I thank you for giving me the opportunity of saying this, and for having listened with patience to this long speech in *two* foreign languages.

DISCUSSION

Mr. G. C. Beresford: 'I should like to ask Monsieur Maurois if he can explain why Bernard Shaw is the English author who is read on the East of the Rhine, and apparently Kipling on the West of the Rhine.'
M. Maurois: 'I think one might say that the main reason why Bernard Shaw is, I will not say unpopular in France (because many of his plays have been staged and acted there), but not an important author for us, is that we already had one Bernard Shaw—that is, Voltaire. What in Bernard Shaw may seem very new to you is not exactly new to us. He attacks things which in France are not to be attacked, because they do not exist. Now in the case of Kipling it is exactly the contrary. We needed Kipling because we have in France the "Kipling" type of man; we have a colonial Empire, and it has never been sung by our writers. They have never written about it, or very little. We have not got our Kipling, and that is why we need yours.'
Mr. Bazley (Hon. Editor) thanked M. Maurois very much, in French, for his lecture, which had been most interesting, and said that when one went through Kipling's works from the beginning one noticed his great and thorough understanding of French mentality.
In reply to a question as to whether Kipling had a parallel in Alfred

de Vigny, M. Maurois said: 'I think it is a very apt point, because it is quite true that Vigny in "Servitude et Grandeur Militaire" is very near Kipling in his ideal of life but Vigny wrote 100 years ago and he has not dealt with the world of to-day. What is interesting to us in Kipling is that in his books we find the heroic point of view. What Kipling has done is to show that these qualities Vigny found in the officers of Napoleon, still exist now, not only among officers, but among engineers, workmen, sailors and men of all trades. He has shown us that the modern man is exactly the same man as the hero of other times. I once asked Kipling himself, because I had just read one of his stories about the Roman Wall in Scotland, how he managed to describe Roman officers and soldiers, and make them so true and alive. Was it not an extraordinary feat of literary skill? He replied: "No, it's very easy, I simply listened to the conversations of British officers in India, and gave them as the conversations of Roman officers and that did the trick." '

In the course of M. Maurois' lecture and at his request, the Baroness van Heemstra gave an excellent reading of the Kipling poems mentioned.

61. 'Rudyard Kipling's Place in English Literature'

25 January 1936

An anonymous obituary article published a week after Kipling's death in the *Times Literary Supplement* (25 January 1936). This seems to be about the best, fullest and most dispassionate of the obituary tributes; it is included here by kind permission of the Editor of the *Times Literary Supplement*. In accordance with the strict rule of anonymity, the author's name cannot be revealed.

Rudyard Kipling was a national institution . . . and regarded as such by all the world. His fame had been long established and his literary activity slight for many years. It was also the case that many had lost interest in him and many others had been repelled. Seldom had a famous national institution been the object of more hostile criticism; some of it, indeed, unfair and marred by lack of understanding, yet some of it damaging enough. There are veterans who were hostile from the first; there are today many thousands of young enthusiasts: but broadly speaking the vocal sections of two generations have been at variance regarding him. Now the time has come for a reckoning; not a final reckoning, for posterity will have its say, but for the verdict of this age, comprising the old and the young, sitting as the jury. The critic writing at the moment must try to assist the jury to find that verdict, not as advocate for or against—they have both been heard at length but, so far as he can and dare, as judge summing up. Conscious of his own limitations and mindful of the disasters of many who have assumed the role, he may also attempt a harder task: that of prophecy. Kipling in life and work alike was downright and decided, without hesitation as to goal or the road that led to it. Let us treat him as he would have chosen to be treated, without timidity or hedging. Let us venture not only to decide what shall be the verdict of our time upon him but to predict boldly what shall be his place in the annals of our letters.

We have to envisage him both as poet and writer of fiction, and in the former aspect our task is, it may be admitted, a difficult one. On the prose side the case is very different. There is, we believe, no heavy risk in the prophecy that Rudyard Kipling will live and be admired as one of the most virile and skilful of English masters of the short story; that if that art, in which we are weak, shows with us no great development in future, he will remain, in years to come, as he now is, unique; that if it goes forward and gives birth to new triumphs, he will still rank among the greatest of the pioneers.

The pioneer has always a special meed of honour, and that honour is Kipling's for more reasons than one. He won it alike for matter and manner. He was definitely the man of the hour, a milestone on the path of letters like Byron and Chateaubriand. He appeared at a moment when literature in this country was being sicklied o'er, not with the pale cast of thought but with the unnatural bloom of cosmetics. We can realize now more fully than was realized then that fine and enduring work was being done in the aesthetic nineties, outside the school of the aesthetes, even outside that of the two giants who had no relationship to that school, George Meredith and Thomas Hardy. Yet the general atmosphere was stale and scented, artistically as well as literally *fin-de-siècle*. There was an extraordinary preoccupation with the artificial, a delight, by no means assumed on the part of many of the 'yellow' world, in 'bought red mouths', 'parched flowers', pallid women, 'delicate' sins.

Before the nineties opened there had spread bruit of a young writer out in India who knew little of this world of opera-cloaks and gold-headed canes and scorned what he did know. Kipling was, as his acute French observer, M. André Chevrillon, remarked, English *d'une façon simple, violente et, de plus, tres nouvelle*; the world which he entered so violently, which he did more than any other to destroy, being, on the contrary, the pale and unsatisfying reflection of a phase in French literature. Kipling was indeed English, but in those early days he was the mouthpiece of classes and types that were not themselves vocal and had long lacked a chronicler. India, with its heat and dust, its diversities of creed and caste was suddenly brought to the door of the stay-at-home Englishman. He learned with a thrill how the more adventurous of his race, from private soldiers to governors of provinces, lived; how they fought and organized and ruled. For this precocious genius had not only observed and recorded for him a great number of interesting and astonishing facts and occurrences; he had also put at his disposal a marvellous power of catching an atmosphere, of summing up an impression of the scenes upon which the writer had looked. This was life indeed, exclaimed the reader in his armchair; this was life as it should be lived, this young seer in India was revealing the highest destiny of the Englishman. Soon it appeared that life could be lived elsewhere than in India. It could be lived in America, in Africa, in the ports of the world, at sea, whether in crack cargo-boats, rusty tramps or the fishing smacks on the Grand Bank, in the cab of a steam-engine; even, for those who knew how, in an unconventional public school. The same vigour, the same brilliant technique, the same power of making mechanism romantic marked each new effort and bound together the spell he had put upon the English public.

And then there came another phase. The worshipper of dangerous living, of physical excitement, of noise, some detractors averred, be-came entranced with the peaceful beauties and with the traditions of the English countryside, and touched upon them with as much originality as he had all the rest. Such are the broad lines of his literary career.

Rudyard Kipling is first of all master of the *conte*. He attempted full-length novels, achieving in *The Light that Failed* and *Captains Cour-ageous* romances to which no adjective higher than 'successful' can be applied: in *The Naulahka* written in collaboration with his brother-in-law, not even that; and in *Kim* his one masterpiece in that province. But in the short story he has had few English rivals, even if we take the best work of others to match against his, and from his take any of forty or fifty which it is hard to separate from the point of view of merit. The short story was suited to his peculiar gifts of compression, of clarity, of characterization that needs no building up but is com-pleted and fixed in a flash. In his stories he has used almost every kind of matter, though the love of the sexes plays a very much smaller part than with most writers. War, adventure of every type, machinery pure and simple, have been his familiar subjects. He has employed the grotesque, the horrible, and very often the eerie in his plots, looking with anxious but never credulous eyes at what may be distinguished or imagined 'at the end of the passage', in the half-world betwixt fact and dream. Nor has he neglected that form of short story which is almost an allegory, among which the Mowgli tales of *The Jungle Book* stand highest. In a great number of the early stories, in those of Mowgli above all, we seem to detect a form of idealism with as little historical justification as that of Rousseau. He sees the savage in man and that it is not far below the surface, and he is disposed to question the benefits of civilization. The sentiment was perhaps with him no more than a phase, but those who study him closely can have little doubt that it existed. They will assuredly not regret the fact. For in the Mowgli stories Kipling achieved a rare feat: he invented a new form of expression. And these tales have a charm, a beauty, a boldness of imagination that we have not often seen equalled in our time. The animals are not, as are those of Kipling's numerous imitators in this vein, creatures with men's minds in the bodies of beasts. The sentiments of beasts may be inaccurately described; that we cannot tell, though we may suspect that their intelligence is exaggerated; but the whole affair is managed with such marvellous dexterity that we are convinced and willingly surrender to him our judgment. Can an animal find enjoyment in the thrill of danger, as many human beings can? Hear his answer and see if you can state the contrary opinion with equal plausibility?

To move down so cunningly that never a leaf stirred; to wade knee-deep in the roaring shallows that drown all noise from behind; to drink, looking backward over one shoulder, every muscle ready for the first desperate bound of keen terror; to roll on the sandy margin, and return, wet-muzzled and well plumped out, to the admiring herd, was a thing that all tall-antlered young bucks took a delight in, precisely because they knew that at any moment Bagheera or Shere Khan might leap upon them and bear them down.

That word plausibility, in fact, gives us the key to one of the chief secrets of his popularity. It also explains a certain impatience felt by those who caught him out. For, excellently documented as he was, he was not always correct—could hardly be so, seeing how wide was his range. But, right or wrong, he was always equally assured, cocksure said the less friendly of his critics. And yet, these slips apart, his plausibility is amazing. The finest of the stories, such as 'On Greenhow Hill', 'The Return of Imray', 'The Strange Ride of Morrowbie Jukes', 'The Man who would be King', 'Without Benefit of Clergy', 'The Mark of the Beast',—have the verisimilitude of chronicles. Let us say that chronicles they are indeed, the chronicles of an epoch of British administration in India, infused with the imagination of a great writer of fiction.

The poetry is another matter. Poetry demands a standard even higher than prose; that is to say, an infelicitous expression, a piece of loose thinking are in it more painfully apparent and bring their own condemnation more swiftly. In his early work in verse Kipling did not fly high. *Departmental Ditties* may have won him his earliest fame, but these popular ballads, parodies, society verses, satires, clever and witty as they are, do not warrant the bestowal of the title of poet. The elevation of Mr. Potiphar Gubbins, the transfer to Quetta of Jack Barrett, may take their place somewhere below the satiric verse of Marvell and above that of Churchill; the rest, if they live, will live because they are Kipling's. Yet on the last page of that volume came a poem, '*L'Envoi*', which few probably noticed, which a bold prophet might have seen as a cloud no bigger than a man's hand. Till that cloud has sailed up we continue in the arid heat of dexterity, of rhetoric, of admonition, of a sententiousness often grating. We are warmed and made happy by wit and humour, we recognize a master of metre, rhythm and onomatopoeia in a line like

'The heave and the halt and the hurl and the crash of the comber wind-hounded.'

But almost always we are either pulled up with a jar by a phrase which is definitely inappropriate, definitely no poetry; or, if we escape that, subsequent reflection seems to indicate a flaw in taste, a thought of which the expression begins well but is not sustained at the level of its early dignity and beauty. But the cloud was drawing nigher and swelling in size. There may be difference of opinions whether the later stories of the English countryside are the equals of the more brilliant exotic predecessors. There can be little doubt that in the lovely songs, strewn among them, buttercups and daisies amid rich green grass, Kipling reached his highest as a poet. The passionate patriotism which had often previously run riot, shocking and offending the weaker brethren, is here even more intense, but purified, purged of that note of brawling.

> Under their feet in the grasses
> My clinging magic runs.
> They shall return as strangers,
> They shall remain as sons.

> Scent of smoke in the evening.
> Smell of rain in the night,
> The hours, the days and the seasons,
> Order their souls aright.

In these songs, with their simplicity, their kindly and gracious philosophy, he reveals at last that lyric sweetness whereof we had had

promise in '*L'Envoi*', and himself as not merely a satirist or humorist
or master of the banjo ballad, but a lyric poet.

> Cities and Thrones and Powers,
> Stand in Time's eye,
> Almost as long as flowers,
> Which daily die:
> But, as new buds put forth
> To glad new men
> Out of the spent and unconsidered Earth,
> The Cities rise again.
>
> This season's Daffodil,
> She never hears,
> What change, what chance, what chill,
> Cut down last year's;
> But with bold countenance,
> And knowledge small,
> Esteems her seven days' continuance
> To be perpetual.

(Even in reading these lines we pause. Is there not something school-
boyish in the irony of that 'almost as long'?)

Yet let us make no mistake. More of Kipling will go down to
posterity than the fastidious literary critic is prepared to pass. The
flaws are those of a great and original craftsman; in the most faulty
productions there is power; one feels everywhere in them the grip of a
strong hand. Often that which is not poetry is life itself. Take a poem
such as 'If'; not poetry at all, some critics may declare. It may not be,
yet it has been an inspiration to many thousands and those not the
most ingenuous or limited in their appreciation of poetical merit. Its
moral maxims are as clean-cut and forcible as those of Pope or Edward
Young. Almost all the patriotic verse, though it may grate often upon
the ears of those whom Kipling called, with rather less than strict
fairness but a large measure of truth,

> Brittle intellectuals who crack beneath a strain,

and sometimes upon any critical ears, represents at least one side of
England. 'Wordsworth,' wrote Lowell, 'never lets us long forget the
deeply rooted stock from which he sprang—*vien ben da lui*.' The words
may be applied with equal justice to Kipling. At his worst as at his
best, the love of England breeds in him a passionate intensity and
sincerity which ennoble even the verse marred by the shouting of

party warfare or by extreme patriotic dogmatism, as by technical faults of like nature.

What verdict England of the future will pass upon England of the last years of Victoria and Edward VII, is uncertain, but it is incontestable that the age will always rank as one of the greatest in our history—great materially and great in national temper. And may one not dare to foresee that when, long hence, that age and its characteristics and products are called to mind, the name of Rudyard Kipling will come first to men's mouths when they talk of its most typical representatives? Is it not likely that then the lesser work will take its place with the greater, as all part of and symbolic of the country which he loved and celebrated?

It were not easy to imagine two writers more widely separated than Rudyard Kipling and Maurice Barrès, but their names are linked by the fact that as contemporaries, born within a few years of one another, each set up a philosophy of nationalism and each was assailed from a point of view in which the political mingled with the artistic. Each might have taken as motto the words of Disraeli: 'Now a nation is a work of art and a work of time;' and each tripped not seldom in the snares which arrogance sets for the feet of the nationalist. Hear them each, Barrès on his beloved Hill of Sion-Vaudemont:

Où sont les dames de Lorraine, sœurs, filles et femmes des Croisés, qui s'en venaient prier à Sion pendant que les hommes d'armes, là-bas, combattaient l'infidèle, et celles-là surtout qui, le lendemain de la bataille de Nicopolis, ignorantes encore, mais épouvantées par les rumeurs, montèrent ici intercéder pour des vivants qui étaient déjà des morts? Où la sainte princesse Philippe de Gueldre, à qui Notre-Dame de Sion découvrit, durant le temps de son sommeil, les desseins ambitieux des ennemis de la Lorraine? . . .

and Kipling on his Sussex Downs:

> See you the dimpled track that runs,
> All hollow through the wheat?
> O that was where they hauled the guns
> That smote King Philip's fleet.

> See you our stilly woods of oak,
> And the dread ditch beside?
> O that was where the Saxons broke,
> On the day that Harold died.

While Barrès, a mystic, heard 'the hushed and timid voices' of the gods of his ancestors at those spiritual points where, it seemed to him, the crust of the material world was thin and the poetry of great deeds and great lives came through it as in a vapour, Kipling, more realistically, conjured up upon the Downs his ancestors, themselves. *Puck of Pook's Hill, Rewards and Fairies,* have in them the very marrow of England. For them, at least, we may prophesy with assurance that death will not come quickly. In these entrancing volumes, in many another tale of the stamp of 'An Habitation Enforced', there is far more than merely the exquisite art of telling a story; there is the recreation of history, the essence of a nation's beginning and early development. The figures of De Aquila and Sir Richard Dalyngridge are not only great characters of fiction but pendants to the works of great historians. 'And so was England born.' The work of Kipling, as of Barrès, at its greatest moments is a flower of national art. It was fitting that the former should have known and loved and been honoured of France; and that the latter, though he said hard words of England, should have been the guest of our fleet in time of war and lauded its traditions to his countrymen.

We have hinted that the young men have less pleasure in the work of Kipling than those who reached manhood at any time between the publication of *Departmental Ditties* and that of *Kim,* though there is some doubt as to how far the young writers represent their generation in this. In any case there is in it nothing uncommon or prejudicial to his eventual fame. At Wordsworth's death, when subscriptions were being collected for a memorial to him Macaulay declared to Arnold that ten years earlier more money could have been raised to do him honour in Cambridge alone than was now raised all through the country. Thirty years later Arnold was bewailing that the diminution of Wordsworth's popularity was continuing, that, effaced first by Scott and Byron, he was now completely effaced by Tennyson. The selected poems of Wordsworth, which Arnold was then editing, to which the essay quoted was a preface, ran through thirteen editions between 1879 and the close of the century, and there have been many others. That which is popular today may be outmoded to-morrow, but if it has the stuff of life in it, it will assuredly not be dead the day after. Yet, where Kipling is concerned, it is improbable that there will ever be unanimity of opinion.

He was a man of strong prejudices, strong political views, with little tenderness for the opinions of others, and—though to lesser extent than now—he may always divide men into camps. So much granted, there will be, we are convinced, in years to come a general agreement upon the high merit of a great part of this man's work. The perfervid admirers will come to admit that there is dross—dross, why he threw it up in a heap about him as he worked, till at times we could scarce see him over the top of it! Those of the type of mind which is antagonized by a loud-voiced patriotism and Toryism will allow those English songs and stories which we last considered to be free from that offence, and will perhaps even pardon it elsewhere for the vigour and skill with which it is presented. Both will proclaim him a magician in the art of the short story, who raised it to a higher station in our literature than it had known before his coming. As novelist they will call him author of one, but one only, of the finest romances of his time. As a poet he will be remembered for a mass of vigorous, pithy, if faulty, work of the second order; for a patriotic hymn that had become part of every national ceremony; last, not least, as the singer of English country beauties and traditions. And if, amid the work he leaves behind him, those juries of the future contrive, to catch a glimpse of the man himself, as his own time knew him, they must add to their verdict a rider that this was a great man as well as a great wirter; and honourable and fearless and good.

Chronological Table

1865   Rudyard Kipling born in Bombay (30 December)

1871–7 At 'Lorne Lodge', 4 Campbell Road, Southsea [Capt. and Mrs. Pryse Agar Holloway]. (To day-school: 'Hope House', Somerset Place, Southsea)

1878–82 At United Services College, Westward Ho! Devon

1882–7 On the staff of the *Civil and Military Gazette*, Lahore

1886   *Departmental Ditties* [after appearing in *C. and M. Gazette* (1886); in the *Pioneer* (1884–6)]

1887–9 On the staff of the *Pioneer*, Allahabad

1888   *Plain Tales from the Hills* (January) [mostly from *C. and M. Gazette*, 1884–7]

1888   'The Indian Railway Library' paper backs: *Soldiers Three, The Story of the Gadsbys, In Black and White, Under the Deodars, The Phantom 'Rickshaw, Wee Willie Winkie* (mostly from the *Weeks News*, Allahabad: a few new)

1889   Left Allahabad 21 February, via Singapore, Hong Kong, Japan, U.S.A. Arrived Liverpool 5 October. 'Ballad of the King's Mercy', November, 'Ballad of East and West' and 'The Incarnation of Krishna Mulvaney' in *Macmillan's Magazine*, December

1890–1 *The Light that Failed* in *Lippincott's*, 1 January 1891, and complete form as book in March

1891   *Life's Handicap* (collected from various periodicals, mainly of 1890)

1892   Marriage. Settled at Brattleboro, Vermont, U.S.A. *Barrack-Room Ballads* (mainly from the *National Observer*), *The Naulahka* (serialized *Century Magazine*, November 1891–July 1892)

1893   *Many Inventions* (mainly from various magazines, 1890–2)

1894   *The Jungle Book* (from various magazines, 1893–4)

1895   *The Second Jungle Book* (mainly from *Pall Mall* and *St. Nicholas*, 1894–5)

1896   Returned to live in England. *The Seven Seas* (from various periodicals)

1897   Settled at Rottingdean. *Captains Courageous* (serialized in *McClure's Magazine*, November 1896–March 1897 and *Pearson's Magazine*, December 1896–April 1897). 'Recessional' in *The Times*, 17 July 1897

1898   *The Day's Work* (from various magazines, 1893–97)

1899   *Stalky & Co.* (mostly from *Windsor* and *McClure's Magazines*, January–June 1899)

1899   *From Sea to Sea* (from Indian papers, 1885–1890, previously issued in pirated or suppressed volumes)

1901   *Kim* (serialized *Cassell's* and *McClure's Magazines*, December 1900–October 1901)

1902   Settled for the rest of his life, at 'Bateman's', Burwash, Sussex. *Just So Stories for Little Children* (mostly from *St. Nicholas* 1897–8, *Ladies' Home Journal*, 1900–2)

1903   *The Five Nations* (from various periodicals)

1904   *Traffics and Discoveries* (from various magazines, 1901–4)

1906   *Puck of Pook's Hill* (serialized in the *Strand Magazine*, January–October 1906; divided between *McClure's* and *Ladies' Home Journal* in U.S.A.)

1907   Awarded Nobel Prize for Literature

1909   *Actions and Reactions* (mostly from magazines, 1899–1909)

1909   *Abaft the Funnel* (American 'pirate' collection of stories and sketches from Indian papers, 1888–90; not published in England until the 'Sussex Edition', 1938)

1910   *Rewards and Fairies* (mainly the *Delineator*, U.S.A., September 1909–August 1910; various in England)

1912–13   *Songs from Books* (1912 U.S.A., 1913 England: collected and expanded verses and poems from the prose volumes)

1917   *A Diversity of Creatures* (mainly from magazines, 1910–15)

1914–18   *The New Army in Training, Sea-Warfare, The Eyes of Asia* and other War pamphlets

1919   *The Years Between* (verse from various periodicals, etc.)

1920   *Letters of Travel* (from *The Times* and *New York Sun*, 1892; *Morning Post* and *Collier's Weekly*, 1908, and *Nash's Magazine* and the *Cosmopolitan*, 1914). *Brazilian Sketches*, from *Morning Post*, November–December 1927, added in 'Sussex Edition', 1938)

1920   *Q. Horatii Flacci Carminum Librer Quintus* (with C. L. Graves, A. D. Godley, A. B. Ramsay and R. A. Knox)

1923   *Land and Sea Tales for Scouts and Guides* (mostly from magazines, 1893–1910)

1923   *The Irish Guards in the Great War.* 2 vols.

1926   *Debits and Credits* (from magazines, 1915–26)

1928   *A Book of Words* (collected speeches 1906–1927. Later speeches in 'Sussex Edition', 1938

1930   *Thy Servant a Dog* (Two stories from *Cassell's Magazine*, 1930, and one new. With two extra stories 1938)

1932   *Limits and Renewals* (mostly from magazines, 1928–32)

1933   *Souvenirs of France*

1936   Rudyard Kipling died 18 January. Buried Westminster Abbey 23 January

1937   *Something of Myself: For My Friends Known and Unknown*
1937–9 The '*Sussex Edition*' (35 vols). Complete edition of his acknowledged
        works, with many hitherto uncollected additions: prepared and
        signed by Kipling
1940   *Rudyard Kipling's Verse: Definitive Edition* (there had been many
        editions of *Collected Verse*, each containing more, since 1912)

Select Bibliography

This short select book list is of volumes containing collected criticism, critical or critical-plus-biographical volumes, and lists of criticism of Rudyard Kipling. For fuller lists see *English Literature in Transition* listed below, and *Cambridge Bibliography of English Literature*, new edition 1969.

A. CRITICAL ARTICLES

GERBER, HELMUT E. *et al.*, Rudyard Kipling: An Annotated Bibliography of Articles about him. *English Fiction in Transition*, Vol. 3, Numbers 3–5, 1960; and *English Literature in Transition*, Vol. 8, Numbers 3–4, 1965.

GILBERT, ELLIOT L., (Ed.), *Kipling and the Critics*, P. Owen, 1965. Reprinted essays, parodies and extracts by Andrew Lang, Oscar Wilde, Henry James, Robert Buchanan, Max Beerbohm, Bonamy Dobrée, Boris Ford, George Orwell, Lionel Trilling, C. S. Lewis, T. S. Eliot, J. M. S. Tompkins, Randall Jarrell, Steven Marcus and Elliot L. Gilbert.

GREEN, ROGER LANCELYN, (Ed.), the *Kipling Journal: Centenary Number*, December 1965. Articles specially written by Rosemary Sutcliff, Bonamy Dobrée, J. M. S. Tompkins, George Calvin Carter, Morton N. Cohen, Elliot L. Gilbert and Nevill Coghill. Reprinted articles by Andrew Lang and Charles Carrington. Centenary poem by Edmund Blunden.

POWELL, FREDERICK YORK, 'Rudyard Kipling—Bibliography'—*The English Illustrated Magazine*, Vol. XXX, pp. 430–2, December 1903.

RUTHERFORD, ANDREW, (Ed.), *Kipling's Mind and Art*, Oliver, 1964. Reprinted articles by W. L. Renwick, Edmund Wilson, George Orwell, Lionel Trilling and Noel Annan; and new articles by Mark Kinkeed-Weekes, J. H. Fenwick, W. W. Robson, George Shepperson, Alan Sandison and Andrew Rutherford.

B. CRITICAL AND CRITICAL-PLUS-BIOGRAPHICAL VOLUMES

BODELSON, C. A., *Aspects of Kipling's Art*, Manchester University Press, 1964.

BROWN, HILTON, *Rudyard Kipling: A New Appreciation*, Hamish Hamilton, 1945.

CARRINGTON, CHARLES, *Rudyard Kipling: His Life and Work*, Macmillan, 1955. [The authorized biography.]

COHEN, MORTON N., *Rudyard Kipling to Rider Haggard: The Record of a Friendship*, Hutchinson, 1965.

CORNELL, LOUIS L., *Kipling in India*, Macmillan, 1966.

DOBRÉE, BONAMY, *Rudyard Kipling: Realist and Fabulist*, Oxford University Press, 1967.

GREEN, ROGER LANCELYN, *Kipling and the Children*, Elek, 1965.

HARBORD, R. E. *et al.*, *The Reader's Guide to Rudyard Kipling's Works*, [Privately printed.] Vol. I, 1961; Vol. II, 1963; Vol. III, 1965; Vol. IV, 1966; Vol. V, 1969; [in progress] Vol. VI, 1970—to be completed in 10 vols.

LÉAUD, FRANÇOIS, *La Poétique de Rudyard Kipling*, Paris: Didier, 1958.

SHANKS, EDWARD, *Rudyard Kipling: A Study in Literature and Political Ideas*, Macmillan, 1940.

TOMPKINS, J. M. S., *The Art of Rudyard Kipling*, Methuen, 1959.

WEYGANDT, ANN M., *Kipling's Reading*, University of Pennsylvania Press, 1939.

C. IMPORTANT UNCOLLECTED CRITICAL ARTICLES

CHAUDHURI, NIRAD C., 'The Finest Story about India in English', [*Kim*], *Encounter*, April 1957.

DUNMAN, JACK, 'Kipling Re-estimated', *Marxism Today*, August 1965.

ELIOT, T. S., Introduction to *A Choice of Kipling's Verse*, Faber, 1941.

KIPLING JOURNAL, (Various), Published quarterly since 1927 by The Kipling Society, 18 Northumberland Avenue, London, W.C.2.

MAUGHAM, W. SOMERSET, Introduction to *A Choice of Kipling's Prose*, Macmillan, 1952.

ROWSE, A. L., 'Blowing Kipling's Trumpet', *Sunday Telegraph*, 19 December 1965.

STEWART, J. I. M., Section on Kipling in *Eight Modern Writers*, *Oxford History of English Literature*, Vol. XII, pp. 223–93, Oxford, 1963.

SUSSMAN, HERBERT L., Chapter on Kipling in *The Victorians and The Machine*, Oxford University Press, 1968.

Index

II TOPICS

THE CRITICAL HERITAGE SERIES

GENERAL EDITOR: B. C. SOUTHAM

Volumes published and forthcoming

Continued